Modern Greece

From Independence to the Present

Second Edition

THOMAS W. GALLANT

Bloomsbury Academic
An imprint of Bloomsbury Publishing Plc

B L O O M S B U R Y
LONDON · OXFORD · NEW YORK · NEW DELHI · SYDNEY

Bloomsbury Academic
An imprint of Bloomsbury Publishing Plc

50 Bedford Square
London
WC1B 3DP
UK

1385 Broadway
New York
NY 10018
USA

www.bloomsbury.com

BLOOMSBURY and the Diana logo are trademarks of Bloomsbury Publishing Plc

First edition published 2001

Second edition published 2016
Reprinted 2017, 2018

British Library Cataloguing-in-Publication Data
A catalogue record for this book is available from the British Library.

ISBN: HB: 978-1-4725-6757-4
PB: 978-1-4725-6756-7
ePDF: 978-1-4725-6759-8
ePub: 978-1-4725-6758-1

Library of Congress Cataloging-in-Publication Data
Names: Gallant, Thomas W., author.
Title: Modern Greece : from the war of independence to the present / Thomas W. Gallant.
Description: Second edition. | New York : Bloomsbury Academic, 2016. |
Includes bibliographical references and index. | Description based on print version record
and CIP data provided by publisher; resource not viewed.
Identifiers: LCCN 2015043871 (print) | LCCN 2015043295 (ebook) | ISBN 9781472567598
(ePDF) | ISBN 9781472567581 (ePub) | ISBN 9781472567574 (hardback) | ISBN
9781472567567 (paperback) |
Subjects: LCSH: Greece–History–1821- | BISAC: HISTORY / Europe / Baltic States.
Classification: LCC DF802 (print) | LCC DF802 .G35 2016 (ebook) | DDC 949.507–dc23
LC record available at http://lccn.loc.gov/2015043871

Cover design: Catherine Wood
Cover image: Photograph from the book *Explorations in Greece: Photographs 1898–1913*.
The Hubert Pernot Collection © OLKOS Publishers Ltd.

Typeset by Deanta Global Publishing Services, Chennai, India
Printed and bound in Great Britain

Contents

Acknowledgements

I began the Preface to my book *Modern Greece* (2001) by stating that 'the burden of history lies heavily on Greek society.' What I had in mind then was the way in which contemporary Greece labours under the burdensome legacy of antiquity. I framed my comments then about the tensions that exist because of Greece being a young state with an old culture. As I was writing the first edition, and as is explained in Chapter 12 of this volume, Greece was enjoying growing prosperity, was in the midst of becoming a full and core member of Europe and, after having just been awarded the 2004 Summer Olympic Games, was gaining the spotlight on the world stage. Accordingly, my analysis written in the late 1990s sought to explain the historical trajectory that brought Greece through the travails of the twentieth century to what seemed to be a triumphant moment. But how things have changed since then. The financial crisis that has rocked the country since 2008 has, indeed, put Greece front and centre on the world stage, but not in a good way, of course. The increased interest in Greek history recently has been driven by the need for people to understand what happened and why in Greece. Those expecting to find an account that teleologically tries to explain how we arrived at 2008 will be disappointed. I address the Greek debt crisis in Chapter 12, but the earlier chapters are not intended as a prelude to the present; instead, they endeavour, as they should in my view, to present the history of Greece over the last few centuries on its own terms (Map 1).

Over the years, many colleagues have provided me with feedback on the first edition of the book. This is, of course, in addition to numerous published reviews of it. On the basis of these comments, suggestions and criticisms, I had had in the back of my mind for some time the idea of doing a second edition. I therefore jumped at the chance when Rhodri Mogford from Bloomsbury Publishing approached me about doing one. In addition to revising the original text, I have added three new chapters; one which provides a much more in-depth presentation of the history of Greece and the Ottoman Empire, another that expands greatly on the history of nation-building during the nineteenth century and a third one that takes the story from 1990 up until the January 2015 election. Over the years many people who teach Modern Greek history have mentioned to me how difficult it is to find primary sources in English that they can use in the classroom. In order to help rectify that problem, I have included in this version forty-two primary sources, which are presented in the form of text-boxes. For the general reader, they are intended to exemplify a point made in the text, while for students and instructors, they are meant to be used as the basis for classroom discussion. Numerous timelines have been included as well. One final change refers to notation and the bibliography. In order to make the book more accessible as a text, the notes section has been reduced substantially from the first edition. Notes in this edition are used to direct the reader to the sources of direct quotes, especially from primary sources, or to sources I consider especially useful for the advanced reader to follow up. In the 'Guide to Further Reading' section, I have restricted the lists mostly to books published since 2000 and which form the basis for the revisions included in this edition; for earlier works, I refer you to the section in the first edition.

I would like to thank Rhodri and his colleagues at Bloomsbury for giving me this opportunity and for all of their hard work in seeing the text through to publication. This is a vastly better book because of the input and feedback I have received from the PhD students I have supervised and worked with over the years. I would like to single out and thank my current group of advisees, Aytek Alpan, David Idol, Kalliopi Kefalas, Leonidas Mylonakis, Emre Sunu, Chris Theofilogiannakis and Juan Carmona Zabala. I have benefited greatly from discussions about Greek history, and about the previous version of my book in particular, with colleagues in Greece, Canada and the United States. They are far too numerous to name. I would, however, like to single out for their contributions Doxis Doxiadis, Sakis Gekas, Antonis Liakos and Emilia Salvanou. As always, Mary Gallant has been my patient partner in our on-going efforts to come to grips with the history of our adopted country. Lastly, recognition is due to my team of canine assistants, Marley, Sadie and Sabrina. Much of this book was written as they dragged me around our neighbourhood on our daily walks.

MAP 1 *Contemporary Greece.*

List of illustrations

List of maps

List of text-boxes

List of tables

List of charts

Timelines

Chapter 1

1345: First Ottoman military involvement in Europe.

1361–1369: Conquest of Thrace.

1370–1388: Conquest of Macedonia.

1389: 15 June. Ottomans defeated the Serbs at the Battle of Kosovo.

1402: Timur the Lame defeated the Ottomans at the Battle of Ankara.

1430: Permanent incorporation of Salonika.

1453: Constantinople captured.

1458–1460: Athens and most of the Peloponnesos incorporated into the Empire.

1520–1566: Reign of Suleiman the Lawgiver.

1522: Conquest of Rhodes.

1570–1571: Conquest of Cyprus.

1669: Conquest of Crete.

1683–1699: The Holy League War.

1699: Treaty of Karlowtiz; Venetian rule of the Peloponnesos began.

1703–1705: Abolition of the Devşirme.

1715: Re-conquest of the Peloponnesos.

1768–1774: Ottoman–Russian War.

1774: Treaty of Küçük Kaynarca.

1774–1810s: Creation of Greek Russia.

1798–1816: Napoleonic Wars.

Chapter 2

1806–1812: Ottoman–Russian War.

1805–1815: The Serb rebellions.

1814: The Philiki Etaireia founded in Odessa.

1815: 9 June. The United States of the Ionian Islands created.

1820–1822: Tepedelenli Ali Paşa's rebellion.

1821: 6 March. Alexandros Ipsilandis's invasion started the Greek insurrection.

1821: 25 March: Rebellion in the Peloponnesos officially declared.
1821: 11 September. Greeks captured Tripolis.
1822: 1 January. First Constitution passed.
1822: 31 March. The Chios Massacre.
1822: 8 August. The Battle of the Dervenakia Pass.
1824: Greek Civil War began.
1825: 26 February. Ibrahim Paşa invaded the Peloponnesos.
1826: 10 April. The fall of Missolonghi.
1826: 15 June. The 'Auspicious Incident': the destruction of the Janissaries.
1826 (August)–1827 (May): Siege of the Athenian Acropolis.
1827: 6 July. The Treaty of London.
1827: 20 October. The Battle of Navarino.
1828: 24 January. Ioannis Kapodistrias elected president of the First Hellenic Republic.
1828–1829: Ottoman–Russian War.
1831: 9 October. Kapodistrias assassinated.

Chapter 3

1832: 7 May. Treaty of Constantinople.
1832: 30 August. The London Protocol created the Kingdom of Greece.
1832–1835: The Regency
1833: 6 February. King Otto arrived in Greece.
1835–1843: Absolute monarchy.
1836: 22 November. Otto wed Duchess Amelia of Oldenberg.
1843: 14 September. Military coup ended absolutism.
1844: 7 March. Greek Constitution ratified.
1847–1850: The Don Pacifico affair.
1849: 8 May. Murder of Captain John Parker. International incident with Great Britain.
1854. 18 May. British and French fleets blockaded Piraeus.
1862: 23 October. Otto deposed.
1864: 7 August. New Constitution ratified.
1874: 29 June. Harilaos Trikoupis published 'Who is to Blame?'
1882: 15 March. Harilaos Trikoupis's first major administration.
1893: 25 July. The Korinth Canal opened.
1893: 10 December. Greece declared bankruptcy.
1895: 16 April. Harilaos Trikoupis lost election and left Greece.
1896: 6 April. The Athens Olympics.
1897: 5 April. The Greco–Ottoman or Thirty Days' War.

Chapter 5

1831–1833 (1838–1839): Ottoman–Egyptian Wars.
1839: Summer. Insurrections in Thessaly.
1839: 3 November. First phase of the Tanzimat.
1854–1856: The Crimean War.
1854: 28 January. Insurrections in Epiros and Thessaly.
1854: 18 May. British and French fleets blockaded Piraeus.
1856: 18 February. Second phase of the Tanzimat.
1864: 21 May. Unification of the Ionian Islands.
1866–1869: Insurrection in Crete.
1870: 12 March. Bulgarian Exarchate.
1877: 24 April (until 3 March 1878). Ottoman–Russian War.
1878: 13 July. The Treaty of Berlin.
1878: 27 October. Pact of Halepa on Crete.
1881: 2 July. Convention of Constantinople between Greece and Ottoman Empire.
1896: 18 May. Cretan insurrection.
1897: 5 April. The Greco–Ottoman or Thirty Days' War.
1903: 20 July. The Ilinden Uprising.
1903: 2 October. The Mürzsteg agreement.
1908: 3 July. The Young Turk Revolution.

Chapter 7

1909: 28 August. The Goudi coup.
1910: 6 October. Venizelos and the Liberals win in a landslide.
1911: 20 May. New Constitution passed.
1912: 8 October. The Balkan Wars began.
1913: 18 March. Accession of King Konstantinos.
1913: 18 July. The Balkan Wars ended.
1914: 28 July. The First World War began.
1915: 24 April. Armenian genocide began.
1915: 31 May. Venizelos won election on a platform for entering the war.
1915: 2 October. King Konstantinos dismissed Venizelos, starting the National Schism.
1916: 30 November. National Defence established alternative government in Salonika.
1917: 13 June. King Konstantinos gave up the throne and left Greece.
1917: 30 June. Greece entered the First World War.
1918: 11 November. Germany surrendered.

Chapter 8

1919: Paris Peace Talks.

1919: 15 May: Greek troops occupied Smyrna.

1920: 23 April. Turkish Grand National Assembly declared independence.

1920: 10 August. Treaty of Sèvres signed.

1920: 12 August. Venizelos shot while in Paris.

1920: 25 October. King Alexander died of septicaemia.

1920: 1 November. Venizelos voted out of office. United opposition government formed.

1920: 19 December. King Konstantinos I returned to the throne.

1921: 23 March. Greco–Turkish War.

1922: August. Greek army defeated at the Battle of Ankara.

1922: 11 September. Military coup by the Revolutionary Committee.

1992: 13–22 September. The Burning of Smyrna.

1922: 31 October–15 November. The Trial of the Six.

1923: 30 January. Greece and Turkey signed the Convention on the Exchange of Populations.

1923: 24 July. The Treaty of Lausanne.

1924: 25 March. The Second Hellenic Republic.

1925: 24 June–29 August 1926: The Pangalos dictatorship.

1928: 5 July. Venizelos became prime minister.

1932: 25 September. Panagis Tsaldaris and the People's Party took power.

1935: 1 March. Venizelos and his supporters' attempted coup failed.

1936: 4 August: Dictatorship of Ioannis Metaxas.

Chapter 9

1940: 28 October. The Greco–Italian War began.

1941: 29 January. Metaxas died.

1941: 6 April. Operation Marita.

1941: 27 September. EAM established.

1941: September–July (1942). The Greek famine.

1942: 25 November. Destruction of the Gorgopotamos bridge.

1943: 3 September. Italy withdrew from Greece.

1944: 10 March. The PEEA established.

1944: 20 May. The Lebanon agreement.

1944: October: The Percentages agreement.

1944: 3 December. The December events.

1945: 12 February. The Varkiza agreement.

1945: Summer. The White Terror.

1946: 28 September. King George II returned.

1946: October. The civil war began.

1947: 12 March. The Truman Doctrine established.

1949: 16 October. The civil war ended.

Chapter 10

1947: 22 March. AMAG formed.

1947: 1 April. King Paul succeeded his brother George.

1952: 18 February. Greece admitted to NATO.

1952: 19 November. Greek Rally under Papagos elected.

1955: 1 April. Violence erupted in Cyprus.

1955: 6–7 September. Anti-Greek riots in Istanbul and Izmir.

1955: 5 October. Konstantinos Karamanlis succeeded Papagos and founded the National Radical Union.

1955–1959: EOKA campaign in Cyprus.

1960: 16 August. Cyprus gained independence.

1961: 17–19 April. Karamanlis in the United States to meet with Kennedy.

1961: 29 October. Karamanlis re-elected amid charges of corruption. Papandreou launched his 'Relentless Struggle.'

1962: Greece admitted to the EEC as an associate member.

1963: 27 May. Grigoris Lambrakis assassinated.

1963: 11 June. Karamanlis resigned and left Greece.

1963: 3 November. Papandreou elected.

1964: 6 March. King Konstantinos II enthroned.

1965: 15 July. Centre Union split by defections. The Apostasy.

1967: 21 April. The Dictatorship of the Colonels.

Chapter 11

1967: 21 April. The Dictatorship of the Colonels began.

1967: 12 December. Royal counter-coup failed.

1968: 13 August. Alexandros Panagoulis' assassination attempt against Papadopoulos.

1968: 1 November. George Papanadreou's funeral.

1968: 15 November. Constitution revised, creating a 'guided democracy'.

1970: 19–23 October. VP Agnew's visit to Greece.

1973: 29 July. Referendum abolishing the monarchy passed.

1973: 14–17 November. Student occupation of the Polytechneio.

1973: 25 November. Military coup. Ioannides replaced Papadopoulos.

1974: 15 July. Greek coup attempt against Archbishop Markarios of Cyprus.

1974: 20 July–18 August. Turkish invasion of Cyprus.

1974: 24 July. Dictatorship fell as Karamanlis returned to Athens.

1975: July–December. The Dictatorship on Trial.

1977: 20 November. New Democracy's electoral victory.

1979: 28 April. Greece gained full accession into the EEC (the European Union after 1981).

1981: 18 October. Papandreou and PASOK elected.

1985: 3 June. PASOK re-elected.

1987: 27–30 March. Greece and Turkey on the verge of war over Aegean oil.

1989: 18 June. PASOK defeated and coalition of New Democracy and the Communist Party formed.

1990: 8 April. New Democracy elected as the ruling party.

Chapter 12

1991: 21 June. Breakup of Yugoslavia.

1991: 16–17 October. Greece protested against name of former Yugoslav Republic of Macedonia.

1991–1992: Massive immigration from former communist countries.

1992: New Democracy implemented austerity program.

1992 (–2000): Construction of the Athens Metro (subway) began.

1993: 10 October: PASOK and Andreas Papandreou re-elected.

1996: 18 January: Kostas Simitis became prime minister.

1996: 31 January: The Imia Crisis brought Greece and Turkey to the brink of war.

1996: 23 June: Andreas Papandreou died.

1998: 23 April. Konstantinos Karamanlis died.

1998 (–2004): Construction of the Rio-Antirrio bridge began.

1999: August–September: 'Earthquake' diplomacy between Greece and Turkey.

2000: 9 April. PASOK re-elected.

2001: 1 January. Greece joined the European Monetary Union (the Euro).

2004: 7 March. New Democracy under Kostas Karamanlis took power; introduced austerity.

2004: 1 May: Cyprus joined the European Union.

2004: 13–29 August: Athens Summer Olympics.

2008: October. Wall Street crashed.

2008: 6 December. Killing of Alexandros Grigoropoulos triggered riots.

2009: 4 October. PASOK and George Papandreou took power.

2009: 20 October. Finance Minister George Papakonstantinou announced public debt crisis.

2010: 3 March: Additional austerity measures passed.

2010: 23 April. Papandreou requested bailout funds from the Troika.

2010: 3 May. Memorandum of understanding between Greece and the Troika signed.

2010: June. Parliament passed austerity package amid rioting.

2011: 25 May. Protesters seized and occupied Sintagma Square.

2011: 29 June. Additional austerity measures passed.

2011: 6–10 November. Papandreou resigned; new coalition government led by Loukas Papadimos.

2012: 17 June. New Democracy won election and Antonis Samaras became prime minister.

2013: November. Greek total unemployment rate rose to 27 per cent and youth unemployment to 62 per cent.

2014: 29 December: ND failed to elect a president and fell.

2015: 25 January. SYRIZA won election and Alex Tsipras named new prime minister.

1

The Greek world in its Ottoman context

The year 1453 is a year that lives in infamy in the Greek collective consciousness. To be more specific, the exact date that exerts such a powerful influence on popular culture is Tuesday 29 May. For centuries, Greeks have considered Tuesdays in general and that particular day in May to be cursed. The reason is that on that fateful day the great city of Constantinople fell to Mehmed II Fatih (the Conqueror) and his Ottoman army. With its capture, the Byzantine state largely ceased to exist and the long life of the Eastern Roman Empire as a Christian polity came to an end. The significance of the city's fall, however, was actually more symbolic than real. By the mid-fifteenth century, the once-great Byzantine Empire had been reduced to a shadow of its former self and, indeed, most of what we can call the Greek world was already under the control of foreign Catholic or Muslim rulers. Though symbolic, that does not mean that the Ottoman capture of the city was not an exceptionally important event. First, it validated the emergence of the Ottomans as a world power and marked their state's transition to an imperial one. Second, it fulfilled a long-held prophecy in Islam that Muslim ascendancy would have been achieved when the 'Red Apple' (Constantinople) became a Muslim city. Third, and conversely, it deprived the Christian world of its greatest capital city. Tuesday, 29 May 1453, then, cast, and continues to cast, a long, dark shadow over the Greek world.

In order to understand the history of Modern Greece, one has to acquire a deep background regarding the major developments between the fifteenth and nineteenth centuries and that means studying Ottoman history. Given the long history of Greece in the Empire and the fact that, even after the establishment of the Greek state, more Greeks continued to reside in the Ottoman Empire than in Greece, Greek history and Ottoman history are fundamentally the same field until 1923. This statement will surprise some and even anger others. This is because nineteenth-century state-formation and culture-building devoted a great deal of attention to demonizing the Ottoman years. Nationalist historiography in the Balkan successor states successfully embedded in popular culture the notion that almost all of the problems and flaws in their states and societies were directly attributable to the sufferings, deprivations and oppression of the 400-year 'Ottoman yoke.' Everything that was deemed wrong in post-independence society was somehow attributable to the 'rule of the Turks' (τουρκοκρατία, as this period is usually referred to in Greece). But like all nationalist myths, this one is largely an invented tradition. This is not to say that, as we will see, Greeks along with other non-Muslims were not systemically and systematically discriminated against, but to assert that we cannot take at face value the totally negative picture that dominates popular culture. One of the problems with post-independence nationalist histories is that they tend to reduce the totality of the experience of Ottoman rule to just the conditions that pertained in the late eighteenth and early nineteenth centuries. This is unacceptable. As was the case everywhere, over four hundred years, conditions in the Ottoman Empire changed radically and repeatedly, and these developments had important consequences for Greeks. In addition to change over time, we also have to recognize that there was a diversity of experience. Different people in different places from different sectors of society experienced Ottoman rule differently.

What I want to do in this chapter, then, is to sketch out those key elements of society, politics and economy that developed during the period of Ottoman rule and that most deeply shaped Greek society on the eve of the revolution of 1821. There are a number of key turning points in the history of the Empire, and we can divide Imperial history into three main phases: the first one covers the period from 1345, when the Ottomans first established a foothold in Europe, to the reign of Suleiman the Lawgiver in the sixteenth century; the second extends from the period of his rule until the end of the Ottoman–Russian War of 1768–74; and the third covers the era from the end of that conflict until the early nineteenth century. We begin with the entry of the Ottomans into Europe.

Building the Empire (1345–1566)

By the middle of the fourteenth century, the unity of the once great **Byzantine/ Eastern Roman** Empire had been shattered, and Constantinople repeatedly found itself at war with various other Christian kingdoms in the region, such as the Serbs and the Bulgarians. Moreover, even among the Byzantine ruling elite, there were destructive struggles for power. It was in 1345 in the midst of one such internecine conflict that the Ottomans entered Europe, having previously established a small polity in northwestern Anatolia. The Ottomans crossed into Europe not as invaders but at the behest of one side in an on-going Byzantine civil war. Once there, they settled in and began to systematically expand their domain in the Balkans. By 1369 all of Thrace was under their control to the extent that Murad I shifted his capital from Bursa to Edirne (Adrianople). Those Christian princes who did not submit and become allies of the rising Muslim power were defeated in combat and reduced to vassalage. After almost two decades of conflict, Macedonia succumbed. A year later, on 15 June 1389, at the head of a mixed Ottoman-Byzantine-Bulgarian army, Murad I inflicted a resounding defeat on the Serbs at the Battle of Kosovo. Even Murad's death in the battle could not diminish the significance of this victory. Had it not been for the Mongolian invasion under the great warlord Timur the Lame (also known as Tamerlane) and his defeat of the Ottomans at the Battle of Ankara (1402), the Balkans and maybe even Constantinople itself would have fallen. As it was, the Ottoman defeat only bought the city a little more time.

The Ottomans quickly rebounded from their temporary setback. During the 1420s, they extended their conquests along the Aegean coast of Anatolia. This was followed by a successful campaign to restore order in the Balkans, including retaking the city of Salonika, which had revolted. In 1451, at the age of twenty-one, Mehmet II ascended to the throne for a second time and set about showing that he belonged in the same company as his boyhood heroes, Achilles and Alexander the Great, by doing something that had only been done once before (in 1204): take the city of Constantinople by force. He set about this task by putting together a combined land and sea force that could invest the city completely. He had built a huge artillery force, including one cannon, the Basilikas, which could fire a 1,000-pound cannonball, in order to smash the city's walls. The siege began on 2 April 1453 and ended with the city being taken on 29 May. From that point on, the Ottoman state was an empire and Mehmet II earned a new nickname: the Conqueror. For almost a decade after this seminal conquest, his armies remained at war in the Balkans; almost all of the remaining Orthodox or Roman Catholic kingdoms and principalities either, like Athens, voluntarily surrendered and were spared the sword, or were defeated in battle and faced the consequences, including enslavement. From the end of Mehmet's reign until the accession of Suleiman the Lawgiver, the story was one of Ottoman expansion and consolidation.

How did incorporation into the Ottoman Empire affect Greece and the Greeks? Before we can answer that question, a few prefatory comments are in order. The first is that by the time the great city fell, much of the Balkans was already in Ottoman hands.[1] In other words, capturing Constantinople was just one of the final pieces in a process of imperial expansion that had been going on for over a century. Second, because so much of the Empire's territory was in Europe, the majority of the population was non-Muslim, including Jews, Catholics, and the largest denominational group, Orthodox. Third, because of the time duration over which these events occurred, the Ottomans had already developed a certain familiarity and understanding of the non-Muslim Balkan populations. Fourth, the governing institutions and policies that the Ottomans implemented to rule this increasingly large and diverse population developed over a substantial period of time and were largely based upon pre-existing models and practices, Sharia law, the Koran and exigent circumstances. When we look back historically at how the Empire functioned, it is easy to assume that imperial statecraft, and in particular its treatment of non-Muslims, were shaped by a conscious set of policy decisions. They were not. Instead, they were the end result of a protracted process that was often driven by ad hoc responses to unanticipated developments. But rather than trace this process chronologically, we will examine the system of rule as it appeared by the sixteenth century.

Let's begin by looking at the social structure. At a macro level, Islam divides all of the world's population into two groups: the **Darülislâm**, those who reside on the House of Islam, and the **Darülharb**, those who reside in the House of War. In theory, those in the second group must convert to Islam or be eliminated. The Koran, however, makes a special exception for those followers of one of the other monotheistic faiths based upon the tradition of Abraham. This meant that Christians and Jews fell in between the two domains, those of Islam or of War. Since the Koran forbids forced conversions, Christians and Jews had the option to voluntarily and of their own volition convert to Islam and enjoy all of the benefits that that entailed (see below) or they could retain their faith but at a considerable cost: systemic and systematic discrimination. But Ottoman society was not divided only along religious lines. Like almost all other Early Modern societies, it was stratified by a judicial status. In Western Europe, there were three legal orders: the nobility, the clergy and commoners; in the Ottoman Empire, the equivalent categories were, respectively, the *askeri*, the *ulema* and the *reaya*. It is important to note that people of all of the different religions fell into one of these groups. As was the case everywhere, one of the most important distinctions between these groups was that two of them, the nobility/askeri and the clergy/ulema, enjoyed many significant tax exemptions. If we think of Ottoman society as being like a pyramid, then the two groups at the bottom were non-Muslim or **Dhimmi** (or Zimmi) reayas followed by slaves. Ottoman society, then, was organized along three axes of difference: one based on religion, another on the judicial category to which a person belonged and the last on gender (Figure 1).

Non-Muslims, including the Greeks, of course, were discriminated against in numerous and important ways. We begin with taxes. In exchange for being able to retain their old religion, non-Muslims had to pay a head tax; this was

FIGURE 1 *Public festival in the Ethiopian Quarter of Late Ottoman Athens. This scene captures the vitality and diversity of life in pre-Independence Athens. Done in the early nineteenth century, it shows Christians, Muslims and Jews, men and women, Europeans and Africans celebrating a festival in the open area just beyond the so-called Ethiopian Quarter in the west side of the city. We see scenes of bands playing and women dancing, of men from different cultural backgrounds smoking and socializing. All around there are merchants hawking their wares and some poor African women begging for money. Note, finally, how almost of the men shown in the illustration are heavily armed.*

John Rodwell (1816). Public Domain. GallantGraphics all rights reserved.

literally a tax that allowed them to keep their head. Called the *Cizye*, this tax was levied on all able-bodied men based upon their net worth and the best estimates are that it equated to between 8 and 10 per cent. In addition, they were subject to an annual land tax, the *Kharaj*, that ranged between 8 and 25 per cent depending on which crops were cultivated on the land being taxed. Also, many families worked land on feudal estates called *Timars* and had to pay a rent equivalent to 10–25 per cent of the crop. Non-Muslims were also subjected to a variety of corporate requisition taxes. The most important of these was the war requisition tax. Since Dhimmis could not bear arms and fight without special dispensation (of which there were many – see below), when the Empire went to war those who did not fight were required to provide food and animals to the military as their contribution. They were also subject to import tariffs and export duties worth 3–6 per cent of the value of their products. They faced other exactions as well, but the ones listed here were the major ones and they suffice to show that the tax burden that non-Muslims had to bear in order to keep their faith was a substantial one and one much higher than that borne by the Muslim reaya.

There were other forms of discrimination as well. Many of these relate to law. Intermarriage, for example, between the religions was strictly controlled and acceptable only between a Muslim man and a non-Muslim woman. Non-Muslims could not carry firearms or bladed implements with a length greater than approximately 6 inches without an imperial dispensation. Dhimmis could not build a house that was taller than the tallest one owned by a Muslim and they could not live at elevations that placed them above Muslims. They had to provide mandatory labour service to the state twenty days each year. Lastly, non-Muslims were at a severe disadvantage in court. In litigation or prosecution that crossed religious lines, the testimony of the Muslim was always taken over that of a non-Muslim. Text-box 1 gives an excellent example of this from a slightly later period. In this case, a Christian, Ivan, sued a Muslim barber named Usta Yumer for appropriating land that belonged to him. Ivan produced two witnesses, presumably Christians, who supported his contention that the land in question was inherited by Ivan from his father. Yumer asserted that the previous owner of the property had died without leaving an heir and so according to the law of the land, it had become state property, and that he had bought it from a government official. He could not, however, produce a single witness who could verify his story. Nonetheless, when he swore a holy oath in the name of God, his testimony was accepted as the truth and the court forbade Ivan from bringing legal proceedings. Legal inequality was just one of the many forms of discrimination imposed upon non-Muslims.

The last extremely important exaction inflicted on Dhimmis was the **devşirme**, or 'child levy.' Later nationalist historiographies have cast this practice as the most iniquitous and painful one suffered by Orthodox Christians. At the time, however, the devşirme represented one of the routes by which Greeks, Serbs and others could obtain positions of power and prominence in the imperial government. It was a way that non-Muslim reaya could become members of the askeri and the ulema. The origin of the devşirme goes back a long way and stems from the tradition of the leader of an Islamic army that conquers non-Muslims receiving perhaps as many as one-half of the prisoners of war as his slaves. As was customary, if an opponent refused to surrender and was defeated in battle, then those who were captured could be legally enslaved. The royal household was to a large extent staffed by slaves. As the Empire ceased to expand into Europe, the supply of slaves dwindled. This led to the adoption of an internal levy imposed upon non-Muslims in the Balkans.

Text-box 1 A Christian versus a Muslim in court (1700)

Ivan, son of Nikola, [an Infidel] from the town of Vidin, in the neighbourhood of Karaman, appeared before the holy [Kadi] court in the presence of the barber Usta Yumer, son of Ali. Ivan brought a lawsuit against Yumer for the following reason:

Ivan had inherited a vineyard of three-quarter acres in the area of Kozlovets, bordering the vineyards of Manush, Yovan the baker, Nikola and the state road. The above-mentioned Yumer had misappropriated it.

During the interrogations, Yumer declared that some time ago, he had bought the vineyard in question for fifteen gurus from a state employee as ownerless property. After the death of its former owner, Ivan Simitchiyata, who died without leaving any heirs, the vineyard became state property.

Nikola objected that what Yumer said was not true and he called two witnesses, both Infidels, who confirmed that the vineyard really belonged to him. As Yumer was not able to find such witnesses within the fixed time, the court suggested that he declare under oath that he had really bought the vineyard as ownerless property. Yumer agreed and took an oath in the name of God. On this basis, the court forbade Ivan to continue any legal proceedings on the vineyard.

Vidin 1770.

B. Murgescu and H. Berktay (eds) (2009), *The Ottoman Empire. Workbook 1*, Thessaloniki: CDRSEE, document II-15.

Periodically (at the peak of the practice during the sixteenth century, it was approximately every four to five years), a commission of Muslim officials would tour the region visiting villages. When they arrived at a place, all of the boys aged eight to fifteen were brought out for inspection. Orphans and only sons were exempted from the levy. The officials, who were joined by local notables and priests, would examine the boys, gauging their physical prowess and development, and their mental acumen, usually by asking them questions in Turkish. Those deemed most suitable would then be confiscated as royal slaves (*Kapikalu*) and converted to Islam. The biggest and the strongest were subjected to military training and became **Janissaries**. They were enrolled in the corps of novices, and those who successfully completed the arduous training were promoted to the regular corps. The Janissaries constituted the core of the Ottoman military and at their height they were considered the finest warriors in the world. The best and the brightest of the corps received the honour of being promoted to be members of the Sultan's personal bodyguards, called *Solaks*. Those boys who were intellectually gifted followed an alternative course of training, that of letters. They would study literature, astronomy, astrology and other sciences, and, of course, would become religious scholars of the Koran. After their training was complete, they took their place among the Empire's clerical elite. Men who entered Ottoman service through the devşirme rose to positions of power in the imperial government, including the post of Grand Vizier. Christian converts, then, formed a sizable and critically important group within the imperial ruling structures. They did not, however, lose touch with their families and relatives back home. Some men were able to obtain administrative positions back in the area that they had come from and it was very common for men to use their position to advance the material interests of their relatives. Through the devşirme, then, Balkan Christians, including Greeks, were able to achieve positions of prominence in the Empire.

During the period that we are discussing, some Greeks were able to participate in Ottoman governance while retaining their Christian faith. One such group comprised members of the old Byzantine aristocracy. In the face of Ottoman military expansion, rather than resisting, some noblemen submitted and became vassals of the Sultan. They pledged their loyalty and military support and in return they received many of the same privileges that were accorded to Muslim nobles; there are well-known cases of Greek nobles converting to Islam and thus acquiring positions of prominence in the government. But the point here is that there were also some who did not do so and remained Christians.

The single most important Christian institution in the Empire was the Orthodox Church, consisting of the Patriarch, the various urban-based Metropolitans and the numerous and oftentimes wealthy monasteries. Since the Ottomans had kept the governmental structures that they inherited from the Byzantines largely intact, this left only the church as a Christian-dominated institution, but one that was also firmly under the Sultan's control. In a world in which religious differences were of paramount importance in social organization, it made sense that the new Islamic ruling elite would utilize the Orthodox Church in the governance of its large Orthodox Christian population. There is some controversy among historians regarding precisely when the head of the Orthodox Church, the **Ecumenical Patriarch**, was granted the privilege of enjoying administrative power over Orthodox Christians, or *Rum* as they were called (they referred to themselves as *Romioi* – Romans), in matters both secular and sacred. According to one version, it was Mehmet II himself who invested the first patriarch, Ioannis Gennadios, with these powers. Others argued that the official institutionalization of the patriarch as head of the Orthodox **Millet** ('nation') developed in a piecemeal process over time. A number of points are clear. The first is that by the seventeenth century, the institution of the Ecumenical Patriarchate was part of the Ottoman state.

Second, the patriarch himself was an Ottoman official who was appointed by a sultan and whose powers were limited to those articulated in the imperial decree that appointed him. Third, the most important privileges granted to the patriarchs were (1) the prerogative to appoint church hierarchs, subject to sultanic approval; (2) exerting control over monastic and church property, subject to certain conditions; (3) legal authority in regard to family law; and (4) the right to collect certain specified taxes from the Orthodox population, some of which stayed in the church coffers while the rest was turned over to the Ottoman treasury. In addition to the Istanbul-based Patriarchate, another religious institution played an important role in Christian life, especially at the local level: monasteries. The best known are the ones on Mount Athos, but there were other important ones scattered across the Empire. Many of the monasteries had their own legal relationship with the Sultan, and because they were large landowners, many peasants were dependent on them for their livelihood. The Orthodox Church as an institution, then, played a vital role in Greek society, the *Millet-i Rum*, in matters both religious and secular.[2]

The way in which the various regions of Greece were administered during this period had an important impact on their historical development. It is important to bear in mind that the nature of Ottoman rule varied across the region depending on a number of different factors, one of the most important of which was whether or not the area had been incorporated into the Empire via voluntary submission or military subjugation. So, for example, communities that had surrendered and accepted Ottoman suzerainty willingly were spared the devşirme. In spite of this diversity, we can still draw some generalizations. As in any pre-modern empire, because of the difficulties of communication, Ottoman rule tended to be decentralized. Though the Sultan was technically an absolute ruler and thus could exercise complete control over his empire, he could not effectively rule his domain alone. Instead, a complex administrative hierarchy developed. Initially, sultans used conditional grants of land as a means of raising an army and of administering conquered areas. **Sipahis,** or cavalrymen, were given a *zimat* or parcel of land. In exchange for control of the land and all those on it, the sipahi pledged to provide the Sultan with troops. These grant-holders tended to live on their estates or in nearby towns and thus assumed many of the responsibilities of local rule. In the early period of imperial expansion, there were both Muslim and Christian sipahis. Over time, this system broke down. Increasingly, it became a more exclusively Muslim position and it lost some of its military efficacy as the estates became hereditary, and so men obtained their grant of land as a right and not because of their martial prowess. The policy, however, left a legacy of massive Ottoman-controlled land holdings worked by dependent Greek peasants. Alongside the sipahi system, there was also a form of provincial administration.

The Empire was divided into various administrative districts or provinces. In many areas, the Ottomans continued to use the geographical system of provinces that they had inherited from the Byzantines. The core areas of the Empire were divided into units called **eyalets** (or *beylerbeyliks*). As is to be expected, over the long history of the Empire, the number and areal extent of eyalets changed; the scheme discussed here pertained during the seventeenth century. The area that is now Greece was included in four eyalets: Rumeli (Thrace, Macedonia, Epiros, Central Greece), the Morea or Mora (the Peloponnesos), the Archipelago (the Aegean Islands) and Crete (after 1669). The governor of an eyelet was called a *Valisi* or *Beylerbey*. The position was term-limited and there was a hierarchy of them, and as a man moved up the ladder in government, he would transfer from the least to the most desirable governorships. In addition to administering his province, the valisi was responsible for collecting taxes and mobilizing the resources of his province in times of war. Eyalets were subdivided into units called **sanjaks** and they were governed by a *sanjakbey*. Lastly, sanjaks were broken up into **kazas**; these were not so much specific territories as they were collections of villages or communities that fell under the jurisdiction of a *kadi*.

To give an example of what the system looked like, here is how the Morea was organized. The entirety of the Peloponnesos constituted the Mora Eyalet and it was governed by the Mora valisis, who resided in Tripolis. The eyalet was divided further into six sanjaks, corresponding roughly to the Argolid (and Corinthia), Arkadia, Achaia, Ilis, Messenia and Lakonia. Each of these, then, was home to numerous kazas; the Argolid, for example, contained eight kazas. In terms of local government, among the Orthodox population, there was a dual administration. On the one side, there were the Ottoman officials, like the kadis who adjudicated civil and criminal cases involving Muslims and non-Muslims, as we saw in Text-box 1. On the other, there were the Orthodox priests and Christian notables (the **kocabaşis**) who collected taxes, settled disputes and effectively governed at the local level. At times, the two systems competed and at times they operated in coordination. At the level of the sanjak, there was a ruling council on which representatives of the various denominational communities sat. There was also a ruling council at the eyalet level. In the Morea, for example, this was the Mora Divani. In the provinces, then, there developed a system that combined a centrally appointed imperial administration with local-level officials who represented the people of different faiths. Real power, of course, rested with the former but still allowed for important input by the latter.[3]

Another legacy of the Ottoman rule was the creation of local communities that developed a very deep sense of local autonomy, inhabited by people who looked on outside institutions with deep distrust. This distrust stemmed from the treatment that the subject Christian population received from those Ottoman institutions that intruded into their lives.

Some Greek communities were able to acquire even more direct control over their own affairs. Providing internal security was of particular importance to the Empire, and so it founded villages called **derbends** in areas that were particularly remote, and thus haunts for bandits, or at specific locations, like mountain passes, that needed protection. Many derbend villages were populated by Greeks, and because they had to provide protection, they had a dispensation to carry weapons. They were also granted a great deal of local autonomy. Other Christian communities were granted special status because they filled particular needs of the Empire. The **Phanariot Greeks** of Constantinople were able to achieve notable success and gain power because of the services they rendered to the Sultan as diplomats and interpreters, or serving as the **Hospodars**, or princes, of Moldavia and Wallachia.

As just mentioned, maintaining order and control over such a vast domain required enormous resources and manpower. Once the feudal system broke down, other means had to be found to do so. A standing army would have been impossibly expensive to keep up. The solution arrived at was the appointment of Muslim militia called the **levend**. During wartime, the levend troops were dispatched to the front. Non-Muslim men of violence were retained and deployed to provide internal security. These men were called **armatoles** and the institution was the **armatolik**. Armatoles were most prevalent in areas where there was a large majority Christian population; mountain Thessaly, for example, was divided into six armatoliks.[4] There was a complex relationship between the armatoles and the levend. When the Empire went to war, often more armatoles were deployed to fill the void left by the levend's departure. At the war's end, the levend troops were demobilized and many armatoles went out of government service. This produced a huge number of unemployed or underemployed armed men. Some were hired by local lords to fill their private gangs, while others were retained for garrison duty. Many, however, took to the mountains and became outlaws, **klefts** in Greek. At times, the fighting between the armatoles and brigands was fierce. So, in some ways, when the Empire's external wars ended, a form of internal unrest took their place. Caught in between the bandits and the agents of the state were the common people. Later, myth-making would turn the bandits into proto-revolutionaries, but to contemporaries, they were a nuisance and a force to be feared.

The developments we have been discussing so far achieved their pinnacle during the reign of Suleiman the Lawgiver (1522–66). He is best remembered in the West for his military conquest; thus, in Western histories, he is usually referred to as Suleiman the Magnificent. And his achievements on the field of battle were exceptional. Under his leadership, the Empire would pretty much attain its greatest territorial extent. He achieved, for example, the subjugation of the island kingdom of Rhodes, which he took from the Knights of St. John. His armies also brought into his domain permanently the Levant, the Middle

East, much of the Arabian Peninsula, including the holy sites of Mecca and Medina, and large parts of North Africa. His other great accomplishment was in the field of law. It was during his reign that the administrative structures and policies discussed above took on a coherent form. Suleiman's rule had three major impacts on Greece and Greeks, two of which were positive and one less so.

The first development resulting from the peace that his rule brought at last to the region was the so-called *Pax Ottomanica*. While much of his life was spent fighting wars, these wars were mostly external, expansionary conflicts. Inside the Empire, and most certainly in its core areas, like Albania, Greece and Rumelia, peace reigned and prosperity flourished. The region of Boiotia in Central Greece, according to a recent study based on archaeological and textual sources, mainly tax registers, experienced a sustained period of unprecedented demographic and economic growth;[5] other regions of Greece did so as well.[6] Second, under Suleiman, probably more Greeks than ever before achieved positions of power and prestige. A good example of this is Ibrahim Pargali Paşa, a convert who was from boyhood Suleiman's close friend and confidant, and who, as his Grand Vizier, assisted him in his conquests. Also, the administrative reforms Suleiman instituted gave Greeks and the Orthodox Church considerable power at the local level. There was a third major development, though its impact would not be felt for some time and it was this: Suleiman's permanent conquest and consolidation of the Middle East and North Africa shifted the geographical balance of the Empire away from Europe. It also changed its demographic composition, rendering it for the first time a majority Muslim state. Lastly, the Ottoman acquisition of the Caliphate elevated to an entirely new level the Islamic character of the Empire. The impact of this last development would not be felt immediately; its consequences would only become manifest over time.

Transitional phases (1566–1768)

While two hundred years might seem like a very long transitional phase, in this case, what transpired was a series of developments, mostly negative, to which the Empire had to respond. And each time it enacted reforms, that themselves were frequently contested, there were consequences both intended and unintended that set in motion new developments. The first set of crises were political and they began shortly after the death of Suleiman the Lawgiver. Including him, the first ten Ottoman sultans ruled for an average of twenty-six years; for the nine who followed that fell to fourteen years. The first ten sultans all came to the throne as mature men: none of them were under the age of twenty, whereas one-third of the next nine were. Only one of the first ten left the throne while still alive, in contrast to the three of the next who did. In short, the century after Suleiman witnessed royal instability that created a crisis of governance. As often happens when an imperial government becomes weak at its core, power devolves to the provinces. In this case, uprisings and insurrections erupted in various parts of the Empire, the most important of which were the Çelali Rebellions (1595–1610) in Anatolia. The centre's loss of control led, then, to unsettled conditions in the provinces that brought to an end the era of peace and prosperity.

Making the situation worse was the disruption to society and economy caused by the advent of the Little Ice Age. The dramatically cooler conditions caused by this climate change had a global impact, and in the Ottoman Empire, it brought with it freezing cold winters and extended, more severe summer droughts: 'The freezing winters of the Little Ice Age propelled hundreds of thousands, or even millions, of Ottomans into famine, flight, and death.'[7] Greece was not spared the ravages to the rural economy caused by climate change. Certainly, more work needs to be done on this topic, but there is good evidence for abandonment of the countryside, as seen in the archaeological record, a drop in population and a severe disruption of the rural economy.

One of the many consequences of instability, unrest, and environmental catastrophe was a shift in the Ottoman treatment of its non-Muslim subjects. In seeking an explanation for what was going on around them, many looked to heaven. Muslim sheiks and imams interpreted the sufferings of the faithful as a sign of God's wrath. The Sultan and society had strayed from the strict teachings of the Koran and had failed to enforce Shari'a law fully. Islamic fundamentalists argued that the most important violation of divine law was that the Empire's infidels were treated too leniently. Related to this, and another cause of unrest among the Muslim reaya, was the fact that Christian converts were able to move up in status to join the askeri and ulema whereas they, native-born Muslims, were not. Together, these created a situation that some sultans thought to correct. Ahmed I (1603–17), for example, issued an imperial decree closing coffee houses and banning the consumption of tobacco and alcohol. Text-box 2 reproduces excerpts from an imperial edict by Murad IV in 1631, which called for the expansion and stricter enforcement of discriminatory laws against non-Muslims and even exhorted the Islamic faithful to insult and humiliate infidels. Another consequence of these developments was the opening up of enrolment into the Janissary corps to native-born Muslims, and this in turn led to a falling off of the practice of devşirme. In sum, the lines of demarcation between Muslims and non-Muslims were becoming sharper and discrimination against the latter was increasing. The social fabric that created a shared world between Christians, Jews and Muslims was becoming frayed.

Text-box 2   Restrictions on non-Muslims (1631)

Insult and humiliate Infidels in garment, clothing and manner of dress according to Muslim law and imperial statute. Henceforth, do not allow them to mount a horse, wear sable fur, sable fur caps, satin and silk velvet. Do not allow their women to wear mohair caps or 'Paris' cloth. Do not allow Infidels and Jews to go about in public clad more finely than the lowest True Believer.

Excerpted from an edict by Murad IV in March 1631 and reproduced in Finkel 2005: 213.

By the third quarter of the seventeenth century, the Empire had begun to recover from the problems described above, but they would soon be followed by new challenges and crises caused this time not by an act of nature but by human frailty. Sultan Mehmed IV and his powerful and competent Grand Vizier, Köprülü Fazıl Ahmed (1661–76), had restored the Empire's fortunes to such an extent that it was able once more to embark on wars of conquest against its neighbours. In 1669, for example, after a long and bitter war, the island of Crete was wrested away from the Venetians. So confident had Mehmed become that he began to interfere in the affairs of his Christian neighbours to the north. He sent troops north to support the Muslim Crimean Tatars in their war with the Cossacks and the Kingdom of Poland, and after a long and bloody campaign, they proved successful. This victory only reinforced his opinion that the time was ripe for him to achieve something that not even the magnificent Suleiman had been able to do: capture the city of Vienna and bring the Holy Roman Empire to its knees. So began the disastrous **Holy League War (1683–99).**

Mehmed IV assembled one of the largest Ottoman armies ever, including over 130,000 cavalry, Janissaries and other troops, as well as over 6,000 pieces of artillery; he also mobilized forces from Muslim allies such as the Tatars from Crimea. At the head of this formidable force, Kara Mustapha Paşa marched on Vienna. The Emperor Leopold refused to surrender and then left the city to its fate. On 12 July 1683, having surrounded the city, the Ottoman army began an unrelenting bombing campaign. In response to the Ottoman invasion, the Pope in Rome called on the Christian heads of Europe to form a Holy League and to launch a new crusade to save the great city. Few answered the call. The largest Roman Catholic country, France, had recently signed a treaty with the Ottomans and so they refused to join. England was in the midst of its own troubles and so did the same. Stepping up to take leadership of the league was the king of Poland, Jan Sobieski. With a force of approximately

48,000 men, he set off to liberate the city. The fate of Vienna, and arguably much of central Europe, was determined on 12 September. The Holy League army scored a stunning victory, crushing the Ottoman army. Kara Mustapha Paşa and his headquarters were captured. After a negotiated truce, he and what was left of his army were allowed to retire back into the Empire, where he was executed by order of the Sultan for his failures. The war would soon come to them.

In the aftermath of the Ottoman defeat at Vienna, other European powers now rushed to join the fray. So, while the Holy League army invaded the Balkans from the north, Russia declared war and marched on Crimea. Other Catholic powers in Western Europe also entered the conflict, the most important of which was Venice. It mobilized an army and mustered a fleet to invade the Morea. Sensing its traditional enemy's weakness, the Shiite Safavid Kingdom of Persia attacked the Sunni Ottomans along their eastern frontier. For our purposes, the most important theatres of operation were the Peloponnesos and the Aegean Sea. In 1684, Francesco Morosini landed in southern Greece at the head of a Venetian and allied army, and over the course of the next two and a half years he waged a successful military campaign that drove the Ottoman forces out of the peninsula. He followed up this victory with an incursion into central Greece. On 21 September 1687, Venetian forces attacked the city of Athens and besieged the Ottoman forces on the Acropolis. After their armoury had been damaged in one of the artillery fusillades, the Ottoman commander moved his remaining gunpowder and shot into the interior of the Parthenon, or, as it was called then, the great Mosque of Ayia Sofia. Five days after the siege had begun, disaster struck. A Venetian artillery shell smashed through the mosque's roof and ignited the gunpowder stores, setting off a tremendous explosion that reduced the Parthenon from an architectural marvel to a ruin. The war dragged on for another decade and the Venetians were unable to make any inroads north of Athens. The conflict finally came to an end in 1699 with the signing of the Treaty of Karlowitz.

The Treaty was a catastrophe for the Ottoman Empire. Never again would the Empire threaten Europe and, indeed, henceforth it would be the other way around. It had to cede considerable territories in the northern Balkans to the Austrians, in addition to other lands that went to Russia. It also saw the creation of the Venetian-controlled Kingdom of the Morea, which consisted of the Ionian Islands, the Peloponnesos and the island of Aegina. The territories in Central Greece that the Venetian military had occupied, including Athens, remained inside the Ottoman Empire. The war had wrought devastation on the Morea, with its pre-war population of close to a quarter of a million people reduced to around 80,000. Defeat in the Holy League War had additional consequences that impacted Greece.

An extremely important one was the reformation of Ottoman governance that began with the overthrow of Mustafa II and the accession of Ahmed III in 1703. 'The practice of devşirme, the levy of Christian children with the view to raising them as administrators and soldiers, which was already in decline in the seventeenth century, was totally abandoned at the beginning of the eighteenth century.'[8] The last recorded mention of the devşirme was a proposed levy to be implemented on the Greek part of Rumelia in 1705; there is no indication that it actually took place. In response to the fiscal crisis created by defeat in war, the Empire revamped its tax-collection system, giving much greater power and influence to tax farmers and by putting greater emphasis on collective liability for the collection of taxes. Another long-term trend that began at this time was the devolution of power and governance from the centre to the provinces. These last two changes set in motion a process that would lead to the creation of communal institutions, particularly in Christian majority areas, and this, as we will see shortly, had important long-term ramifications. These, and other reforms, restored somewhat the fortunes of the Empire to the extent that it was able to mount a successful military campaign that drove the Venetians out of the Peloponnesos in 1715. Their attempt to wrest away from the Austrians the territories they had lost in the northern Balkans, however, was less successful, and so the Empire achieved both gains and losses in the Treaty of Passarowitz (1718) that ended this latest round of conflicts. For Greece, besides the restoration of the Morea, the extremely important development that occurred at this time was the practice of appointing Phanariot Greeks as the Hospodars, or governors, of the Empire's northern provinces of Moldavia and Wallachia.

New Greek realities (1768–1810s)

A new period in the history of Greece and the Greek world began in 1768 with the most important of the many wars fought between the Ottoman and Russian empires (Figure 2). Until that year, the Ottoman Empire had experienced its longest continuous period of peace in its history. Not since the 1739 signing of the Treaty of Belgrade that ended the three-year-long Ottoman–Hapsburg War had the Empire been at war with any of its European rivals. A respite from armed conflict with its rivals gave the Empire an opportunity to introduce internal reforms. After the debacle of the Holy League War and the loss of significant territories, such as the Morea, the Empire had made a comeback of sorts, reclaiming that region in 1715, as we saw. After almost half a century of war, the Empire was finally at peace and that gave it an opportunity to deal with the economic and political fallout from the wars and to rebuild its social

FIGURE 2 *The bear eats 'the Musselmen'. Between 1684 and 1917, the Ottoman and Russian empires fought one another repeatedly; indeed, their on-going and persistent wars were of major importance to world history. The scene here is an allegory that captures the animosity between the two. The artist depicts Russia as a giant bear devouring the Ottomans, who are represented as mussels; the artist is making a pun on the word 'Musselmen', as Muslims were often called at the time, and mussels.*

Artist Unknown (1828). Public Domain. GallantGraphics all rights reserved.

and administrative foundations. So, while the rest of Europe was engaged in costly and brutal conflicts, such as the Seven Years War (1756–63), following the advice of a number of competent Grand Viziers, until 1768 the Ottoman Empire remained outside the fray.

On 23 October the Ottoman Empire declared war on Russia, with disastrous consequences. The reasons why Mustafa III made this decision were many. Though she had been on the throne only for a short time, Catherine II of Russia was making it clear that she would pursue a very aggressive, expansionist foreign policy. This set her on a collision course with her southern neighbour, which resulted in war. This was a curious conflict, with two years, 1770 and 1774, of intense military activity, interspersed with lengthy periods of inactivity during which negotiations took place. There were three primary theatres of war: the trans-Danubian region, the Aegean and the Morea. In 1770, the Ottomans suffered major defeats in the first two of them. On 7 July, the Ottoman fleet was almost completely destroyed in the Battle of Çesme (the straits between the island of Chios and Asia Minor). Coincidently, at exactly the same time that its warships were going up in flames, the army was routed at the Larga River in what is now Romania. Though the war would drag on for another four years, its outcome was largely determined in 1770.

Another significant development that took place that year was an insurrection in the Morea known as the Orlov Rebellion or the Morean Rebellion. As part of its grand strategy, the Russian military command sought to incite uprisings by Ottoman Christians in the Balkans. Fydor Orlov, the younger brother of Count Aleksey Orlov, the commander of the Russian fleet, was given the task of organizing the rebellion in the Morea. The call to arms resonated especially strongly with one of the most powerful of the Greeks in the region, Panagiotis Benakis. According to one source, he was the wealthiest man in the Morea; in addition to owning as private property six agrarian estates near the city of Kalamata and another four near Patras, he also controlled much of the southern Morea's external trade and the collection of its taxes. As befitted a man of his wealth and power, Benakis controlled a patronage network that included both Muslim ayan and Christian kocabaşis, as well a very large number of armed men. It was Benakis whom the Russians chose to lead the rebellion, and according to one rumour, he had even been commissioned into the Russian army with the rank of general. Working with Fyodor Orlov, Benakis mobilized men and materials for an uprising in February 1770.

The Orlov Rebellion ended in a crushing defeat. At its height, Benakis had put together an alliance of supportive kocabaşis and their followers, having at one point mobilized a force of close to 5,000 men. And they even enjoyed some limited success. They attacked all of the major Ottoman garrisons at places like Patras, Koroni, Leondari and Kalavryta, and even managed to capture the important city of Mistra. But the rebellion was crushed at the Battle of Tripolis on 9 April. There were many reasons for this lack of success. First, the vast majority of the population, who were reayas, failed to respond; instead, they remained loyal to their lords, be they ayan or kocabaşis. Second, many kocabaşis decided not to join the rebellion, while others, like the powerful Zaimes family from Kalavryta, actively opposed it, mainly because it was being led by their political enemies. What the Russians did not realize was that they were about to become entangled in a fierce, long-standing power struggle between competing factions. So, the minute they picked one side as their ally, they alienated the other factions. The Russians unsuspectingly stepped into a hornets' nest and it cost them. Third, the rebels had neither the manpower nor the resources to storm the Ottoman fortress, or the luxury of time to besiege them. Fourth, unfortunately for the Russians and the Greek rebels, one of the Ottoman Empire's most competent military men was resident in the Morea when the rebellion broke out, and he took the lead in crushing it. Muhsinzade Mehmed Paşa had been Grand Vizier up until the start of the war with Russia. Because he opposed it, he was dismissed from his post. After a brief retirement to the island of Lesbos, he was commissioned in July 1769 as commander of the garrison at Nafplion. He mustered a sizeable force of Albanian militiamen, Greek kocabaşis who remained loyal to the Empire and their armed gangs, and Ottoman garrison troops with which he crushed the rebellion. Though the insurrection failed, the 1768–74 Ottoman–Russian War had wide-ranging and important consequences for Greece and the Greeks, many of which stemmed from the pact that ended the war: the Treaty of Küçük Kaynarca.

The Treaty of Küçük Kaynarca, signed on 21 July 1774, is one of the most important documents of the modern age. The main conditions laid down in the treaty are the following: first, Russia gained territories both in the Caucasus and in the northern Balkans. Second, greater autonomy was given to Moldavia and Wallachia. Third, other articles gave Russia additional rights and prerogatives in the Ottoman Empire. For example, Russian merchants were given unrestricted access to the Black Sea and the Mediterranean via both sea and overland routes; they were also given special dispensations in regard to import duties and tariffs. Moreover, Russian consuls obtained the right to dispense '*berats*' or protégé status to Ottoman subjects, thus affording them all of the legal rights and economic privileges, including those just mentioned. And, since the treaty also gave Russia the right to establish consular office anywhere in the Empire, this practice quickly became widespread, especially, as we shall see shortly, among the Empire's Greek subjects. Lastly, the Porte had to pay a massive war indemnity, and this, on top of the colossal financial burden already caused by the war, exacerbated the Empire's economic woes.

Two other articles, numbers 7 and 14, proved to be far more significant than most of he substantive clauses discussed previously. In Article 7, the Porte promised to provide protection to the Christian religion and to its churches. Moreover, by compelling the Sultan to make this promise, Article 7 implied that Russia had the right to set the conditions for the treatment of his Orthodox Christian subjects. Article 14 likewise was susceptible to a similar interpretation. This clause stated that Russia had the right to construct a 'Russo-Greek' Orthodox church in Istanbul and to make a representation to the Porte on its behalf. Later Russian leaders took Article 14 to mean that Russia could interfere in Ottoman affairs on behalf of the Orthodox Church.[9]

All told, then, the events between 1768 and 1774 had a tremendous impact on all of the peoples of the Ottoman Empire, and none more so than the Greeks. The situation of Orthodox Greeks within the Empire changed dramatically. And Russian policies towards its new territories, called 'New Russia', ushered in a new relationship between it and the Hellenic world.

Catherine the Great was a **Philhellene** and student of Ancient Greece, and she had a dream. She would recreate the Eastern Orthodox Roman (Byzantine) Empire with a member of the Russian royal family on its throne, and its capital in the great city of Constantinople. By re-creating the Byzantine

Empire under Russian protection, she would not only unite the two most important Orthodox nations – Russians and Greeks – but she would also liberate from the 'yoke' of Islam the venerated heartland of the Classical Greek world so dear to the heart of supporters, like herself, of the **Enlightenment**. Even before her project had achieved its final form, she had already solidified links between Russia and the Greeks through her policy of settling Greeks in the territories of New Russia. Between the mid-1770s and mid-1810s, tens of thousands of Greeks immigrated to Russia, and specifically to a few cities and areas on the shores of the Black Sea and the Sea of Azov.

The initial settlement of Greeks occurred while the 1768–74 war was still in progress, and the immigrant population consisted mostly of refugees from the Peloponnesos and the Aegean Islands who had taken refuge with the Russian forces. Some of these people were transported and settled in the Crimea, while others were taken to the city of Taganrog on the northern shore of the Sea of Azov. It had been captured in 1769 and the settlement of Greek refugees there began the following year. They were soon joined by people fleeing their homeland out of fear of reprisals for their actions during the Orlov Rebellion. This group consisted mostly of men who had fought on the losing side. In 1775 alone, for example, over 2,000 families were settled in Sevastopol. In exchange for grants of land and financial support, the heads of these households were enrolled into militia battalions; there were two in the Crimea, called the Spartan Brigade and the Balaclava Brigade. Soon this unplanned settlement policy was replaced by an official, systematic and well-financed one.

The Russian government issued manifestos in 1784, 1785 and 1792, aimed at recruiting Christian immigrants from the Ottoman Empire, mostly Greeks, to repopulate New Russia. These immigrants settled mostly in the towns around the coast of the Sea of Azov. The Russians provided them with mortgages to buy land and grants to build houses, and mandated that repayment of the loan began only after a period of ten years. In addition, immigrants were exempted from property taxes for between 10 and 30 years and as an inducement to merchants, they were exempted from many tariffs and duties. Greek men who agreed to serve in a militia received additional benefits. Not surprisingly, Greeks (mostly from the Peloponnesos and the Aegean Islands) left the Ottoman Empire in droves and migrated to New Russia, settling mainly in three cities and their hinterlands: Taganrog and Mariupol on the northern shore of the Sea of Azov, and Odessa in the northwestern corner of the Black Sea.

By 1805, about 45,000 Greeks were residing in Taganrog and they dominated much of the economic and political life of the city. While not as large, Mariupol was even more of a Greek city, having been founded by immigrants. But it was Odessa that emerged as the most important city in Russia for Greek-Russians. By 1816, the Russian government estimated that almost 12,000 Greeks lived in Odessa, accounting for approximately one-third of the population. More important than the size, however, was the Greeks' role in the economy. By the 1820s, Greek merchant houses had assumed a commanding position in the commercial life of the city. In 1832, two of these houses alone accounted for almost 10 per cent of the Odessan import–export trade. These family businesses created commercial networks that connected Odessa to major markets of the Ottoman Empire, Western Europe, the Middle East, and even across the Atlantic to the United States. In addition to controlling foreign trade from the Russian Empire, Greeks also played a critical role in the financial sector, founding banks and maritime insurance companies. Southern Russia, then, became home to the wealthiest Greeks in the world. In sum, one of the most important developments for Greeks between 1774 and the outbreak of the great insurrection of 1821 was the establishment and development of Greek Russia.

One of the other important consequences of the establishment of Greek Russia and the development of a prosperous Greek merchant elite was the involvement of Greeks in service to the Russian state. Many of the men who were to play critical roles in the 1821 rebellion had experience as soldiers and politicians in Russia or as servants of the Empire abroad. Men like Skalartos D. Sturdza, Spyridon Destunis and Ioannis Kapodistrias all served the Russian state in various capacities, and some, like Kapodistrias, rose to high office. In the latter's case, he served as joint foreign secretary of the Russian Empire from 1815 to 1822. These three statesmen were clearly exceptional, but they represent a much broader group of men of Greek descent or of Greek immigrants who assimilated into Russian society and who served the Empire faithfully. Greeks also joined the Russian military, and some of them, like the Ipsilantis brothers, rose to the highest ranks. Many of these soldiers would play important roles in the 1821 insurrection.

Thousands of Greeks who resided outside of Russia, mostly in the Ottoman Empire, also entered into service on behalf of the Tsar, primarily in two areas: as members of irregular military units and as consular officers in the major Eastern Mediterranean cities. It became routine when Russia went to war with the Ottoman Empire for it to mobilize and organize Christian subjects of the Porte into irregular units. We saw this policy taken to the extreme during the Orlov Rebellion. But the practice really reached its zenith during the Napoleonic Wars (1797–1816). This militarization of Ottoman and Ionian Greeks had important ramifications. First, it established personal bonds between Greek and Russian soldiers that would prove consequential later on. Second, it created even more Greeks proficient in the art of war. Third, it made available ever-increasing quantities of firearms, as well as the building of armouries and gunpowder mills. From 1774 onwards, this increasingly meant using Ottoman Orthodox men, especially Greeks, to act as the Empire's consular officers. This development had serious and important consequences. First, it meant that St. Petersburg received intelligence about what was happening in the Ottoman Empire as perceived through Greek eyes. Second, it enabled increasing numbers of Greeks to obtain special privileges as protégés because the Russians issued them berats. Third, the practice obviously helped to reinforce the idea that Greeks had a special bond with Russia. And this, in turn, fostered the expectation that Mother Russia would eventually deliver the Greeks from the grip of Ottoman control.

One of the other most important developments for Greece after 1774 was the formation of a Greek Diaspora merchant elite. By the end of the eighteenth century, Greeks dominated merchant shipping between the Black Sea, the Mediterranean and beyond to Europe and America. We have already discussed the situation in southern Russia and on the Black Sea and, as we saw, Greeks plying trade under the Russian flag came to have mastery over maritime commerce between Russia and the West. Greeks controlled Ottoman-flagged shipping as well. Greek captains and crews also plied the waters flying the flags of Austria, Venice, Great Britain and Ragusa. So ubiquitous were Greeks in Mediterranean shipping that Greek, and in particular Ionian Greek, became the lingua franca of the Eastern Mediterranean and Greek became almost as important as Italian in the Western Mediterranean. Every major city in Western (Liverpool, London, Paris, Amsterdam, Livorno), Central (Vienna, Berlin, Trieste) and Eastern Europe (Moscow, St. Petersburg, Kiev) hosted flourishing communities of Greek merchants. And the merchant Diaspora extended not just to Europe but also elsewhere, for example India.

From the 1770s to 1821, the economies of Russia, the Ottoman Balkans and the Eastern Mediterranean became ever more tightly bound with the emerging Eurocentric world economy. Related to this phenomenon was the development of a vast Greek Diaspora trading network that literally spanned the globe from Southeast Asia to North America. Much of this international trade and commerce was in the hands of Greek trading houses. Domestically in the Ottoman Empire as well, Greek merchants and traders, artisans and craftsmen were of vital importance. The economic development of the Empire during this period had three important consequences for Greeks. First, there emerged a large and wealthy Greek merchant elite both inside and outside of the Empire, and these were not separate and distinct groups but, in fact, were tightly connected. The expansion of maritime trade was of particular importance in this regard. Second, the prosperity of the times was not restricted to just the upper class, and so, a new group emerged on the scene: the Greek bourgeoisie, consisting of petty merchants, middling commercial brokers, and artisans. Third, the Greek Diaspora grew in size and expanded in distribution, not only contributing to the material betterment of their lives but also exposing them to the ideas, ideologies and contemporary trends that were sweeping Europe and the West in the age of revolution.

The last major development of importance to the history of Greece during this period was a political one. The ability of the imperial government in Istanbul to effectively control such a huge territory with pre-modern communication technology was always a formidable challenge, but because of the numerous and severe crises of the eighteenth century, its capacity to do so was lessened even more. The result was that many of the core aspects of governance had to be delegated into local hands. The most important of these functions, for our purposes, was (1) tax-collection and other fiscal matters, (2) dispute resolution, (3) military mobilization and (4) the maintenance of law and order. The first of these enabled local men to gain great wealth through life-lease tax-farming, while the other three opened up new spaces for them to acquire power. As a consequence, there developed across the Empire (though we shall focus just on the Balkans and especially on those in the Peloponnesos, called Mora ayanlari) new groups of power brokers and an elite consisting of Christian kocabaşis and Muslims ayans. Moreover, because of the on-going crises, the Porte had lost much of its capacity to control and hold accountable these provincial notables.

Ayans were Muslim notables who constituted a local-level elite. Sometimes, ayans held positions in the government as appointees of the Porte, but government service was not a prerequisite for being considered an ayan. Some were members of the Ottoman military order, askeri, and received grants of land in exchange for their service in the imperial cavalry, but others were not. In sum, this was a very mixed bag of individuals. Their role in local society was more clear-cut: they acted as both a buffer and a bridge between the reaya, both Muslim and Christian, and the organs of the state. Many were landholders and played vital roles in the local economy as well. During times of war, they were expected to mobilize manpower, coordinate the collection of materials and supplies, either through the requisition tax or by purchase, and to go to battle themselves, depending upon their status and position.

During the eighteenth century, and especially after 1774, the position of the ayans in society changed dramatically, particularly in the Morea and Rumelia. Decentralization was certainly important, but it was more the form that this devolution of power took that matters most. Changes to the fiscal and military organization of the Empire contributed most to the rise of ayans to power, transforming them from local big men into state officials – even governors – as well as notables, warlords, landlords, plantation owners, fiscal agents and business entrepreneurs.

The same fiscal and military reforms that led to the ayans flourishing also benefited the Greek kocabaşis in the Morea and Rumelia. In the Morea and in much of Rumelia as well, especially in the countryside, Muslims were in the minority, and so, it is not surprising that Christian-dominated villages and communities produced their own leaders. Prominent local men were selected or elected to councils that regulated communal affairs, adjudicated local disputes and organized the collection of communal taxes. Structural changes in the administration of the Ottoman Empire, especially in Greece and the Balkans, led to the emergence of new Christian and Muslim power-brokers and warlords, who could threaten imperial rule at the local level. That threat became even more acute and imminent when the Empire became embroiled in the wars being fought in the West to decide the fate of Europe and as radical, indeed revolutionary, ideas arrived in the region. When Napoleon Bonaparte came east, the game changed dramatically, and ayans and kocabaşis would henceforth play extremely important roles in the power struggles that the French intervention unleashed. By the early nineteenth century, then, there had developed a wealthy mercantile Diaspora Greek elite, as well as a class of powerful Christian landowners in Greece. Both groups were becoming increasingly dissatisfied with Ottoman rule, and by the early decades of the nineteenth century, they were obtaining greater means and the will to do something about it.

2

The war for independence, 1821–1832

The modern state of Greece came into existence as a result of a protracted, bloody insurrection against the Ottoman Empire between the years 1821 and 1827. The significance of the Greek War of Independence transcends the bounds of Greece and Greek history. It was, in fact, of global significance. First, the insurrection was the first major successful war of independence by a subject population against an imperial power since the American Revolution of 1776. In spite of its enormous importance, the French Revolution did not create a new country but only introduced a totally new form of governance to a pre-existing one. The Greek insurrection was also the first successful nationalist revolution and it provided a model for later nationalist struggles in many parts of the world. The Greek War of Independence had a profound impact on the Ottoman Empire. Indeed, arguably it was the most important event in the history of the Empire since the reign of Suleiman the Lawgiver. At first, because the struggle quickly took on a pointedly religious dimension – Christians versus Muslims – the war strengthened the position of the Islamic establishment. However, in dealing with the rebellion, Mahmud II and his supporters had to initiate radical reforms, such as the abolition of the Janissaries, which changed the fundamental fabric of the Empire. The era of Ottoman reform really begins with the Greek War of Independence. The Ottoman move towards modernity had a profound impact on its people, including the huge Greek population that remained in the Empire even after the creation of the independent Greek state. Lastly, the conflict was the first real test of the conservative **Concert of Europe** that emerged out of the great power Congress of Vienna in 1816. The Greek War of Independence, then, was an event of transcendent importance.

The conflict started as an uprising aimed at liberation or the overthrow of the ruling regime. Because it succeeded, the rebellion became a revolution rather than being forever remembered as a civil war. Revolutionary movements, whether successful or not, inevitably lend themselves to myth-making. Revolutions make men and women into either heroes of the glorious struggle or martyrs to the lost cause. Following the lead of the sources, it is easy, therefore, to romanticize revolutions and revolutionaries, and to see the result of the national struggle as in some way inevitable. Certainly, this is the case with Greece. When participants in the struggle later penned their memoirs, as they did in large numbers, they actively wove the fabric of the myth of revolution, which shapes interpretations of the war even to this day. We must, however, avoid the pitfall of *post hoc* interpretations, which impute motives and plans that only became evident after the fact.

Like any historical event, the Greek War of Independence was the end result of a wide range of factors and influences, and its successful outcome was far from preordained or inevitable. Much of what occurred was contingent on past events and on contemporary developments in the Europe of the 1810s and 1820s. The Greek war for liberation must be seen in the context of Europe during the heyday of the conservative counter-revolution that dominated the great power politics after the defeat of Napoleon.

The pre-revolutionary context

The first of these contexts focuses on ideology and the formation of Greek nationalism, a development that took place through a sustained engagement with the body of ideas and writings emanating from the Western European Enlightenment. A useful way to trace the development of the Enlightenment in the region is to discuss the most important scholars chronologically and to think of them as generations. The most important writer in the first generation was Nicholas Mavrokordatos (1680–1730). In works published in the 1720s, he challenged the older system of learning that was based upon Orthodox religious texts and the writings of ancient authors, especially Aristotle, and of education that called on students to receive, not challenge, the ideas contained in them. Mavrokordatos argued in favour of science and scientific inquiry and he called on his fellow intellectuals to challenge the received wisdom. His work triggered a debate between those called the Ancients, who supported the older knowledge regime, and those called the Moderns, who shared his perspective. The debates between the two took place exclusively within the confines of the Orthodox Christian Academies, involved primarily a small group of intellectuals, who were also clerics, and had little impact outside of the confines of higher education. Indeed, even within the confines of the Orthodox Patriarchal schools, they gained little traction.

Exemplary of the next generation, which spans the period from the 1740s to the 1780s, were Evgenios Voulgaris (1716–1806) and Iossipos Moisiodax (1730–1800). The former championed the cause of Enlightenment philosophy and scientific inquiry; the latter did so as well, but he added three new dimensions to the debate: the secularization of knowledge, rational humanism and liberal progress. The leaders of this second generation were truly transnational scholars, whose educational formation took place both in the traditional centres of orthodox learning and also in the universities of Western Europe, and especially in Italy. Though still opposed by the church hierarchy, their work tipped the balance in favour of the Moderns and strongly influenced the next generation of scholars, who would take what had previously been a debate between intellectuals and turn it into a public discourse.

The third generation of intellectual scholars flourished from the 1790s onwards. They were a transitional group, bearing some resemblances to the previous generations, but also important differences. The most important distinctions were that this cohort of writers had a greater familiarity and engagement with the West, and many important Greek thinkers resided in the Diaspora. Second, far fewer of them were religious clerics and, third, as a consequence, more of them had no connection to the Orthodox academies. Lastly, and most importantly, their works were much more overtly secularist and political, particularly after the French Revolution of 1789. Predicated on Enlightenment ideas, the overthrow of the absolutist Bourbon dynasty and the establishment of a republic founded on the principle of popular, 'national' sovereignty had a profound impact on Christian intellectuals in the Balkans. It showed that regime change was possible; to use the language of the time, 'tyranny' could be toppled and the oppressive political systems of the Old Regime could be cast off and replaced by ones founded on the Enlightenment principles of liberty, equality and social justice. For people, like members of the Millet-i Rum, living in an absolutist state and subject to legal discrimination based on religion, these ideals were profoundly influential. Lastly, if the legitimacy of the new, post-revolutionary state rested on popular sovereignty, then this raised the critical question as to identity, belonging and national consciousness. In sum, it raised the issue as to what the nation was and what criteria determined inclusion in it.

The origin of a specifically 'Greek' national consciousness cannot be pinned down to a precise moment in the past but, instead, must be seen as part of an ongoing process. As we saw in the last chapter, discerning specifically ethnic or national identities among the subject populations of the Ottoman Empire is not easy, and care must be exercised in projecting nineteenth-century national identities on to the past. Nonetheless, it is evident that the development of a national consciousness among the subject populations of the Balkans took on a greater coherence and developed more rapidly in the latter part of the eighteenth century and the first part of the nineteenth century, especially after the French Revolution of 1789. Diasporic Greeks had grown in affluence and prominence during the eighteenth century, and because of the greater freedoms accorded them and their exposure to intellectual currents in Western Europe, it is not surprising that the intellectual basis of Greek nationalism was most coherently formed among this group.

The voluminous writings of these men constituted a Greek extension of the ideas and philosophies of the Enlightenment. Moreover, 'the Greek Enlightenment has left an indelible mark upon the full extent of Greece's *development* – upon both Greece's actual historical development and *the history of the discourse* on Greece's development.'[1] This intellectual movement had, then, a lasting impact on Greece. Among the contributors to the Greek Enlightenment, two men in particular stand out: Adamantios Korais (1748–1833) and Rigas Velestinlis (ca. 1757–98).

Adamantios Korais was born in Smyrna to a Chiote father and a Smyrniote mother. After receiving an eclectic and unconventional education, as befit a member of the burgeoning Greek merchant elite, Korais was sent to Amsterdam to oversee his father's silk trading interests there. He was to remain abroad thereafter. From his home in Paris, Korais played a leading role in formulating the intellectual foundation of Greek nationalism. Repulsed by the violence he witnessed during the French Revolution but steeped in hatred for the Ottoman Empire, he was thus torn by his firm belief that Greece must be freed from the 'yoke of tyranny', but that it must not be by violent revolutionary means. Instead, he preached a middle way of emancipation through education.

Through his work in Classical philology, Korais aimed at inculcating in Greeks a sense of their ancient heritage. His emphasis on the need to resurrect Greece's ancient glory stemmed in large part from his intense hatred of the Orthodox higher clergy – 'monkish barbarians' as he once called them – whom he blamed for the degraded state of the populace. For Korais, then, the model for a new Greece had to be ancient Athens rather than medieval Byzantium. It was, thus, through his efforts as a linguist and in particular his contribution to the development of *Katharevousa* (a purely literary language that combined elements of ancient Greek with the popular spoken language called demotic Greek) that he intended to give Greeks a means to invigorate that heritage. Though he had much to say about the 'moral' regeneration of the Greeks, he was strangely mute about the type of polity he foresaw rising from the ashes of the Ottoman Empire. Of course, it was to be liberal, but beyond that he never addressed issues such as its size, composition and governmental system. He lived to see the creation of an independent Greek state, though he played no major active role in its creation and, in fact, worried when hostilities broke out that the rebellion was premature.

Rigas Velestinlis was more than anyone else the father of the revolution. A Hellenized Vlach, Velestinlis had a chequered career; his most notable post was that of secretary to Alexander Ipsilantis, the *dragoman* of the Porte, in Constantinople. Rigas spent much time in Wallachia in the service of Phanariote *hospodars.* Highly educated and a gifted linguist, he was well suited to act as the conduit for the transmission of revolutionary ideas and ideals from the West to the East. Based in Vienna and imbued with the revolutionary fever emanating from France, he actively sought to spread the contagious creed of liberation to the Balkans.

In a series of works, Rigas both spread the gospel of revolution and sketched out a vision for the new Balkan republic that would emerge from the ashes of the Ottoman Empire. In his *The Rights of Man,* he transferred some of the key aspects of the French *Declaration of the Rights of Man and the Citizen* into a Balkan context. In Article Three on the equality of all men before the law, for example, he explicitly stated that this included both Christians and Muslims. Other articles as well emphasized that these fundamental, natural rights appertained to all groups and all religious denominations. He also called for the abolition of slavery and for the use of Greek as the common tongue of the new motherland.

In his most important work, the *New Political Constitution of the Inhabitants of Rumeli, Asia Minor, the Archipelago, Moldavia and Wallachia,* he provided a more detailed blueprint for the new state's constitution (see Text-box 3). The new polity was to be a secular, democratic republic. He referred to it as a 'Greek Republic' but, as he clearly noted, Greek in this context meant citizen, not ethnicity: 'The Greek People [consists of all] those living in the Empire, without distinction of religion or language ...' (Article Two). He was even more explicit in Article Seven: 'The sovereign people consists of all inhabitants of this Empire, without distinction of religion and speech, Greeks, Bulgarians, Albanians, Vlachs, Armenians, Turks and every other kind of race'. A sign of how progressive his thinking was that he wanted mandatory education specified in the Constitution and that it be required of both boys and girls. In sum, Rigas wanted a secular, multi-ethnic, liberal democratic state that geographically resembled the Byzantine Empire. This was a noble vision that was not to be. Finally, he recognized that the rabble needed more than political ideals to be roused to action, and so he penned a revolutionary anthem: the *Thourios.* This stirring poem became the Greek *Marseillaise*, and it was widely disseminated and sung. It ends with the following call for action:

Let us slay the wolves who impose the yoke,
Who cruelly oppress both Christians and Turks;
Let the Cross shine over land and sea;

Text-box 3 Rigas's 'new political constitution' (1797)

Constitution of the Greek Republic

Article 1

The Greek Republic is one, for all that it contains within it different races and religions. It does not look on differences in worship with a hostile eye. It is indivisible, for all that rivers and seas divide its provinces, which constitute a unitary, indissoluble body.

Article 2

The Greek People, that is to say those people living in this Empire, without distinction of religion or language, is divided into primary assemblies in the districts, to put into practise its sovereign authority. That is to say they assemble in every province, to give their opinion on any problem.

Article 4

Every man born and inhabiting the Republic, of the age of twenty-one, is a citizen.

Article 7

The sovereign people consist of all the inhabitants of this Empire, without distinction of religion and speech, Greeks, Bulgarians, Albanians, Wallachians, Armenians, Turks and every other kind of race.

Article 22

All, without exception, are obliged to know letters. The Motherland must establish schools for boys and girls in all the villages. From letters is generated progress, with which free nations shine. The ancient historical writing should be interpreted. In the big cities, the French and Italian languages should be taught. The Greek language is mandatory.

Article 122

The Legislative Administration assures all Greeks, Muslims, Armenians, Jews and all nationalities (who find themselves inhabitants in this Republic) equality, freedom, security, the control of the landed property of each, the public loans, which may be incurred for Freedom, the freedom of all religions, a common upbringing, public contributions there, where they belong, the unhampered freedom of the press, the right of each to petition and to complain, the right to gather in public companies and, lastly, the enjoyment of all the Rights of Man.

Paschalis Kitromilides (ed.) (2000), *Ρήγα Βελεστινλή Απαντα τα σωζόμενα*, Athens: IEI.

Let the foe kneel down in the face of justice;
Let men be purged of all this sickness;
And let us live on earth, as brothers, free! (lines 121–6)

While attempting to spread the gospel of national revolution, Rigas was captured in Austrian-controlled Italy. He was transported to Vienna where he was imprisoned. After intense lobbying by the Porte, he and seven other Greek radicals were extradited to the Empire. On the night of 24 June 1798, Rigas was executed by strangulation in a Belgrade prison. With the following words, Rigas became the first martyr to Greek independence: 'This is how brave men die. I have sown; soon the hour will come when my nation will gather the ripe fruit'.

Rigas's was not the only vision of what a liberated Greek state should look like, nor was his the only voice calling for rebellion. The anonymous author of the *Greek Rule of Law, or A Word About Freedom* published in 1806, for example, framed his call for revolution with a detailed catalogue of the horrors suffered by the subject Christian population of the Empire. But unlike many others, he viciously attacked fellow Greeks for their roles in perpetuating the suffering of their people. He saved his most savage diatribe for the clergy. For this writer, the war of liberation meant not only throwing off the yoke of Ottoman rule, but also the tyranny of the Orthodox Church and the heavy-handed domination of the 'Turkified' Greeks of the ruling class. Conversely, another widely held view was that it was the church that held the key to liberation.

Proponents of this idea argued that Orthodoxy was the only force capable of mobilizing the mass of people to rise up against the infidels. They looked back to the past to chart the future for their new Greece. What they foresaw was a new Byzantine Empire: Greek, theocratic and monarchical. The idea of Byzantine Hellenism resonated most loudly with the Phanariots of Constantinople. That there was not a single revolutionary vision is not surprising. What is significant is that all shared in the belief that the time was ripe for some form of relief from the worst aspects of Ottoman rule.

If a revolution is to be successful, three conditions must be met: there must be an ideological framework that gives aims and a direction to the movement; there must be an organizational structure that can coordinate and lead the movement; and, finally, there must be adverse material conditions among the populace that make mass support for action possible. In the Balkans of 1821, all three of these conditions were met.

Between 1804 and 1815, there were two connected episodes of civil violence in Serbia that led to the province obtaining greater autonomy within the Ottoman Empire. Since Serbia formed the frontier between the Empire and Austria and since Serbs were subjects of Austria on the other side of the border, the Sultan Selim III found it expedient to accede to the calls from Serbian leaders for certain reforms. Among the privileges accorded to the Serbs was the right to collect their own taxes and to bear arms and form militias. Also, the Porte granted them certain land rights and protections from abusive officials. Lastly, the balance of power at the local level was shifted through the formation of local Christian councils that dealt with internal matters and that liaised with the Porte's officials. Thus Serbians obtained greater local autonomy and influence in government. These created tensions with local Ottoman officials, and especially the Janissaries, who resented their loss of power. This led to a conflict in which Serbs fought alongside forces representing Istanbul against local Ottomans. Once they were victorious, a split developed between the two sides, and the Serbs, seeking greater local autonomy, revolted against the Ottoman state. With the great power intervention in 1815, the Serb rebellion was brought to an end.

The Serbian insurrection and its settlement had important ramifications for Greeks in Ottoman Europe. First, they led to the establishment of yet another semi-autonomous territory in the Empire, in which Christians largely ruled themselves. It may not have been large in size but it was significant because it showed others that home rule was possible and that the partitioning of the Empire was feasible. Second, the new Serbian principality was strategically located at the crossroads of the Balkans and Europe: at its centre was Belgrade, the gateway to Europe on the Danube; it bordered Austria and the Danubian Principalities, and it was relatively close to Russia. In short, Serbia further entangled the great powers in Ottoman Balkan affairs. Third, there was now a well-armed and battle-hardened Christian militia in the region that could potentially provide the vanguard for a larger insurrection. And lastly, it stood as an example. Other groups asked themselves: if the Serbs could gain self-rule, why not us? In regard to this last point, as important as Serbian semi-autonomy was as a beacon of hope, it paled in comparison to what happened at approximately the same time on a group of islands off the coast of Greece. The creation of the independent United States of the Ionian Islands had far-reaching consequences for Greeks everywhere.

Fuelling further the belief that independence was possible was the creation in 1815 of the first independent Greek state since 1453: The United States of the Ionian Islands. The seven islands of Corfu, Paxos, Lefkada, Kefalonia, Ithaki, Zakinthos and Kythera had for centuries been part of Venice's Levantine Empire. After the demise of the Serenissma Republic in 1797, the islands were passed back and forth between the various great powers – France, Russia and Great Britain. With the defeat of Bonaparte, their status was in limbo. Each of the great powers wanted them, but none would let the others have them. The solution struck upon was to declare them a sovereign state under the protection of Great Britain. This landmark event had two immediate consequences: first, the islands stood as an example that independence could be achieved, and second, the way that the Ionians had gained their independence raised hopes and expectations that the Western powers would intervene in Greek affairs on the Greek side.

During the 1810s, three other major developments helped bring matters to a head. The first was the global economic crisis that followed the cessation of the Napoleonic Wars. Napoleon's continental blockade of Britain had provided a great opportunity for those willing to risk violating French reprisals. Numerous Greek merchants and captains had seized the moment and made huge profits. The boom in Greek shipping came to an abrupt end. First, immediately after the war, all of Europe, and Britain in particular, was plunged into a depression as industries tried to cope with the greatly reduced demands of a peacetime economy.

Second, compounding this crisis of the manufacturing sector, severe weather conditions, in part caused by a series of volcanic eruptions in the South Pacific, greatly reduced the yields of most major food crops. The last great subsistence crisis of the Western world, as one historian has described it, struck. The Balkans were not spared these traumas.

Third, when conditions began to ameliorate, the mercantile fleets of England, Holland and the others who had suffered under the French blockade, regained their former prominence. Greek merchant shipping between 1815 and 1820, for example, fell by almost 40 per cent on average. Prices for subsistence grains soared as supplies declined. Across much of the Balkan Peninsula near-famine conditions obtained. The general economic crisis and the singular inability of government at any level to address the widespread distress exacerbated the existing feelings of resentment among the rural populace. Indeed, rather than taking active measures to alleviate the suffering, the Porte raised taxes. As the experience of France during the 1780s had shown, hungry bellies and revolutionary discontent went hand in hand. Only one final element, that of organizational leadership, was needed before the situation in the Balkans would be truly ripe for revolution, and that also developed during the 1810s.

There could be no Greek insurrection without an organization to lead it, and one emerged in the 1810s. The European 'age of revolution' was also the era of secret societies. Revolution is impossible without leadership and since revolt is treasonous, men dedicated to the cause had to operate in secret. All across Europe such organizations appeared. In Italy, there was the Carbonari and in Russia, the Decembrists, for example. Liberal movements to resist the conservative counter-revolution's attempt to restore the *ancien regime* in the aftermath of the French Revolution and Napoleon flourished everywhere. Diaspora Greeks were members of some of them, and they formed their own national liberation groups as well. And there were many of these, though most never amounted to much. Two, however, did: the Filomouso Etaireia and the **Philiki Etaireia**.

The Society of the Friends of the Muses was a philanthropic and educational organization established in Vienna in 1814. The organization soon founded branches in almost every major European city, but especially important were those in Russia. The society gathered funds to build schools and other educational and cultural establishments in Ottoman Greece and to support Greek students studying at European universities. While not an explicitly political organization, the Society had the goal of fostering Greek liberation through education. They believed that by elevating the moral character of the Greek population through the study of Classical texts and ecclesiastical writings, Greece would eventually be liberated with Russian assistance. Liberation for them was a long-term goal that would come gradually and without violent revolution.

The *Philiki Etaireia*, or 'Friendly Society', was the most important of the many clandestine revolutionary groups that had sprung up since the 1770s. Emmanouil Xanthos, Nicholaos Skoufas and Athanasios Tsakalov, three merchants from different regions of the Ottoman Empire, founded the Philiki Etaireia in 1814 in Odessa on the Black Sea. Xanthos was initially the driving force behind the organization. Though based in Odessa, he travelled widely in the Balkans because of his olive oil business. One of his trips took him to the island of Lefkada, one of the Ionian Islands. The ideas of the French Revolution had taken root there during the period of French rule. Not only did Xanthos become stirred by the notions of liberty and freedom while staying on the island, but he was also introduced to the murky world of secret societies when he was enrolled in the island's Masonic lodge. Like many members of the diaspora communities, Xanthos believed that liberation for the Greeks would be achieved through the actions of the major Western European powers. The Concert of Europe crafted by Klemens von Metternich at the Congress of Vienna dashed any such hopes. The conservative crowned heads of Europe combined to maintain the status quo, and that policy extended even to relations with the Ottoman Empire. The Philiki Etaireia was established when it became clear that if freedom was to be attained, the Greeks and the other Christians in the Balkans would have to attain it themselves.

If the Philiki Etaireia was to have any chance of success, it would have to appeal to a wide spectrum of Balkan Christians and would have to recruit as members as many prominent men as possible. Accordingly, the central committee appointed twelve men, the Apostles, and assigned them the task of recruiting as many leaders as possible in their assigned regions. After this move, the organization's membership expanded rapidly both in size and in geographical scope. Influential men both inside and outside of the Ottoman Empire joined the organization.

Organizationally, the membership was divided into four hierarchically ordered civil ranks and two military ranks. The ranks were based on wealth and responsibilities. In order to maintain secrecy, only members from the highest ranks knew the identities of members outside of their immediate cell. This compartmentalization meant that, unlike other such groups, the Philiki Etaireia was able to both attract a substantial membership and elude detection and suppression. It brought together men from many levels of society – merchants, professionals, large landowners (kocabaşis), members of the clergy, klefts (bandits) and kapoi (warlords), and even some prominent Phanariots, like the former Russian general Alexander Ipsilantis, who eventually emerged as the group's paramount leader. It was not a real mass movement in the truest sense of the term; according to the membership lists that have survived, very few peasants, shepherds or workers were members. This should not, however, be interpreted as a sign that they did not support the goals of the organization, but only that the leadership was reluctant to include them in the membership.

The Philiki Etaireia grew to be the largest secret society, and it provided an organizational base for the dissemination of revolutionary ideas and for coordinated action. But there was a very significant downside to its large size. Along with size came diversity of aims, ambitions and viewpoints. Ideologically, except for the goal of liberation from the Porte, little else connected the membership. Some prominent leaders envisioned a new Byzantine Empire, based on a Greek theocratic monarchy; others fervently wanted to create a multi-ethnic secular republic founded upon the principles of the French Revolution. These fissures would only emerge after the actual onset of hostilities. Initially at least, because of its size and the number of important leaders whom it counted as members, the Philiki Etaireia had emerged as a Balkan-wide revolutionary organization. By 1820, all of the pieces were in place for a Christian uprising in the Balkans. Only a spark was required to set ablaze the conflagration of war.

The Greek War of Independence, 1821–1828[2]

The precipitating factor in the Greek War of Independence was the revolt of **Tepedelenli Ali Paşa** of Ioannina (born 1744(?), died 1822) against his master, **Sultan Mahmud II**. In a cultural landscape littered with colourful characters, Tepedelenli Ali Paşa stands out as larger than life – though his story has until relatively recently been curiously neglected by historians. An enormous man with enormous appetites, the so-called 'Lion of Ioannina' left a lasting imprint on the history of Greece and the Balkans. Ali was born at Tepedelen in 1744 into a very powerful Albanian Muslim family. His father was Bey of a small sanjak, but he was killed when Ali was seven or eight. Influenced by his domineering mother, he began his career as a sheep-rustler and brigand at the tender age of fourteen. The experience made him a hard man and he soon rose to lead his own gang. As often happened in the Ottoman Empire, his reputation as a man of violence led to his being appointed as a keeper of peace. He rapidly climbed the ladder of politics and in 1786 he was appointed Valisis of Trikala. Soon thereafter, Epiros was added on. He moved his base of power to Ioannina, leaving his son Veli in Thessaly.

Tepedelenli Ali Paşa had created a mini-kingdom stretching from central Albania, through Epiros and Thessaly into central and even southern Greece. He was in total control, having either co-opted or driven out all of the armed armatoles, or border guards, and klefts, or outlaws (though in reality they were often the same men). He had also surrounded himself with an excellent staff, including many well-educated Greeks and Christian Albanians: Alexandros Noutsos, Ioannis Kolettis and Manthos Oikonomou and his brother Christos, for example. During the period from 1800 to 1815, Ali skilfully played the game of power politics, putting down all opposition to his rule, consolidating his hold over continental Greece and playing the great powers, especially France and Great Britain, off against one another. Eventually, Ali began to rival the Sultan in his power. He then began to flex his muscles against the Sultan's appointees to the north, but by so doing, he went too far.

In 1820 Mahmud II gave the Balkan upstart forty days to appear before him in Istanbul or else face the consequences. The Lion smelled a rat, and demurred. The Sultan duly ordered another provincial governor, Ismail Paso Paşa, to attack his hated rival and neighbour. The conflict so initiated provided the opportunity for the Philiki Etaireia and its leader Alexander Ipsilantis to launch the Greek insurrection.

Tepedelenli Ali Paşa had known of the existence of the Philiki Etaireia for some time. Indeed, some of his key advisors were among its high-ranking members. Recognizing the need to forge alliances against the coming storm, Tepedelenli Ali Paşa negotiated pacts with warrior groups like the Souliotes and various Albanian bandit gangs, and he made covert overtures to the leadership of the Etaireia. Each side saw an opportunity to achieve its objectives by exploiting the opportunities created by the other's actions. There was also deep distrust on both sides. The winter of 1820–1 was a busy time. Ismail Paso Bey had proven himself not up to the task of taking on the Lion of Ioannina and so he was relieved of his command. Hurşid Paşa, the valisis of the Morea, was promoted to the rank of serasker (commander-in-chief) of Rumeli, given a war-chest of one million piasters (US$20,000,000), and the authority to levy levend troops from no less than thirteen paşas. Hurşid was a formidable opponent. He had commanded the army that ended the Serbian rebellion, and before that he had performed outstandingly during the 1806–12 war with Russia. Also, having previously been Grand Vizier (1812–15), he knew how things worked in Istanbul and had valuable allies (and opponents) at court. Ayans formerly attached to Ali switched sides; military commanders like Omar Vryonis and Androutsos along with their men were persuaded by Hurşid's largesse to join his army. Hurşid Paşa's elevation to commander of the army sent to defeat Ali had three important consequences. First, it assured the outcome: Ali would fall within a year. Second, the imposition of the war requisition tax on an already destitute and desperate peasantry elevated the level of mass discontent in the region to a new high. Paying the war tax was for many farmers and shepherds a life or death issue. Third, the mobilization of so many warriors depleted the garrison forces along the Danubian frontier and in the Morea. Ali's rebellion had presented the Philiki Etaireia with an opportunity. The time for plotting was over; now was the time for action.

The onset of the war of liberation appears far more coherent than it really was. Though the various groups of revolutionaries and secret societies were in contact with one another, there was little coordination: mutual distrust and the difficulties of communication saw to that. As the war clouds gathered, the aims of the major participants seemed to have been these: Tepedelenli Ali Paşa wanted to withstand the initial assault against him by Hurşid Paşa. Then, depending on the outcome of the fighting, he could open negotiations with the Sultan either as a submissive supplicant begging for forgiveness or as a powerful leader who could restore peace in the Balkans on his terms. The etairist leadership sought to ride the coattails of Ali's war. Assuming that the bulk of the Ottoman forces would be arrayed against Ioannina, the plans were to foment rebellions by Christians in three regions – the Danubian Principalities of Moldavia and Wallachia, Constantinople and the Peloponnesos. Each strategy had its own rationale and its own set of problems.

An uprising in the Peloponnesos was crucial. Its remoteness from the centre of the Empire, the very high ratio of Christian to Muslim inhabitants, the number of powerful Greek kocabaşis resident there and the considerable number of Christian and Muslim Albanian armed bands operating in the region whose allegiance was up in the air elevated the chances that a rebellion would be successful. It could then, the argument went, provide the rump of a Greek-Christian state or, at worst, provide a base of operation for further attacks against the Porte. Riots were planned that would spill blood on the streets of Constantinople, thus bringing the rebellion right to the Sultan's doorstep, and this development would force the hand of the Orthodox Patriarch to support the movement. Finally, the Danubian Principalities were key.

Alexander Ipsilantis was headquartered with his forces in southern Russia. Given that the Principalities already enjoyed a special, quasi-autonomous status within the Ottoman Empire and that Russia had a special interest in their affairs, the idea was that Ipsilantis would invade Moldavia. At the same time, forces under the command of local leaders, like Tudor Vladimirescu, Ali Farmakis, Georgakis Olimpios, and perhaps even the Serb leader Milos Obrenovich, would join them in what would amount to a rebellion of the Millet-i Rum. With the entire region up in flames, Tsar Alexander I would have no choice but to bring the might of Russia into play on their behalf.

Among the etairist leadership, then, there clearly was a rough plan and some crude assumptions about how the revolt should proceed, but these masked a multiplicity of aims, intentions and interests among the various groups throughout the region. Moreover, there were formidable logistical obstacles that had to be faced, the most important of which was that the vast majority of the subject Christian population did not possess firearms, and so initially at least, the bulk of the fighting would have to be done by small groups of trained troops and by much larger numbers of former klefts and armatoles, and others who had gained experience, and weapons, fighting in the Napoleonic Wars. If, and at the time it was a big if, the masses of peasants joined the insurrection, then arms, powder and supplies had to be found for them. In addition, the costs of financing an uprising would be huge, and no secure source of money had been found. Victory would come only if the initial success was quickly followed by Russian intervention.

From its inception, little about the uprising went according to plan. First, the Lion of Ioannina proved to be a paper tiger. His forces melted away like spring snow before the Ottoman army and by the middle of February, he was on the brink of defeat. Besieged in his island retreat, he put up a stubborn defence until being slain in what was, by all accounts, a valiant last stand. Hursid Paşa dispatched Ali's severed head to the capital. Now the bulk of the forces under his command were free to be deployed elsewhere in the Empire. Second, the proposed riots in Constantinople never materialized. To be sure, after the insurrection had begun, there was violence in the capital city; most of it was carried out by Muslims and was directed against the Greek Orthodox population. Third, the pillars of power, on which the insurgents had pinned their hopes, denounced them. Shortly after the insurrection had begun, Tsar Alexander announced in no uncertain terms that he would not support the rebels and Patriarch Grigorios V excommunicated them. As a consequence of these developments, the campaign in the north was a debacle.

The early morning fog on the Pruth River was pierced by a ferryboat crossing from the Russian to the Ottoman side. It was 6 March 1821 and Alexander Ipsilantis along with twenty of his closest advisors was invading the Ottoman Empire. Resplendent in his general's uniform, the one-armed leader of the Philiki Etaireia disembarked from the ferry and set off for the Moldavian capital of Jassy. Upon arrival he met with Hospodar Michailis Soutzos, who agreed to give him his support, placing his household guard under the general's command. Ipsilantis made it known that 70,000 Russians would soon be crossing the border. He issued his own proclamation, calling on everyone to join him and proclaiming that with the assistance of a 'tremendous power', they would soon be free (see Text-box 4). Some Serbian, Albanian, Bulgarian and even Romanian militiamen answered the call. Nicholas Ipsilantis, Alexander's younger brother, arrived from Russia with 800 infantrymen and engineers dressed in their black Russian uniforms. A few days later, 1,200 members of the recently disbanded Greek militia of Odessa joined them. Then, the Sacred Band, a special force made up of Greek students from the military academies in Odessa, Taganrog and Mariupol arrived. On balance, however, the vast majority of the Christian population refused to answer the call to arms. The local Romanian peasantry had little sympathy for the Greek cause and, indeed, saw the Greek elite of the Principalities as their oppressors. In addition, Grigorios's action of excommunicating anyone who joined the rebellion put paid to the idea that the uprising was to be a pan-Christian rebellion, and this also eroded support among the non-Greek Christian population. In the absence of the Tsar's support, Vladimirescu switched sides but Ipsilantis had

Text-box 4 Ipsilantis proclamation (1821)

Fight for Faith and Motherland

Alexandros Ipsilantis's Proclamation of Insurrection in the Danubian Principalities, 24 February 1821.

Fight for Faith and Motherland! The time has come, Greek men! Long ago the people of Europe, fighting for their own rights and liberties, invited us to imitate them. Those men, although partially free, tried with all their strength to increase their freedom and through their action, their prosperity.

Our brothers and friends are everywhere ready. The Serbs, the Souliots, and all of Epiros, bearing arms, await us. Let us enthusiastically unite with them. The Motherland is calling us!

Europe, fixing its eyes upon us, wonders at our inertia. Let all the mountains of Greece resound, therefore, with the echo of our battle cries, and the valleys resound with the clang of our weapons. Europe will admire our valour. Our tyrants, trembling and pale, will flee before us.

The enlightened peoples of Europe are occupied in restoring the same well-being, and, full of gratitude for the benefactions of our forefathers towards them, desire the liberation of Greece. We, seemingly worthy of ancestral virtue and of the present century, are hopeful that we will gain their aid and assistance. Many of these freedom lovers want to come and fight alongside us. Arouse yourselves, old friends, and you will see a Mighty

Empire defend our rights! You will see even many of our enemies, moved by our just cause, turn their backs on our enemy and unite with us. ... The Motherland will embrace them! Who then restrains your manly arms? Our cowardly enemy is sick and weak. Our generals are experienced, and all our fellow countrymen are full of enthusiasm. Unite, then, O brave and magnanimous Greeks! Let national phalanxes be formed, let patriotic legions appear and you will see those old giants of despotism fall by themselves before our triumphant banners.

All the shores of the Ionian and Aegean seas will resound to the sound of our trumpet. Greek ships, which in times of peace have learnt both how to trade and to fight, will sow terror and death, by fire and the sword, in all the harbours of the tyrant! ...

Turn your eyes, O fellow countrymen, and look upon our miserable state! See everywhere the ruined churches! See there our children seized for the degrading abuse of the shameless hedonism of barbarous tyrants! Our houses are stripped bare, our fields are laid waste, and we ourselves made miserable slaves!

The time has come to overthrow this insufferable yoke, to liberate the Motherland, to throw down the [Ottoman] Crescent from the skies, in order to raise up the symbol by which we will always conquer, namely the Cross, and thus liberate the Motherland and our Orthodox faith from the impious scorn of the heathen. ...

Fellow countrymen, with unity, with respect for our Holy Religion, with obedience to our laws and our generals, with boldness and steadfastness, our victory is certain and inevitable. ... The Motherland will reward her loyal and genuine children with prizes of Glory and Honour. Those who disobey and turn a deaf ear to the call to arms will be declared bastards and Asiatic spawn, they will be labelled as traitors, they will be anathematized and cursed by later generations.

Let us then once again, O brave and magnanimous Greeks, restore Liberty to the classical land of Greece! Let us do battle between Marathon and Thermopylae! Let us fight on the tombs of our fathers, who, so as to leave us free, fought and died there! The blood of the Tyrants is acceptable to the shades of Epaminondas the Theban and Thrasyboulos the Athenian, who crushed the thirty tyrants, to the shades of Harmodios and Aristogiton, who destroyed the yoke of Pisistratos, to that of Timoleon, who restored freedom to Corinth and Syracuse, certainly to those of Militates and Themistocles, of Leonidas and the Three Hundred, who cut down the innumerable armies of the barbarous Persians, whose most barbarian and inhuman descendants we today, with very little effort, are about to annihilate completely. To arms then, oh friends! The Motherland calls us!

B. Murgescu (ed.) (2009), *Nations and States in Southeast Europe. Workbook 2*, Thessaloniki: CDRSEE. document I-8.

him executed before he could pose a threat. Thus, isolated in hostile territory, the rebels stood no chance. Though they gamely fought on, they stood little chance of winning and were finally wiped out at the battle of the Dragatsani River on 2 June 1821. Ipsilantis fled into Austria, where he was captured and imprisoned, and died. His forces scattered. Some managed to escape back into Russia. Others remained in Moldavia, but by the end of the summer, they too were wiped out. The fighting in the North was at an end. The wider insurrection, however, was not.

On 25 March 1821, as legend would have it, Bishop Germanos, the Metropolitan of Patras, raised the flag of revolution at the Monastery of Agia Lavra near Kalavrita, and the second theatre of hostilities was opened. In large part, Germanos's act only solemnized actions that were already underway. The clouds of war had been gathering over the Peloponnesos since mid-winter. Gangs of armed predators had robbed Muslim tax collectors and attacked farms and villages. By late March, Petrobey Mavromichalis, leader of the powerful Maniate clans, was marching with his forces against the important town of Kalamata in Messenia. The noted kleftic chieftain, Theodoros Kolokotronis, had assembled his warriors and was closing in on Tripolis, the capital city of the region. Germanos's proclamation, coming as it did at a meeting of the leading wealthy landowners and officials, gave a stamp of approval to these actions and symbolically served as a signal to begin in earnest the assaults on the Ottoman-controlled towns and fortresses.

The initial phase of the war in the south resembled a civil war, characterized by the awful bloodletting that such internecine conflicts cause. In 1821, approximately 40,000 Muslims inhabited the Peloponnesos, as opposed to about 350,000 Christians. Most of the Muslims were civilian families who had lived in the region for a long time. As hostility towards them increased, many sought refuge in the walled towns and fortresses at Patras, Tripolis, Kalamata, Corinth and Nafplion. Stationed there to protect them were relatively modest numbers of troops, mainly Albanian mercenaries that Hurşid Paşa had left behind when he marched north to face Tepedelenli Ali Paşa. The combination of irregular bands of former brigands thirsting for booty and oppressed Christian peasants hungry for revenge against their overlords was a lethal one. When the Ottoman-held fortresses capitulated, bloodbaths ensued: as much as one-third to one-half of the Muslim population fell to the insurgents' bullets and blades.

To be sure, each side could tell its tales of butchery and slaughter. The Greeks recoiled in horror when news of the pogroms in Constantinople, Smyrna and Salonika and the massacre on the island of Chios reached them. The ignominious death inflicted on Patriarch Grigorios V was so awful that it blinded many to the fact that he had not supported their revolt. On the Ottoman side, the news of the massacre of thousands of men, women and children at Kalamata, Nafplion and Tripolis, in some cases even after the Greek leaders had promised them safe passage, fuelled the cries for a *Jihad* against the Greek infidels. In the period from March 1821 to December 1823, it is estimated that the combined casualties were of the order of 50,000, mostly unarmed non-combatants. Each round of massacres only served to make finding a political solution to war even more difficult.

Militarily, 1821 saw the insurgency meet with success in some places. Soon after the insurrection in the Morea erupted, it spread across the Balkans and the Eastern Mediterranean as community after community decided to join the cause. By mid-April most of the Greek and Albanian Christian villages of Boiotia and Attika had risen, soon followed by those in Western Greece (Aitolia and Akarnania). In June, Greek Athenians rose up and besieged the Ottoman garrison on the Acropolis. The Aegean islands, beginning with Hyrda, Poros and Spetsis were not far behind. Greeks in Cyprus and Crete attacked Ottoman forces and Muslim civilians. To the north, the banner of rebellion was unfurled in Thessaly and Macedonia. To be sure, there were Greek communities that decided not to rebel. On the rich and prosperous island of Chios, the Orthodox leadership denounced the rebellion and pledged their loyalty to the Ottoman government. The collective leadership on the Catholic islands of the Cyclades, such as Tinos, Syros, Thera and others, did so as well. Nonetheless, by the summer of 1821, the Ottoman government was confronted with insurrections from the Danubian region in the north to Crete in the south, and from the Adriatic Sea in the west to the shores of the Levant in the east. The Empire, however, responded vigorously, and in many areas effectively, to these challenges. The Greek uprisings in areas such as Thessaly and Macedonia, where the Ottomans had sizable military forces, were easily put down. As we have already seen, by the end of the summer, the insurrection in the North had been completely crushed. While fighting persisted slightly longer, the rebellions on Crete and Cyprus were also largely extinguished. Could even the Peloponnesos avoid this fate?

In February, Hurşid Paşa captured and beheaded Tepedelenli Ali Paşa. A new commander, Mehemd Dramali Paşa, was given the task of crushing the revolt in the Morea. From his base in Yanya (Ioannina), he planned a campaign for the summer of 1822 that would end the Greek rebellion. He would command one army that would march down the east coast of Greece through Boiotia and Attica, relieving the Ottoman garrisons along the way. Then, he would cross the Isthmus and rescue the men trapped in the impregnable fortress of Acrocorinth. From there he could launch an assault on Nafplion, where the leadership of the Greek rebel state was located. At the head of a force of 12,000 infantrymen, 600 regular cavalry and 200 deli cavalry (light-armed skirmishers), Dramali left Larissa in early July. He seized control of the coastal and inland roads and his forces swept across the plains of Boiotia. Quickly marching southwards, he took the isthmus and marched on Corinth, driving off the Greek rebel forces. By 17 July, he secured Acrocorinth as his base of operations. Giving his troops only a brief rest, one week later Dramali crossed the mountains that separate the Corinthia and the Argolid and marched on Nafplion. Believing that the Greeks would surrender, flee or fight and lose, he planned on a very quick campaign. Consequently, he did not outfit his army adequately with supplies.

Marching through the narrow defiles, his forces entered the Argolid. While doing so, he made his most serious mistake: he failed to post guards to protect the mountain passes. Contrary to his expectation, the Greeks would not face him in battle on the plain. Instead, they divided their forces into three groups. One, under Dimitrios Ipsilantis, marched south and encamped at the Mills on the coast road. Theodoros Kolokotronis mobilized a sizable force in the mountains on the western side of the plain, and Papaflessa and Nikitas Stammatelopoulos concentrated their men in the mountains to the east of the plain. A deadly trap was forming. Greek peasants burnt their crops and spoiled their wells before taking refuge in the city. Dramali could neither compel the Greek troops to give battle nor could he take the city by force. As his supplies dwindled, he had no choice but to retreat.

On 8 August, he walked into the trap. The Greeks had blocked the Dervanaki pass and arrayed their men on the heights above the narrow road through the mountains. It was a slaughter. Dramali and about 800 men made it out alive. Dramali committed suicide rather than face disgrace and what was left of his army fled north, harassed by rebel forces along the way. Eastern Greece and the Morea were now secure.

Divisions regarding the political goals of the war existed among the Greek rebel leadership from the start, and the rifts only became deeper and more diverse as Greeks from the diaspora, from the disbanded court of Tepedelenli Ali Paşa and from the Phanariot community of Constantinople arrived in the Peloponnesos. In addition, there were the Greeks of the diaspora who flocked to the 'motherland' with heads filled with republican ideologies and dreams of a resurrected democratic past. Keeping these competing and disparate interests together proved one of the greatest challenges of the war.

All parties agreed on a few issues. That political victory, in the form of independence, required great power intervention was one. Another was that they had yet to face the full might of the Ottoman Empire, and that they had to take advantage of the Porte's indecisiveness. A third was that they needed money and arms desperately and quickly. As we have seen, a cold wind blew from St. Petersburg. And in the midst of the ongoing political unrest in Portugal, Spain, Piedmont, Naples and Belgium, the other great powers were equally unsympathetic to the Greek cause. In order to garner the support of the Western powers, the Greek leadership had to declare their independence unilaterally and to promulgate a constitution creating a government, which could then open negotiations with the great powers. All the while they had to cast their cause not as a national struggle based on liberal principles, which would have won them few supporters in post-Napoleonic Europe, but as a religious conflict of an oppressed Christian population against their Islamic oppressors.

Three days after Germanos raised the banner of revolt, Petrobey Mavromihalis issued a proclamation that served as the Greek declaration of independence:

> The insupportable yoke of Ottoman tyranny has weighed down for over a century the unhappy Greeks of the Peloponnesos. So excessive had its rigors become, that its fainting victims had scarcely strength enough to utter groans. In this state, deprived of all our rights, we have unanimously resolved to take up arms against our tyrants... . Our mouths are opened; heretofore silent, or employed only in addressing useless supplications to our tormentors, they now celebrate a deliverance which we have sworn to accomplish, or else to perish. We invoke therefore the aid of all civilized nations of Europe, that we may the more promptly attain to the goal of a just and sacred enterprise, reconquer our rights, and regenerate our unfortunate people. Greece, our mother, was the lamp that illuminated you; on this ground she reckons on your philanthropy, Arms, money, and counsel, are what she expects from you. We promise you her lively gratitude, which she will prove by deeds in more prosperous times.[3]

Six weeks later, the Maniate chieftain convened a congress in Kalamata to draft a constitution and establish a government. Representing almost exclusively the Peloponnesian ruling elite, the congress created a senate and elected Petrobey as president. Neither enjoyed much legitimacy anywhere else in Greece. The bandit chieftains and the other warriors bearing the brunt of the fighting, for example, felt that they had been cheated out of power. Dimitris Ipsilantis, brother of Alexander, claimed that he spoke for the Philiki Etaireia and, since it was the body representing the interests of the rebels, on its behalf he refused to accept the writ of the new government. Finally, as other areas of Greece became liberated, the leaders in each formed their own ruling councils, until there were no less than three regional assemblies. All, of course, claimed to represent the interests of liberated Greece.

To deal with the situation, a National Congress at which all parties would be represented was convened in Epidavros in December 1821. After weeks of intense debate, the delegates passed a new national constitution, modelled on the French constitution of 1795. The new Greece was to be a democratic republic founded on the principles of civil liberties and equality for all. The constitution had to also define what exactly the criteria for membership in this new state were. Text-box 5 reproduces the formulation they arrived at as it was adumbrated in the 1827 Constitution of Troezen, which was based on the Epidavros charter. Two points stand out: first, that religion was to be a central element and second, that Greece was clearly to be a nation-state. Gone was Rigas's vision of a grand multinational, multi-denominational country; replacing it was a nationally and religiously homogeneous one. Alexandros Mavrokordatos, a learned Phanariot and the chief drafter of the constitution, emerged as the first president. The new government's main goals were to mobilize the peasantry and prosecute the war, press the Greeks' appeal for assistance from the West and end the factional squabbling. It succeeded somewhat with the first but failed utterly with the others.

A second National Congress was called in April 1823 to modify the constitution and to elect a new government. The Peloponnesians, and especially the military captains, dominated this session. Petrobey emerged as the new president and Kolokotronis as his vice president. The virtual exclusion of leaders from Western and Central Greece and of Western-orientated diaspora Greeks, who with the exception of Mavrogordatos were actually forbidden to hold high offices, doomed this national government as well. Unity was absent

Text-box 5 Definition of citizenship in the Troezen constitution (1827)

In the Name of the Holy and Indivisible Trinity …

Article 6. Greeks are:

a. The indigenous people in the Greek territory who believe in Christ;
b. Those under Ottoman rule who believe in Christ and have come or will come into the Greek territory to join the struggle, or live in it;
c. Those living in foreign territories and who were born to a Greek father;
d. Indigenous or non-indigenous persons and their descendants, who became citizens of foreign states before the publication of the present Constitution, who came into the Greek territory and took the Greek oath;
e. Any foreigners who come and take the citizenship oath.

B. Murgescu (ed.) (2009), *Nations and States in Southeast Europe. Workbook 2*, Thessaloniki: CDRSEE. document II-11.

even within the administration. Shortly after his election, Petrobey turned to his reluctant second-in-command and cryptically asked him, 'So, are you going to dance, Kolokotronis?' To this the warlord menacingly responded, 'As long as you are singing, I shall dance. Stop the song and I stop the dance.'[4] The song and dance did not last for long.

Frustrated by the actions of the executive council members who were not military men, Kolokotronis seized and imprisoned them. Open conflict between factions in the government erupted soon thereafter. This lack of political unity, at times lapsing into actual armed conflict, was to prove very costly.

A pivotal point in the war occurred in 1824. Militarily, the gains of the previous three years soon began to slip away and were finally lost. The masses of peasants who had initially joined in the fighting lost their enthusiasm as the war dragged on. They had not signed on to serve garrison duty besieging walled towns, especially not while land was lying free for the taking back home. Many returned to their farms and villages to reap the immediate benefits of the departure of Ottoman landlords. Only very reluctantly, and often by threat or coercion, did they rejoin the fighting. This left the fighting to be done by the bands of irregulars, former bandits and border guards (see Figure 3 for a depiction of a revolutionary war fighter). While they could be an effective guerrilla fighting force, they were ill-suited for sustained, disciplined military campaigns; they owed their allegiance to their captain; and they were largely interested in pay and booty. From such a foundation, military machines were seldom built. Politically, internecine discord erupted between the various factions. Some warlords even switched sides and joined with the invading Ottoman forces, further jeopardizing the future of the revolution. Internationally, however, for a variety of reasons, the Greek cause became far more visible and took on a new importance in the diplomatic deliberations of the European powers. One of the great ironies of the war was that success was achieved at a time when the Greeks were, in fact, losing on almost all fronts.

On 5 January 1824, Lord Byron arrived in liberated Greece. He had been on the scene for some time, residing on the British-controlled Ionian Islands. But his actual arrival on Greek soil was rife with both practical and symbolic importance. The Greek War of Independence struck a chord in North America and Europe. Romanticism and Christian humanitarianism motivated many idealistic European and American young men either to go to Greece and join the conflict or to remain at home supporting the Greeks by raising money and by lobbying with their respective governments. Romanticism's glorification of ancient Greek culture easily elided into eager support for the oppressed, 'enslaved' and debased contemporary Greeks. Leading Romantic artists and writers, such as Lord Byron and Alexander Pushkin in Russia, lent their names, gave money and, in some cases, their lives, in support of the Greek cause.

FIGURE 3 *A Cretan fighter in the Greek War of Independence (1826). Le Blanc's portrait vividly depicts a Cretan warrior during the War of Independence. He carries with him the full array of the warrior's craft: his doufeki (flint musket), his pistol and his slashing sword (yataghan). He wears the typical waistcoat, meant to protect him from attack, and around his waist is a long bolt of silk cloth that serves to hold his weapons, as well as containers for powder and shot, religious amulets to keep him from harm and his tobacco for smoking.*

Theodore Le Blanc (1833–4). Croquis d' après nature faits pendat trois ans de sejour en Grèce et dans le Levant, *Paris: Gihaut. Public Domain. GallantGraphics all rights reserved.*

Their vision was shared by countless university students who had been reared on the Classics and who had embraced liberalism. Disillusioned by the stifling intellectual environment of conservative counter-revolutionary Europe, they saw in the Greek uprising a great and noble cause: to repay the debt that the West owed to the Greeks. Philhellenes, as these men and women came to be called, played a critical role in the war. Military men left without a war since the demise of Napoleon, romantic youths seeking their classical roots, liberal reformers who saw in the Greek struggle a chance to strike a blow for liberty, religious zealots who likened the struggle against the 'infidel' to the Crusades, and other assorted freebooters and misfits rallied to the Greek cause as fundraisers or donors, soldiers and sailors, lobbyists and advocates. The Philhellenes were responsible for raising monies to support the insurgents, bringing the conflict to the attention of the wider world, and keeping it there until the great powers could be cajoled into intervening.

The military gains made in the first phase, however, were soon lost. A new strategy came to dominate the Sultan's approach to the Greek rebellion. Mahmud II remained as wedded as ever to the plan to destroy the Greek rebellion by 'fire and sword', but it had become painfully obvious to him and his advisors that the old-style military, based on Janissaries, mercenaries and irregulars, was obsolete and ineffective. A complete overhaul of the war machine was required, but this would take time and money and he was running short of both.

During the winter of 1824, Mahmud II struck a bargain with Mehmet Ali of Egypt. Though nominally his vassal, Mehmet Ali was to all intents and purposes a ruler in his own right. The bargain they arranged was that in exchange for control of Crete and the appointment of his son, Ibrahim Paşa, as governor of the Peloponnesos, Mehmet Ali would deploy his French-trained Western-style army and navy against the Greeks. Shortly after the agreement had been reached, Mahmud introduced measures to reform the Janissary army and to create a new one manned by troops trained in the European manner. Janissaries, especially those in Istanbul, resisted and threatened to topple the monarchy. But Mahmud struck first. In an event known as the 'Auspicious Incident', on 16 June 1826, the Janissary Corps was abolished and thousands of Janissaries were executed. The creation of a new Western-style army called 'The Trained Triumphant Soldiers of Muhammad' commenced. While the reform of the Ottoman military was taking place, the war to crush the Greek rebellion continued with Ibrahim and his Egyptians playing the leading role. This allowed him to launch a two-pronged attack. The Sultan's forces, totalling almost 20,000 men, marched from the north, one branch down the Ioannina–Arta corridor in the west, the other through Boiotia towards Attika and the Isthmus along the east. Meanwhile, the army of Mehmet Ali under the able leadership of his son Ibrahim Paşa had already successfully established a beachhead and was, in fact, a permanent army of occupation in control of much of the Peloponnesos. Soon, Ibrahim advanced from the south with the aim of catching the remaining Greek forces in a vice.

The strategy worked. The fall of the fortress at Missolonghi in the spring of 1826 gave the Ottoman forces control of Western Greece and of the Gulf of Patras. After Missolonghi, matters went from bad to worse. Reşid resupplied his army and marched eastwards. He took the cities of Boiotia and in summer laid siege to the Greek forces on the Acropolis of Athens. In a last chance gamble to keep the revolution alive, another national assembly was convened to try and restore unified leadership. A new provisional government was formed that appealed for aid from Europe. It also deployed whatever monies remained in the coffers to purchase supplies and to hire experienced fighters like Sir Richard Church and Lord Thomas Cochrane. The new leadership rallied the remaining rebel forces to try to save Athens. In this endeavour, they were unsuccessful. Led by General Ioannis Makriyannis, the besieged put up a valiant defence but numerous attempts to break through the Ottoman lines failed, in one of which the commander-in-chief of the Greek army in Central Greece, General Yiorgos Karaiskakis, was slain, depriving the revolution of its best general.

Political unity proved to be short-lived, and civil discord hampered the war effort once again. After almost a year's siege, Athens fell in 1827 and with its capture, Reşid restored Ottoman control over all of central Greece. Out-gunned, out-manned, and running desperately short of money and supplies because of the horrendous devastation wrought in the countryside by Ibrahim's army of occupation, the Greeks found themselves in a grim situation, and especially one group of people – the women.

The burden of the war increasingly fell most heavily on Greek women. In contemporary Greek popular culture, the women best remembered from the war are heroic figures like Laskarina Bouboulina and Manto Mavrogenous, who actually took part in the fighting. But far more prevalent were the thousands of nameless women who had to deal with the myriad challenges that the war presented. Women, no less than men, bear the burdens of war, but this is especially the case with rebellions, like the Greek War of Independence, where the battlefront and the home front occupy the same space. Women whose husbands, brothers and sons were off fighting had to take over the job of running the farm, undertaking all of the jobs usually done by men. And as war needs consumed ever more resources from the countryside, it was women as household managers who had to devise ways to keep their families fed. Increasingly, this was becoming harder to do. Poverty and destitution spread across the region and affected thousands.

Women also had to confront the physical ravages of war. Thousands of women were brutalized and raped by Ottoman troops, and sad to say, occasionally by Greek fighters as well. When villages were captured, the men were often executed and it was the women and children who were left to face the horror of slavery (see Figure 4, which shows a Greek woman about to be sold in the Istanbul slave market). Tens of thousands were sold in the slave markets of Istanbul, Smyrna and Alexandria; some were ransomed back by relatives but institutionally, because of the poor financial state of the Greek revolutionary government, outsiders had to step in, like the Austrian emissary at Messenia who ransomed thousands of women and children or the American missionary Jonathan Miller who helped to redeem scores of

FIGURE 4 *Greek women in the slave market (1830). This painting shows a Greek woman who had been captured during the war about to be sold in the Istanbul slave market. While Darondeau's depiction is clearly romanticized and stylized, it still captures vividly the fate that befell thousands of women over the course of the insurrection.*

Stanislas-Henri-Benoit Darondeau (1830). GallantGraphics all rights reserved.

people (Text-box 6 reproduces excerpts from Miller's diary and they vividly capture the horrible acts perpetrated on female captives). In sum, the war was wreaking terrible havoc on Greeks in the war zone, and by the end of 1827, the fate of the uprising itself hung in the balance. What had started as a Balkan-wide conflagration was quickly being reduced to a series of brushfires. If not for the intervention of the great powers, the rebellion would have been extinguished that year.

Great power interest in the Greek rebellion can only be understood in the context of the conservative counter-revolution exemplified by Metternich's Concert of Europe. Stability and maintenance of the status quo were the order of the day, but eventually, the disruption to the economic interests of each of the powers, as well as their mutual distrust, led them to intervene in the Eastern Mediterranean. Over time, Great Britain came to play the leading role in the search for a solution. Even though the British government had been

Text-box 6 The horrors of war (1827)

Diary Entry, 21 June 1827.

There arrived at this place last evening six females, who had just escaped from an Arab slave ship. Early this morning they were brought to my quarters. On going out, O, God of mercy! What a sight was presented to my view!! A girl of eleven or twelve years of age stood before me, with her nose cut off close to her face, and her lips all cut off, so that the gums and jaws were left entirely naked. All this had been done more than a year ago, and the poor creature was yet alive. Her refusal to yield to the embraces of an Arab was the cause of this horrid and shocking barbarity.

The other five females had submitted to numerous hardships, abuses, wounds, and sufferings. One of the five, a woman about twenty-five years old, gave me, in the presence of Jarvis, who arrived about ten minutes after Capt. Kearney had left, a relation of her captivity. After having had her husband killed before her eyes, she was taken by a party of Muslims, who inflicted wounds and such personal abuses as cannot be related. 'God forgive me', said she, 'for my sins, that I had not died rather than have ever submitted to such treatment'. The poor creature wept, and I kept her company.

J. P. Miller (1828), *The Condition of Greece in 1827 and 1828*, New York: J. & J. Harper, 71–2.

unsupportive of the rebellion at the start, many prominent political figures personally were sympathetic to the cause. Also, the widespread Philhellenic sentiment of the British people created a climate supportive of British intervention.

In the summer of 1825, the Greek government passed an 'Act of Submission'. In this petition, the Greeks agreed to place themselves under the protection of His Majesty's government and they accorded Britain the right to select a ruler for the Greek state. Even though Foreign Minister George Canning rejected the petition, the door was now open for more direct European involvement. It swung wide open with the death of Tsar Alexander I in December and his replacement by the much more ambitious Nicholas I early in 1826.

The new Tsar's more aggressive stance towards the Ottoman Empire and his more open sympathy to the Greeks increased the risk of a Russo–Ottoman war and of much greater Russian dominance in the region. To prevent these things from happening, Canning sent the Duke of Wellington to Russia to open negotiations. The result of these talks was the Anglo–Russian Protocol of 4 April 1826, in which the British proposed that Greece become an autonomous state within the Empire, that it pay a tribute to the Porte, and that its ruler be designated by the Sultan. In return, the Sultan was to withdraw his troops.

A number of developments made the negotiations more difficult and more protracted. First, the war was going so well militarily that Mahmud II hoped to make the negotiations moot by reconquering Greece before he would have to face an ultimatum. Second, Canning was in failing health. In the summer of 1827, he informed King George IV that he was withdrawing from active politics, and his successor, the Duke of Wellington, had the Eastern Question much lower on his foreign policy agenda. On the plus side for the Greeks, however, was the election of Ioannis Kapodistrias as the new president of Greece by the tumultuous Third National Assembly on 11 April 1827. Because he enjoyed much greater credibility with the Western powers and, in fact, resided in Geneva, he was a more effective advocate for the Greek position. In addition, Nicholas I was becoming ever more impatient with the lack of action and the reactionary Charles X began to push for greater French involvement in the region.

The result of these developments was the Treaty of London signed by Great Britain, the Russian Empire and France in July 1827. This agreement reiterated many of the key aspects of the April Protocol, but it also called for an immediate armistice, set a time limit for compliance, promised great power protection during the armistice and authorized the dispatching of a joint fleet to guarantee the peace.

The signing of the Treaty of London set up the likelihood of direct military intervention by the guarantor powers in the face of the Porte's intransigence. In the end, it was the combined might of the British and French fleets that decided the issue. Sent to the region to ensure that the stipulations of the agreement were enforced, Admiral Lord Codrington and his French counterpart de Rigny deployed their forces along Western Greece. Ibrahim, fearful that unless an agreement was reached soon his entire force of 40,000 men might be lost, called on his father to lobby the Porte on his behalf. But matters dragged. Finally, in autumn of 1827, Codrington had run out of patience. Together with the French and Russian forces, he entered the bay of Navarino in southwestern Greece and then issued an ultimatum to Ibrahim: quit the Peloponnesos or face the consequences.

The Battle of Navarino on 20 October 1827 witnessed the destruction of the Ottoman fleet with the loss of sixty out of eighty-nine ships and a casualty roster of over 10,000 men. With Navarino, the die was cast. There would be an independent Greek state; foreign intervention had seen to that. The exact boundaries, nature and disposition of the new polity remained to be determined, but, nonetheless, by the spring of 1828, a free Greece had been established.

The presidency of Ioannis Kapodistrias

Ioannis Kapodistrias was elected president of the fledgling state and took up the post in January 1828. Kapodistrias had enjoyed a long and fruitful career in the foreign service of the Russian Empire, at one point holding the rank of Privy Councillor to Tsar Alexander. Greek nationalists, including the Philiki Etaireia, had long wooed Kapodistrias, a native of the island of Corfu; he did not join them, though both of his brothers did. When Ipsilantis launched his invasion and started the rebellion, Kapodistrias spoke out against him, expressing his belief that the time for action was not right. Consequently, though he supported the idea of Greek independence, he remained above the fray throughout the wars.

For a variety of reasons, then, he seemed an ideal choice for governor at that crucial moment in 1827 when the great powers were equivocating on what action to take and still deliberating on the fate of Greece. First, he was not associated with any of the existing factions and so was not caught up in the highly charged political vendettas that the civil strife had created and which continued to hamstring every effort at creating a united government. Second, he was an accomplished diplomat and so had credibility with the foreign offices of the great powers. In the end, his tenure proved to be as short as it was turbulent.

The problems facing Kapodistrias were tremendous. First, the Ottoman Empire had still not given up hopes of carrying the day. Indeed, even after Russia declared war and invaded the Danubian Principalities, Mahmud II continued to press the hard line even though some of his advisors were now telling him that the best course of action would be to seek 'peace at any price in the name of saving the remaining part of the Empire'. With the continued ascendancy of the war party within the inner circle of the Porte, hostilities continued. Inside Greece, various factions, each revolving around a cluster of 'big men' or patrons, continued to control what amounted to private armies. Much of Greece lay in ruins, the war still dragged on and the coffers of the state were empty.

In addition, the Constitution that Alexandros Mavrodgordatos had drafted at the Third National Assembly was deliberately intended to circumscribe the powers of the executive branch of government. It required, for example, that all executive orders had to be countersigned by one of the cabinet ministers. It gave the Legislative Assembly broad powers of impeachment, denied the president the power of the veto and forbade presidential access to legislative sessions. So, the newly elected leader could not use his powers of persuasion to present his agenda to the lawmakers; he could not stop them from passing new laws, which he might oppose; and finally, his own position could be easily challenged. Kapodistrias was able to introduce modifications to the Constitution that shifted the balance slightly towards the executive, but, nonetheless, the difficulties of governing an already fractious group were only compounded by the power-sharing scheme established by the Constitution.

In spite of these formidable obstacles, he introduced many reforms aimed at solving some of Greece's most pressing problems. He pushed through legislation for land distribution, awarding grants of land to some, providing loans for the purchase of state lands and awarding legal recognition to lands usurped during the first days of the war. New taxes were imposed. He facilitated the development of the regular army, and allowed French troops and officers to form the backbone of the new army. Local administration was radically reformed, shifting the balance of power from the local community to the central state. In short, within a relatively short span of time and during an on-going war, Kapodistrias tried to mould revolutionary Greece into a 'modern' Western polity.

He failed. By temperament, Kapodistrias was ill-suited to play the role of mediator and conciliator; tired of having to barter with indigenous Greek powerbrokers, he opted, instead, to rule through enlightened despotism even though this entailed his eventually abrogating the constitution on the basis of which he had been elected. Exasperated by the incessant opposition to his efforts to establish a Western-style, centralized, bureaucratic administration, Kapodistrias finally concluded that 'Greece is now in the hands of God, and the great powers.'[5] His own fate lay in the hands of assassins who claimed his life on 9 October 1831. That of Greece was more than ever in the paternalistic care of European powers.

Three agreements, the Treaty of Adrianople (September 1829), the London Convention (May 1832) and the Treaty of Constantinople (July 1832), vouchsafed once and for all the existence of an independent Greek state by placing it under the protection of France, Great Britain and Russia, defining its boundaries, establishing its systems of government and determining its first ruler – Otto, son of Ludwig of Bavaria. In 1832, then, Greece came into existence. A pale comparison to the lofty 'new Byzantium' dreamed of by men like Rigas, it was a tiny, foreign-ruled and utterly dependent polity. Nonetheless, for the first time in history, there was a state for the Greek nation.

3

Building the modern state, 1832–1898

This was the spectacle when the newly anointed monarch of an independent Greece arrived at Nafplion (Text-box 7). Jubilation and optimism characterized popular feelings on that August winter's day. Neither, unfortunately, would last for long. The second son of the Philhellene ruler of

Text-box 7 King Otto's arrival in Greece (1833)

6 February 1833 … formed an era in the history of Greece, nor is it without some importance in the records of European civilization. A new Christian kingdom was incorporated in the international system of the West, at a critical period for the maintenance of the balance of power in the East. The scene itself formed a splendid picture. Anarchy and order shook hands. Greeks and Albanians, mountaineers and islanders, soldiers, sailors, and peasants, in their varied and picturesque dresses, hailed the young monarch as their deliverer from a state of society as intolerable as Turkish tyranny. Families in bright attire glided in boats over the calm sea amid the gaily decorated frigates of the Allied squadrons. The music of many bands in the ships and on shore enlivened the scene, and the roar of artillery in every direction gave an imposing pomp to the ceremony. The uniforms of many armies and navies, and the sounds of many languages, testified that most civilized nations had sent deputies to inaugurate the festival of the regeneration of Greece.

G. Finlay (1971 [1877]), *History of Greece From Its Conquest by the Romans to the Present Time, B.C. 146-A.D. 1864. 7 volumes*, London: Zeno, Volume V, 108.

Bavaria, Otto was a mere seventeen years old when asked to ascend the throne of the newly formed Kingdom of Greece. His reign spanned three decades and, because of developments we shall discuss shortly, it falls neatly into two periods: the first from 1832 until 1844 and the second from 1844 until his forced abdication in 1862. Otto had many faults – he was vainglorious, stubborn and frivolous – but he grew to love his adoptive kingdom and saw the state through some very difficult times (Figure 5). After Otto's overthrow, a new dynasty was established. Members of the Danish Glucksberg family would rule Greece off and on for almost a century. In this chapter, we examine the process of state formation in newly established Greece up until the end of the nineteenth century. Our main goal is to understand how and why the

FIGURE 5 *King Otto. This depiction of King Otto shortly after his arrival in Greece captures his youthfulness and his arrogance. Dressed in traditional Greek garb, the young German monarch tries to strike a regal pose. Despite all of his attempts to become 'Greek', Otto never fully became accepted by the people, with whom he had a love-and-hate affair for over thirty years.* Illustrated London News, *15 May 1834.* GallantGraphics all rights reserved.

institutions of the new state developed as they did and to assess their relative strengths and weaknesses. We also want to consider how developments in Greece compared to what was going on in the rest of Europe. Lastly, we need to consider how the flawed process of state formation during the nineteenth century created conditions that persisted, and that we will explore in subsequent chapters, over the course of the twentieth century.

Regency and absolutism: the political settlement of liberated Greece

The second son of King Ludwig I of Bavaria, Otto emerged from the great power negotiations as an attractive possibility to become ruler of Greece. Among the advantages of Otto's candidacy were, first, that his father was not firmly aligned to any of the major powers; second, that the youthful prince was an ardent Philhellene; third, that his political views were moderately conservative; and fourth, that he was young and malleable. The powers, however, initially passed him by in favour of Leopold, Duke of Saxe-Coburg, because of two drawbacks to his candidacy – his inexperience and his Catholicism. When Leopold removed himself from consideration and other possible candidates demurred, the great powers turned once again to the Bavarian monarch to inquire about his son. After a series of lengthy negotiations, on 7 May 1832, Ludwig signed the London Protocol with Russia, France and Great Britain that installed Otto as the first King of Greece. Later that year, on 21 July, an agreement was reached between the great powers and the Ottomans (The Treaty of Constantinople) that defined the new country's borders. The most important terms under which the young Bavarian would come to the throne were these. Otto, or Otho as he came to be called in Greece, became absolute monarch and his crown was to be passed on through hereditary succession based on the customary aristocratic practice of primogeniture (whereby the crown is passed on to the male heirs in order of age from eldest to youngest). Concerned about his son's safety because of the ongoing conflict and in order to guarantee as well as possible his future security, Ludwig insisted that the treaty mandate that a force of 3,500 Bavarian troops accompany the new King and that Bavarian officers be appointed to supervise and train the regular Greek army. Lastly, the three powers guaranteed the sovereignty of the new state and pledged loans totalling 60,000,000 francs; the money was to be distributed in three payments, only the first of which was actually scheduled in the treaty. Thus secure in its borders, protected by the shield of the West, and bankrolled by Western loans, liberated Greece greeted its youthful ruler and the Regents who would rule in his name. It would not be too long thereafter that they would all be sucked into the vortex of Greek partisan politics.

Since Otto was a minor, the treaty gave Ludwig the authority to appoint a three-man Regency to rule until his son came of age on 1 June 1835. To carry out this challenging task, he selected Count Joseph von Armansperg, Law Professor Georg Ludwig von Maurer and General Karl Wilhelm von Heideck. This troika exercised almost complete control over the Greek government. Von Armansperg assumed executive control; von Maurer was charged with devising the system of local and central government, promulgating codes of law and designing a system of civil and criminal justice, and overseeing the daily operation of the government; Heideck, of course, had the daunting task of administering the military affairs of state. Though an absolute ruler, Otto's role in the government was rather minor – this was to be on-the-job training for him – and, instead, it was his father who acted as advisor to the Regents.

Greek leaders played only subsidiary roles in the governance of their own state. Westerners were appointed to almost every major position of importance. This 'Bavarokratia' (the term by which Greek critics referred to the period of the Regency) became a source of much friction among Greek politicians. Compounding the Greek dependency on the Bavarian protectorate was the considerable influence exerted by the representatives of the great powers. The factionalism that had developed during the war continued, and each party looked to the French, English or Russian delegations as their protector.[1]

The so-called Russian Party had at its core men who had been important supporters of Ioannis Kapodistrias. Prominent among them were the old warrior Theodoros Kolokotronis, the Ionian Islands magnate Andreas Metaxas and military men such as Konstantinos Tsavellas and Dimitrios Kallergis. Its core membership came primarily from the wartime military leaders. What united this group and its followers was the belief that because of their shared religion, Russia was the great power most likely to further Greek interests. The movement was socially conservative and anti-liberal, and economically they sought to further the interests of small landowners.

Ioannis Kolettis led the French Party. He had been an advisor to Tepedelenli Ali Paşa and in that role he had had numerous dealings with French representatives during the Bonaparte years. A curious combination of military warlords from Central Greece, Peloponnesian kocabaşis and island ship owners constituted the core of the party. Kolettis brought them together by promising to address the demands of each group: land and estates for the Moreotes; open commerce and restitution of wartime losses for the islanders, and military commissions and back pay to the warlords. The link to the French delegation was through Kolettis himself.

The English Party was the movement of the Western-orientated progressives. Led by Alexander Mavrogordatos, it brought together those who favoured liberalism and Westernization. It found its strongest followings in the towns and cities (Athens, Nafplion, Hermoupolis and Patras) and among bureaucrats, intellectuals and the 'commercial class'.

Each of these parties was constantly in contact with, and some were used by, the foreign delegation of the country they looked to for support. In many ways, then, the war for 'liberation' from a foreign yoke had resulted merely in a change of masters. Finally, further exacerbating the political turmoil was the persistent power struggle between the Regents, which led eventually to two of them being recalled.

During the brief period of the Regency, Armansperg emerged as the dominant leader. When Otto became monarch in his own right on 1 June 1835, Armansperg stayed on for a brief period as Arch-Chancellor and was then replaced by another German, Count von Ruduck. Whether it was under Armansperg or Otto, the government of Greece was autocratic and its administration dominated by Germans and other Westerners. To be sure, there was some participation by Greeks as members of a cabinet of advisors to the crown, but as was made evident on numerous occasions when important actions were taken and key decisions made without even a nod in their direction, the Greeks' role in practical governance was largely irrelevant. Finally, and perhaps most importantly, the appointment of Greeks to any governmental position was based on royal patronage doled out by the functionaries surrounding the Regency and the monarchy.

A good example of the cavalier attitude that the Bavarians evinced towards the Greeks and their traditions in regard to crafting the institutions of the new state was the legal system. After taking into account the customs, traditions and laws that had shaped the process of dispute resolution and jurisprudence in the past, the Bavarians cobbled together a hybrid system that drew its structure and trappings from the French system, and its philosophical basis from German thought. The legal pluralism that had existed under the Ottomans was replaced by a unitary one. Though the legal reforms supposedly created a national system of civil and criminal courts, including a system of justices of peace who were to adjudicate minor disputes, the system never effectively functioned outside of Athens, Syros and a few other major towns. In other words, for much of the nineteenth century, the state-mandated writ of law lacked legitimacy in local eyes, and it was only after a very long time that this situation began to change. And even then, many people continued to cling to the old ways of adjudicating disputes.[2]

The political scene in post-war Greece was turbulent to say the least. A convoluted triangle of factions and power groupings developed that made for some very strange bedfellows. Factions developed within the Bavarian administration and each of them forged alliances of convenience with one of the Greek parties and with one of the foreign delegations. The Greek factions likewise sought the support of one of the big three – France, Britain or Russia – which were themselves intensely active in promoting their countries' vested interests in the Eastern Mediterranean. Any endeavours to reconstruct war-ravaged Greece, then, had to negotiate these turbulent political waters.

Rebuilding a broken land

Notwithstanding the complicated political situation, the problems facing Otto and his advisors from 1832 to 1843 were formidable. Economically, the country was in ruins. Politically, the Bavarian regime faced a serious crisis of legitimacy. Westernized Greeks who had fought for the ideals of the American and French Revolutions were profoundly disappointed to find themselves saddled with a foreign absolute monarchy. Phanariots and indigenous kocabaşis who saw it as their right to succeed the Ottomans as rulers of the land were furious at being frozen out of power. Granted that the more thoughtful of the Greek leaders recognized that only a foreign leader not tied to any of the entrenched factions could possibly salvage the situation, many still resented the Bavarians. In addition, the wounds from the civil unrest of 1832 were still fresh, and with thousands of armed warriors still roaming the land, the cauldron of internecine conflict could easily boil over again.

Bread and butter issues topped the Bavarian agenda. During the course of the war of liberation and the subsequent events of 1832, over 662 villages had been devastated. In spite of the significant strides made during the presidency of Kapodistrias, there were still thousands of refugees who needed food and shelter. In towns such as Patras, Kalamata, Tripolis and Athens, few houses stood above their foundation (see Figure 6). Visitors to these ruined settlements paint stark pictures of the devastation and of Greeks living like beasts in makeshift hovels and shacks. Homeless men wandered the land seeking employment, while war orphans and widows sought some kind of protection and sustenance. Thus, in despair, a destitute and displaced rural populace looked to their new king for assistance.

The agricultural infrastructure on which the economy was based lay in ruins. Over two-thirds of the olive trees and three-quarters of the vineyards had been destroyed. Three-quarters of the olive and flour mills had been reduced to rubble. Of the estimated pre-war flocks of over 100,000 goats and sheep, only approximately 10,000 remained. Vast sums of money were needed to rebuild the infrastructure of the agrarian economy. But above all, economic reconstruction depended completely on the redistribution of land. The peasants, then, looked to the young king for bread, land and peace.

FIGURE 6 *Returning to War-ravaged Athens (1831). In this moving painting, we see a young couple and their children returning to their devastated house in Athens. The man lays his hand on what are presumably the remnants of the walls of his house, while his spouse sobs at his side. Just behind them, a man and a woman are gathering up what remains of their belongings. To set the scene, von Hess painted a panoramic view of an Athens in ruins.*

Peter von Hess (1840). GallantGraphics all rights reserved.

Other groups felt that they were owed much because of their roles during the war. The primates who had led and paid for the war wanted land, power and pay for their men. The ship owners who had been the backbone of the fleet and who had spent a great deal of cash on the war wanted indemnity payments. The men at arms who had fought the war wanted regular pay as soldiers, or land, or both. Satisfying all of these claimants, even with the monies available through the foreign loans, was impossible.

Throughout his reign, Otto faced fiscal crises. Dwelling within his kingdom's bounds were only 750,000 Greeks compared to over two million still under Ottoman rule. Most importantly, in respect to the economic future of the kingdom, the fertile plains of Thessaly and lacustrine basins of Macedonia lay outside the kingdom. The major Greek cities and entrepôts of Salonika and Smyrna and the island of Crete remained in the Ottoman Empire. In spite of the expertise and connections that the Greeks of the diaspora brought with them as they migrated to the new kingdom, manufacturing and trade remained underdeveloped. The economic conditions in Greece presented the government with a major challenge: how to stimulate growth, satisfy the immediate needs of the population and pay the war indemnity owed to the Porte. The only feasible internal source of revenue entailed taxing the very thing that needed to expand – agriculture. Even before that could become an issue, the government had to deal with the complicated but crucial issue of land redistribution.

The land situation in Greece was chaotic. As we have seen, during the period of Ottoman rule, 65–75 per cent of the cultivated land in Greece was in Muslim hands, either through private ownership or in one of the conditional tenures bestowed by the Sultan. By the war's end, the vast majority of the Muslim population had either fled or been killed. The land of the deceased was up for grabs, and while some of those who fled the carnage had managed to dispose of their land, many others had not. The revolutionary governments nationalized all such property and used the newly confiscated lands as collateral for international loans. At the war's end, some Greeks possessed land that they had legally purchased before the war. Others held legal title to estates they had purchased from Muslims during the war. And still others were in possession of land that they had usurped as war booty or that had been given by Greek warlords in lieu of payment for their services. When Kapodistrias came to power, one of his top priorities was to commission a survey to determine who legally owned which lands and thus to determine the location and extent of the national lands, and to calculate the amount owed as compensation to the previous owners. Kapodistrias's programme met with stiff resistance and had not progressed very far at the time of his assassination. The land issue was of such crucial importance, however, that it quickly became a priority for the new Bavarian regime.

On 7 June 1835, less than one week after he had become sole ruler, Otto issued the 'Law for the Dotation of Greek Families.' The culmination of many years' labours, this legislation was to be the capstone of the Bavarian economic and social policy of reconstruction. While thoughtfully crafted in theory, the law paid scant attention to the realities on the ground in the Greek countryside, and so it produced results very different from those intended by the lawmakers.

The law stipulated that all native-born and foreign-born Greeks, and all non-Greeks who had fought in the war and continued to reside in Greece, were eligible to receive a 2,000-drachma government credit certificate with which to purchase national land. Each head of a household, and this included war widows, could bid on parcels of land varying in size and quality up to the limit of their certificate. No one could obtain more than four hectares of national land. Once purchased, the land became private property to be held in perpetuity. In return, the owner incurred a mortgage that mandated a payment of 6 per cent of the purchase price annually for thirty-six years. Two successive defaults in payment and the land was returned to the state for reallocation. The crown claimed an additional 3 per cent of the purchase price in taxes that was to be paid in cash and not in kind. This then was the scheme that the government hoped would create a stable landholding peasantry and that would set the state on the road to fiscal responsibility.

The programme, however, was fraught with difficulties. First, the four-hectare maximum was too low. Even under the best of conditions, this amount of land would barely provide basic subsistence to the average family, let alone cover the mortgage and taxes. Moreover, the 2,000-drachma allocation was predicated on the average price for a hectare of cultivable land being 500 drachmas. This proved to be unrealistic. Prices at the land auctions varied on average from 1,350 drachmas per hectare for basic arable land to 2,600 for land with vines to over 5,000 drachmas per hectare for irrigated gardens.

As a result, those peasants who had to rely solely on the government certificate were able to acquire farms of only between one and three hectares, and usually the land they purchased was of the lowest quality. Even in the best of years, such *minifundia* would not have fed the average family. But Greece possessed a very high-risk agricultural environment in which even a six-hectare farm would have failed to provide subsistence one-sixth of the time. Peasants either had somehow to acquire non-national lands – almost an impossibility – or they had to find other sources of income, of which there were precious few in post-war Greece. In addition, as mentioned above, since landholders had to pay in cash a three per cent tax based on the purchase price, many proprietors were compelled to find non-agricultural sources of cash income or borrow the money to pay their taxes.

The family farms created by the dotation scheme were born into dependency and debt, and that soon translated into poverty. At the same time, the auction system was very susceptible to manipulation and corruption. A few wealthy men were able to exploit the loopholes in the system to acquire sizable estates with the best land. In short, the rich got richer and the poor poorer. Land, debt and poverty remained persistent features of the Greek countryside throughout the modern era.

Otto's government then found itself in a difficult situation, on the one hand passing land reform laws in order to distribute land to the peasants and providing low-interest loans to enable families to cultivate that land, while on the other having to claim back these resources in the form of taxes. In addition to the taxes on the national lands, a tithe of 10 per cent was levied on privately held land. The collection system combined the older mechanism of tax-farming with one operated by government civil servants. Both were open to manipulation and corruption. Evasion by tax payers became rampant, and peculation by tax collectors rife. The result was a very insecure income to the state. Since internal sources of revenue were inadequate, borrowing from Greeks abroad, foreign banks and European states was repeatedly resorted to. Indebtedness was the result in both cases. Debt remained a serious problem throughout the modern epoch and resulted in Greece going bankrupt more than once.

In spite of the obstacles, the reconstruction of Greece from the devastation of eleven years of war did occur. The merchant marine recovered from the wartime losses and once again much of the sea-borne freight of the Mediterranean was in Greek hands. According to one estimate, the value of mercantile trade handled by Greek ships rose by 194 per cent between 1833 and 1840, and by 1840, the value of that trade was in the order of 80 million drachmas. Not surprisingly, given the low level of agricultural production and very modest industrial output of the Kingdom of Greece, most of the commerce handled by Greek ships was transit trade between the Ottoman and Russian empires and Western Europe. Because of the development of the mercantile sector, islands such as Syros and port cities like Patras began to flourish once again.

Syros in the Aegean literally became the crossroads of the Mediterranean. By 1837 the majority of commerce between East and West passed through the island. Its capital city of Hermoupolis grew in size, from a population of 150 in 1821 to over 12,000 in 1840, and in wealth. Patras on the northwestern tip of the Peloponnesos also witnessed a remarkable recovery during the age of Otto. The first decade of Otto's rule, then, witnessed an economic recovery of sorts, but the nature of that recovery, based on mercantile trade rather than a solid base of production, was to have a lasting impact on the Greek economy.

After the economy, the paramount issue facing the royal government was security. The war of liberation had been fought by a combination of a very small army made up of Western-trained regular troops and much larger bands of former bandits, ex-paramilitary police and armed peasants. Military warlords held sway over their band as their own personal army. The Bavarians, as had Kapodistrias before them, recognized that no national government was secure so long as warlords commanded personal armed bands. They faced roughly the same options as the ill-fated first president: either incorporate or eradicate the rootless gangs of irregulars. If anything, the situation facing them was even more acute than it had been for Kapodistrias. The civil war of 1832 had elevated the level of militarization of the countryside and its outcome left stranded large numbers of disgruntled veterans of the war of independence who wanted their back pay, land and a livelihood. They looked to the boy king to give these things to them.

Otto and his Regents had other ideas. They believed that a modern army, trained in the Western style and loyal only to the monarchy could ensure the government's security. The 3,500 Bavarian troops that accompanied the king were soon augmented to 5,000, all German volunteers. They were to form the core of the new regular army. On 2 March 1833, the Regency issued a decree disbanding the irregulars; another law that banned the possession of firearms without a government licence quickly followed it. Enforcement of these laws, however, could easily have plunged the nation into civil discord yet again.

So the Regents offered some inducements for compliance. Older warriors would be enrolled into an honorary battalion and be provided with retirement benefits. They could send their sons free of charge to the newly established military school in Aigina. More generally, the disbanded irregulars could join the new regular army. The idea was that Greek troops, trained and commanded by German officers, would complement the Bavarian mercenaries in the new modern army. Still others were offered the opportunity of enlisting in the new gendarmerie that had been established to police the countryside.

Few Greeks responded positively to these measures. Warlords were loath to relinquish the stick that gave them leverage in their struggles to gain political power locally. Uniforms, strict discipline, hard training and low pay were anathema to the proud and independent mountain warrior/brigands who made up the rank-and-file of the irregulars. For many old warhorses of the revolution, it was preferable to sleep on the mountains in a goatskin cloak as a bandit than to wear the hated uniform of the Germans. Consequently, only a handful of able-bodied men enlisted in the regular army. More became gendarmes because this gave them complete discretion to exploit the local peasant villages in ways that they already had been doing.

One old warhorse at least saw as a sham the government's other schemes to disarm them by offering medals and honours, characterizing them as 'a bone to lick until their teeth finally fell [out]'.[3] Most reverted to the old ways, and became brigands and gunmen for hire. Some bands crossed over into Ottoman-controlled northern Greece and plied their craft there, using the border as a means to play the Porte and the government in Athens off one another. Others formed bandit gangs that roamed the countryside of Attika and the Peloponnesos. Armed conflict between them and the forces of the state was inevitable.

Between 1834 and 1840, numerous armed uprisings occurred. Some, like those in the Mani in 1834 and in Akarnania in 1836, involved hundreds of men and required a sustained campaign by government forces before peace was restored. Just as significant was the endemic banditry that flourished throughout the peninsula. Otto made a number of concessions, like dismissing the Bavarian troops and replacing them with Greeks, and this helped to alleviate the situation somewhat. But brigandage and unrest would continue to plague his government and insecurity was a perennial problem, especially in the border zone. Just as disgruntled, demobilized members of the revolutionary army proved a powerful destabilizing factor on land, so too did pirates at sea. During the war, the Greek fleet had systematically preyed on Western-flagged ships that were sailing to Ottoman ports, arguing that they were preventing supplies from reaching the enemy. Though reasonable, this line of argument carried little weight in Western capitals. After independence, Greek piracy was indefensible and a source of contention between Athens and the European powers. Moreover, as Aegean pirates increasingly became less discriminating about whom they attacked, piracy proved detrimental to the Greek economy as well as providing a flashpoint for conflict with the Ottoman Empire. Issues over law and order, then, proved critical in the formative years of the new Greek state.

Political stability proved elusive in the first phase of Otto's rule. He and his advisors showed little sensitivity to indigenous traditions in politics, law and education as they attempted to impose Western models. Increasingly, the Greek elite split between *heterochthons*, Greeks from the diaspora who had migrated to Greece, and *autochthons*, the descendants of the old elite families or *tzakia*. Old cleavages from the war years remained and new ones developed connected to the struggle for power in local administration and for influence with the King. But, as Edmond About noted in his commentary on Greek life and politics, 'the future belonged to the men in black coats [i.e., the westernized Greeks]'.

The old-timers, however, would not go down without a fight; and the political system established in 1834 made such partisan conflicts inevitable. The kingdom was divided administratively into 10 *nomarchies* (prefectures), 59 *eparchies* (sub-prefectures) and 468 *demes* (counties) (see Map 2). Nomarchs and eparchs were nominated directly by the king; demarchs were appointed by him from a list of three elected by a small number of the wealthiest men in each deme. The absolute power invested in Otto rankled with the men who had fought the war in the name of republicanism. The extreme centralism at the heart of the new administration trampled on the long and storied tradition of local rule. And it challenged, in theory at least, the power of the local elites.

Adding further fuel to the political fire was the religious question. A decree by the Bavarian Regency in 1833 established an autocephalous Orthodox Church of the Kingdom of Greece with Otto at its head, and this led to a rupture with the Patriarchate that would only be healed in 1850. The young monarch, however, remained a Roman Catholic and showed no inclination to alter that fact. After his marriage to the Duchess Amalia of Oldenburg in 1836 and his failure to sire a child, the issue of the religion of his heir became a controversial one. Greeks wanted an Orthodox ruler, and Otto persisted in showing disdain for that widely felt sentiment. This stance infuriated, in particular, those of the 'Russian' party who believed in the vision of a greater Orthodox Greek state, and a group of them re-invigorated a secret organization called the

MAP 2 *The Kingdom of Greece, 1833.*

Philorthodox Society to force change, if necessary. Fiscal chaos, failed land reform, increasingly violent factionalism and resentment at unfulfilled agendas, all spelt trouble for the young monarch. Tensions came to a head in 1843.

Constitutional monarchy

The second period of Otto's rule officially began on 7 March 1844, the day on which the new constitution was promulgated. The age of absolutism in Greece was officially over. Since he had returned from Germany with his new bride in the spring of 1837 (they were wed in November 1836), Otto had become ever more the absolute ruler. He dismissed many of his top-ranking German advisors; he showed disdain bordering on contempt for the Greek cabinet. He strove to concentrate sole power in his own hands. Pushing him in this direction was Amalia, who proved to have a stronger character and will to rule than her husband. Otto was neither ruthless enough to be feared, nor compassionate enough to be loved; nor was he competent enough to be respected. He thus commanded the loyalty of no sector of society. Lacking any support among the general populace, at odds with the leaders of the major political parties and estranged from the representatives of the great powers, the King found himself increasingly isolated, a condition only exaggerated by his dismissal of all of his most independent-minded advisors. As discontent rose to open rebellion against his reign, Otto had no one to turn to and so had to compromise.

Colonel Dimitrios Kallergis, the cavalry commander of the garrison of Athens, who was also related to powerful men in Russia and in Greece, led the coup that toppled the absolute monarchy, in what was to be the first, but by no means the last, time that the military would intervene in civilian affairs. Plots against Otto had been hatching for some time and their existence was well known, even as far away as London. When Otto's attempt to have the ringleaders arrested failed, Kallergis called out the troops and marched on the palace. The square in front of it soon filled with people. Shouts of 'Long live the constitution' and 'Death to the Bavarians' rang out from the crowd. After consultations with Kallergis and other military leaders, meetings with heads of the major parties and audiences with great power delegations, Otto saw that his position was untenable. Without a drop of blood being shed, the Bavarian absolute monarchy came to an end.

In the wake of a military coup, Otto reluctantly agreed to convene a national assembly to draft a constitution. The constitutional assembly met on 20 November 1843. When it finally finished its work that spring, a new system of government was established by an overwhelming majority on 7 March 1844. Otto would rule as a constitutional monarch. There would be a bicameral legislature. One chamber, the *Vouli* or Lower House of Parliament, consisted of deputies elected on the basis of mass enfranchisement (any male property holder over twenty-five years of age could vote), and the other, the *Gerousia* or Upper House or Senate, had members appointed by the king. Greece became, in theory, one of the most democratic states in Europe.

Intense debates ensued, however, over the question of who actually was a 'Greek.' The division between autochthonous Greeks (those who had been born in the territory of the new state) and heterochthonous Greeks (those who had moved to the kingdom from outside) led to rancorous debates when it was proposed that essentially there would be two categories of citizenship based on one's origins. In the end, the distinction based on place of origin was dropped. Otto, however, retained the power to appoint or dismiss government ministers unilaterally, to dissolve parliament and to veto legislation. With the counter-signature of a minister, he could issue executive decrees as law, and with the agreement of the prime minister, he could appoint for life members of the Gerousia. He agreed, in turn, that his successor to the throne would be Greek Orthodox.

Political parties did not arise in the wake of parliamentary democracy. Instead, factionalism took a new form. Hierarchical pyramids of power centring on a single prominent man developed and were held together by patronage. This is not particularly surprising given that personal relations had been a central element of the political system from the very foundation of the new state. No one played the power politics under the new constitution better than Ioannis Kolettis and he left his imprimatur on mid-century Greek politics. He was able to form working alliances with both the Western modernizers and the traditional power brokers while not becoming closely tied to either. Politics by personalities as exemplified in the career of Kolettis set the pattern for the political culture of Greece until the 1870s.

This crafty veteran of the political intrigue was appointed prime minister of Greece under the new system in 1844 because he enjoyed the support of the king. His faction occupied only 22 of the 127 seats in the Lower House. Through the lavish use of favours and appointments, cajoling and intimidation, Kolettis managed the new parliament. His faction grew in size and he personally monopolized power, holding the portfolios, at one point or another during his three-year term, of Foreign Affairs, Justice, Interior, Culture and Public Instruction and Finance, as well as that of Prime Minister. Coupled with his autocratic inclinations were his populist tendencies: he knew the value of popular support in a democratic system. As a contemporary, George Finley, noted about Kolettis: 'He could hear the first whispers of public opinion, and he knew to avail himself of its support as soon as it made its voice heard.'[4]

During his administration, he implemented some important measures to help develop the economy and to build the country's infrastructure, but financing such moves put the country further into debt in light of the country's declaration of bankruptcy a few years before (1843) when Greece was forced to default on some of its war loans. Kolettis is best remembered as the man who first gave a coherent focus to the widely held belief among Greeks that the Greeks still residing in the Ottoman Empire had to be redeemed; this vision became known as the **Megali Idea**, or Great Idea. Kolettis had been able to manipulate the various parties and the king so as to strike a 'balance of forces'. No one faction was able to gain ascendancy because the wily old veteran of the politics of patronage was able to play each side against the others. When he died in September 1847, the political situation changed for the worse. A series of episodes over the next few years served to expose the weaknesses of the system and began the slide in Otto's popularity that would end in his overthrow.

In 1848, the year of European liberal revolutions, even Greece could not escape the infectious spirit of rebellion. However, with the exception of a demonstration on 25 March 1848 during which university students gathered before the palace and shouted 'Long live the republic!', the uprisings in Greece did not challenge the institution of royal rule as the revolutions elsewhere on the continent did. There were, nonetheless, a number of rebellions; some, like the peasant revolt in central Greece, involved very large numbers of men. All of the uprisings had their origins in local causes. Disgruntled politicians who had lost their positions in the uncertain days after the death of Kolettis led some of the revolts. Many more were uprisings of peasants in protest over high taxes, skyrocketing debt and foreclosure, and the increasing poverty of the countryside (see the discussion of the rural economy in Chapter 6 for the reasons behind these developments). So, even though the rebellions did not directly threaten the government and the monarchy, as happened elsewhere in Europe, they clearly highlighted the growing disaffection with them among the people. Developments over the next few years only made matters worse.

On 15 January 1850, a British naval squadron under the command of Vice Admiral William Parker laid anchor just off the port of Piraeus and an ultimatum was issued to Otto and his government. Two episodes that generated great tensions between London and Greece, and which lost Otto a great deal of British support, marked the turn of the mid-century. In 1847, the house of a man named David Don Pacifico, a Portuguese Jewish merchant who had been born in Gibraltar and so was a British subject, was attacked by an anti-Semitic mob in Athens. With the ardent support of Sir Edmund Lyons, the British minister in Greece, Pacifico sought compensation from the Greek government for damages to his property and effects and for the suffering endured by his wife and children. While a fruitless dialogue was going on between London and Athens, another episode involving a Briton made matters worse. Captain John Parker was a former British soldier who had retired to the Ionian island of Kefalonia, where he had married Kiara Assani, the daughter of a Greek aristocratic family and taken up employment as the forest ranger on the island's Black Mountain. At this time, the Ionian Islands were a self-governing state under the protection of the British Crown. On 8 May 1849, assassins brutally murdered Parker and his pet dog while they were patrolling the mountain. There was at this time a radical movement on the island that sought unification with the Kingdom of Greece and it was actively inciting insurrection. The year before Parker's murder, there had been an outbreak of anti-British violence, and there was every indication that another rebellion was in the offing. The police investigation uncovered evidence that suggested that officials in the Greek government were complicit in Parker's killing. That Greek officials impeded the murder investigation seemed to confirm British suspicions, thus escalating further tensions between London and Athens. Having already alienated both France and Russia, Greece was on the verge of losing the support of the third of its protecting powers. Moreover, it was fast gaining a reputation as the 'bad child' of the Mediterranean. By 1850, Lord Palmerston had grown tired of the endless negotiations and was now demanding that the Greek administration make good on the monies owed to Pacifico and a few others, or else the fleet would blockade Piraeus, Syros, Patras and Nafplion. The blockade lasted for three months until at last, under the threat of an actual bombardment of Athens, Otto gave in. The episode led to widespread anti-British feelings and generated, in the short term, support for Otto; in the long run, however, it also showed how weak and dependent the kingdom was. The debacle of 1854 exposed that situation even further.

The outbreak of the Crimean War seemingly presented Greece with an opportunity to gain major territorial concessions from the Sultan (see also p. 103). In anticipation of an Ottoman defeat at the hands of Russia, Otto declared, in effect, that as the only Christian king in the Near East, he had a sacred duty to protect the Christians of the Balkans and exhorted further that God in His greatness would never abandon the 'Christian cause'. With these words he signalled his wholehearted support of the Megali Idea and his approval of Greece's participation in the conflict. Greek irregulars streamed over the frontier into Thessaly and Epiros with the blessing of the Monarch, the Parliament and the Greek people.

When Great Britain and France intervened in the war on the side of the Porte, everything changed. Greece was now embroiled in a conflict that pitted two of its protecting powers against the third one. Yet again, the Western powers issued an ultimatum to Greece: stand down or face the consequences. After a humiliating occupation of Piraeus by French and British forces in May 1854, Otto had to ignominiously give up the 'Christian cause' and had an administration selected by the foreign legations imposed on him.

On the anniversary of Otto's twenty-fifth year on the throne in 1858, his popularity with the Greek populace rebounded slightly but was still not great. It should occasion no surprise, then, that within a matter of a few years he would be driven out of the country. A number of factors contributed to his demise. First, Otto had by and large reduced constitutional government to a sham, effectively ruling as an autocrat at the head of a royalist faction of sycophantic politicians. Opposition to the way the political system was being manipulated grew, especially among younger and university-educated politicians whose political sympathies were more liberal and democratic. Second, Otto's initial response to the emergence of the Italian unification struggle, the *Risorgimento*, in 1859 eroded his popularity with the general public and provided his opponents with fodder to fuel the fire of discontent. The public at large supported the Italian cause, seeing in it a reflection of their own irredentist dreams; Otto, on the other hand, openly favoured Austria in its attempts to put down the Italian uprising. Third, many Greeks looked at the support Great Britain and France were giving the Italian insurgents and speculated that Otto was the reason that the Western great powers continued to look on the Greek nationalist cause unfavourably. Fourth, the issue of succession continued to plague Otto. The royal couple remained childless, and so in the event of Otto's death, the throne would be passed on to one of Otto's brothers, all of whom refused to convert to Orthodoxy and so openly stated that they would decline the throne. Otto continued to refuse to reveal whom he would nominate to be his successor and the succession issue remained a source of unpopularity with the Greek people and with the Russian government, which was worried that the lack of an Orthodox heir would have a serious impact on their position in the region.

In a vain attempt to stem the tide of opposition to his rule, Otto attempted to foment a military venture against the Ottoman Empire. He inaugurated talks with Serbia and Montenegro, and even with Garibaldi in Italy, regarding a concerted campaign against the Sultan. But these efforts failed, plunging public assessment of his rule even lower and, further, incurring the displeasure of France and Great Britain. Symptomatic of the rising opposition to the Bavarian monarchy were the attempt by radical university students to assassinate Queen Amalia in 1861 (which nearly succeeded) and the military revolt centred in Nafplion in early 1862, which was only marginally suppressed. In mid-October, Otto and Amalia left Athens to tour the Peloponnesos; they wanted a respite from the political hothouse in Athens and they wanted to hear firsthand the opinions of 'real' Greeks. While they were away, revolts broke out at numerous garrisons around the country, and when they tried to enter the port of Piraeus, the Royal Navy blocked them. In their absence, a bloodless coup had taken place. A provisional government had seized power, declaring the abolition of the Bavarian monarchy. Amalia, the stronger of the two to the end, urged her husband to fight, but he would not; his will to resist had evaporated when he was informed that none of the guarantor powers would come to his rescue. Otto left Greece a broken man. He spent the rest of his life, which turned out to be only a few years (he died on 26 July 1867), in Munich, often seen still wearing the traditional Greek fustanella. He had come to love his adopted country but its people never loved him back. There would, then, be a new administration in the Kingdom of Greece and this momentous political change would come at a time when the entire Greek and Ottoman worlds were in a state of flux.

The age of liberal reform, 1864–1909

The overthrow of Otto created both constitutional and successional crises. The former focused on the relative balance of power between sovereign and Parliament; the latter touched directly on the question of sovereignty and autonomy. A constituent assembly was called in 1863 to address both issues, but it soon became evident that the protecting powers had no intention of relinquishing their prerogative to appoint the new king. Therefore, the assembly spent its energies debating the constitutional question.

While, in theory, the Constitution of 1844 shared power between King and Parliament, in reality, it had given the monarchy sufficient powers to control the government. A national assembly was convened on 22 November 1862 to draft a new constitution, which was eventually promulgated in 1864 and which was far more democratic than its predecessor. For a start, sovereignty was invested in the Greek people, not the monarchy. This was to be a *vasilevoméni dimokratía*, a democracy with a monarch or a 'crowned democracy'. Second, rather than being open ended, as they were in the 1844 charter, in the new constitution, the monarch's powers were restricted to those specifically adumbrated in the document. Structurally, there was to be a single-chambered parliament vested with full legislative powers and elected by direct, secret ballot of all Greek men over the age of twenty-one who owned some property or who followed a trade or occupation. As the debates in the constituent assembly made clear, the king's powers, however, were still going to be considerable. He would have the power to appoint and dismiss ministers, dissolve parliament, disburse funds, declare war and contract treaties. Because the new king would thus wield considerable power, the question of who would sit on the throne of Greece was an extremely important one.

The people of Greece made clear whom they preferred as their new leader. In a plebiscite in December 1862, 241,202 votes were cast; 95 per cent of them were for Queen Victoria's second son, Prince Alfred. But having a member of the British royal family on the throne of Greece was completely unacceptable to the other protecting powers, and so the search for a suitable king continued. It had to be someone from a prominent, yet not too partisan, royal house. Chosen eventually was Prince Christian William Ferdinand Adolphus George of Holstein–Sonderberg–Glücksbrug, the son of the future king of Denmark. He would reign as George I, King of the Hellenes, until his death at the hands of an assassin in 1913.

George was eighteen years old when he ascended to the throne. Determined to learn from the mistakes of his predecessor, he did not bring with him a large entourage of foreign administrators, he did not fall prey to the factionalism that so beset Greek politics and he made it explicitly clear from the start that, though he intended to adhere to the Protestant faith, his children would be Orthodox. Finally, he was a firm believer in constitutionalism, and so he readily accepted in principle the idea that while he reigned as monarch, he did not rule the state. At times, his impatience with Greek politicians gave him pause, but he never really challenged the separation of powers. He enhanced his position with the Greek people further by taking an Orthodox, albeit Russian, bride and then solidified it by siring an Orthodox son and heir, and by auspiciously naming him after the last emperor of Byzantium – Konstantinos.

In spite of the arrival of a new ruling dynasty and a new constitution, little seemed to change in the rough-and-tumble practice of Greek politics. Powerful personalities continued to hold sway through their networks of clients held together by bonds of patronage. New cleavages did appear, however, based on broad differences regarding economic development and liberalism. One group, called the 'montaigne', tended to be more liberal, supporting economic growth through industrialization and urging greater government intervention in both the social and economic spheres; this group drew its support primarily from younger, educated men who had a more Western outlook and the growing urban middle class and entrepreneurs. The other group, referred to as the 'plaine', was conservative in orientation 'preferring security through stagnation rather than progress through friction'; its base of support tended to be among the large landowners of the Peloponnesos.

More important in defining Greek political culture in the second half of the nineteenth century than these loose, volatile groups were the political clubs, which sprang up in increasing numbers. Clubs like the 'Korais', the 'Athanasios Diakos' and the 'Rigas' united like-thinking men and enabled more coherent political discourse to develop; they also linked Members of Parliament with the local power brokers in their constituencies.

A good example is the club 'Athanasios Diakos' based in Lamia, Phthiotis. In 1875, this club had fifty-nine members: twenty-five lawyers, thirty large landowners and four physicians. The group was 'plaine' in orientation and so their leader Konstantinos Diovouniotis, whom they got elected in three successive elections, was a follower of Dimitrios Voulgaris. Diovouniotis was client to Voulgaris, seeking from him perks and privileges; Diovouniotis, in turn, answered to the members of his club by looking out for their interests; the members of the club shared their leader's ideology and promised their support by mobilizing votes.

The large landowner, Nikolaos Papalexis, for example, guaranteed in 1885 at least 350 votes for his patron; how he could make such a boast was simple: that was the number of agricultural labourers employed on his large currant plantation near Olympia. The implication was clear. Those of his workers who did not vote as he instructed them would soon be looking for other employment. Intimidation, extortion and other strong-arm tactics made up what was referred to as the 'system' through which powerful men created their factions.

In urban areas, artisans' associations and merchants' guilds, like the Athens-based Guild of Green Grocers, also provided vehicles for political acculturation and acted as vehicles for mobilizing electoral support. Out of this patchwork of clubs and guilds, political factions were formed and parliamentary democracy practised under the 1864 Constitution.

In spite of the changes, the political system was deeply flawed. An examination of the period 1865–75 shows these defects clearly. During that decade there were seven general elections, and more importantly, eighteen different administrations: the longest lasted twenty months and the shortest a mere fourteen days! The difficulty was that King George had the power to appoint or dismiss ministers, and so he could create or collapse administrations at will. If a key piece of legislation became blocked or if the budget failed to pass, then the monarch dissolved the government. Political leaders constantly juggled a variety of demands in order to keep their fragile ruling coalitions together.

Most importantly, since the King could appoint as the Prime Minister whomsoever he desired, men with only a handful of MPs supporting them were asked to form governments, and conversely, the leader of the largest group of members might have found himself denied the leadership of the chamber. This was a recipe for a political gridlock as well as a mockery of the democratic process.

In 1874, a 37-year-old politician addressed the problem of gridlock and set himself on the path to becoming one of the most important leaders in the history of modern Greece. Harilaos Trikoupis was born in the same year that the nation was formed, 1832. He was, then, a 'new man', born into the first generation after the War of Independence. Trikoupis came from a prominent family and he spent the first thirteen years of his life in England. Fluent in English (throughout his life his Greek was heavily accented) and Western educated, he firmly believed that in order to modernize, Greece had to emulate the countries of Western Europe.

Trikoupis rose politically as a follower of Alexander Koumoundouros, the leader of the liberal 'montaigne', and he was appointed foreign minister by his patron in 1866. He entered the political fray on his own with the publication in 1874 of his anonymous article 'Who Is To Blame?' in the newspaper *Kairoi*, in which he examined the causes of Greece's political turmoil (Text-box 8). The response to his rhetorical question was manifestly evident to him: it was the King who was to blame by not appointing only majority governments. In the firestorm that followed the article's publication and Trikoupis's subsequent arrest for treason when his identity as the author became known, King George eventually relented and recognized the principle of *dedilomeni*. By so doing the King agreed that in future he would ask only the leader of the declared majority of Members of Parliament to form a government. If no one could obtain the pledged support of a plurality, then the King would dissolve Parliament and call for a general election.

The ramifications of the new policy were far-reaching. In the last twenty-five years of the nineteenth century, there were only seven general elections and a much greater stability of administrations. Greater continuity of governance was the result. Two figures, Trikoupis and his conservative rival Theodoros Deliyiannis, dominated Greek political life in the last few decades of the nineteenth century. But it was Trikoupis more than any other who shaped the age and made it into an era of reform.

Text-box 8 'Who is to blame?' (1871)

Since the institution of the principle of the minority governments in 1868, each new step of the power reveals the objective it aims at; ... Mr Voulgaris, Mr Zaimis and Mr Deligiorgis were organs of the same policy, executors of the same plan. None of them was invited to the power on the suggestion of the representatives of the Nation, no one represented totally the aspirations of the Nation; all three of them were presidents of a personal government, that is servants of the same desire acting sometimes for this and at other times for something else.

The Nation does not bear any moral responsibility for the conduct of these persons ... but the administrative insufficiency during the election irregularities is not a work of the power, which represents the majority of the Parliament that should be responsible for its actions before the Nation. It is the work of people who owe their ministerial existence to the only absolute use of the right of the Crown, which is written in the Constitution, to appoint and dismiss ministers ...

Therefore, the responsibility of what has occurred belongs completely to the element in which the entire power has been concentrated because of the distortion of our constitutional institutions... . In order to remedy this, the fundamental principle of the parliamentary government must be sincerely admitted, that is that the ministries should be attributed to the majority of the Parliament.

Καιροί, 29 June 1871.

Trikoupis was utterly convinced that in order for Greece to become a 'modern' state, it needed to develop economically and to become more liberal socially. For reasons discussed in the next chapter, it had also to be strengthened militarily. During his nearly continuous term of office in the 1880s, he set about the task of reforming and modernizing Greece. His reforms can be divided into two groups, economic and social.

The Greek economy perennially operated with a trade deficit and it fluctuated widely in its performance, in large part because of its linkage to the more advanced economic systems of Europe, especially Britain and France. Chart 1 depicts the balance of trade between 1850 and 1900. Even during the decade of the 1880s when Trikoupis enacted his reforms and we can see a marked growth in the export sector, imports still ran far in excess of exports. Greece imported both manufactured products and basic foodstuffs, in particular, food grains. The major Greek export commodities were currant grapes and olive products, making the agricultural sector the backbone of the economy. Through the nineteenth century, Greece remained a nation of

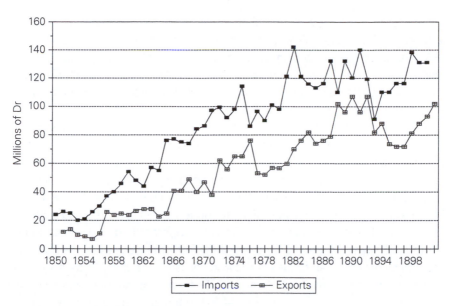

CHART 1 *Greek balance of trade, 1850–1900.*

agriculturalists. Roughly 75 per cent of the adult male population was involved in agriculture, fishing or forestry in 1870; the figure fell slowly but steadily through to the end of the century to the figure of 62 per cent in 1907. There were two countervailing forces at work in the Greek agricultural sector, and both inhibited economic development.

Since the War of Independence there had been a constant clamour among the peasantry for land redistribution. At issue was the disposition of the formerly Ottoman-held land and monastic properties. Otto had attempted a variety of land reform schemes over the years. Between 1835 and 1857, under the land dotation programme of 1835, individual household heads had purchased nearly 20,000 hectares. Two additional laws in 1871 attempted to rectify the deficiencies of the previous programmes and accelerated the distribution of national lands. All of the land allotment schemes had drawbacks, and land redistribution remained a major issue into the twentieth century.

One result of the land allotment schemes was the establishment of a large number of small family farmers whose productive aims were focused on self-sufficiency rather than marketability. As studies of the Greek peasantry have shown and as I shall discuss in more detail in Chapter 6, subsistence security rather than profits made them risk averse. Consequently, one very large sector of the rural economy participated only marginally in the market as either buyers or sellers, and so offered little prospect of economic growth. The other result of the land dotation schemes was the formation of large agricultural estates or plantations. These were formed through manipulation of the land allotment laws and through foreclosures and expropriation of peasant families. In the western Peloponnesos, the Ionian Islands and Thessaly (after 1882), large estates producing export commodities, especially currants, were worked by tenants and/or hired labour. This was the only sector that offered any hope of sustained growth, but as we shall see, reliance on monocropped export items was to prove a very precarious base.

Trikoupis focused his economic reforms on facilitating the growth of the export sector. He hoped to reduce overhead costs by expanding the transportation network. New roads, railroads and other public works were to allow for a more rapid movement of goods from the countryside to the cities and the ports. In addition, the cultivable area of Greece was to be expanded through the drainage of waterlogged areas like the Kopais Basin. The Corinth Canal, begun under the Roman Emperor Nero, was at last to be completed, greatly speeding up travel time from the Aegean to the Adriatic. The transition from sail to steam allowed for larger cargoes to be delivered at cheaper prices. Between 1875 and 1895, steamship tonnage under Greek ownership rose from 8,241 tons to 144,975. Industrialization also developed under the paternal eye of the Trikoupis government. Between 1875 and 1900, the average number of workers per manufacturing establishment rose from 45 to 71, and steam horsepower increased by over 250 per cent. Much of this growth centred in the textile trade. Trikoupis's reforms facilitated economic development, but at a cost.

Echoing back to Korais, Trikoupis believed in advancement through education and under his tutelage, public education was greatly expanded: the number of university students between 1860 and 1900 rose from 1,100 to 3,300; the number of boys attending high school increased from 6,000 to 24,000; the number of boys enrolled in primary schools increased from 44,000 to 178,000 and that of girls, from a mere 8,000 to over 82,000. In addition to direct legislation, Trikoupis helped to foster a new cultural climate. During the latter part of the nineteenth century, a bourgeois culture developed, self-consciously drawing on Western trends in dress, architecture, art and manners. Part of becoming Western was to look the part. It was, indeed, a time of change.

The single greatest challenge facing Trikoupis and his administrations was how to finance their programmes of reform. Like his predecessors, he had to chart a treacherous course between the need to raise revenues and the danger of strangling economic growth in the process. Foreign debt was the engine that drove his reform programme. Between 1879 and 1890, six major foreign loans were arranged totalling 630,000,000 drachmas; by 1887, 40 per cent of the total government expenditure went towards servicing the national debt. Internally, sources of revenue that did not have a direct deleterious impact on one sector of society or another were simply not available. In the end, Trikoupis had to tax the Greek populace heavily in order to pay the bills. He levied taxes on wine, tobacco, sheep, goats, oxen and donkeys; the tithe on all agricultural produce was increased, as was the tax on land holdings. He established state monopolies on salt and matches, and the prices of both soared. High import tariffs raised revenues and prices but failed to abate the people's appetite for foreign goods. Consequently, export duties had to be raised on precisely those commodities that formed the economy's lifeblood. The impact of Trikoupis's fiscal policies on the average Greek citizen was profoundly negative. And still the debt grew. Chart 2 presents a diachronic view of the government revenue surpluses and deficits between 1850 and 1900. The sustained deficits evident through the 1880s caused the collapse of the 1890s.

The Greek economy had been buoyed for some time by the rapid expansion of the international market in currants following the phylloxera epidemic that had destroyed many of the vineyards of France, Spain and Italy. Through the 1870s and especially during the 1880s, Greek exports of currants soared as prices on the international market rose (Chart 3). Cultivation expanded as demand grew. Profits from agricultural exports were converted into investment capital. Government revenues derived from export duties were a critical component in financing the reform programme. Many of the foreign loans that Trikoupis contracted were guaranteed by the revenues from currant exports. It is not going too far to say that the financing of his entire programme was underwritten by a raisin. So long as these conditions of high prices and great demand for Greek grapes lasted, Greece's creditworthiness remained

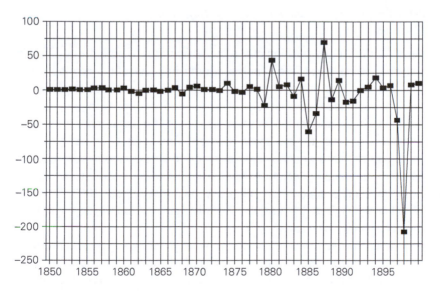

CHART 2 *Greek national primary budget surplus or deficit, 1850–1900.*

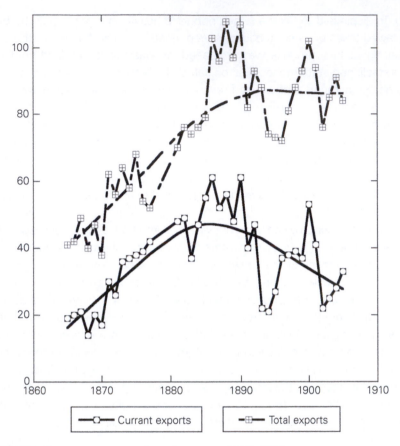

CHART 3 *Currant exports and total exports, 1865–1905.*

high, and the precarious position of the public fisc could be maintained, but in 1893, the bottom fell out of the Greek economy. Because of the confluence of numerous factors, currant prices plummeted and, as a consequence, so did government revenues (see Chart 3). A massive budget deficit loomed, but the final nail in the budgetary coffin was that a number of major bond issues were becoming due at precisely the same moment. And Greece did not have the money to pay back the bondholders, let alone to service the annual interest on the other outstanding loans. In what was one of his shortest and surely his most memorable speech to Parliament, on 10 December 1893, Trikoupis informed his colleagues, 'Regretfully, we are bankrupt' [Δυστυχώς επωχεύσαμ εν]. The boom times were over.

The worst, however, was yet to come. After a royally appointed caretaker government failed to make much headway in dealing with the crisis, Trikoupis once more became premier, and his last term in office ran from November 1893 until January 1895. The challenges his government faced were formidable and the opposition to his administration was intractable. Greece's economic situation continued to deteriorate. Globally, the Great Depression worsened as markets continued to contract and as more countries found themselves on the verge of bankruptcy. Thus, the prices for dried fruits on world markets, especially for currants, continued to plummet. Correspondingly, Greek government revenues from the tariffs on exports fell precipitously. Trikoupis endeavoured to make up the difference by borrowing from international financial markets, but his entreaties fell on deaf ears, especially after he proposed imposing a 70 per cent reduction on the existing foreign debt. Even Ottoman Greek entrepreneurs and financiers, who had played so important a role during the 1880s, refused to lend to Greece in the face of such economic uncertainty. He had, then, to address the financial situation internally. This meant dramatic spending cuts and a firm policy of austerity. All sectors of government felt the axe, but none more so than the military. On the revenue side, the government raised almost all of the existing taxes, thus rendering even more onerous the burden on Greek taxpayers, who had already seen their taxes double over the previous decade. Then he introduced other fiscal exactions, and none that was more despised than the new property tax. It is fair to say that Trikoupis's financial policies managed to alienate almost every sector of Greek society. Not surprisingly, then, his Modernist Party was swept out of office in the April 1895 election, with Trikoupis himself even losing his seat. After his humiliating defeat, he moved to Paris where he died in the spring of 1896.

With his old rival driven off the political stage, Theodoros Deliyiannis had the spotlight all to himself. The year 1896 saw Greece get some respite from its troubles and that was due to the 1896 Summer Olympic Games. While Athens was basking in its 'golden' Olympic moment, ominous developments were occurring in the Ottoman Empire, specifically in Macedonia and Crete, which would soon overshadow it. The National Question once more came to dominate public discourse and drive government policy, and the government found itself hostage to the very nationalist forces that it helped foster. Even the populist, Deliyiannis still believed that he could play the nationalist card as a means to stay in power and still remain in control of the situation. But times had changed. In Greece, a radical nationalist group called the National Society, riding a wave of Romantic Nationalism (see pp. 89–90), became even more influential. Like many a politician before and after him, when faced with a restive populace and hard economic times, Deliyiannis played the nationalist card, as much out of necessity as anything else. Tensions were rising in both Crete and Macedonia and huge street rallies were held to demonstrate the public's support for the liberation movements there. I discuss the background to the Cretan revolution of 1896 in detail in the next chapter. What needs to be appreciated here is that the elevation in nationalist sentiments gave

Deliyiannis an opportunity to deflect criticism of his administration for its economic policies. When fighting broke out in Crete, the National Society sent arms, men and supplies. Sultan Abdul Hamid II demanded that Greece cease and desist its activities in both areas. Unadvisedly, with dreams of territorial gains both to the north and the south, Greece mobilized for war. The ill-fated war began on 17 April 1897 and lasted for only thirty days. (See pp. 108–10 for a description of the war.) The Greek army under the leadership of Crown-Prince Konstantinos was routed as the Ottoman forces took Thessaly and stood poised to march unopposed on Athens. Timely and forceful intervention by England and France prevented a total collapse, and even managed to salvage Greece from complete disaster. In the end, Greece lost little territory but had to pay a large war indemnity, which only compounded the kingdom's already terrible financial situation. This was not, however, just a defeat. This was a humiliation.

One year later, insult was added to injury. In April 1898, the International Financial Control Commission (IFCC) was established in Athens to deal with Greece's bankruptcy. The commission consisted of six members, representatives of the great powers, and it was given the power to collect and then expend monies to retire the loans. The IFCC retained a Greek company to collect and to convey to it these revenues: the customs duties of the ports of Piraeus, Volos, Corfu, Lavrion and Patras; taxes from state monopolies over salt, matches, playing cards, cigarette paper, kerosene and emery from Naxos; and various 'sin taxes', especially on tobacco products. The IFCC laid out the repayment schedule, and any revenues collected that exceeded the stipulated amount were transferred to the National Bank of Greece to be used internally. But, to be sure, the foreign bondholders came first. Lastly, the commission had considerable input on Greek taxation and fiscal policies. In the long term, IFCC policies stabilized the drachma on the foreign exchange markets and allowed Greece to re-enter the international bond markets, and by so doing helped to foster economic growth during the first premiership of Eleftherios Venizelos (see below). In the short term, however, the commission's austerity regime further depressed agricultural exports, triggered a rise in the prices of imports, including foodstuffs, and thus drove the economy further into depression, all of which inflicted great pain on the Greek people.

With the debacle of the 1897 war and the take-over of the Greek economy in 1898, the age of reform had come to an end. In spite of all the beneficial changes enacted during the previous twenty-five years, changes that left an indelible mark on the development of Greece, at the turn of the century Greece stood on the verge of collapse.

4

Constructing the modern nation: Cultures, identities and diversity

The previous chapter focused on the most important development of the nineteenth century and that was modern state formation. But going hand in hand with that was a second and equally important development, and that was nation-building. These were the two complementary processes that were absolutely essential to the creation of nation-states as we know them. State formation was all about creating the institutional structures that regulated the state and governed society. But one of the unique characteristics of the nation-state was the creation of the Nation as well. National identity and national culture were not something people were born with or states were endowed with. Both had to be invented. In the case of Greece, small as it was, at the moment of independence it was home to a very diverse population. About the only aspect of culture in which there was homogeneity was religion; the vast majority of the population was Christian, and that was because during the war the Jewish population was driven out and the Muslims were killed, or they fled or converted to Orthodoxy. Turning the diverse Rum population into Greek nationals, then, was a contested process, and one that we explore in this chapter.

Nationalism and identity

One of the most 'remarkable achievements of modern Greece is to have forged in a relatively short period of time an extremely cohesive nation-state of which Greek national identity, despite all political cleavages, is the cornerstone. And it has forged this out of what was geographically, historically, culturally, linguistically and up to a point even religiously, a diverse population whose allegiances and loyalties up until the beginning for the nineteenth century were small-scale and localized.'[1] As the quote from one of Greece's leading intellectuals, reproduced in Text-box 9, makes absolutely clear, nation-building was a totalizing process that involved nearly every aspect of popular culture and material culture. National identity was reflected in dress, speech, behaviour and just about everything else, including what one ate and drank.

Before the war of liberation, there really was no Greek nation, let alone people possessing a fully formed national consciousness. There was an awareness, either acute or vague depending on a person's station in life, of being a member of the Millet-i Rum, of being a Christian (Orthodox), and of speaking the Romaic language, that is, Greek. But such awareness did not constitute a consciousness of being nationally Greek. Instead, peoples' primary identity was rooted in their local village community and in the nexus of real and fictive kinship networks that bound them to others. In the remainder of this chapter we explore how a Greek national identity was forged both within the Kingdom of Greece and among the Greek communities of the Ottoman Empire.

Religion played an important but complex role in the construction of Greek national identity. From the time of the revolution, there were marked tensions between the church, the leadership of the national liberation movement and the people. The ideological foundation that undergirded the movement was rooted in Western European Enlightenment thought, a key element of which was secularism. For thinkers such as Voltaire, for example, religion was the bastion of the *ancien régime* and was synonymous with ignorance and oppression. Greek intellectuals like Adamantios Korais thus argued for the

Text-box 9 Greek national dress (1843)

In the interests of economy and national pride and in order to avoid foreign luxury and corruption, which is what has brought Greek affairs to their current situation, it would be expedient … to create a national dress: cheap, comely, elegant, made of local materials and by local craftsmen … which would identify our nationality, link everyone in national unity and promote the ongoing formation of the nation. It is certain that as a distinctive nation, part of Asia and Europe and honoured for its distinguished ancestry, *the Greeks must have a national dress, education and diet* (italics mine).

A. Politis; reproduced in B. Murgescu (ed.) (2009), *Nations and States in Southeast Europe. Workbook 2,* Thessaloniki: CDRSEE, document III-14.

creation of a secular Greek state and for a new Greek society that drew its inspiration from the glories of pagan antiquity.

Yet, the masses who rose to the banner of rebellion did so first in the name of religion and only secondarily from a sense of local grievance and discrimination. This was to be, after all, in theory at least, an uprising of the Millet-i Rum. What transpired then was a revolt based on religious divisions led primarily by liberals with the intent of creating a secular state. Another strand of tension developed when the Ecumenical Patriarch of the Orthodox Church and *Ethnarch* of the Christian population denounced the uprising and excommunicated its leaders. The establishment of a specifically Greek National Orthodox Church in the kingdom only created further difficulties that took decades to sort out (see below). This schism raised a fundamental and exceptionally important question: Which Orthodox church, the one based in Athens or the one in Istanbul, was the church of the Greek Nation? This dispute we will refer to as the Church Issue.

A third level of complexity regarding Greek identity appeared before the war and persisted long after its end, and this one revolved around the legacy of ancient Greece. During the long period of Ottoman domination, Renaissance Europe had appropriated the Classical age as its own legacy, seeing in fifth-century Athens the primordial roots of its own civilization. It was the allure of the Classics that drew many Philhellenes to support the cause of the Greeks. Out of this situation, the roots of two opposed Greek identities thus emerged, one as 'Hellenic' that emphasized Western values that derived from antiquity and that de-emphasized the importance of Orthodoxy, and the other as 'Romioi', Roman, that emphasized Orthodoxy, the oriental characteristics of Greek culture and traced its roots to the Orthodox Byzantine Empire.

With the establishment of the Kingdom of Greece and the enthronement of a foreign, Catholic ruler, these tensions over identity and national consciousness had to be resolved, if the new state and the 'nation' that constituted it were to endure. In other words, peasants who conceived of themselves as Christians (*Christianoi eimaste*) and speakers of Greek had to be reformed to think of themselves as members of the Hellenic nation who were both Christians and Greek-speaking. As part of this process there had to be a transformation from a religion-based identity to one grounded in a secular national identity. The process was neither easy nor quick, but over the course of the nineteenth century, it was achieved.

There were two especially important means by which it was accomplished. One focused on the appropriation of Orthodoxy by the Greek state in such a way that the ecumenical aspect of it was downplayed, and by so doing it wedded religious identity with a Greek nationalism centred on Athens. It was from this construct that the Megali Idea emerged. But there was a critically important dilemma here: from 1833 until 1850, there were two Orthodox churches, one centred in Constantinople and the other in Athens. Before religion could become one of the pillars of a Greek *national* identity, the Church Issue had to be resolved. The second dynamic revolved around the purposeful construction of a public culture that emphasized the Hellenic as opposed to the Romeic dimension of Greek identity. Through a process of acculturation of this ideal, Greeks began to internalize deeply a Hellenic national identity that coexisted with, but took precedence over, the Romeic one. Let us begin with the Church Issue.

On 4 August 1833, a Royal Decree drafted by von Maurer, Spyridon Trikoupis, a prominent politician, and Theoklitos Farmakides, a leading Orthodox cleric, established an autocephalous Orthodox Church of the Kingdom of Greece with Otto as its titular head. This was to be an explicitly 'national' church, that is, a church of the Greek nation. It would be governed by a Synod headed by the Archbishop of Athens, but as an institution, the church was a branch of the Greek state. This step was in keeping with actions taken by each of the revolutionary governments, beginning with the very first, which stated in its constitution that the Orthodox Church was inseparable from the Greek state.

The establishment of the autocephalous (independent) church had manifold consequences. First, it set a precedent for linking nationalism and religion institutionally that many of the secessionist movements in the Ottoman Balkans would follow. Second, it raised the vexing question regarding what the relationship between the new Greek national church and the Ecumenical Patriarchate in Constantinople would be. After all, the Patriarchate had vehemently opposed the Greek uprising and, moreover, it remained a multinational religious organization under the control of the Ottoman state. The question, then, was this: What would be the relationship between the two Orthodox churches? Text-box 10 reproduces some of the main arguments put forward by supporters of each side on the issue.

There were powerful voices in the kingdom which, from the moment of independence, pressed for unity with the Great Church. After 1834, this faction was led by the powerful cleric Konstantinos Oikonomos. He had earned a reputation as being a powerful preacher and news of his charismatic following reached Constantinople. In 1808, Patriarch Gregory V invited him to the capital. He was in Constantinople when the rebellion erupted. He moved to the Kingdom of Greece in 1834. When he arrived in Greece in 1834, there was widespread suspicion that he was acting as an agent of the Russians. He led the conservative faction that wanted to embed the new Kingdom in the greater Orthodox community.

In addition to this split, there was another faction, led by Theophilos Kairis, which argued that the new state should have its own religion. Kairis was born on 19 October 1784 to one of the most prominent families on the island of Andros. At age eight, he was sent to the Virgin Mary of the Orphans

Text-box 10 The Church Issue (1833)

In favour of an autonomous Greek national church

In June 1833, the Church of the Kingdom of Greece declared its Autonomy and Independence... . The Greek nation, having declared its political independence before God and men from the beginning of its glorious Revolution ... also declared its church as Autonomous and Independent, for the aim of the sacred struggle was ecclesiastical as well as political (in order to gain independence). ... No permission or approval was required [because] political autonomy goes hand in hand with ecclesiastical autonomy, as per the beliefs of the Eastern Orthodox Church ... without the need for any particular act or agreement, for territory and church are one and the same thing.

Theoklitos Farmakides (1835)

In favour of remaining tied to the Orthodox Patriarchate of Constantinople

What sufferings have the brothers left outside undergone for the sake of a free Greece? And yet you demand that they be called neither Greeks nor brothers, but inhabitants of Turkey and subjects of what you call the Enslaved Church! Thus, you sever (as far as you can) Greece from Greece and the Greeks from each other, fragmenting the nation and inducing religious discord, which results in internal maladies and dire wars among brothers. Thus, finally, you shrink the state of Greeks within too narrow limits, and hinder the progress of the God-succoured kingdom of Greece, cancelling (again, as far as you can) the hopes and the desires of an entire nation, and so many centuries and so many philhellenic Christian nations! O men, how can you behave like that?

Konstantinos Oikonomos (1839)

B. Murgescu (ed.) (2009), *Nations and States in Southeast Europe. Workbook 2*, Thessaloniki: CDRSEE, documents II-18 A and B.

School, also known as the Oikonomou's School, located at Kydonies/Aivali in Asia Minor. He continued his studies, working with some of the leading Orthodox intellectuals of the time. He particularly excelled in the sciences. When he completed his studies, he relocated to Paris where he became a close confidant of Adamantios Korais. Kairis, unlike Korais, viewed the French Revolution positively and during his time in France, he developed a deep love of liberalism. In sum, he was a true child of the Enlightenment. As a liberal dedicated to the idea of Republicanism, he was profoundly disappointed by the presidency of Kapodistrias. Not surprisingly, he was an ardent foe of Bavarian absolutism, and on one occasion even refused to accept a medal from the King.

During the 1830s, he was active as a teacher and as a religious agitator. He believed that the new country needed a new religion. He developed a doctrine of belief that he labelled 'theosebism.' Based upon Deism, this new faith espoused a belief in God as the creator of the universe but rejected the idea that God interfered in human affairs, much less that the Bible was the received word of God or that Jesus Christ was his son. Theosebism promoted the idea that the Bible was just one of many texts that could guide human morality. Kairis opposed all organized religions and saw the Orthodox Church as an oppressive force. Not surprisingly, he ran afoul of the church hierarchy, and the Holy Synod placed him on trial on 21 December 1852. He was found guilty and sentenced to a prison term, though he served less than a year of it before he died.

In addition to these disputes among Orthodox clerics, there were other dimensions to the Church Issue as well that caused dissent. One had to do with the Catholics. There was a sizable Catholic population in the new kingdom and this raised the issue of their spiritual needs and their relationship to the Papacy. Implicated in this matter, of course, was the fact the Royal Family was Catholic and had no intention of converting to Orthodoxy. Finally, the activities of Protestant missionaries aroused opposition because of the widespread suspicion that they were proselytizing the youth through their supposedly educational endeavours. On numerous occasions, the religious question led to eruptions of violent unrest; the most important of these was the Papoulakos affair.

Christoforos Panayiotopoulos, also known as Papoulakos, was a butcher and a pig merchant from central Greece. While suffering from a typhus-induced hallucination, he received a vision from God, in which he was told that he was to lead a mass movement to restore traditional Orthodoxy. When he recovered, he became a messianic preacher, travelling around the Greek countryside standing up to the King, whom he accused of being an atheist and of sharing with the French and the British the goal of destroying Orthodoxy. He also assailed the institutions of the new state, like the University of Athens, which he referred to as 'the devil's tool,' and Jews, whom he accused of being 'crypto-Muslims' and defilers of Christ. His zealous message resonated with religiously conservative peasants and, at the height of his movement, he had over 6,000 followers. In addition, he drew the attention of the Philorthodox Society, which supported his opposition to Otto's regime. On 26 May 1852, he actually mobilized his followers into a rebel army and marched on the city of Kalamata, where he was defeated by the Greek army. He was arrested, convicted and sentenced to prison, but because of his ongoing popularity, the government opted to release him rather than making him into a martyr. Episodes like this show that the persistent and heated contestation over the religious question bedevilled the Bavarian monarchy throughout its duration.

In sum, the first few decades after independence saw a playing out of forces aimed at creating some sort of collective national identity, but it remained an impaired and incomplete process. It was really only in the second half of the century that a more fully formed national identity emerged. By the mid-1850s, the Church Issue had gone a long way towards resolution. The two churches in Athens and Constantinople had been reconciled, and the last religiously inspired revolt suppressed. The centrality of Orthodoxy to the Greek national identity was assured and, indeed, remained so to such an extent that even in the year 2000, a threat to that connection was enough to spark public unrest (see p. 309). From mid-century onwards, a new engine was driving the process of nation-building and that was Romantic Nationalism.

The second half of the nineteenth century witnessed a transformation in the idea of nationalism. It began to take on a new and more virulent form, sometimes referred to by historians as hyper-nationalism; it postulated that the nation was the greatest social good and that all aspects of life, both public and private, were sublimated to the greater national good. A concomitant development was the racialization of nationality, whereby it was believed that different nations were, in fact, also different races. By essentializing nationality as biological, hyper-nationalism reified group boundaries and rendered cultural assimilation impossible. The fluidity of identities that was prevalent earlier no longer pertained. There was a cultural dimension to this process as well, one that romanticized the nation. For this reason, some scholars speak of Romantic Nationalism, the term that I prefer to use. Romantic Nationalism emerged from the confluence of nationalism, constitutionalism and the idealization of popular society, especially the peasantry, as the glorified repository of national culture. National belonging was based upon blood descent, as well as shared religion, culture, language and history. The political expression of Romantic Nationalism was made manifest in constitutions such as the 1864 Greek Constitution that enshrined the principle of popular sovereignty. The people, that is, the nation, were now the font of legitimate authority, and so, while it was the laws as enshrined in the Constitution that made the state, it was the people who organically constituted it. The nation was now the paramount political body.

Greek Romantic Nationalism was based upon three essentialized unities: The first of these we can call the Greek Unity. This was the cultural dimension of the Greek nation. It was culture as preserved in popular society, called in Greek the λάος, that connected the Greeks of today with their glorious ancient ancestors. The second element we can call the Christian or the

Orthodox Unity. The shared bond of religion gave the nation a unique spiritual core that was the expression of divine providence. The third element was the Roman Unity. This referred to the political inheritance of the medieval Byzantine Empire that framed Greece's imagined national space. Finally, Romantic Nationalism emphasized that the nation-state was the highest form of social organization, that it was divinely inspired, quintessentially modern and a manifestation of a distinct set of unities that made each nation unique. Lastly, it postulated that the greater national good superseded everything else, including the truth.

> The [historian's] duty is both scientific and national. It is only the historian's pen that can compete with weapons. Therefore, those nations which have not yet accomplished their high mission and achieved national unification should tie their potential national grandeur to two anchors: military organization and the development of historical studies; these are both necessary for claiming national rights. ... Indeed, there is no greater companionship than the one between the historian's desk and the military camp. On both, one and the same flag waves, the country's.[2]

History and indeed all of the social sciences were sublimated to one single and unitary goal and that was not the furtherance of scientific truth, but instead of the National Truth. Romantic Nationalism was a powerful force that shaped world history, culminating with the First World War.

Along with changes in the realms of ideas and ideologies, new public practices were adopted that helped to disseminate, and to inculcate Greeks with, new, proper national sensibilities. A series of events in 1871 and 1872 symbolize, I believe, the solidification of a Hellenic national identity and definitively situated Athens as the centre of Hellenism. From the moment that Athens was selected to be the capital of the new kingdom, there had been a palpable sense that it needed to become *the* centre of Hellenism. Over time, the need for it to play that role became even more urgent. In 1861, for example, the newspaper *Athena* noted: 'The capital of Greece, Athens, is the focal point and centre of light and culture for two ... concentric nations, the nation of liberated Greece, and the larger nation of greater Hellenism, which is still under foreign rule.'[3] The jubilee year in the life of the Greek Kingdom was 1871. The festivities planned for the celebration of the fiftieth anniversary of the start of the Revolution were to commemorate the war but also to recognize the progress that Hellenism had made over the previous decades. A central element of the celebration was to be the transportation and the interment in Athens of the body of Patriarch Gregory V. He was, as previously noted, the Patriarch at the start of the Revolution who was killed during the anti-Greek pogrom in Istanbul. How ironic it was that the Patriarch who had excommunicated anyone who joined the rebellion was now being recognized as one of its heroes and one of the greatest national martyrs. And yet in 1870, the decision was made to feature the re-interment of the cleric's body in Athens as a central element in the jubilee. The entire ceremony was redolent with symbolism. The body was transported to Greece in a Greek warship named *Byzantion*, the casket was greeted at Piraeus by the church hierarchy who conveyed it to Athens where it was received by King George and Queen Olga. Huge crowds attended at every stage. Just as in antiquity, where the re-interment of the bones of the Athenian hero Theseus symbolized the emergence of democratic Athens, so did the transportation of the bones of the Patriarch represent the emergence of Athens as the centre of modern Hellenism.

But there was an additional element to the jubilee ceremony: the wedding of Orthodoxy to the Revolution. The following year, at another public ceremony, a statue of Gregory V was unveiled at the University of Athens. It joined one of Rigas and, in 1875, one of Korais as well. Here was the 'holy' trinity of the Hellenic Revolution and revival: one who had espoused an ecumenical, secular new Greece, another who believed in a secular Greece whose taproot was the Classical age, and a third who opposed the Greek Revolution. Yet, in the invented tradition of nationalism, they became united as symbols of Hellenic liberation. Orthodoxy as religious identity had now been transformed definitively into a secular Greek national identity.

There were, however, other dimensions to the process of turning peasants into Greeks. A very important one was language. The so-called 'language question' in Greece has a long and contentious history, and the issue was resolved only as recently as 1976. In this section, I provide just a brief survey of it, highlighting how it relates to the formation of Greek national identity. For most of its history, there has been a situation of *diglossia* in Greece. Two different versions of the same language, one spoken and the other written, existed side by side. At the time of independence, the language spoken by Greeks was called *dimotiki* or demotic Greek. While related to ancient Greek more closely than, say, modern Italian is to Latin, it was still very different from the ancient tongue, and from the language of the church.

Not surprisingly, given that it was a living language, over the centuries Turkish, Albanian and Slavic words became incorporated into the popular spoken vernacular. Because the spoken tongue highlighted the cultural distance between modern Greeks and antiquity, particularly in the eyes of Western Europeans, intellectuals like Adamantios Korais and his followers pushed for the introduction of a new, pure form of the language that would emphasize the Hellenic heritage of a liberated Greece. Some argued for the wholesale re-introduction of ancient Attic Greek as the official language of the new state.

The compromise, a language called *Katherevousa*, was a hybrid of the ancient *koine* (the language of the New Testament and the liturgy) and demotic Greek. Katherevousa was to be the language of the new Greek state and resurrected Greek nation. It did, in fact, become the written language of public discourse, in government, in the newspapers and in education. But there remained an inherent tension between it and demotic Greek. Each of them suggested a slightly different version of Greek identity, one – katharevousa – emphasized the Hellenic, the other – demotic – the Romaic. The two competing visions were not reconciled and at times led to violent clashes. Nonetheless, language played a crucial role in the invention of Greek national identity.

Related to both language and religion in this process was history. After all, all national or ethnic identities have at some point to evoke the past to give pedigree and legitimation to a group's claims to common roots. As in the other areas we have discussed so far, in the case of Greece there were two competing visions of the past – the Hellenic with its lineage ground in the Classical age, and the Romaic with the Byzantine Empire as its wellspring. Greek history became a particularly contested terrain during the 1830s. In addition to all of the aspects we have analysed so far, in 1830, a new one was introduced. In that year, the German philologist Jacob Fallmerayer published a study in which he claimed that the Greeks of his day were not racially descended from the ancient Greeks, but were, instead, Slavs. Not only did this deny to the Greeks any claim on antiquity as their heritage, but it also divorced the Byzantine Empire from it. The legacy of Classical antiquity thus belonged to the West, of which the modern Greeks were *ipso facto* not a part.

For the next few decades, Greeks responded to this challenge in a number of ways. The immediate response among historians and linguists was to mobilize data to support the idea of a connection to antiquity. Folklore studies developed in Greece as urban intellectuals scoured the countryside looking for survivals of ancient customs, practices, stories and beliefs that resembled ones described in ancient texts. Archaeology in Greece, both by Greeks and by foreigners, was called on to produce the 'symbolic capital' that demonstrated the linkage between the Greeks of 'today' and those of the distant past.

These efforts did not wholly or even partially bridge the chronological gap of the Middle Ages. The historian Konstantinos Paparrigopoulos accomplished that task. Starting in 1860, he published a five-volume *History of the Hellenic Nation from the Ancient Times Until the Modern*, in which he reconciled the dual identities of the nation and gave them a historical grounding. There was, he argued, a direct and unbroken history of the Greek nation, or *ethnos*, divided into three phases – Classical, Byzantine and Modern. Each phase built upon the others. Greeks were neither Eastern nor Western, but both. They could legitimately lay claim to the pagan/secular and liberal legacy of ancient

Greece as well as the ecumenical, Orthodox Christian one of Byzantium. In so doing, Paparrigopoulos created a unity out of the Greek past and, of equal importance, a unity of all the Greek people.

Finally, through the conscious modification of popular culture, the state and the intelligentsia facilitated the internalization by the masses of this invented Greek identity. This new vision of Hellenism was literally inscribed on to the landscape. In rebuilding the towns that had been destroyed during the Revolution, city plans were designed specifically to make the new urban areas look Western. Built on a grid system and adorned with public buildings and houses in the neoclassical style, the new towns were to give concrete form to the new Hellenic national identity by obliterating all traces of the Ottoman past and reviving the memories of the Classical past. With a similar purpose in mind, the names of hundreds of rural villages were changed from 'Slavic' or 'non-Hellenic' names to names that were 'totally' Greek.

From the 1870s onwards, there was an explosion of clubs and associations. During the height of 'syllogomania' (association-mania) as it was called at the time, numerous voluntary associations (sports clubs, reading societies, drama clubs, athletic associations, working men's clubs, etc.) developed. Some were intended explicitly to propagate the national mission; in others, furtherance of the national mission was a by-product. All of them, however, furthered the creation of a unified national identity. Print media and literature were called on to propagate the vision of the new national identity. Popular posters combined visual images that drew on various elements – historical, pagan mythical and religious – that thus reinforced the central elements of the national identity. A superb and representative example of how visual art helped shape national consciousness is presented in Figure 7. The visual arts, theatre, literature and music were implicated in one way or another in helping to craft the national identity.

Lastly, and perhaps most importantly, public education became a major vehicle for transmitting this as well (see Text-box 11). The history texts used in elementary schools told a simplified version of Paparrigopoulos's story of national continuity. In the secondary schools, students spent more time studying ancient Greek than any other subject. Not only was nationalism embedded in the school curricula, but as Kallia Kalliataki Merticopoulou has recently shown, whether or not parents sent their children to school was affected by their perception of the importance of education to the national cause. Religious instruction was also part of the school curricula.

Thus, through architecture, education, art and literature, in public festivals and celebrations, Greeks came to internalize the new national Hellenic identity that incorporated both the Hellenic and the Romaic, the heritage of both the Classical world and the Orthodox Christian one. So successful was the process that all sense of it being an 'invention' was lost. Instead, an identity grounded

FIGURE 7 *The Sortie of Missolonghi (1853). As part of nation-building and romantic nationalism in the second half of the nineteenth century, artists like Theodoros Vrysakis painted highly stylized and romanticized images of episodes from the War of Independence. Illustrations like this one sought to glorify the Greeks while demonizing the 'Turks'. They also created the imaginary visual memory of the war that pertains in popular culture to this day. In this scene, the besieged Greeks of Missolonghi are attempting to break through the Ottoman blockade, and, in a moment of great sacrifice, most would die in the endeavour. Note the prominent presence of women in the fighting, the scenes of carnage involving women and children, and the array of symbols suggesting that while this battle might be lost, the war would be won.*

Theodoros Vrysakis (1853). National Gallery and Alexandros Soutzos Museum, with permission.

in 'history' became timeless and primordial. As a popular expression has it, 'we have always been Greeks'.

There was one additional development that contributed to Greek nation-building and it deals not with internalized feelings and sensibilities, like the developments we have traced so far did. But, instead, this last one focuses

Text-box 11 A public school (1845)

Livadeia, Thebes, July 1845.

I first visited the Demotic school, attended by 140 boys. The school-room was large and airy, arranged on the Lancastrian plan, and the instruction was given in reading, writing, arithmetic, geography and religion. The first class was reading passages from the Scriptures when I arrived, and a little boy of eight years old, in fustanella and goatskin, gave the passage from the gospel … this little boy read with more truth and discernment than all the literati I had heard read orations at Athens … the Lancastrian system is still in use, and all the regimentation of it [was] in full vigour. The classes are divided by boards, placed with the numbers at the end of each division, comprising a certain set of benches, the walls hung around with tables of reading and arithmetic on the most approved plans, and made use of by the pupils. … In all these outward appliances, and the healthy, clean, and fresh character of the school-room itself, there is no perceptible difference between this and the best country schools in England or Ireland.

Sir Thomas Wyse (1871), *Impressions of Greece*, London: Hurst and Blackett, 99–100.

on how Greeks responded to external perceptions of them, and thus how their culture appeared to the outside world: this was banditry. One of the images that Westerners had of Greeks portrayed them as Europe's aborigines or as the Irish of the Mediterranean.[4] A critically important element in the construction of this stereotype, and for the consequent demotion of Greeks on the league table of civilizations, was lawlessness and banditry. Brigandage became the measuring stick of modernity and Greece was falling further behind as banditry became even more widespread and more violent during the 1850s and 1860s. There were numerous instances of wealthy Greeks being kidnapped by bandit gangs and held for ransom, or of villages being attacked and looted. Text-box 12 contains an eyewitness account of just such a bandit raid. So prevalent did the practice become that there even developed an unwritten set of rules that both kidnappers and victims and their families understood and adhered to.

Sotiris Sotiropoulos, a wealthy politician and future prime minister of the country, left a detailed and scathing account of the thirty-five days that he spent as the 'guest' of a bandit gang. But it was not only the rich who fell prey to brigands. The latter terrorized villages, and there are numerous accounts of women, for example, being tortured to be forced to give up the location of their jewellery and their dowry cash. Banditry flourished both because the

Text-box 12 A bandit raid (1855)

This day's events have almost turned my hair grey. We have been for upwards of four hours in the hands of a band of robbers, who surprised this house and village; and what we had to suffer, expecting to see the children tortured or killed, you may imagine. It was fortunate that I had a large sum of money in the house or my poor children would've been orphans. Every moment I was threatened with being scolded or slashed with their yataghans (knife); and one of our peasants was cut severely before our eyes. Another had his head cut open, and the third was tortured with boiling oil. The poor girl who waits on the children [Irene] narrowly escaped [being raped], but the money and rich booty saved us. They spent four hours breaking open every drawer and knocking everything to pieces. I lost about $200 in cash. All our linen that they did not carry off they tore into pieces. They broke up the furniture and smashed the looking glasses and the panes of glass in the windows. Every house in the village has been plundered and all the hard earnings of years are gone, leaving many families wretched.

Can you imagine the scene, with these yelling monsters cursing and destroying everything? Why do we work and toil in this country on which God's curse seems to rest? I had a peaceful and honourable occupation; many hundreds were living happily and prospering under my undertakings, and this is the upshot. Thank God we have escaped with our lives, though poor Irene [his Greek servant maid] may never recover from the shock. What is the government about? Honest men are prohibited from having arms; so my wood cutters are unarmed. I had twenty wood cutters in the forest, and there were many peasants in the fields, and some builders in the village; but numbers could do nothing without arms. The wood cutters came down with their hatchets but were driven back by the fire of the brigands. One had a ball through his capote [traditional cape made out of sheepskin], another had the handle of his axe broken in his hand.

Letter from Edward Noel to George Finlay, 2 April 1855. Edward Noel was a British citizen who spent most of his life in Greece. The village of Achmetaga, where he lived, was attacked by the bandit gang of Nikolaos Koukovinas. He and his men had only recently been released from prison where they had been held on the charge of sheep stealing.

state was unable to suppress it and because it actually needed such men of violence. As we saw earlier, these men of violence could be deployed as border guards and occasionally they were even hired to keep the peace. In the period after the introduction of democracy, men of violence like these were often employed by politicians to coerce votes and to intimidate their opponent. Unable to suppress banditry by force, the state often resorted to granting amnesty to get them to cease their activities. So prevalent had this practice become, that the new constitution of 1864 actually contained an amendment that forbade it.

The issue came to a head in 1871. A bandit gang kidnapped a group of Western tourists, including aristocratic members related to the British royal family. The British government placed great pressure on the Greeks to resolve the matter and to get the hostages released. The negotiations went awry, and the hostages were killed in an episode that became known as the 'Marathon Murders' or the 'Dilessi Murders.' The brutal slaying of British blue-bloods

Text-box 13 Banditry and its suppression (1855)

The difficulty of securing the borders, since they were not established along high and inaccessible mountain ranges, was the main reason that the province ... was scourged by brigandage. The means of pursuit were inadequate as well, for as the Armed Forces comprised irregulars, local volunteers who were related to brigands and themselves occasional outlaws, they were in no hurry to pursue their kin or friends seriously, managing usually to arrive after the brigands had left the place, and preferred to desert rather than submit to discipline.

But when the evil became intolerable, special measures were necessary, and these varied ... . Some used political craft by recruiting the bravest men into the Army and thus undermining the brigand groups, occasionally managing to isolate and to capture or kill the chieftains themselves. Most of the leaders escaped, however, and found refuge among the Ottomans beyond the mountains ...

But the newly assigned Captain didn't use either tactic, devising instead a system that aroused general panic. ... He suspected everyone and was seldom wrong. He blamed the government and the laws, which hindered him from examining the soundness of the members of every class, but especially of those in high social positions. ...

Following his principles and disposition, he proceeded to hunt down brigands systematically. Once he learnt of a brigand, he seized his parents, kinsmen, and friends, who, being handier, were subjected to cross-examinations and torture until they revealed the brigand's location and offered suggestions for tracking him down. Some were whipped, some were hanged by their feet, some had large stones set on their chests. Among other devices, he denied his victim sleep for days, ... and made use of the rack and the red-hot irons.

P. Kalligas (2000 [1855]), *Thanos Vlekas*, Evanston, IL: Northwestern University Press, 16–17.

reinforced the image of Greece in Western eyes as a land of barbarism. It also threatened the country with retribution from the great powers. But it also hit deeply at home. It made manifest the close connection between the government and violence, and even corruption. It also hit upon Greeks' self-image. It tainted the view of the nation. Over the next few years, banditry would be largely eradicated in Greece. This was achieved through a combination of forcible suppression, by deploying military forces to destroy bandit gangs. Text-box 13 recounts how the Greek state endeavoured to suppress banditry. One of the measures it introduced was holding households and kin groups collectively responsible for the actions of its individual members. If a son turned to banditry, for example, then his parents, siblings and even more distant relations could be persecuted and prosecuted for his actions. And eventually the harsh measures taken by the state proved successful. One rationale for the concentrated effort to eradicate banditry related to state formation; one of the hallmarks of the state is its monopoly over legitimate violence. But the reason why the discussion of banditry is being conducted here is that it shows how totalizing a process nation-building was. No aspect of social or cultural life was left untouched in the efforts to create a modern Greek nation.

5

The 'National Question': Irredentism and foreign policy

No account of the development of Greece during the nineteenth century can be complete without an examination of foreign policy and the role of the Megali Idea in shaping it. In spite of all the factionalism and the multitude of regional differences and identities that continued to characterize the new kingdom, one thing that increasingly united the vast majority of its inhabitants was the ideology of irredentism. The War of Independence had been fought on the ideal of liberation of all Greeks in the Ottoman Empire and their inclusion in the Greek nation-state. As we saw, in the end only a fraction of ethnic Greeks dwelling in a small part of the Eastern Mediterranean were constituted as the new state (see Map 3). Even before the prominent politician Ioannis Kolettis gave coherence and vision to the irredentist ideal, moves had been made to continue the struggle to redeem the remaining 'Greek' lands (see Text-box 14). All foreign relations during the nineteenth century and the early twentieth century were in one way or another viewed through the lens of the Megali Idea. Moreover, both the very identity of the nation and the development of the state became bound up in the ideology. Identity, nationalism and irredentism, then, formed an essential core that influenced almost every aspect of the development of Greece during the nineteenth century. The same, however, cannot be said about Greeks outside of the kingdom. There were multiple and competing identity narratives to the Athenocentric one. In the Greek communities of southern Russia, among the Ionian Islanders, and for Ottoman Greeks, what it meant to be 'Greek' and what the key markers of identity were, were rather different. Since they had a different interpretation of what the Greek Nation was, it is not surprising that they held divergent views on what should be the Greek nation-state. In sum, the National Question was answered differently depending on which Greek community was doing the responding. The Megali Idea was the one adopted in Greece.

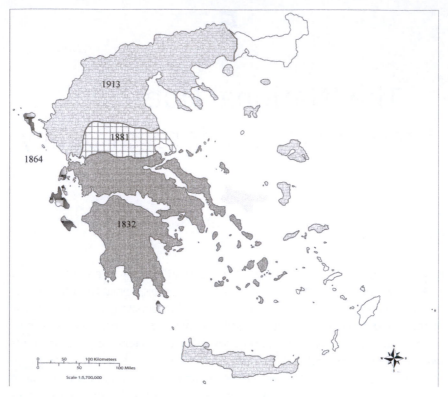

MAP 3 *The expansion of Greece, 1833–1948.*

Text-box 14 The Megali Idea (1844)

The Greek Kingdom is not the whole of Greece, but only a part, the smallest and poorest part. Autochthon [indigenous] then is not only someone who lives within this Kingdom, but also one who lives in Ioannina, in Thessaly, in Serrres, in Adrianople, in Constantinople, in Terbizond, in Crete, in Samos … in general, every inhabitant of land that is Hellenic historically and ethnically … . The struggle did not begin in 1821; it began the day after the fall of Constantinople; [freedom] fighters were not simply those of 1821; fighters were and are always those continuing the struggle against the crescent for 400 years.

Ioannis Kolettis, address to National Assembly, 1844. Quoted in G. Augustinos (1977), *Consciousness and History: Nationalist Critics of Greek Society, 1897–1914*, New York: Columbia University Press, 14.

The Megali Idea and the struggle for territorial expansion

The so-called Arta-Lamia line that formed the northern border of the kingdom was an artificial demarcation that delineated no meaningful boundaries. To be sure, the team of British surveyors given the unenviable task of determining the border did their best, but the result was far from satisfactory. Geographically, the border did not follow along any topographical features that would have created a readily visible division between Greek and Ottoman territory; rather, it cut across some important ones. Nor did it conform to any significant cultural boundaries; instead, it divided villages into two zones, with some families residing on the Ottoman side and others on the Greek side of the border. In other cases, peasants and their land were located on opposite sides of the border, and in others, villages and their water supply were located in different countries. Not surprisingly, the frontier region became a zone of contention that defied easy solutions.

As we saw earlier, the cessation of official hostilities left many warlords and their men in great difficulties. Some found themselves on the Greek side of the border where they confronted a hostile government that was refusing to recompense them for their efforts during the war and that was now making them unemployed. Many returned to their brigand ways. Others who had fought on the Hellenic side but whose homelands remained part of the Ottoman Empire had to submit to their Muslim lords, or face the executioner, or take flight as outlaws. Banditry flourished on both sides of the border, but was especially troublesome on the Greek side. Ottoman officials also turned to a past practice and employed some of the bandit gangs to be the police and the border guards. The Greek government followed suit and frequently hired prominent bandit chiefs and their followers to be the national guards.

In addition to the movements of brigands through the fluid frontier zone, there were the transhumant shepherds, like the Vlachs and the Sarakatsanoi, whose annual movements from mountain pastures to lowland fields constantly compelled them to violate the border – or else to pay hefty duties to the border guards for legal passage. Caravanners and merchants also preferred to smuggle their goods across the frontier, and to ensure their safety they often hired armed guards. The result of these developments was the paramilitarization of the borderland. Given that most Greeks believed that the border artificially separated them from their Hellenic brethren to the north, the area became a flashpoint for further nationalist conflicts in pursuit of the irredentist dream.

As early as the late 1830s, Greek nationalist secret societies were actively hatching plots to foment rebellion in Thessaly, Epiros and southern Macedonia, taking advantage of conditions along the frontier. An opportunity presented itself in 1839. The Porte was facing an internal crisis with Mehmet Ali of Egypt. Mahmud II and he had already gone through one round of fighting in 1831 that stopped only when the great powers intervened. But the peace between the two rivals was short-lived. When civil war broke between Mehmet and Mahmud's successor, Greek secret societies struck. With the tacit backing of Athens and the direct support of some key political figures, Captain Ioannis Valentzas, a well-known bandit/border guard, led a force of men across the border into Thessaly. The hope was that the oppressed Christian population would rise up and join them. At the same time, a group of monks were to lead a rebellion on Mount Athos and a Greek bandit chieftain named Karatasos led an attack on Salonika.

Since some of the leaders of the insurgents were closely tied to the palace in Athens and to the Greek political elite, it was impossible for the government to deny plausibly that there was no official support for their activities. When the great powers demanded that the rebel activities cease or the much-needed loans that had been promised to Greece would vanish, Otto, though a supporter of irredentism, found himself in a difficult position. The young Bavarian had no choice but to relent and thus his popularity with the people began to suffer even more. This episode helped contribute to the constitutional revolution of 1843. It also demonstrated how vulnerable the Greek irredentist cause was to the dictates of the great powers.

The Crimean War (1854–6) presented Greece with its first real opportunity to gain territory from the Ottoman Empire. The early stages of the war saw successive Russian victories, and, as it had done repeatedly in the past, Russia sought to foment uprisings by the Ottoman Empire's Christian populations, including the Greeks. As discussed previously, Otto seized the chance to join the fray verbally and to turn a blind eye once again to the activities of the outlaws and the National Guard; to the end, he remained reluctant to commit contingents from the regular army. The nation firmly believed that the year 1853, marking as it did the 400th anniversary of the fall of Constantinople, was a propitious one for the restoration of a 'Greater Greece'. And so they girded for war.

Between 4,000 and 5,000 armed warriors had already infiltrated well into Thessaly, Epiros and Macedonia, and they were able to generate sufficient popular support to lay siege to the town of Arta and even to threaten the walls of Ioannina. The intervention of France and Britain on the side of the Porte led to Otto facing the humiliating need to recall all of the forces and break off the struggle. Once again the port of Piraeus was blockaded and, on this occasion, unlike in 1850, foreign troops even occupied Athens. Yet again, the cause of Greek irredentism was sacrificed on the altar of great power political expediency. Moreover, this proved to be the case even when the Megali Idea met with success.

Greece's first major territorial gains on the continent came in 1881 with the acquisition of Thessaly and Arta. The irony was that these additions came about inadvertently rather than through the aggressive action of Greek governments. The change of dynasties and the adjustments to the political system had had little or no impact on popular nationalism. As we saw in the last chapter, the middle decades of the century witnessed the crystallization and dissemination of a more uniform Hellenic identity. An even more radically expansive view of the Hellenic ecumene accompanied it.

At the same time, during the 1870s, Greek attention was increasingly focused on developments in the Balkans to the north. In the wake of the Cretan revolution (see below) and the expansion of more militant nationalist movements among various groups in the Balkans, the Porte attempted to play the game of divide and rule. A major initiative along this line was the creation in 1870 of an autocephalous Bulgarian Orthodox Church led by an Exarch, and thus called the Exarchate. The establishment of a Bulgarian Exarchate accelerated the process of Bulgarian nationalism. It also created tensions and competing interests between Serbia and Greece, and between them and the Bulgarian nationalists. Greece was also compelled to reassess its relationship with Russia because Pan-Orthodoxy, the idea that had previously been the rationale of Russian interest in the region, came to be replaced by Pan-Slavism: the former included Greece, the latter did not.

Greece, then, was not overly enthusiastic about joining with Serbs and Montenegrins in the summer of 1876 when they declared war on the Porte after an insurrection in Bosnia. Russian intervention in the face of Serbian defeat led to a change in Greek policy. Fearful of being left out of the settlement if the Russians were victorious and cognizant of the growth of anti-Ottoman sentiment in Britain over the 'Bulgarian Horrors', Athens had to adopt a more aggressive policy. This was a case as well of a government following the lead of their people. Greek popular opinion was overwhelmingly in favour of direct action.

Revolutionary societies, the most important of them being the National Defence, funded by domestic and diasporic merchants, artisans and labourers, channelled money and materials to the frontier. Irregulars under the command of recently decommissioned regular army officers streamed into Thessaly, Epiros and Macedonia. Text-box 15 reproduces a report from a field correspondent for the *London Times* that vividly captures the nature of the guerrilla tactics used by the Greek forces.

In Thessaly and Epiros, guerrilla tactics proved remarkably successful in tying down considerable numbers of Ottoman troops and they effectively laid siege to the larger garrison towns by completely dominating the countryside. Moreover, unlike during earlier incursions, many Greek and other Christian peasants rose up and joined in the fray. Wherever the Greek forces drove

Text-box 15 Greek guerrilla warfare (1878)

The mode of warfare adopted by the insurgents is the only one suited to the circumstances. It is necessary to them to economise men and to avoid the disheartening effect of a decided defeat. The object kept in view is not so much the defeat of the Turkish army as the expulsion from the land of the machinery of the Ottoman government and the affording of an opportunity to the inhabitants to express their true sentiments. They should, and generally do, strike no blow without a fair chance of gaining some tangible strategical or political advantage. The Greeks, with few exceptions, have no idea of fighting in the open. They are too intelligent to stand up and be shot at; and this, with the political considerations already mentioned, determines the nature of the tactics that they have recourse to. They keep to the mountains, descending into the plain only to capture Turkish convoys of provisions – an operation that they effect with great success, even under the castle. Posted on the heights, behind rocks and breastworks of loose stones, they fire with deliberate aim at the advancing battalions, and retire with scarcely any loss before they can be surrounded. However strong a village may be, they never occupy it, but take up positions on the surrounding heights, to avoid, as they express it, being taken as rats in their holes. In this way the defence is sometimes successful, sometimes not; but it is never disastrous. The Turkish troops shut up in a few towns are massed from time to time for the attack of some position held by the insurgents. The strategical disposition is often good, and they advance in overwhelming numbers; but the only result is that their losses are in overwhelming proportion to those of the enemy. That which is technically a victory becomes practically a defeat, and the work of suppression has to be begun over and over again.

London Times, 19 March 1878.

out the Ottoman troops, they immediately set up local governments loyal to Athens. As the nineteenth-century observer Lewis Sergeant noted, this practice, more than anything else, influenced the European powers into making territorial concessions:

The thing [restoration of the liberated zones to the Ottoman authorities] was physically, as well as morally, impossible. The Turkish system was destroyed throughout the provinces affected by the wars of 1876–8. The valis, the mutessarifs, the caimakans, the mudirs, had fled, or had been driven away; the whole civil administration of the vilayets, the whole military organization and the police of the country, so far as Turkish authority is concerned, were at an end. Not a pasha, not a bey, not a zaptieh, could return to his post and resume the power which he was wont to exercise.[1]

The uprisings in Macedonia, however, were not faring as well. Not only were the Greek forces up against better-trained Ottoman troops, but the complexity of the situation among the local Christian population also complicated matters significantly. In February 1878, following in the wake of the successes of the irregulars in Thessaly and the uncertainty of the situation in Macedonia, King George gave Prime Minister Alexandros Koumoundouros the go-ahead to launch an invasion of Thessaly by the regular army. Unfortunately, the pace of events elsewhere had overtaken them. Shortly after the Greek mobilization, an armistice was declared between Russia and the Ottoman Empire. If official Greek troops had occupied the liberated territories, then Greece would have been in a stronger position at the bargaining table. As it was, Greece came away from the war with almost nothing.

The subsequent Treaty of San Stefano left Greece out of the picture when a 'Greater Bulgaria', which included Macedonia and Thrace, was formed. Greeks and Serbs felt betrayed by Russia. Fortunately, the other great powers, in particular Great Britain and Austria, were also most displeased with the settlement. Diplomatic machinations continued until three months later, a new conference was called by Otto von Bismarck and a new treaty negotiated. Greek diplomats and the King lobbied strenuously for Greek interests, while sabre-rattling in Athens continued in the background. Ottoman intransigence to the Berlin Treaty led to greater pressure being placed on the Porte by the great powers.

Finally, in 1881, a bilateral agreement between the Sultan and Greece was reached. The territories where the Greek forces had been most successful and where they had liberated territories, Thessaly and southern Epiros (the area around the city of Arta), were ceded to the Hellenic Kingdom. A major step towards the realization of the Megali Idea had been taken with the addition of approximately 213,000 square kilometres of territory and 294,000 people. The diplomatic victory was marred in the public's view because the section of Epiros given to Greece did not include the capital city of Ioannina, no territory in Macedonia was included and the great island of Crete remained outside of the national fold. For the remainder of the century, the irredentist struggle focused on these unredeemed regions.

The Cretan and Macedonian questions

The story of the struggle for the liberation and incorporation of Crete into the nation-state of Greece began during the 1821 rebellion. Cretan Christians had joined their fellow members of the Millet-i Rum across the sea in the uprising and had been largely successful in the fighting against the Ottoman forces on the island. The tide turned, however, when Ibrahim Paşa invaded the island as part of his plan for the invasion of the Peloponnesos. The Porte was adamant that Crete should not be included in the new Greek Kingdom, and the European powers agreed. The Sultan then granted the island to Mehmet Ali of Egypt as a reward for his efforts during the war.

Egypt ruled the Christian population harshly and inter-communal relations on the island remained very tense. Taking advantage of Mehmet Ali's uprising against the Sultan in 1839 and his consequent fall from grace, a delegation of Cretan leaders petitioned the great powers for *enosis,* or union, with Greece. Instead, the island was returned to the Ottoman Empire. In 1858, a group of Christian and Muslim Cretans petitioned the Porte, calling for full implementation of the new edicts. When this failed to happen, Cretans split into three factions and began to mobilize for action. One group wanted to remain in the Empire but only if the reforms were fully enforced. Another wished to see the island remain in the Empire but on very different terms. They sought local autonomy and home rule, much like that enjoyed by Serbia and the Danubian Principalities. Yet another faction arose, and it sought nothing less than the unification of Crete with the Kingdom. All of them shared a desire for the island's situation to change, but they had radically different visions as to what that change should be.

On 3 August 1866, the general assembly of Cretan leaders met at the village of Apokorona. A force of 14,000 Ottoman and Egyptian troops confronted them and demanded capitulation. Shots were fired from the Ottoman ranks. Seeing no other choice, the Cretans returned fire. In this manner, the first of three Cretan revolutions was begun. Crete is the fifth largest island in the Mediterranean and since antiquity, it has been eagerly coveted by any power with pretensions to control the region. Consequently, as the Eastern Question took on increased prominence in great power international relations during the second half of the nineteenth century, so did the status of Crete become more problematic. The island was simply too important strategically for it to fall into the hands of any of the European powers, though the British in particular sought to be the island's 'protector' on numerous occasions. Ceding the island to Greece would, it was argued, have brought war to the region. The solution repeatedly opted for was to leave it in the hands of the Sultan, but to ensure that the lot of the Orthodox population was improved.

In the 1860s, matters came to a head for a number of reasons. First, the successful 'Risorgimento' of Italy, and the great power acquiescence in it, raised hopes that a similar unification of Greece would also find favour. Second, in 1864, Great Britain had ceded the Ionian Islands to the Kingdom of Greece after having occupied them for almost fifty years; if they could be united with the motherland, why not Crete, many argued. Third, the Orthodox population had been steadily growing as the Muslim population declined so that by 1866, the former outnumbered the latter by 200,000 to 62,000. Moreover, nationalist sentiments among this group were also rising. Fifth, the government of Dimitrios Voulgaris in Athens was whispering to the leaders on Crete that assistance was assured, and as tensions mounted even King George let it be known that he was prepared to lend moral and material support. For all of these reasons, the time seemed ripe for rebellion.

The rebellion on Crete took on the contours of a guerrilla war. From their mountain strongholds, the Cretan rebels and their Greek supporters pledged 'to fatten the eagles of the White Mountains [of central Crete] on the bodies of Turkish Pashas and Beys. ...'[2] Unchecked, they roamed the wilder regions of the island with impunity while Ottoman forces focused their attentions on the towns and villages. In many ways, this conflict resembled the one in Thessaly we discussed earlier. Volunteer brigades formed in Greece and street demonstrations drew thousands of Athenians from their homes. Men, material and money were collected and sent to Crete, with the active encouragement of the government. Initially, the rebels were extremely successful, inflicting approximately 20,000 casualties in the first year of fighting. Since the Ottoman and Egyptian forces could not engage the insurgents in open battle, they took out their ire on the civilian population. The reports of atrocities, and in particular the self-immolation of over 400 men, women and children in the besieged monastery of Arkadi on 21 October 1866, aroused great sympathy in Europe and the United States. But once again the hard realities of great power politics were to prove cold comfort to the cause of Greek irredentism.

Other groups in the Balkans, in particular the Serbs under Prince Michael Obrenovic, sought to gain advantage and so made demands on the Porte for concessions. This led to extensive bilateral negotiations between Greece and Serbia that resulted in the signing on 26 August 1867 of a treaty with seventeen clauses, the most important of which dealt with the size of the military contingents each side would provide in the event of war with the Ottoman Empire, the territories each side would acquire if the war was won and the formation of confederated states in some areas if necessary. Russia was also using the pretext of the Cretan rebellion to extend its influence in the Balkans. This served to heighten Franco-British sensitivities and pushed them towards adopting measures to maintain the status quo.

By early 1869, the military tide was turning as the Ottoman fleet, through its blockade of the island, was depriving the insurgents of much-needed supplies. Simultaneously, the diplomatic currents had also turned against the irredentist cause. With the assassination of Prince Michael and the continued opposition of King George, the Serbian alliance fell apart; France, Great Britain and Austria were pressuring Athens to compromise; the Sultan was threatening to declare war on Greece; the Russian Empire was adopting an ever more conciliatory tone. Finally, the volatility of the issue domestically had brought down three governments in three years. Compromise was the only solution. In the Paris peace talks of 1869, it was agreed that Crete would remain part of the Ottoman Empire but that there would be significant changes in how the islanders were to be governed and in their legal status within the Sultan's domain. The reform package was referred to as the 'Organic Laws'. Cretan unification, however, remained a key issue for the next forty years.

An uneasy calm had reigned on Crete from the late 1860s. There had been periodic outbursts of nationalist agitation, particularly during the 1877–8 wars in the Balkans, discussed previously. Nonetheless, the expanded scope for local rule awarded to the Christian population in the wake of the first Cretan revolution had eased tensions somewhat. The so-called Halepa pact of 1878 had addressed many of the Cretans' grievances and had provided for much local autonomy. It was the erosion of those powers in the 1890s that brought revolution to the island once again. In 1895, for example, the Porte announced the suspension of all civil liberties for the Christian population. As civil unrest escalated, reports of atrocities began to be circulated. Then, in 1896, the Cretans rose in open rebellion once more.

The news sent shockwaves through Athens. Secret nationalist groups like the National Society collected money and arms and men to aid the rebellion. Mired in economic turmoil, the rebellion provided the hard-pressed Deliyiannis government with a means of diverting popular discontent. The nation readied for war.

Yet again, however, the issue lay in the hands of the great powers. But at this juncture, the configuration of national interests among them had shifted. The German Empire had decidedly thrown its weight behind the Porte as had, increasingly, Austria. Russia was still keen to take advantage of any Ottoman reversals so long as doing so did not threaten their influence in the Slavic areas. Britain and France looked warily at any moves that changed the balance of power in the region and so threatened their vital trading interest.

Active Greek support for the Cretan rebellion elevated tensions between Athens and the Porte and led only to full-scale, national war. The 1897 Ottoman–Greek War was one that the Ottoman Empire did not want, the great powers tepidly sought to prevent and the Deliyiannis government in Athens could not stop. Abdul Hamid's government found itself in a quandary. A war with Greece would inevitably result in great power intervention and that was the last thing it wanted. The recent episodes of anti-Armenian violence had already brought on international opprobrium. Plus, the Empire's financial situation had only recently begun to improve. War would jeopardize those gains. But national honour and international credibility were on the line. On the other side, war fever gripped Greece and there was no stopping it.

Peasants from the countryside flocked to Athens to join the reserves. Throngs gathered in Sintagma Square daily, exhorting the government to act. Even the royal family joined in the clamour for war. There was a mania bordering on blind faith stoking the belief that a war of liberation against the Ottoman Empire would cure all of the country's ills. Thus, Greece entered into a fray that would see the nation's fortunes turned upside down in a matter of weeks. The Thirty Days' War had begun.

The war was fought along two fronts on the Ottoman–Greek border: Epiros and Thessaly. The latter would be the more important of the two. Under the leadership of Crown-Prince Konstantinos, Greece mobilized three divisions, two of which were dispatched to the Thessalian front. The Greek forces in this critical area consisted of 45,000 infantry, 500 cavalry and 96 small field artillery pieces. From his headquarters at Elassona, the Ottoman commander, Edhem Paşa, marshalled 58,000 infantry, 1,500 cavalry and 190 pieces of artillery. The Ottoman numerical advantage in numbers, especially in cavalry, proved decisive. But numbers alone did not account for the Greek defeat. The Ottoman army was equipped with newer and better armament. The infantry, for example, now carried German smokeless Mauser repeater rifles, whereas the Greek infantry still used much inferior single shot French Gras carbines. The German Empire had also sold to the Ottomans far superior modern field artillery. In addition to logistical superiority, the Ottoman forces were much better organized, trained and led. On the other side, from the very beginning there were problems in the Greek military leadership. The professional soldiers, such as Colonel Konstantinos Smolenskis, had little confidence in the royal princes, and their reservations proved well-founded. Konstantinos and his staff made numerous critical errors that cost the Greek side dearly. Outmanned, outgunned and poorly led, the Greek forces were quickly routed.

In order to get his army across the mountain ranges that separated Thessaly and the Empire, Edhem Paşa had to force two passes – the Nezeros Pass to the east and the Melouna Pass in the centre. Both mountain defiles witnessed some of the fiercest fighting of the war. Of the two passes, Melouna was the more important because it guarded the main road from Elassona, Ottoman HQ, and Larissa, where Konstantinos had his command centre. For four days, the two sides ferociously contested every inch of the pass, until finally on 21 April, the Ottoman infantry broke the Greek defences. The Greek army regrouped and made a stand at the village of Tyrnavo, but soon it also fell. With a secure beachhead and the mountain passes in his hands, Edhem Paşa marched the main army on to the Thessalian plain, where his numerical superiority in cavalry gave him a marked advantage. Larissa was indefensible and so the Greeks evacuated. Thus, after only a span of less than two decades, the city was back in Ottoman hands.

Konstantinos retreated, dividing his army in two. One group marched to Farsala, where it could use the hillier topography to its advantage and also defend the mountain passes that protected the city of Lamia. The other sector of the army regrouped at Velestino, a site that controlled the main passage southwards to the coastal road, along which the modern National Highway runs, and that protected the main route to the critically important city of Volos. In response, Edhem divided his forces in three. Two followed the Greek forces southwards, while the third marched to the city of Trikala to the west. By seizing it, he could threaten the rear of the Greek forces in Epiros. Ottoman forces were successful in all three areas. Smolenskis, Greece's most able commander, devised a brilliant plan and his forces put up a fierce resistance at the Battle of Velestino before finally being defeated on 30 April. Just over a week later, Volos was taken. The Greek army was now cut off from the sea. On 5 May, the forces at Farsala were beaten. Konstantinos fled to Lamia to regroup, and then, following the advice of his staff, he marched the remnants of his army south to make a final stand at Thermopylai. He would not have the chance to see if he would be modern Greece's equivalent to the Spartan King Leonidas, leader of the famous 300, because on 20 May, under pressure from the European powers to protect Greece from total defeat, an armistice was declared (see Figure 8). The war was over after only thirty days.

In the broad settlement that ended that conflict, Crete's status was changed. It was to become an autonomous polity under the sovereignty of the Ottoman Empire, but governed by a High Commissioner, Prince George of Greece, and a chamber of Christian and Muslim deputies. In Chapter 6, we shall examine in more detail the period of Prince George's limited rule.

No issue dominated Balkan foreign relations more than Macedonia during the last decades of the nineteenth century. The definition of the region referred to as Macedonia in modern times defies precise delineation. Under Ottoman rule, it did not constitute a single administrative district, but, instead, was composed of three Vilayets: Salonika, Monastir and Uskub (Kossovo). Delineating its geographical boundaries is also difficult because there are no topographical features that create a single coherent spatial unit. As a working definition, we could define Macedonia geographically as the territory bounded on its western side by lakes Ochrid and Prespa, the Shar, Rila and Rhodope Mountains and the Crna Gora to the north, the river Nestos (Metsa) to the east and the Pindos Mountains, Mount Olimbos and the Aegean Sea to the south. But we need to bear in mind that the area thus defined contained a variety of different geographical regions.

Neither was there a single cultural or ethnic group, the distribution of which we could employ to demarcate an area as constituting Macedonia. For centuries the region was home to Jews, Muslims and Orthodox Christians, to

FIGURE 8 *A small job for Six Big Policemen (1897). Published while the Greco–Ottoman War of 1897 was still in progress, this cartoon shows Greece as a little boy in traditional costume surrounded by six oversized policemen, each representing one of the great powers. Arrayed around little Greece are England, Russia, Hungary, France, Germany and Austria. There is some ambiguity in the cartoon as to whether the Six Big Policemen are protecting or arresting little Greece. It also captures Greece's ambiguous relationship with the European powers on whom the little country was dependent. At times they protected it, while at others they persecuted it.*

Udo J. Kepler, Punch, *14 April 1897. GallantGraphics all rights reserved.*

Ladino, Greek, Serbian and Romanian speakers. Many and diverse were the groups that made up the 'Macedonian Salad' of the nineteenth century.

What is incontrovertible is that the region, however loosely defined, is one of the most important in the Balkans. Macedonia contains some of the richest farmland in a part of the world where arable land is at a premium. Geographically, it is the southern gateway into the Balkans, and thence into Central Europe. Macedonia also stands at the crossroads of the major overland communication routes that link Asia and Europe. The region was home to one of the most important commercial and manufacturing centres in the Eastern Mediterranean – Salonika. In addition to this jewel of the East, there were other towns of economic importance in their own right, such as Florina, Monastir, Edessa and Kozani. From antiquity to the present, then, Macedonia has been one of the most important regions in the Eastern Mediterranean.

At the time of the war of liberation in 1821, some Greek leaders fervently hoped that when the war was won, the resulting state would have Macedonia as a core region and that Constantinople would be the new polity's capital, or if that city could not be liberated, then the honour would fall to Salonika. Such was not to be. Though many in the region participated in the rebellion, at the war's end there was never any serious possibility of Macedonia being included in the settlement. Through the middle years of the century, there were bouts of unrest, usually related to the operation of Greek bands in the border zone between Greece and the Empire, but none of them posed a serious threat to Ottoman suzerainty over the region.

There were, nonetheless, some important developments during this period. The first was the accelerated economic development of Salonika. The city grew dramatically in size, the volume of commercial traffic through the port increased substantially and industrialization commenced. The second was the increased migration of Greeks from the kingdom into the region; some of these were peasants in search of land and others were irregulars in search of booty. Almost all of them were imbued with the spirit of Greek irredentism. Tension between Greek- and Slavic-speaking groups escalated. One reflection of this was the numerous petitions by Slavic community leaders to the Patriarch and the Porte for permission to have the Bulgarian language used in church. These overtures were rebuffed until 1870.

In that year, a firman from the Sultan created a Bulgarian Church called the Exarchate, and it further stipulated that the Exarchate leadership could establish a church in any community in which two-thirds of the people professed allegiance to the new organization. Along with the new churches, of course, would come new Bulgarian-speaking schools. Shortly thereafter, the Orthodox Patriarch responded by declaring the new church schismatic. A battle was now under way for the hearts and minds of Macedonian Christians between the Exarchate, the Patriarchate, and in some areas, the Serbian Orthodox Church. Across the region, people were being forced to choose between one of the rival churches, and it was through making that choice that they began to espouse a specific ethnic identity. The stakes of making such a decision soon got much higher.

We discussed the Russo–Ottoman war of 1877–8 earlier in this chapter, focusing our attention in particular on the role of the Greek irregulars in Thessaly and Epiros. The war, however, had a much greater scope than just that theatre of operations. Massive uprisings also occurred in Serbia, Bulgaria and Macedonia. The treaty of San Stefano, which not only created an autonomous principality of Bulgaria but also included in it the lion's share of Macedonia, shook the Greek world. The revised settlement imposed by the subsequent Treaty of Berlin restored most of southern Macedonia to the Ottoman Empire. But it also served to escalate the struggle between the rival Christian nationalist movements.

Pavlos Melas, a prominent Greek nationalist who lost his life fighting in Macedonia, captured the feeling of many of his compatriots when he stated that Macedonia constituted the lungs of the body of the Greek nation: without it, Hellenism would expire. Over the last two decades of the nineteenth century, fierce rivalries developed between partisan groups like the Greek National Society and the pro-Bulgarian and Macedonian groups such as the Internal Macedonian Revolutionary Organization (IMRO). In a struggle over culture, language and identity, each side sought to 'Hellenize' or 'Slavicize' inhabitants of the region. They endeavoured to establish as many areas as possible in which they could claim that their group predominated numerically. Maps could then be produced that showed the spatial distribution of ethnic groups and this would strengthen each side's claim to the area.

Recent studies have demonstrated that the process of identity formation in Macedonia was complex and which of the competing identities a person subscribed to was based on a variety of factors. Given the intensity of emotions that accompanied this struggle, it is not surprising that violence often erupted. Open conflict between the rival bands became even more prevalent and the level of violence inflicted on the local communities became even more horrific after 1897.

The Greek kingdom's disastrous war against the Ottoman Empire and the shifting currents of great power foreign policy positions opened a window of opportunity for the pro-Bulgarian and pro-independence groups in Macedonia, and they were quick to seize on it. IMRO and exarchist bands stepped up the level and intensity of their efforts to 'win over' areas to their side. After his appointment as metropolitan bishop of Kastoria in 1900, Germanos Karavengelis spearheaded the efforts of the Greek patriarchists to confront them. The situation on the ground, however, cannot be seen as simply a struggle between patriarchists and exarchists. There were divisions among the exarchist groups over whether there should be an independent Macedonia or one attached to Bulgaria, and this split occasionally erupted into open conflict. Among the patriarchists, there were some whose vision of Hellenism was shaped by perceptions emanating from the Patriarch in Istanbul, while others were wedded to a view coming from Athens. Albanian nationalist groups were also rising up in arms and their activities added an additional complicating factor. The final players were, of course, the police and military forces of the Ottoman Empire. The conflict, then, was many-sided and the fighting, conducted largely by guerrilla bands, was fierce. Purported atrocities by all sides contributed to the volatility of an already explosive situation. The fighting became even more intense and widespread after an IMRO uprising during the festival of Saint Elijah, or Ilinden in Slavic, on 2 August 1903 that centred on the city of Monastir in Western Macedonia. The revolt involved both guerrilla bands and Christian peasants. After a two-month-long conflict, it was brutally suppressed by Ottoman troops, assisted by some Greek patriarchist bands. Fearful of a wider Balkan conflict and repulsed by the horrors of the Ilinden uprising, the emperors of Austria and Russia persuaded the other great powers regarding the need to intervene. Following a meeting in October 1903, they imposed on the reluctant Porte a series of reforms known as the Mürzsteg Programme. Some of its most important aspects were the appointment of two officials, one Austrian and one Russian, to monitor the programme's implementation; the reformation of the gendarmerie whose leadership would be made up of officers from each of the European powers; and the redrawing of administrative boundaries to produce districts with the most ethnically homogeneous composition possible.

For a Greece scarred by the catastrophe of 1897, the conflict in Macedonia, especially after 1903, provided a source of national hope. The Greeks, as did others, misread the administrative reform of the Mürzsteg Programme as a signal that the powers might be supportive of the division of Macedonia along ethnic lines and that this move was but a prelude to those districts' incorporation into the appropriate national state. Funds and fighters in increasing volume began to flow into Macedonia. Although it maintained to the great powers that it was not responsible for the escalation of the conflict, the Greek government was clearly involved. Attachés and consular officers attached to the Greek embassy in Salonika were instrumental in directing the activities of the Greek bands. Greek military officers and warriors who fell in the conflict, like Pavlos Melas, were elevated to the status of national heroes. At a time of national malaise, the 'Macedonian struggle' provided a focus of national unity and purpose. When in 1908, however, the Committee for Union and Progress, led by a group known as the Young Turks, staged a 'revolution' in the Ottoman Empire and inaugurated a period of reform, the fighting in Macedonia subsided and the Greek dream of fulfilment of the Megali Idea in Macedonia was dashed – for the time being at least. The disappointment at this setback to the irredentist cause would contribute, as we shall see shortly (see pp. 166–7), to a major political upheaval within Greece.

Understanding a state's foreign policy over any length of time is always difficult and requires simplification of complex realities. In the case of Greece during the nineteenth century, the Megali Idea formed a type of ideological core that implicitly or explicitly shaped foreign policy decisions. Greco–Ottoman relations, for example, could never be 'normalized' so long as Greece continued to claim Ottoman lands as its own. The issue clouded all aspects of interaction between the two – political, diplomatic and economic. Moreover, adding an additional layer of complexity was the increasing tensions between Greece and the other Balkan secessionist states, particularly Serbia and Bulgaria. Each of them had its own irredentist vision and its own Megali Idea, and all three claimed many of the same territories as belonging to their national space. The Balkan states' irredentisms clashed with one another, and, of course, all were antagonistic to the Ottoman Empire's fierce opposition to territorial partition. These conditions created a Balkan powder keg that had global implications. The imperial ambitions of Russia, Great Britain, France, Austria and Germany after 1878 became tied to the Balkans. For Greece, its relations with the various great powers ebbed and flowed depending on the needs and dictates of the Megali Idea. No other issue exerted as great an influence on the development of the Greek state and society during the nineteenth century, and by that era's end, the dream of a 'Greater Greece' seemed more distant than ever.

6

Society and economy in the nineteenth and early twentieth centuries

Greek society underwent many profound changes during the nineteenth century. There were, however, substantial continuities with the Ottoman past as well. In this chapter, we explore the social history of Greece during its first century of existence. Social history differs from its sister disciplines of political and economic history in the way in which it views the importance of time. Political history and economic history lend themselves to sequential narrative analysis, resembling in this way a motion picture where one frame follows another to tell a coherent story: events can be linked into a consecutive sequence and chronological relations of one episode to the next can be appreciated. Social history marches to a different chronological drummer. Social changes appear in the historical record less as events than as processes, and consequently it is difficult to delineate them as discrete moments in time.

The sources for social history are also not well suited to a sequential analysis; the records of society in the past are patchy and filled with gaps over both time and space, especially for the largest groups in society – peasants and workers – who for the most part have left us few written accounts of their lives. For these reasons, social history often appears less like a movie and more like a series of snapshots taken at different points in time. These problems are all evident in the case of Greece where the sources available, for example, on peasant life are disparate and incomplete. The rich anthropological literature on Greece, while based on the recent past, can help us to transcend the limitations of the historical sources, but we have to be careful that we do not create an impression that Greek society, especially rural society, has not undergone profound changes over the last 200 years. Therefore, in spite of the obstacles that confront us, without a history that includes the peasants – male and female – the labourers, the sailors, the street vendors and the beggars, our understanding of Greek society will be incomplete.

I begin with an examination of the basic structures of Greek society during the nineteenth century, such as demography and household structure. Since Greece was predominantly a rural society, we shall next move on to discuss various aspects of village life. We also need to examine how the people worked the land and how agrarian practices changed over time. Then, using gender as our organizing axis, we can explore the social worlds of men and women. In the penultimate section of the chapter, we move from the country to the city.

One of the most important social developments in Greece during the second half of the nineteenth century was the remarkable growth of Athens and its port city of Piraeus at the expense of both the countryside and the other cities of Greece. Once again, we shall begin our discussion with the structural aspects of urbanization and then move to the experiential: How did the move to the city affect peoples' lives? In Greece, as it did elsewhere in Europe, rapid urbanization generated a host of 'social problems': crime, violence, prostitution, poverty, sanitation and the like. We shall examine how the Greek state responded to these pressing social issues. Finally, I examine the great exodus of Greeks to the United States and elsewhere at the end of the nineteenth and the first two decades of the twentieth centuries.

Demographic change

The revolutionary war had been a long and bloody affair. Caught between the savage scorched earth policy of Ibrahim Paşa and the continual depredations of the Greek irregulars, the peasantry suffered horribly. Though it is impossible to determine the exact numbers of fatalities, we can be sure that tens of thousands died. Yet, if the earliest demographic data available after the war are to be believed, a combination of in-migration from the Greek communities outside of Otto's kingdom and a vigorous rate of population growth among the indigenous Greeks recouped the war losses in a relatively short time. Table 1 and Chart 4 provide an overview of population growth from 1833 to 1920.

If we focus first on the kingdom as a whole, it appears that the years immediately after the war, roughly from 1832 until 1835, witnessed a modest but steady growth in population. This was followed by a very sharp increase

TABLE 1 Population growth in Greece, 1821–1920

Population	Country	Peloponnesos	Central Greece	Aegean Islands	Ionian islands	Thessaly
1821	766,477	389,709	206,356	161,412		
1828	600,000					
1835	674,185					
1843	915,000					
1848	987,000					
1853	1,036,000					
1861	1,096,810	552,414	318,535	225,861		
1870	1,436,141	611,861	356,865	238,784	228,631	
1879	1,638,850	709,245	441,033	259,056	229,516	
1889	2,187,308	813,154	556,254	235,050	238,783	344,067
1896	2,434,000	902,181	758,385	234,747	235,973	385,520
1907	2,632,000	937,366	897,773	230,378	254,494	448,618
1920	5,021,790	915,204	1,125,073	222,347	224,189	491,159
		Crete	**Macedonia**	**Thrace**	**Epiros**	**Other islands**
1920		346,584	1,090,432	199,470	213,784	263,248

during the late 1830s and 1840s, with the population size expanding from about 650,000 in 1835 to almost one million in 1848. Indigenous growth rates remained at moderate to high levels for the remainder of the nineteenth century. Table 1 also shows the impact of the addition of the Ionian Islands in 1864 and Thessaly and Arta in 1881 on the size of the population of Greece. The territorial expansions resulting from the Balkan Wars and the First World War, as a result of which the population rose to just over five million people, are reflected in the census of 1920 (Table 1 and Chart 4).

All told, these figures suggest a large increase in the population of Greece as a whole; this was partly due to the addition of new territories and partly to the indigenous demographic growth. Within the territory of 'Old Greece', that is, those areas that constituted the kingdom in 1832, there was a 295 per cent increase in population. The actual growth rate was even higher than this figure suggests because it does not take into account the half million Greeks who left the country between 1880 and 1920 – about whom more will be said shortly. To place the Greek case into a comparative framework, over the same period, the population of Spain grew by 183 per cent and that of Italy by 185 per cent, while the major powers of France and Great Britain expanded by 127 per cent and 233 per cent, respectively. Like the rest of Europe during the nineteenth century, Greece experienced population growth.

A number of factors control the rate at which a population grows. At a very basic level, of course, the primary one is the ratio of the live birth rate to the death rate. Quite simply, if there are more births than deaths, population increases. The live birth rate, using the standard measure of births per 1,000

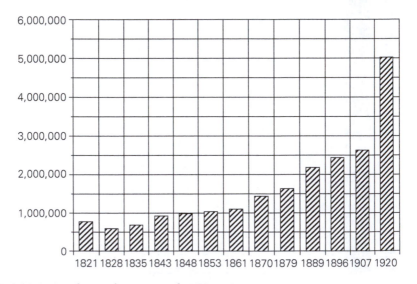

CHART 4 *Greek population growth, 1821–1920.*

persons, in 1860 was 38.6, while the mortality rate was 26.5. The live birth rate rose over the next few decades, reaching its zenith during the 1880s (40.8/1,000), while the mortality rate fell at a corresponding rate, sinking to its nadir of 20.3/1,000 at the turn of the century. In the absence of national-level data before 1860, we have to rely on archival studies of specific localities, and the few studies that have been carried out suggest that figures of the same magnitude pertained before 1860 as well. So more Greeks were being born while the rate at which others died fell. Why?

The key demographic variables controlling the birth rate are the female age at marriage, life expectancy, fertility rate, artificial fertility control, the percentage of women and men who marry and the infant mortality rate. If, for example, few women marry and they marry late in life and die shortly thereafter, and if many of the children they give birth to die, then the birth rate will be low. What transpired in Greece during the nineteenth century was the development of a demographic regime that produced population growth but one which was subjected to periodic shifts as a result of factors such as massive emigration.

One critical factor contributing to this development was the low age at marriage for women. From the available data, it appears that throughout the century women married in their early twenties. The average age at marriage for men was the late twenties. Over the course of the century, both of these figures fluctuated, but the trend was for the vast majority of women, over 90 per cent, to be married by age 26 and the average age for men declined to 26–27, with over 80 per cent of men having taken a bride for the first time by age 30. Simultaneously, life expectancy for both men and women increased from 35.7 in 1860 to 45.2 by the 1920s. Effective artificial birth control was not widely practised by Greek couples and so a natural fertility rate predominated.

Two additional factors of importance were that, first, almost all Greek men and women married, meaning that everyone contributed to the reproducing population, and second, the infant mortality rate was falling. According to one study, for example, the infant death rate fell from 198.2 in 1860 to 148.1 by the 1920s. We can conclude, then, that almost all Greek men and women married; they married somewhat younger and lived longer than their forebears; and in the absence of birth control, they produced more children, a greater percentage of whom survived to adulthood. It was the combined effects of these and the other developments discussed above that created a demographic regime of growth that produced the population increase recorded in Greece during the nineteenth century. Some of the more important social consequences of this growth will be examined shortly. I want to turn next to an examination of the nature of the family and household in nineteenth-century Greece.

The Spiti: family and household structure

Throughout history, Greeks have drawn no difference between the house in which they reside and the people who reside there with them. In antiquity, the word *oikos* captured this dual sense of house and household, while in the modern era the word used most often is *spiti*. *Oikogenia,* a word whose origin is evident, is employed to capture the sense of family, but in everyday speech, one hears people most often using spiti when they talk about their family.

As in other agrarian societies, the household constituted the primary social unit on which the communal and the national social structures were built. It was both the centre of production and reproduction, and the most basic unit for the socialization of the young. A man's overarching obligation was to protect and further the interests of his household, his spiti, and after that, it was to the extended network of men to whom he was related by blood. Outside of their households and kin groups, men, of course, had other duties and obligations, but should a conflict arise between household and community, between kin and non-kin, the former always took precedence. Household interests come before all others in the Greek peasant worldview. However, no household is an island unto itself. The spiti was also the locus for the union of two groups of kindred – the husband's and the wife's. We shall see repeatedly throughout this chapter just how central the spiti was in Greek society. It is important at this juncture to examine the structure of the household and the processes by which it was formed.

The most basic question we need to answer about the household is simply this: What did the average one look like? Was the typical Greek household large, consisting of many generations or groups of brothers and their families living under one roof? Or was it more like the structure normative today, in which the household usually consists of a married couple and their unmarried offspring? Answering this question is not as simple as it might initially appear. First, there is yet again the problem of the paucity of information. We need fairly detailed census data or other types of family records in order to reconstruct the structure of households. Second, we have to be aware that the average household may have been prevented by demographic factors from achieving its culturally idealized final form. Nonetheless, we can venture some generalizations.

The first point of significance is that no single form of household or family structure predominated in all regions and among all classes in the Greek world. Table 2 presents the data derived from studies of different communities during the nineteenth century. We can see clearly from the table the variety of forms manifest both between communities and even within the same community. Among the pastoralists in the Epirote village of Syrrako, for example, about half

TABLE 2 Household structure in various regions. The figures represent the percentage of households recorded for each structural type

	Syrrako 1905	Syrrako 1905	Aristi 1905	Hermoupolis 1879	Mykonos 1861	Kythera 1788	Preveza 1780	Krokylio 1915	Çukur 1884
	Pastoralists	Permanent							
Solitaries	2	12.6	8.8	13.6	11.2	14.4	36	2.6	1.5
No family	0.6	5.4	1.3	7.2	4	2.6	16	1.3	0
Nuclear	50.1	46.2	28.9	72.4	76.8	75.7	40	62.6	45.5
Extended	21.1	21.5	25.2	4.5	3.9	4.5	4	16.7	4.5
Joint	23.9	11.7	32	0.5	3.8	2.7	4	12.1	47.9
Other	2.3	2.7	3.8	1.8	0.3	0.2	0	5.6	0

Note: See Gallant (2015: 194) for the sources of these data.

of the households contained only a nuclear family (by which we mean parents and their offspring). Another 45 per cent consisted of extended families, in which there was a nuclear family that was joined by one or more relatives, or joint families, in which one or more married siblings, usually brothers, and their families co-resided. This pattern flourished frequently in the past among groups that practised large-scale animal husbandry. The reason for this would seem to be that larger, more complex households were better able to pool resources and to manage labour in a way better suited to the needs of shepherding, especially where transhumance was involved.

Theodore Bent, an English traveller, for example, visited an extreme example of this type of household on the island of Gatharonisi (today called Agathonisi) adjacent to the island of Patmos in the Eastern Mediterranean in 1865. He found that only one family inhabited the entire island and that it consisted of an elderly couple, three married sons and their families, three unmarried sons, one married daughter and her family, and six other unmarried daughters. All together twenty-two people shared bed, board and flocks on this remote islet.[1]

A similar tendency towards forming joint or extended households flourished among the richest and the poorest Greeks on the Ionian Islands. Complex households were found among sharecropping families, which were attached to the great feudal estates on the islands of Corfu, Zakinthos and Kefalonia, and among the aristocratic families who owned the plantations. In the case of sharecroppers, as with pastoralists, it appears that it was the ability to muster a larger labour force that explains why two or more nuclear families would choose to co-reside. Also, by continuing to live and work together after the death of their father, brothers were able to keep intact the leasehold that was bequeathed to them as their inheritance.

The reason why aristocratic families formed complex households was related to property and patrimony as well. Like nobility elsewhere in Europe, the Ionian bluebloods practised unigeniture, a system of inheritance whereby only one child received the family's property. In exchange for obtaining legal ownership of the family's villa, plantation and townhouses, the primary heir was obligated to house and support his younger siblings. It was, therefore, not uncommon on the islands to find four or more brothers and sisters and their families living together along with their domestic servants in one mansion.

The villagers of Aristi in Epiros also showed a similar tendency towards forming more complex households (57.2 per cent), but for quite different reasons. The people of Aristi were not pastoralists but agriculturalists in an area where arable land was scarce, and what there was of it was of poor quality. Like many upland communities in Greece where a very delicate balance between people and resources existed, village men would temporarily migrate as itinerant labourers, artisans or merchants. In the case of Aristi, they specialized as innkeepers and bakers, and men from the village worked in cities all across the Balkans. The female-headed households of the absent men would combine with siblings or in-laws on a temporary basis or co-reside in some other arrangement that produced joint households.

The pattern manifested among the permanent members of Syrrako typifies the more normal Greek peasant household in which the entire family worked the land on a more or less continuous basis. The nuclear household was overwhelmingly the most frequently occurring form among the peasantry and there were relatively few joint households. Extended households formed, if they did at all, when a widowed parent continued to reside in the family's house. Because of the differences in age at marriage and in the average life expectancy between men and women, this meant that almost invariably it was the mother who lived out the rest of her life with one of her married children. The comparatively higher number of solitaries among farming households represents widows and widowers who either chose not to live with one of their children or whose offspring had left the village.

This general pattern in which the nuclear household predominated was the norm among peasants in most of southern Europe. Newly wedded peasant couples created a new household by combining the land that the husband received as his inheritance with the property that the woman brought into the union in her dowry. Among peasant families, the formation of a joint household between siblings does not appear to have been common, and when it did occur, it was in all likelihood as an emergency measure. Finally, contrasting with the patterns we have discussed so far, all of which involved rural folk, was the one that emerged in nineteenth-century cities.

The cosmopolitan port city of Hermoupolis on the island of Syros manifested a pattern of family structure typical of urban areas elsewhere in Europe in which the nuclear household predominated. A variety of factors shaped this practice. With the exception of Salonika, all of the cities of Greece were essentially new foundations, and thus, the result of in-migration usually of people from the countryside. These young migrants would marry, and in the absence of already established households to which they were related, families would set up a dwelling of their own. This practice was facilitated by the ease with which families could build illegal dwellings in the city. Also, elderly parents would more than likely have remained in their rural village and so the possibility of creating extended households was lessened. Finally, the number of 'solitaries' appears to be the same as among the peasants of Syrrako, but for different reasons. The sizeable number of people living alone in the city was not widowed men and women but rather merchants who had set up house temporarily.

In nineteenth-century Greek society, then, there were three predominant forms of family structure. The most common pattern pertained among the

Greek peasantry where the nuclear household was the normative form. Another pattern, most common among pastoralists and sharecroppers, featured a greater proportion of extended or joint households. And finally, there was an urban pattern in which nuclear households were the overwhelming favourites. Related to the structure of the household and to how the household operated as a social unit was the pattern of residence.

Three different types of post-marital residence patterns have been observed in Greece. Not too surprisingly, each of them was related to a number of factors, such as household structure, the nature of the kinship system and the way property was transmitted to the next generation. One prominent post-marital residence pattern was virilocality or patrivirilocality. In the regions where this was the custom, the newly married couple would set up residence either in the household of the husband's father (patrivirilocal), thus creating a complex household, or they would build a house in very close proximity to the father's abode, often even in the same compound. Over time, this custom produced a spatial geography characterized by clusters of men related to one another by blood. It was found most frequently among pastoralists and in other areas like Crete and Epiros, regions with a tradition of autonomy and militarism that placed a premium on having numerous fighting men connected to one another like the Mani and the central mountainous regions of the Peloponnesos, and in places such as the Ionian Islands where sharecropping created common economic interests between agnatic kinsmen.

This system placed great emphasis on the kinship relationship between men, and agnatic kin groups often formed tightly organized groups. Property transmission focused on men as well. Upon the death or retirement of the *pater familias*, the adult sons would share equally in the inheritance, but there were considerable social pressures placed upon them to continue to operate their holdings as a unit. Women traditionally did not receive land as part of their dowry or share in any inheritance. Instead, they received their share of the parental estate in their dowry, usually in the form of a trousseau that included cash and moveable property.

The second post-marital residence pattern practised in the past was uxorilocality. In this case, the married couple went to live either with the wife's family or in close proximity to them. In other words, uxorilocality is more or less the mirror image of the system that we just discussed, only in this instance, the focus was on kindred women rather than men. Kinship lines tended to be traced bilaterally, in other words along both the husband's and the wife's families, and strong bonds were formed between kinswomen. Regarding the intergenerational transmission of property, the custom was for one of the daughters to receive her parents' house as part of her dowry, but the practice regarding which girl, if there was more than one daughter, varied.

In some places, it was the eldest, in others the youngest, and in yet others, it was decided on the basis of filial affection. This custom was seen most frequently on the Aegean Islands or in other maritime communities where the men would be absent for long periods of time.

The third system fell somewhere in between the other two, and while it had a long history, it really developed into the predominant custom only during the nineteenth century. In this instance, couples practised neolocality, in which the newlyweds would establish their own household spatially distinct from either's parents. Since the parents would more than likely be leaving behind a house, one of the children would receive it as their patrimony, usually in exchange for agreeing to care for the aged parents. Property transmission among agriculturalists tended to be partible, meaning that each child received an equal share of the parental estate, and women frequently received land as part of their dowry. This was the practice among the vast majority of peasant farming families across Greece. It became the custom in the newly emerging urban areas as well, with an apartment or a similar dwelling space substituting for arable land.

Whether large and complex or simple and nuclear, the spiti was at the centre of Greek life. Before examining the traditional social roles that men and women played in their household, I want to examine first the place of the spiti in the material world posing two questions: What sort of community did most Greeks live in and how did the household operate as a unit of production in the past?

Farms and villages

The visitor to Greece today is immediately struck by the degree to which cities, especially Athens, dominate Greek society. Such an impression is amply supported by a glance at the most recent census figures, which show that over one-half of the entire Greek population resides in the greater Athens area alone. Yet, the predominance of cities and their urban lifeways is a relatively recent phenomenon. For most of its history, Greece had been a country of rural folk who lived in villages. For example, according to the first census that recorded occupational information, taken in 1861, 74 per cent of adult men were agriculturalists who earned their livelihood from working the land. Moreover, the pattern remained fairly consistent through time. By 1920, for example, the proportion of heads of households listed as farmers had barely changed, dropping only to 70 per cent. Before examining the agrarian systems of nineteenth-century Greece, we need to make a few observations about where Greeks lived and how that built environment of the village helped shape their social world.

Table 3 gives a very clear idea about the distribution of human settlements in Greece before the arrival of the Asia Minor refugees in 1922 (see Chapter 8), but after the incorporation of the northern regions of Epiros, Thrace and Macedonia at the end of the Balkan Wars in 1913 (about which, see Chapter 7). In 1920, almost 52 per cent of the entire population resided in villages comprising less than 1,000 individuals, and villages of this size accounted for nearly 94 per cent of all human habitations. Hidden within these aggregate figures is the fact that the majority of villagers (approximately 35 per cent) lived in villages of less than 500 people, and over 150,000 people lived in settlements of fewer than 100. The typical village had a population of either 200–300 or 600–700 people. If we consider that settlements with between 1,000 and 5,000 inhabitants were also populated predominantly by peasant families, then over 70 per cent of the population lived in villages. The data also suggest that by 1920, the population distribution of Greece was sharply divided between rural villages and larger cities, and that towns (i.e. settlements with between 5,000 and 10,000 people) were of relatively modest importance. Moving back in time, the picture of Greece as a land of rural villages only becomes more apparent. The general pattern can be exemplified through a more detailed examination of one well-studied region in the Peloponnesos.

Karytaina is an upland district in the central Peloponnesos. Mountains and hills divide the region into numerous basins where the best arable land is concentrated. In terms of its physical geography, it resembles many areas of

TABLE 3 Distribution of population in Greece by settlement size, 1861

Size of settlement	Frequency	Population
0–1,000	10,050	2,703,539
1,001–2,000	510	689,012
2,001–3,000	107	263,697
3,001–4,000	38	119,677
4,001–5,000	23	101,613
5,001–10,000	33	230,210
10,001–50,000	26	466,154
50,001–10,0000	1	51,598
<100,000	3	593,281
Total	10,791	5,218,781

Source: Gallant (2001: 86).

Greece. In 1879, Karytaina contained a population of 56,017 people residing in 140 settlements (Map 4). As a glance at the distribution map indicates, the region was blanketed by a dense network of villages, 93 per cent of which were occupied by fewer than 1,000 people and fully 80 per cent contained fewer than 500 inhabitants. Assuming that the average household contained five people, then the overwhelming majority of inhabitants lived in villages of 100 or fewer families. Indeed, almost 10 per cent of the settlements were hamlets in which fewer than ten families lived.

The farther back in time we go, the more pronounced the pattern becomes. In 1829, according to the census conducted by the French expedition to the Peloponnesos, the region contained 34,223 people residing in 127 villages with an average size of 269 people per village. Twelve of the villages held less than fifty people, and a sizeable number of hamlets were occupied by only one or two families. Going back to the Venetian census of 1700, it appears that Karytaina was occupied by only 11,773 people who lived in villages with an average population of ninety-seven, and almost one-half of them were inhabited by fewer than fifty people. In sum, accepting that the settlement history of Karytaina was fairly typical of the rest of mainland Greece, then it would seem that for most of its history, Greece has been a land of villages, and often very small villages and hamlets. As a consequence of this, the physical and social environment that shaped peoples' lives was that of the small face-to-face community.

It is impossible to describe *the* typical Greek village. Village design varied from region to region and from place to place within regions depending on a variety of localized factors. The same can be said for house design as well. In addition to the purely physical factors, there were social ones as well, especially wealth, that influenced village and house construction. We can, however, posit some generalizations regarding the common factors that influenced the physical layout of villages.

First, given that so much of the Greek landscape is hilly or mountainous and that arable land was at such a premium, villages tended to be built on hillsides and slopes rather than on farm land. Second, because of the very hot, dry summers, villages were sited with an eye to water sources. Some other recurring features were the presence of a church and an open space or square around which the village's houses would be clustered. Regarding house design, the fact that these were functioning farms also created some recurring features such as storage facilities, spaces for penning animals and areas reserved for food preparation.

Text-box 16 reproduces a lengthy description of a village and its houses of the poorest class in rural Greece, that of dependent sharecroppers (see below pp. 137–9), and it vividly captures the nature of one type of rural settlement. This description captures well the simplicity and rudeness of

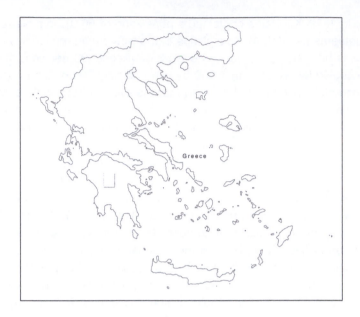

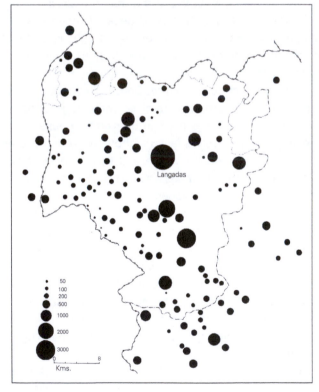

MAP 4 *The settlement system of Langadas, Achaia.*

Text-box 16 A peasant house (1892)

Let us look more closely at a village of the first category [sharecroppers]. I will take one with which I am tolerably familiar, Achmetaga, in the island of Euboea, as typical of a village occupied by Metayers, and it will serve for a model of any other such village in Attica and central Greece. The houses grouped round the little church are all one-storied oblong cabins built of stone, which is almost everywhere ready to hand, from thirty to thirty-six feet in length by about twenty-four feet in width. Two-thirds of this area is devoted to the dwelling part, while the other third is reserved for the stabling of the beasts in winter; and there is seldom any partition wall to screen it, for the peasant likes to keep them in sight. ... The family live in common – men, women, and children together, often, indeed, several generations of them – in the habitable end, which has a dried-clay flooring or, in some cases, a wooden planking raised a foot or two above the ground. The fire, on a hearth of stone, is against the wall in the more recent and better-built cottages, which boast of a chimney, though in many villages it is still in the middle of the room, the smoke escaping as best it may through the holes in the roof. Furniture there is generally none, unless it be a rude cupboard, or a wooden chest, or, perhaps, a few shelves to hold their simple cooking utensils. In one corner is a stack of rugs, mattresses and cushions. These laid upon the ground form their beds at night. The mattresses, stuffed with maize husks, are covered with a rough carpet material, which the women weave, and so are the square cushions, which serve as seats by day when the simple meal is spread upon the ground. Sometimes there is a table, but not often, in the genuine peasant's huts. ... Strings of onions and bunches of golden maize hang from the rafters, and a large earthenware water-cooler, with a number of smaller red jars and bowls of classic pattern, make up the humble equipment of the cottage. No house is complete without its ikon, generally a picture of the Panaghia or Virgin, but occasionally representing the saint whose name the householder bears, or in whose especial protection family tradition has confidence. Sometimes a little rude shrine is built up round the picture, and in front of it is always a lamp, which many families keep burning night and day, often stinting themselves of oil to keep the saint supplied. Outside the door is the oven, a beehive-shaped structure of clay, which is heated well-nigh red-hot with wood, after which the fire is raked out, and the dough wrapped round with leaves is introduced for baking. There are also generally without supporting posts for a primitive loom. Sometimes the loom is arranged with cross-bars between two young trees, behind which the lower hind-posts are driven into the ground, so that the weaver sits in the shade of the trees at work, or else a little thatch is built to shelter her from the sun, for the houses are only occupied at night or during bad weather, and village life is entirely in the open air.

Rennel Rodd (1892), *The Customs and Lore of Modern Greece*, London: D. Stott, 56–7.

the houses and villages of the poorest stratum of Greek society. But it also conveys some very important insights into the multifaceted functions that the house served.

Slightly more elaborate than the crude village and the simple one-storey stone or mud hovels of the sharecroppers were the larger and more elaborate villages and houses found among freeholding peasants. Whether in the mountains or on the plains, villages of peasants who owned their own land tended to be more elaborate and their houses were usually larger and more complex than those of sharecroppers. In mountainous or hilly regions, the houses were well built of stone masonry, usually two or more storeys in height, and the space within them tended to be divided into separate activity zones, often based on gender. The ground floor was reserved for keeping animals and storing equipment; the first floor was the primary dwelling space for the family; and the second storey usually contained more storage space and the sleeping quarters. In some regions, this basic form was augmented by a stone tower or some other similar type of defensive structure and it usually incorporated a walled-off courtyard. Houses tended to be inward looking, and through their design they demarcated sharply between domestic and public space. The house provided the family with protection from the outside world, but it also articulated them to it.

Figure 9 depicts the interior of a typical peasant house in the Argolid in the 1870s. The type of house depicted here is called a 'long house.' In addition to providing us with information about things like gender roles, the drawing can also tell us a great deal about material culture and the domestic space. The first thing to note is that the main residential area was a relatively large undifferentiated space. The houses were not divided into separate rooms, but, instead, all inside activities took place in a single area. During the course of a day, then, the same space served as the dining room, as in Figure 9; a workshop, especially for women's work; and as the bedroom. That this was a multi-activity space is reflected by the lack of furniture. Conspicuously absent are storage cupboards, tables, chairs and even beds. The furniture that is present is portable and can be removed quickly. So, the communal dining table consists of a large, round metal plate that rests on a short wooden base. The family sat around it on the floor, making it easy to convert the

FIGURE 9 *Interior of a typical peasant house (1877). This drawing by the* Illustrated London News' *'roving correspondent' depicts the interior of a peasant house in the Argolid. In addition to suggesting the rustic construction of the typical house, it also conveys a vivid sense of the importance of gender in rural Greece.*

Illustrated London News, *28 February 1877. GallantGraphics all rights reserved.*

area into the bedroom when the meal was finished. The tray and its base would be stored, probably hung on the wall, and then sacks filled with straw would be laid on the floor and covered with woollen blankets. The family slept together in this communal area, along with some of their livestock. Domestic goods that needed to be stored were hung on the wall, from the rafters, or placed on shelves. The residential area was heated either with a fireplace, as shown in Figure 9, or with a portable brazier. Dark, smoke-filled and redolent with a variety of scents and smells, this type of house was at the centre of Greek life.

Farming the land

Greece was a land of farmers, and so in order to understand their society, we need to examine the agrarian systems that both shaped their lives and formed the backbone of the national economy. An agrarian system consists of a number of related elements, the most important of which are land tenure and ownership, technology, labour arrangements and production aims.

Scholars of the rural economy during the nineteenth century have tended to focus on only one type of agrarian system and then to assume that it aptly characterized the entirety of the Greek countryside. Some, for example, have reconstructed a rural past dominated by small, independent peasant proprietors who used a primitive technology not much different from the one described by the poet Hesiod in the eighth century BCE to produce the bare subsistence needed to feed their family. For scholars of this persuasion, the rural economy was 'pre-capitalist' and was responsible for the retardation of the Greek economy. Others accept the primacy of the small family farm, but they see it as having been capitalist and market orientated in its production goals. Some argue that the lot of the average peasant family was a grim one, marked by poverty, poor yields, debt and low wages for the relatively little paid work that was available. Others paint a rosier picture of family farming; in their view, most peasants were relatively well off. They argue that land was readily available, that rural wages were high and that social mobility was a desired and attainable goal.

Historians on both sides agree that Greece was different from other European countries, especially Spain and Italy, in not having a landed aristocracy that controlled vast tracts of land and in not having to contend with the onerous legacy of feudalism. In fact, some pretty much dismiss the plantation form of agriculture as irrelevant to the Greek case, allowing only for a couple of notable exceptions like Thessaly.

While the debates make for interesting reading, they are largely misdirected because in each case the participants have a propensity for portraying the agricultural landscape of Greece as monolithic, whereas it was anything but uniform. Aspects of all of the scenarios are correct, but what needs to be appreciated is that there were a number of agrarian systems in operation simultaneously and that the fortunes of those operating within any one of them varied tremendously on a case by case basis. We can identify, I suggest, three primary agricultural systems, and within each also, there were a number of variations.

The first type of farm was the single-family peasant household estate. In its general characteristics, it resembled peasant farming from anywhere else in Europe and is the archetype that commentators from modern anthropologists to nineteenth-century travellers and politicians have focused on.

The salient features of the peasant agrarian system are the following: First, the labour force was drawn only from the household members. The adult head of the household provided the primary source of labour; as his sons got older they would assist him in the fields until such time as they left the paternal estate to start their own household or moved abroad. Female members of the household would assist in the fields on a seasonal basis, to help with the harvest or with weeding – the latter back-breaking task was especially considered to be 'woman's work.' Second, the production aim of the farm was first and foremost to meet the subsistence needs of the household. In practice, this meant that farmers would cultivate small amounts of numerous crops. So, each farmer would cultivate a few olive trees, some plots of wheat and barley, maize and legumes, a scattering of fruit trees and a couple of plots of vines. The family's land holdings would be fragmented into numerous small plots scattered across the landscape. This practice reflected the family's strategy of risk minimization; because by scattering their crops across a range of micro-environments, they reduced the risk that a single natural trauma would destroy all of their crops.

The technology and tools required by such a farm were rudimentary, and most of them would have been simple wooden hand tools. The high labour intensity and the relatively modest productivity of this technology was more than balanced by its suitability to the terrain and soils of Greece, and the production goals of the peasant farm. The peasant household would also have possessed some livestock. There would be the mandatory donkey, a few sheep and goats for milk, cheese, wool, hides and meat, and, if the family was sufficiently wealthy, a team of plough oxen.

Though subsistence may have been its primary production goal, no household could get by without some connection to the market. There was, for example, a range of goods that the family could not produce on its own – salt, tea, coffee, gunpowder (if the man of the house could have afforded to acquire a firearm) and metal for tools – and so the family had to purchase them from the local market town or from the itinerant merchants who traversed the countryside.

There were agencies like the Church and the State that made claims on the household's resources and which often required their payment in cash. Finally, there was the family's need to provide the wherewithal for dowries for its daughters, to underwrite the costs of weddings and funerals and to cope with all those unexpected expenses that arise during the lifespan of any family.

Consequently, all peasant households had to devise strategies for generating some cash income. For many, it was the production of a cash crop: in some areas, this was the currant grape, in others it was tobacco or cotton; most farmers also tried to produce a surplus of consumables like olive oil or wheat (substituting maize for the dietary needs of the family) that they could sell in local towns. Greek peasant farms, then, were neither anti-market nor fully commercialized. Instead, their goal was as far as possible to meet their basic needs and to get ahead as much as they could, and as long as by doing so they did not place the family's future at risk.

The type of farm we have discussed so far was the ideal. And there were, of course, many families that achieved that ideal. But the vagaries of fortunes over time meant that many families failed to meet the ideal, while others exceeded it. One key in determining which of the two it would be was land. As we saw in Chapter 3, the land donation scheme enacted under King Otto was fraught with difficulties and susceptible to corruption, and produced a stark disparity between a relatively small number of sizeable estates and a much larger number of peasant minifundia. A second major redistribution of national lands began after the passing of legislation in 1871, and then of additional laws that endeavoured to clarify the complex, not to say Byzantine, land tenure arrangements that had developed in the countryside over the ages.

The aim of this legislation was to secure firm legal ownership of the land for as many families as possible. It was estimated that over 50,000 families occupied and cultivated land to which they did not have verifiable legal title. This placed them in a very vulnerable position vis-à-vis creditors; it made them less likely to make long-term investment in the productivity of the land; it also meant that they had to pay the state a burdensome usufruct tax in addition to the other mandated exactions. Giving them legal title to the land, it was hoped, would solve all of these problems. But the main emphasis of the 1871 laws was to provide land to the landless and to allow those who owned only a small amount of land to expand their holdings. Learning from the mistake of the earlier scheme, peasants did not purchase the land parcels through auctions, in which the prices could rise outside of the range that they could pay, and, instead, government assessors set the prices.

Though approved in 1871, the land redistribution programme was implemented over a period of time and most intensively during the early 1880s. Eventually, the scheme proved largely successful in creating new peasant farms. But some of the old problems persisted. Corruption by assessors led to a maldistribution in some areas. Even where the system worked fairly well, this second round of land distribution still left thousands of households in possession of land holdings insufficient to meet their basic needs. The great interannual variability of crop yields in Greece meant that even farms that could sustain a family during a good year soon fell prey to debt and all that went with it after any one of numerous bad years. The consequences of the continuing small size of the average peasant holding and its continued vulnerability to debt were first the persistence of what agricultural economists refer to as 'pluriactivity', meaning that household members needed to undertake economic activities like seasonal wage labour or they were compelled to cede part of the produce of their land to creditors, which effectively turned them into sharecroppers on their own land.

In sum, while the family farm was the predominant unit of agricultural production, there was a great range of variability within the peasant agrarian system. Some households were able to take advantage of the opportunities that arose and became wealthier, while many others fell into a cycle of debt and dependency that left them destitute. Moreover, the continually increasing size of the rural population that we discussed earlier served only to exacerbate the fragility of many families' situations.

The second category of agricultural production, tenant farming and sharecropping, was in some ways related to the tenuousness of the peasant agrarian system. There were three predominant varieties of sharecropping in Greece during the nineteenth century. Two were inherited from older arrangements that had existed for years in regions that were added to the kingdom later in the century, the Ionian Islands and Thessaly, and the third developed in Central Greece and the Peloponnesos after independence.

The Ionian Islands had been possessions of the Venetian Empire for centuries, and during that time a system of feudalism had been introduced. In the northern islands of Corfu and Lefkas, the emphasis had been on the production of olives, while on the more southerly islands of Kefalonia and Zakinthos, the preferred crop was the currant grape, but on all of them, the organization of production was roughly the same. In exchange for their support of the regime, noble Ionian families had been given title to feudal estates by the Venetians, including not just the land but the people on it as well.

What was entailed under this feudal system was that peasant proprietors were given the right to work specified parcels of land in perpetuity under the following arrangement: One-fifth of the land was given to the tenants as *emphyteusis* land that they were free to cultivate, and whatever they grew was theirs to keep. The tenant was required to cultivate the remainder of the land with crops mandated by the landlord, and the harvest was divided in one of the two ways. If the landlord supplied everything (equipment, tools, seeds, cuttings, etc.) but labour, then the split was two-thirds to the owner and one-third to the tenant. If the peasant supplied all of the materials needed to produce the crop, then the split was fifty-fifty. The tenants were also required to sell their share of the currant crop to their lord, and they had to have their grain and olives ground at mills controlled by him for an additional payment of 10 per cent of the crop.

Under the period of British rule from 1815 to 1864, a new wrinkle was introduced whereby annual contracts were issued specifying which of the above arrangements would obtain and what the exact division of the estate's production would be. The tenants who enjoyed feudal tenure kept possession of the land in perpetuity. So, for example, in the dowry contracts that Ionian Island aristocrats drew up for their daughters, it was clearly specified that they and their new husbands would not take over occupancy of land but only the share owed by the peasant family. When Greece took possession of the islands in 1864, it inherited the feudal regime. But not for long: after a series of tumultuous rural revolts, feudalism was abolished, but the remnants of the sharecropping system remained in place.

A not dissimilar situation occurred when Greece obtained Thessaly in 1881. In this case, wealthy Greeks, often from the diaspora, purchased the çiftlik estates from the departing Ottoman owners. Depending on the status of the land under Ottoman law, the land was either held in freehold or the new owner enjoyed a form of feudal right. In this case, the owner was required to contribute nothing to the production process, yet was awarded one-third of the total production from the land.

In Boiotia, Evvoia and the Peloponnesos, the nature of the sharecropping system depended on whether the tenants willingly took up occupancy on the landlord's land or whether they had fallen into debt. In the former case, the tenant enjoyed access to a house (subject to the payment of one bushel of grain as rent) and a garden, and the family supplied all of the seeds, equipment and labour in exchange for a two-thirds share. In cases where a debt was involved, creditors would take over legal possession of the farm but would leave the owners on their land. They would then provide the seeds or other supplies needed to produce a crop and in exchange for doing so, they would take the produce equivalent to their investment plus 15 per cent of the remainder. Sharecropping was a despised practice. As we saw earlier, villages of sharecroppers tended to be the poorest and meanest in the land. But for many driven by debt or their inability to acquire land in any other way, it was a necessary evil. Given the increasing size of the rural population and the increasing pressure on the land, it was young men and women from sharecropping families who were often the first to seek alternative work off the farm, migrating either to the cities or abroad.

The plantation of Sotirios Sotiropoulos exemplifies the last category of agricultural enterprise we find in nineteenth-century Greece. Sotiropoulos came from a wealthy family and was very active in national politics, holding various ministerial portfolios during his career. He owned an estate in Messenia that consisted initially of 15 hectares, 12 of which were planted with currant vines; in 1861 he acquired an additional 9 hectares by a combination of purchase and debt foreclosure. On his plantation were also 250 mulberry trees for the production of silk, 40 pear trees and three vegetable gardens. He grew wine grapes on another one-hectare plot and had set aside half a hectare as a drying ground for his currants. On another part of the grounds he had built a villa where his family resided during the summer months. Sotiropoulos was an absentee landlord. In comparison to the latifundia of Sicily or southern Spain, this was a small plantation; nonetheless, within a Balkan context, it was a sizeable estate, worked by hired workers.

Sotiropoulos employed an overseer who along with his family lived on the estate year round. The latter was permitted to grow food crops in the gardens, was provided with a house and was paid a monthly wage. Two unmarried hired workers also lived on the estate with the overseer and his family. The job of the three men was to tend the vines and the other tree crops throughout the year and keep up the villa. A gang of fifteen workers was hired for a two-week period during the spring to assist with the job of hoeing the vineyards, and a group of thirty or more was employed in July or August to harvest the grapes. Plantation owners often also hired small gangs of armed guards to protect their field during the summer months. This was explicitly a commercial farm, the aim of which was the production of cash crops for an international market. It provided a nice complement to the peasant sector of the economy by providing a source of wage labour and a cash income. Smallholders, like those we discussed earlier, could supplement the income from their minifundia or obtain cash for dowries by working on commercial estates like this one. This type of plantation was found in the northern and western Peloponnesos, the Ionian Islands and, after 1871, in parts of Boiotia and Thessaly.

The other Greeks: shepherds, sailors and artisans

Historians are fond of reproducing the following passage from the memoir of the old warlord Theodoros Kolokotronis as an accurate assessment of the isolation in which most Greek peasants lived: 'There were men [in the villages] who did not know of a village more than one hour distant from their own. They thought of Zakinthos [the southernmost Ionian Island] as we now speak of the most distant parts of the world. America appears to us as Zakinthos appeared to them: They said it was in France.'[2] The impression sentiments like these created was that rural men and women were born, lived and died without ever transcending the narrow confines of their village and its surrounding fields. The reality was that the Greek countryside was alive with movement.

When anthropologists began writing about the remote villages they had studied during the 1950s and 1960s, they either implicitly or explicitly reproduced this assessment. The view of the Greek village as isolated in space and frozen in time has thus had a long history. But, at best, it is misleading and, at worst, inaccurate. For one thing, as we have already seen, villages were enmeshed in very extensive networks of settlements that spread over fairly wide regions.

There were frequent and regular movements of men and women between villages for *Panigyri* (festivals) and weddings, for commerce and marketing, and for the mundane aspects of social life like visiting relatives, helping kinsmen and finding spouses. Furthermore, each region had one or more towns or large villages that connected the various villages and hamlets together by providing markets for goods like coffee, tea, salt, gunpowder and the few other items that peasant households could not produce for themselves, and that served as administrative centres, including the courts. In addition to this fairly constant movement of people on a regional level, there were numerous occupations and sources of livelihood that required people to move about regularly and often.

We saw in the last section that many peasant households could not be sustained by the production from their farms. This meant that they had to seek ways to augment their household incomes. In some cases, groups of male kinsmen – brothers, fathers and cousins – and in others, entire families would make a circuit around the Peloponnesos or central Greece working as seasonal wage labourers harvesting grain or picking grapes. In some regions, especially those involved in the production of currant grapes, peasants would move on a seasonal basis between the village where they lived most of the year, usually in an upland area, down to the coastal zone where they had acquired vineyards.

Another strategy for generating an extra-household income was for men to acquire craftsmen's skills as smiths, knife sharpeners, carpenters and masons. They would then traverse the countryside offering their skills in small villages and hamlets that were incapable of supporting a full-time artisan on their own. In some villages, usually ones located in particularly inhospitable areas, almost all of the men in the village would become specialized craftsmen. Such was the case with a number of settlements in Arkadia, which produced some of the finest masons in the Balkans, and whose handiwork is still on display in many of Athens' nineteenth-century public buildings. Becoming an itinerant merchant was another way to make ends meet that required men, and sometimes their families, to take to the road periodically.

Adding further complexity to the myriad of movement across the countryside were those groups whose livelihoods kept them much more constantly on the move. Two in particular stand out. The first one was the transhumant shepherds. There were certain ethnic groups, like the Sarakatsanoi, who specialized in large-scale animal husbandry. Twice a year, they would undertake a relatively long-range movement of their flocks, moving from the lowland and coastal plains where they spent the winters to the upland pastures for the summers. In addition, while situated in their seasonal camps, they would be constantly moving their animals around the locale to take advantage of the available food supply.[3]

The other group consisted of caravanners. Some Vlachs, for example, made a living out of transporting goods over land on donkeys. Given that through most of the Balkans, the road networks were poorly developed and that railroads did not come to play an important role until much later on, the easiest way to move goods long distances over land was on the backs of beasts of burden. This form of transportation was even more important in moving goods between lowland ports like Patras, Missolongi, Arta and Nafplion, to upland towns and between upland towns as well. Finally, in terms of livelihoods that required mobility, each year thousands of men answered the siren song of the sea and flocked to the ports to join the merchant marine.

Lastly, from the 1870s onwards, there was a massive exodus of young men and women from the countryside to Athens, Piraeus and other cities, and from the 1890s on to the United States as well. Those who migrated to the cities often traversed back to their natal village and this added another source of mobility of people across the landscape.

In sum, the image of the nineteenth-century Greek villagers as ensconced in their little villages, isolated from and ignorant of the wider world, is grossly inaccurate. No village was an island unto itself. The Greek countryside was a fairly dynamic place characterized by a relatively constant movement of people across it and periodically punctuated by the larger-scale arrival and departure of work gangs, itinerant merchants and artisans, donkey caravans, shepherds with their families, and flocks, and of course, the dreaded bandit gangs, which continued to be a menace to society until late in the century.

The social world of men and women

So far we have examined the key structures of Greek society – household forms, family organization, means of livelihood and the like. It is now time to move beyond the purely structural and try as best we can to reconstruct the experiential. How did men and women during the nineteenth century think, act and behave in their daily lives? What cultural factors shaped their interactions with one another? What social ideologies underpinned their ideas about what it meant to be a man or a woman in Greek society at that time? In endeavouring to answer these questions, the deficiencies of the historical sources become all too obvious.

The contemporary nineteenth-century accounts of 'traditional' society by Greek urban folklorists contain many fascinating details, but their utility is limited by the political agenda of the scholars and their class bias. The vivid descriptions left to us by foreign travellers can be very useful, but they too have severe limitations. One of the most important was that foreigners frequently lacked any local knowledge – from language to customs – and so their view was shaped by their past experience of rural folk in their homeland. Another was that their perspective about modern Greeks was almost invariably shaped by the foreigners' studies of ancient Greece, and this meant that they were almost always disappointed when the reality of village life failed to match their image of Classical Athens. Finally, the brevity of their stay in one place meant that they never developed a rapport with the local people that would have enabled them to probe beyond their superficial exposure to Greek society.

It is on the topic of rural society, however, that the rich anthropological studies of rural Greece in the more recent past can be most valuable to us, provided that we are careful not to allow the past and the present to fold together and produce a picture of a seemingly unchanging rural society. One very important area in which there is meaningful continuity from the past to the present is the role of gender in shaping the social world. I begin with the world of men.

At the core of nineteenth-century notions of masculinity was the concept of *timi*. This term is usually translated as 'honour.' Honour has become such a loaded term that we must employ it with care. A better way of conceptualizing timi is as reputation. A man of honour or timi was someone who was held in high esteem by his peers, by the other men in his community. And it appears that the attribute that more than any other provided the yardstick by which a man's reputation was measured was control. A man should demonstrate at all times a firm command over all of those things that mattered in the lives of Greek peasant men: land and property, animals and the people in his household. We should also add that he needed to demonstrate control over himself as well. Exercising control of resources defined his role as *nikokyris* (literally, lord of the household). He was to see to the material needs of those residing in his household. This included the mundane wherewithal of daily existence but also entailed ensuring that there would be enough goods to vouchsafe the future survival of his sons and daughters.

A man was to use every means at his disposal – deception, prevarication, intimidation and even violence – to defend the social standing, and enhance the material welfare, of his household. A popular metaphor at the time compared the plebeian household to the celestial order, with the head of the household playing the role of the Supreme Being. In carrying out his 'divine' duties, a man was to manifest complete control of everything in his spiti, and he was to ensure harmony within it as well. His reputation among his peers was based on their collective assessment of how well he lived up to this culturally inscribed set of expectations.

To be sure, the ideal of a man as absolute master of the domestic realm and of the household being as harmonious a realm as the celestial order was often far from reality. As in any society, conflicts between brothers and between fathers and sons were not uncommon occurrences, and the court records are replete with examples of litigation between members of the same household and even of homicidal violence in the house.

Take the case of a young man on the island of Lefkas in 1853 who went to his family's olive grove one evening and cleaved his father's head with an axe. At his trial, he broke down and confessed that he had slain his father because the *pater familias* was threatening to disinherit him if he went through with his plans to marry a girl of whom his father disapproved. The son hoped to strike before the father could visit the notary and change his will. The incident itself is not especially remarkable. Interfamily fights over land, dowries and inheritances were not uncommon. What is noteworthy here was the reaction to this heinous deed.

Before the killer met his fate at the end of a rope, he was forced to march through his village and then from his village to the town of Lefkas wearing a placard around his chest that branded him as a 'father killer'. While violence and conflict within the household did occur, it was socially reprehensible. Violence directed from the spiti outwards in defence of its interests, however, was not only acceptable, but even mandatory, if a man did not want to lose face.

A central element of nineteenth-century masculinity, then, was the ethos of vengeance. Most observers of Greece during the nineteenth century ascribed murder, banditry and feuding to the deep-seated ethos of vendetta or blood revenge. Moreover, the thirst for vengeance in the name of honour was, they believed, an inherent – almost indelible – trait of the Greek character, going back to the time of Homer. While essentially correct, by reducing violence to a single and base cause, nineteenth-century observers presented an oversimplified view of a far more complex reality. I suggest that instead of seeing vendetta, duelling and feuding as separate and distinct or as essentially interchangeable categories of masculine violence, we need to envisage them as closely related forms of ritualized violence undergirded by a common ethic, that of honour or reputation.

Nineteenth-century masculinity also dictated that if a man or his family were insulted or wronged in any way, he had to respond with aggression or risk seeing his reputation diminished. But the type and the amount of socially accepted violence differed depending upon the context. The knife duel, the vendetta homicide and the feud were integral components of masculine violence; they were hierarchically related, but each also manifested a very different set of rituals that shaped the nature of each form of violence. In other words, the vendetta was a form of ritualized violence that operated according to fairly strict rules of engagement and that was connected to other types of violent behaviour through a shared ethos, which I call the ethos of vendetta, and all of these were manifestations of self-help justice. Given the ubiquity of knives in Greek society (see Text-box 17), it is not surprising that one of

Text-box 17 Men and knives (1859)

Perhaps it will seem to many a very extraordinary thing that the people should be able to drive away robbers. But we must remember that almost every Greek is armed. You will see a little boy who has no means to buy bread, begging money in order to buy a knife. And often when he has not the means of procuring this, he steals one from a shop. This he wears in his zoni [waist sash]. In Athens, where the people cannot arm themselves [with firearms], almost everyone wears a large knife in his zoni, or in the cover of his legs; and they use this as the ancient Greeks did the maxaira, for other purposes than that of a weapon. Often, in a contention they draw their knife, and kill their enemies.

In Athens there are very few fountains, and on account of this, during the summer the people suffer much. At every fountain there are always more than fifty persons, with their barrels and jugs, wanting water. In those places they often fall out, one endeavouring to take it before another and a struggle ensuing, when the one draws his knife and kills the other.

J. N. Abbott (1859), *Sketches of Modern Athens*, London: A. M. Pigott, 50–2.

the most common forms of honour-related violence was the knife fight, the essence of which is captured in the following tale.

On a hot summer's eve in 1836, Tonia Theodoros was sitting in his small village's wine shop on the island of Corfu. Men had gathered, as was their wont, for a few glasses and some conversation. Theodoros and a co-villager named Mokastiriotis, to whom he was not related, got into an argument, the cause of which none of the five witnesses could remember. Suddenly, Theodoros called Mokastiriotis a fool and a braggart. Mokastiriotis loudly replied that he would rather be a fool than 'the lord of a house full of Magdalenes'. Theodoros erupted from his chair, drew his knife and demanded that Mokastiriotis stand and face him like a man. None of the other men in the room intervened as the knife-fighters traded parries and thrusts. Finally, Theodoros with a flick of his wrist delivered a telling blow that cut his victim from the tip of his chin to half way up his cheek. As blood flowed from his face, Mokastiriotis fell to his knees cursing his assailant. When asked by the presiding magistrate at the Police Magistrate's court in the town of Corfu why he had caused the fight, Theodoros sternly replied that no man would call his wife and daughters whores and get away with it. His reputation would not allow it. As a man, he would not stand for it.

Thousands of similar episodes took place all across Greece. Men engaged in ritualized knife duels in order to defend their reputation. Most frequently, the insult that inaugurated a duel was calling a man a cuckold or branding his wife as a *Magdaleni* (a word in Greek that could mean either an adulteress or a prostitute), which would, of course, make the man a cuckold. Calling into question a woman's sexual reputation cut so deeply in this culture because it struck at the heart of masculinity: a man's ability to control the most important element in his household – his wife's or his daughter's reproductive behaviour. A man who could not control that aspect of his domain was, in their view, no man at all.

When confronted with such an insult or any imputation that the women of his household were anything less than chaste, a man had either to rise to the challenge and fight, or be humiliated. This form of violence was socially sanctioned and accepted. Take the episode from 1852 involving a flower vendor in Athens who, while selling flowers at the parade grounds one Sunday afternoon, saw a man approaching his wife, and making advances to her. Grabbing his knife, he confronted the man and in the ensuing fight stabbed him through the heart.

Not only did the assembled crowd not intervene in the fight, but they also made no effort to stop the vendor and his wife from leaving, and some of the male onlookers even commended the man for the precision of the fatal stroke. Finally, by allowing two men to settle their dispute with a mano-a-mano duel served another function as well: it prevented disputes over honour between two men from expanding into violence that would involve all of their kinsmen.

Another consequence of the ethos of vengeance was the vendetta. In the world of Greek men during the nineteenth century, the shedding of the blood of another initiated a vendetta in which the family and the kin of the deceased were required to shed the blood of the killer or one of his kinsmen. The following case from Athens in the 1850s is not atypical.

An old man, a veteran of the War of Independence, learnt that his eldest son had been killed in a fight in a wine shop. Inquiries by him and his kinsmen convinced him that the fight in which his boy had died had not been fair. Blood vengeance was sworn. The old man waited for forty days during which time peacemakers, including the police, failed to broker a peaceful resolution. Meanwhile, throughout this period, the grieving man neither shaved his beard nor cut his hair. Come the forty-first day after the killing, and with his red blood boiling and his white hair grown longer, the old warrior took vengeance. He slid four flintlock pistols and two curved sabres into his silk sash, went to the house of his foe and slew every man in the place. He killed everyone so that the vendetta would not go any further. If he had not massacred them all, then the kinsmen of the deceased would have been bound by blood to exact vengeance on the old warrior or his kinsmen.

In theory, a feud would persist until the men on both sides, save one, were killed. Few did, though. Usually a form of arbitration would take place and one side would pay blood money to the other, and, not infrequently, the families would exchange marriage partners to seal the pact. The vendetta and the feud, even as the state authorities tried to stop them and the urban bourgeoisie denounced them, remained features of Greek society well into the twentieth century.

There was one other circumstance in which the community of men absolutely demanded blood: seduction and betrayal. The story is told about a young man from a village in the Peloponnesos who courted a young girl from a good family and betrayed her. The couple became betrothed and, as was often the case after a match had been formally made, they became intimate. On the eve of the wedding, the groom got cold feet and ran away. The bride's family swore revenge. They soon learnt that the absconding Lothario had joined the merchant navy. Since the code of honour demanded that the bride's brothers could not rest until they had caught up with the man and killed him, they set off in pursuit. Eventually, they tracked him to Portugal and on the Lisbon waterfront, they cut him to ribbons.

A well-known homicide from the island of Kefalonia gives us some sense of the degree to which this form of interpersonal violence was socially sanctioned. Two brothers from a 'good' (honourable) peasant family learnt that one of their sisters had become pregnant out of wedlock. They discovered, by means we can only imagine, that it was the son of the wealthy family in whose house she was a servant who had seduced her. To avenge the deflowering of their sister, on a balmy summer's eve the two brothers waited until the young man was home alone. They climbed on to the balcony that led to the upstairs dining room where the man was enjoying his evening repast, and they shot him repeatedly.

The more important element of the story is what occurred afterwards. Over twenty people – servants, gardeners and others attached to the estate who were working in and around the house – witnessed the killing, and yet, even under intense questioning by the police, not a single person would reveal the brothers' identity, and some even commented that the deceased had got what he deserved. It was very common for a wall of silence to descend on Greek villages when the police arrived to inquire about slayings that popular custom determined to be legitimate. And even if they were not, people believed that vengeance was the prerogative of family and kinsmen, and not the state.

From the foregoing stories, one gets the impression that violence was highly prevalent during the nineteenth century, and compared to most other areas of Europe at the time, it was. Yet, it was not violence so much as aggression that was crucial to honour. A related dimension to the code was that a man should act on his own to achieve his goals. To rely on others, to be dependent, was a sign of weakness, 'to be like a woman'. Yet, the reality, of course, was that such a situation was impossible. Wealth and class stratified

Greek society by the nineteenth century. Even within the hamlets and small villages, and certainly within the large ones, there were households that were larger and wealthier than the others.

So while men shared an ethical system that emphasized equality, their world was one rife with inequalities. How did they reconcile ideology and reality? One mechanism involved honour itself. As I mentioned earlier, a man's reputation was made or lost through the assessment of his peers, that is, those co-villagers and neighbours and kinsmen who subscribed to the same ethical system. This process determined the boundaries between those who were part of the group that mattered, Us, and those that did not, Them – the bourgeoisie, the landlords, the bureaucrats, etc. The ideology of equality pertained to those in the group.

Peasants coped with the reality of inequalities in a number of ways. One was to make useful outsiders insiders through the practice of fictive kinship, blood brotherhood and godparenthood, for example. Reliance on men who shared the same blood, even metaphorically, did not diminish a man's reputation. Finally, men formed strategic alliances with those from the higher strata of society in which they willingly adopted the subservient position in order to obtain material benefit and protection. These bonds between a client and his patron provided the weaker partner with an important insurance policy in the unsure environment of rural Greece. Because the dominant party came from a higher social class and because the client benefited from the arrangement, becoming a client did not diminish a man's stature among his peers. The key here was that the client obtained goods and services that increased his family's fortunes, and so it enhanced his reputation as a man who could take care of his own. Thus, there was often intense competition between peasant men to forge a bond with a powerful figure.

The social world of men, then, was marked by intense and often violent contests over goods, resources and reputations. We can now examine the social world of women.

Man is endowed with strength to meet life's challenges whereas a woman's strength is toward the tending and feeding of the child. Powerful is the man who takes risks; weak and cautious the woman. He is clever and has imposing and sweeping plans. She is a demon and loses herself in details.[4]

Thus did a late-nineteenth-century women's periodical summarize some of the differences between men and women. During the nineteenth century, the roles and prescribed behaviours of men and women were sharply defined, in theory at least. As examinations of gender roles in more recent times have suggested, there is often a gap between what the cultural rules mandated and how real people acted in their daily lives. This certainly seems to have held true in the past as well. Let us look first at the ideal.

In reconstructing women's roles in the past, the paucity of sources presents a formidable obstacle. Not only is there the usual problem of the thinness of the sources but also compounding it is the fact that the lion's share of them was penned by men. Nonetheless, using the information found in the travel literature, in the memoirs and commentaries by women, folksongs and folktales, and official documents combined with the ethnographic studies, we can get some sense of both the image and the reality of women's lives in the past, lives that revolved above all around the household. In many ways, a woman's life only began when she got married. Marriage signified not just her transformation from child to woman but it also marked the union between two households and between two sets of kinsmen. Weddings, then, were a huge affair, and Text-box 18 captures what it was like for a bride on the day of her marriage. Once a wife, a woman had to conform to roles society defined for her.

The first element that stands out was the spatial segregation of women from the outside world. The house was the domain of women, and especially if they were young and unmarried, they were not to leave it without good cause. Second, modesty and shame provided the moral framework that dictated women's comportment and the Virgin Mary (in Greek, the *Panayia*) was supposed to be her model. Third, the woman was to be the source of sustenance in the household; it was her job to prepare the food and to see to the material needs of her family. Fourth, she was also to be the source of spirituality; women were supposed to keep the family icons and attend church. All of these aspects emphasize the positive roles that woman played in society. But men believed there was a dark side as well. Women were believed to be closer to nature and to have the ability to perform magic and witchcraft. Since women lacked self-control, they were always at risk of falling to prey to their baser, sexual instincts. Hence the great concern among men about their wives' reputations. In short, women's roles in society were shaped by their domestic duties and their need to ensure that their reputations remained unsullied.

The reality of women's lives was more complex and varied greatly between classes. The daily lives of a peasant woman were dominated by domestic duties. Preparing her family's food, especially bread, took up a considerable portion of her day. Fetching water was also a very time-consuming task that was gendered as women's work. The care and nurture of children was obviously of importance as well. The women of the household were also to spin and weave the cloth consumed in the household and they were to produce the goods that constituted the trousseau the daughters of the house would include in their dowries. And while these activities were mainly

Text-box 18 A Peloponnesian bride (1847)

The solemnities of the wedding opened with the attiring of the bride and bridegroom, which was not commenced until all the party was assembled to witness it. Manolis's [the bride's father] house, like all others in the village, consisted of a single room, divided into two portions, the one raised above the other by a flight of wooden stairs. In the upper part was Xanthi [the bride], seated on the floor, surrounded by all the women of the village. The task that she had to perform throughout the day, according to the inviolate custom, was certainly no easy one, for it was considered absolutely necessary from the time she became a 'nymph', or bride, that she should literally enact the part of a statue, and allow herself to be dressed, married, kissed and congratulated, without so much as lifting her eyes from the ground, or moving a muscle of her continence. Two women were appointed to hold her by the arms, and lead her about as occasion required, while another held the corner of her veil, and stood ready to put her hair out of her eyes, or perform any other little offices that such an utter renunciation of personal independence might render necessary. The lively little woman had already entered on this arduous duty, and really seemed, with her classical dress, and cheeks somewhat more pale than usual, to have been transformed into some beautiful piece of sculpture. ... Perfectly motionless she sat, while all the old women – talking, laughing, screaming and quarrelling – crowded around her, arranging and rearranging the minutest details of her dress. Every single lock of her dark hair, carefully separated, was spread out on her shoulders, and interwoven with silken threads of a similar length, fell down past her knees; her forehead was bound with a string of silver coins, one of the hereditary possessions of the family, and when her little stocking-less feet had been thrust into the embroidered slippers, much resembling the sandals of old, the finishing touch to her toilette was given by the mother herself, who made her eyes seem preposterously large, by drawing a black line from beneath the eyelid to the temple, an operation to which the poor little bride submitted without winking, as she did everything else.

Anonymous (1847), 'Life in an Arcadian Village', *The Dublin University Magazine* (July–December): 24.

conducted within the house, there were a variety of activities that took them out into the world.

The labour needs of the peasant household, for example, invariably required women's participation (Figure 10). In large villages and in towns, unmarried women were often employed as domestic servants and perforce had to venture out in public. Lastly, there were a whole variety of female-dominated

FIGURE 10 *Women harvesters in Epiros (1930). This photograph by Nelly captures the complex realities of women's lives. Here we see a group of Epirote women assisting with the grain harvest while also engaged in child care. For women, much more so than for the men, there was not much distinction between domestic duties and farm labour.*

Nelly and the Photographic Archives of the Benaki Museum, with permission.

social gatherings that took place in public. Female seclusion then was an unrealizable ideal, except perhaps among the upper classes for whom women's labour was not vital. What was crucial was that women comported themselves in public in a way that conformed to cultural expectations and that the reason she was out in public needed to be related to one of her domestic roles.

Finally, women were supposed to be active defenders of their own and their family's reputations. There was an ethical code for women similar to men's honour and, like men, women engaged in contests over reputations. But whereas men often waged their combat with knives, women employed words. Gossip and slander were the weapons of choice and the stakes were high. If a woman did not contest malicious gossip about sexual comportment, the cleanliness of her house or her devotion to the church, her sons might have a harder time to find a good match, her daughters might require a much larger dowry to secure a husband or her spouse might find himself drawing the blade to defend her and his reputation.

In sum, the social world of the little communities of Greece in the past was shaped by the gendered roles of men and women. But in many ways, those roles served a common purpose – enhancing the material wealth and social reputation of the households that men and women made up together.

So far we have examined Greek culture largely in a village context, and given that throughout the nineteenth century, Greece was predominantly a society of rural dwellers, that is appropriate. But there was another important development during the long nineteenth century that had a profound impact on society, and that was urbanization. By 1920, a sizeable portion of the Greek population resided in Athens and its port city of Piraeus. This began a process that would end with the greater Athens being home to almost one-third of the country's population and lead to a situation in which one megalopolis effectively dominated the life of the nation.

Athens ascendant

From its foundation as the new capital in 1834, Athens was a peculiar city. Unlike many nineteenth-century cities – Manchester, Birmingham or Lyon, for example – it did not develop as an industrial centre that grew by attracting manufacturing and workers. Nor was it similar to cities like London, Paris or Madrid that enjoyed a long tradition of being national capitals. Indeed, in spite of its antiquity, modern Athens was literally a new city. Granted, during the period of Ottoman rule, Athens had served as a regional marketing and administrative centre, but it could by no stretch of imagination be considered a conurbation in any meaningful sense of the word. In addition, it had suffered greatly during the war of liberation, and was reduced to ruins at the contest's end.

Looking at the sprawling metropolis of over five million people today, it is hard to imagine that, but for the chance of fate, it could have remained a modest provincial city. This proposition seems even more outrageous given the prominent position that ancient Athens plays in the imagined identity of modern Greece. Nonetheless, the observation is accurate. As late as the middle of the nineteenth century, a caustic observer of the Greek scene, Edmond About, noted that if the capital of the kingdom was moved elsewhere, back to Nafplion or to Corinth, Athens would, in short, order become a ghost town of little consequence. Though cast in his usual hyperbolic fashion, About's point is a telling one. Athens became the premier city of Greece because it was selected to be the capital, and not the other way around. And this had a very profound impact on the way it developed as a city. Before examining the character of the new city's development, we must first get a picture of its demographic development.

Table 4 charts the growth of Athens and its port of Piraeus from 1821 to 1920. As we can see, on the eve of the revolution Athens was a modestly

TABLE 4 Population growth of Athens and Piraeus, 1821–1920

	Athens	Piraeus	Total
1821	7,000		7,000
1836	17,600	1,001	18,601
1840	18,535	2,033	20,568
1850	24,278	5,286	29,564
1860	41,298	6,452	47,750
1870	44,510	10,963	55,473
1880	84,903	24,883	109,786
1890	114,355	36,000	150,355
1900	123,001	50,200	173,201
1910	167,479	73,579	241,058
1920	292,991	133,482	426,473

sized provincial town. The population was roughly split between Muslims and Christians, and though it operated as a market town, many of its inhabitants were farmers. A few huts hugged the shore around the bay of Phaleron, but Piraeus, as we know it, did not even exist. Between the mid-1830s, when it was made the kingdom's capital, till mid-century, Athens grew from 17,600 to 24,278 inhabitants and Piraeus was established as the main port to service the new city. During this first phase of growth, Athens expanded through in-migration of wealthy Diaspora Greeks, office holders and the new clerical middle class, and those members of the lower social orders needed to provide services to them. In other words, the initial expansion of Athens disproportionately involved members of the middle and upper classes.

A second, and far more profound, period of urban expansions began during the 1860s and then took off during the 1870s and 1880s. Between 1870 and 1890, Athens and Piraeus grew by 271 per cent and manifested annual growth rates of an astonishingly high 5.17 per cent. Unlike the early phase of urban in-migration, this second growth spurt was fuelled by the movement of rural peasants and workers to the city in search of work. As we saw earlier in this chapter, the Greek rural population grew at a fairly consistent and high rate for much of the century, but economic growth did not keep pace, nor could the material conditions of the countryside provide for the increasing numbers. The pressure on land and the oversupply of labour created a rural pressure cooker that could only be relieved by a rural exodus. By the fin-de-siècle, Athens and Piraeus had become a large urban complex that was radically different in character than it had been even at mid-century. As it grew in size and complexity, so too did Athens change in character.

King Otto and the Bavarian Regents decided to make Athens the capital of the new kingdom because of its connection to the glories of classical antiquity – a connection that was openly visible in Athens more than in other cities like Nafplion and Argos. A series of architects were employed to draft blueprints for the construction of a city that would both pay homage to the past and reinforce the connection of Greece to the West. Neoclassical public buildings in marble, like the Royal Palace, the Royal Academy and the Parliament building, began to adorn the wide boulevards like Ermou Street and Panepistemiou Street. When the seat of government shifted to Athens in 1834, hundreds of people flooded the city in search of housing. One newspaper of the time bemoaned how old Athenian families, some even with pregnant women and infant children, were being turned out into the streets to make way for the rich and the powerful, for the bureaucrats, officeholders and government hangers-on.

Conforming to the grand vision set out in the various master plans, splendid townhouses adorned with neoclassical facades soon began to appear on the major streets and avenues around the new centres of power. As home to the cultured elite and as the centrepiece for the 'Westernization' of Greek society, Athens quickly became a very cosmopolitan city. The latest styles in clothes, for example, would soon find their way from the salons of Paris, London and Milan to the shops of Athens. On the city streets, then, one would see side by side living vestiges of the legacy of Ottoman rule along with self-consciously crafted displays of European-ness.

Alongside bourgeois Athens, another city developed. This other place was home to the lower classes of society. After all, the upper and middle classes could not get by alone. They needed servants and shopkeepers, haberdashers and hairdressers, carters and coachmen. Carpenters, masons and other construction workers were needed to meet the demands of contractors. Dockworkers and deliverymen were needed to shift the ever-increasing volume of goods that now began to appear at Piraeus. People, especially from the Cyclades, began moving to Athens to fill these roles. With the influx of migrants, land and housing prices in Athens soared. In addition, because this was to be a planned city, permits were required to build within the city limits. The high cost of accommodation and the tight restrictions on building new houses put lower-class people in a bind.

The story is told of an old woman who was standing in an Athenian street, staring at a plot of land with tearful eyes. In her hand she held a piece of paper. An elderly gentleman approached her and inquired what circumstance had driven her to such a state. She needed to build a house for her family, she replied, but she did not have the permission of Athens' planning board and did not expect to hear back from them for many months. And in the meantime, she bemoaned, they would have nowhere to live. Not to worry, the man replied, he knew the architect. He asked her to give him her petition and he would see what he could do. Within days she received her building permit. She was a lucky woman, indeed. Not many people could get King Ludwig of Bavaria, the father of their own King Otto, to intervene on their behalf.[5]

Most people who found themselves in that situation simply disregarded the law and built illegally, risking a confrontation with the authorities, or they built outside of the city limits and thus were not covered by the planning laws. Some threw together shacks to house their families. Others built multiple dwelling houses with an eye to renting one or more of them to newcomers at very steep rents. The housing difficulties rose to crisis levels during the 1870s and 1880s as tens of thousands of people poured into Athens and Piraeus. The central core of bourgeois and 'respectable' Athens became ringed with poorer neighbourhoods. Piraeus, in particular, developed as a working-class city because this was where the hard jobs of working the docks and of carting the goods were concentrated, and also because it was in and around Piraeus that industry began to develop.

As Athens and Piraeus grew in size and complexity, the usual 'social problems' that accompanied nineteenth-century urbanization developed. The rates of crime and violence, for example, soared. During the period of peak in-migration, the greater Athens area experienced one of the most profound increases in homicide ever recorded. For the years 1888–91, when the homicide indictment rates in cities like London, Paris, Berlin and Amsterdam were less than two killings for every 100,000 people, Athens recorded a rate of 107. The overwhelmingly young and male migrants to Athens and Piraeus brought with them the propensity to violence inculcated during their rural upbringing, except that circumstances in the city brought their violent tendencies more frequently to the fore.

Thrust together in a hostile environment, men from various regions of the country found themselves in new contentious situations. Absent, however, were many of the social control mechanisms that existed in the village – limited though they were. Kinsmen were not there to pull disputants apart; nor were there village elders who might prevent disputes from reaching violent ends – though as we saw above, they were often unsuccessful mediators. And in the struggle to create new social hierarchies, men became, I would suggest, hypersensitive to slights, real or imagined, to their honour. Thus, as we saw earlier, much of this violence took place in taverns and cafes. One episode reported in the newspaper *Avgi* epitomizes the new street violence. Two men were standing in line to get water at a pump. One cut in front of the other. They exchanged angry words. One pulled a razor and slit the other's throat.[6]

The numerous wars and irredentist conflicts waged by Greece during this period introduced another dimension: cheap firearms. The impression is that pistols came to account for the majority of homicides in this period.

Along with violence, other public order issues emerged. Street crimes like robbery and larceny became a constant problem in Athens. Beggary and vagabondage, and prostitution also became issues of social and political importance. Other social problems emerged as well. Infant abandonment, for example, became a grave concern, as did a whole variety of environmental issues like the need to supply water, build sewers, provide streetlights and pavements, and regulate traffic. One problem that contemporaries continually complained about was the horrendous amount of dust that basically enveloped the city at various points of the year. This was not surprising given that the roads were unpaved and the climate so dry. Text-box 19 presents a prominent Athenian's view on the dust of Athens, while Figure 11 shows us one of the responses to it: the ubiquity of bootblacks.

Text-box 19 Athenian dust (1905)

The wide, shapeless streets and the glare of the marble houses may not be so well suited as narrow lanes and Turkish buildings to the heat of summer; it might have been better if the plan of modern Athens had been made in Byzantium rather than in Germany. But, undoubtedly, it can boast of magnificent houses ... which no European capital would scorn to own. But there is no prospect without a cloud, and in the case of Athens, the cloud is of dust. The 'thin soil' of Attica has not grown deeper since the days of Thucydides, and the lack of water makes it impossible to cope with the myriad of fine particles, which penetrate into the most hidden recesses, and carry infectious germs hither and thither. In a high wind an Athenian Street resembles the desert during a sandstorm; in ordinary times, it is thought necessary to station small boys with brushes to flick the boots of the visitor as he enters a hotel. The ordinary Athenian has his boots cleaned many times a day; if he had only a penny in the world, he would spend half of it on having his shoes polished and the other half on a paper to read during the operation. Hence the vast army of [boot]blacks who form so marked a feature of Athenian life, and who are constantly knocking their boxes to attract the notice of the passerby. They are excellent little boys, extremely honest, industrious. ... They run errands, sell papers and lottery tickets, act as porters and make themselves generally useful.

W. Miller (1905), *Greek Life in Town and Country*, London: George Newnes, Limited, 184–5.

FIGURE 11 *Bootblacks in Athens. The massive influx of young men and women from the countryside to Athens during the last two decades of the nineteenth century could not be absorbed by the underdeveloped industrial economy of the time. Many men, and especially boys, found work in low-level service occupations, like shining shoes, as depicted here. The urban migration stream would soon flow out of the country to the United States.*

H. A. Franck (1929), I Discover Greece, *New York: The Century Co, photo facing 172. GallantGraphics all rights reserved.*

All of these issues required direct state intervention, and in responding to them, the power of the state over civil society and the capacity of the government to intervene in peoples' lives, often at the expense of civil liberties, expanded ominously.

Harilaos Trikoupis, as in so many areas of late-nineteenth-century Greece, led the reform movement. In each of his long administrations, for example, Trikoupis enacted reforms of the criminal justice system. With regard to the police, he initiated a variety of comprehensive reforms that helped to modernize the various forces. He appointed the ruthless Bairaktaris as chief of the Athens police and gave him sweeping powers to deal with urban crime. Bairaktaris doubled the number of policemen in Athens, increased their pay, and inaugurated more careful screening and training of recruits. Law 2509 of 21 July 1892 gave the Athens' chief of police the power to use regular army troops to patrol the city, and Bairaktaris employed this tool vigorously. Trikoupis also suspended *habeas corpus* on two occasions and allowed known offenders and 'shiftless young men' to be rounded up, detained without trial and exiled to deserted or sparsely populated Aegean Islands – often for a considerable period of time. While helping to deal with the immediate problem of urban crime, these actions set dangerous precedents for the future. Trikoupis was just as active in other areas as well, passing laws regulating housing, sanitation and public welfare. He built new hospitals and orphanages and refurbished older ones. However, while these measures did help to alleviate some of the most pressing problems caused by rapid urbanization, many more remained unsolved.

Coming to America

Between 1890 and the 1920s, over half a million people, almost 90 per cent of them men between the ages of eighteen and thirty-five, left their homeland and migrated to almost every corner of the globe. Some crossed the Mediterranean and moved to Ethiopia, the Sudan, Tanganyika and South Africa; others gravitated to places where long-standing Greek communities existed like Britain and Russia; but the vast majority looked to both the northern and southern hemispheres of the New World, and above all the other places combined, they immigrated to the United States. During the decades around the turn of the century, more than 500,000 men moved to the United States. Many returned to Greece; others stayed and carved out a living, eventually bringing over a bride from their *patrida* (homeland).

Text-box 20 reproduces a lengthy account of why people emigrated to the United States. The factors driving the exodus are for the most part the same ones that caused the shift in population from the countryside to Athens. Relative rural over-population, a scarcity of labour and low wages made it simply impossible for households with more than one or two sons to make ends meet and to provide for the continuation of the family into the next generation by providing dowries and inheritances that could sustain new households. The collapse of the currant market in the 1890s, which pushed Greece into bankruptcy, as we saw in the last chapter, devastated the rural economy. Larger estates that employed thousands of wage labourers either went out of business or dramatically scaled back production, thus putting more people out of work. Sharecroppers who paid their rents in currants now found themselves defaulting on their payments, and many were evicted. Small private landholding peasants who grew currants as their cash crop with which to pay their taxes and to meet household expenses were devastated.

Text-box 20 Why we leave for America (1908)

There are few manufacturing plants and none of any great importance. ... Female and child labour are very generally utilized in Greece, whenever they can be made serviceable. ... There is not much hope for a labouring man to save money in Greece, where three to four drachmas a day are good wages and where seven drachmas are regarded as a high wage for a master workman. A labourer earning five drachmas per day will pay ten drachmas per month for a room for himself and his family. 'The workman's breakfast consists of bread and black coffee; his luncheon of a piece of bread, or if he can afford it, a piece of bread and some black olives, which he usually takes with him in a little round, covered box. Sometimes he buys a half cent's worth of inferior grapes, or a tomato. Thus his lunch would cost, say, six cents for bread and two cents for olives.' At night the family dines on a few cents' worth of rice, boiled together with wild greens and olive oil, and bread, or wild greens boiled in olive oil and eaten with bread, or some similar inexpensive dish. ... Meat is eaten by the labouring classes as a general thing three times a year: Christmas, Easter and on the so-called 'Birth of the Virgin,' which the church has set down for the month of August. Such a family as I am describing, the average labouring man's family of Greece, rarely if ever see such things as butter, eggs and milk. There are 180 fasting days in the Greek religious year, which are rigorously observed by the labouring class, without, however, causing any marked degree of abnegation in the matter of diet. People living under conditions of this sort are ripe for emigration, especially if, like the Greeks, they are of a stock that has always displayed great readiness in severing home ties. All that is needed to start an enormous exodus is some immediate stimulus, some slight turn in the condition of affairs, provided that a favourable outlet presents itself, and the process of migration is not too expensive or difficult. As an American gentleman of long residence in Athens remarked, 'The wonder is not that the Greeks are now emigrating to America in such numbers, but that they did not begin long ago'.

H. P. Fairchild (1911), *Greek Immigration to the United States*, New Haven: Yale University Press, 72–3; the internal quotes refer to material that Fairchild cited from a report by the US Consul to Greece, George Horton, 'Report on Industrial Conditions in 1908'.

A new wave of men and women were driven out of the countryside looking for work. The slow pace of industrialization meant that there were not sufficient jobs in the cities to absorb the rural refugees. In addition, as the passage cited above suggests, many of those who had been part of the migration flow to Athens and Piraeus during the 1870s and 1880s and who found jobs and established families suffered as well during the depression of the 1890s. Some determined to stay and fight for better conditions by joining the labour movement or one of the emerging left-wing political parties. Others chose to seek a better life in America.

Three different migration flows brought people from Greece to the United States. The largest one consisted of men and a few women who had either already lived in the cities for some time or had recently arrived there but could not make ends meet. According to the best available figures, over 63 per cent of the immigrants to the States were either unskilled workers or servants. Another stream swept up people who moved abroad directly from the countryside. Included in this group would be those 16 per cent who considered themselves to be farmers and some of those who listed their occupation as labourers. There was a third and smaller group that consisted of merchants and skilled workers. Most of these folks moved from the city, and constituted the majority of those who moved as couples or as complete families.

The move abroad, or what in Greek is referred as *xenitia*, was financed in one of three ways. In some cases, men paid for their own passage with funds that they had been able to save or to borrow from kinsmen. In a large number of instances, agents called *padrones* would make an agreement with young men whereby the agent would provide them with passage to America and in return the men would be obligated to work for whomever the padrone contracted them out to. Obviously, this system was susceptible to corruption and abuse, and many Greek migrants recalled the horrors of the transatlantic crossing that were only compounded when they arrived in the United States to be shipped in cattle cars to the Western frontier to work laying railroad track or digging mines. The last mechanism for emigration consisted of chain migration. In these cases, one member of a family who had made the sojourn previously would send money back to Greece to pay the passage of a kinsman. In this way, more than one member of a kin group could move abroad without falling into the clutches of a padrone.

One last final group of migrants completed the creation of Greek America and it consisted of women, who were sent to the United States to marry. These women were called *nifes*, which is the Greek word for brides, but in this instance it referred to a special type of bride. Because the initial wave of migration was almost comprised mostly of, unmarried males, Greek men found themselves in a position of having to find mates. Some did marry American women, but the vast majority did not. The cultural divide and the intention of many migrants to return to their homeland debarred most of them from doing so. Instead, they relied on their family back home to make an arranged marriage for them. These women were often called 'postcard brides', because the only way that their intended spouses could recognize them at the immigration entry points to America was from the postcard picture of them that they had been sent. A wonderful, fictional depiction of the plight of the postcard brides is presented in the 2004 film *Nifes* by Pandelis Voulgaris. Not all Greek women were happy at the prospect of being forced from their home to travel halfway around the world to marry a man that they had never met. Text-box 21 reproduces a beautiful song by the famous **Rebetika** singer Rita Abatzi that captures the anguish and anxiety of the postcard bride. Comparing herself to a lamb about to be sacrificed, she bemoans her fate to be buried in a distant land with her broken heart.

The mass migration of the late nineteenth and early twentieth century had a profound impact on the development of Greek society. Could it be otherwise when a country loses almost 40 per cent of its adult male population? But the impact of the exodus had both positive and negative dimensions. The most important of the positive results was the massive amount of money injected into the Greek economy by remittances sent home by foreign emigrants.

It is estimated that on average Greeks sent home approximately $5,000,000 each year between 1903 and 1914. The huge outflow of people relieved the population pressure and underemployment in the countryside – perhaps too much so. Some large landowners found themselves having to bring in migrant farm workers from Albania to meet their labour needs. Wages in some industries also rose as companies competed for workers. The levels of interpersonal violence were reduced substantially as the most violence-prone sector of society had migrated to the United States, where they were equally violent.

Text-box 21 'Mother, Don't Send Me to America' (1936)

Mother, don't send me to America
I'll wither away and die there.
I don't want dollars, why don't you understand?
I want bread, onions and the one I love.
Mother, I love someone from our village,
He's a beautiful man and an only son.
He has kissed me down in the gully,
And hugged me under the willow tree.
My Giorgios, I'm leaving you and going far away.
They are sending me to get married in a foreign land.
Like a lamb to slaughter they are sending me,
And they will bury me with my broken heart.

Rita Abatzi

But there were numerous negative consequences. Factory owners and others replaced male workers with women or children, to whom they paid low wages. The demographic growth of the country slowed. The number of men in their prime who were eligible for service in the military fell. Large sections of the countryside went out of cultivation, and numerous small villages became deserted.

Many of the migrants would eventually return to their homeland, but from the turn of the century onwards, a new chapter in the long history of the Greek diaspora had been opened.

7

From a nation united to a nation divided, 1898–1919

No single figure casts as long a shadow over the history of Greece in the twentieth century as Eleftherios Venizelos. For a quarter of the century, he dominated the political life of the nation. He led Greece to some of its greatest accomplishments and was part of its most cataclysmic defeats. He came closest to fulfilling the Megali Idea, but was partly responsible for the dream coming to an end. He did more than anyone else to foster the social and economic development of Greece; but he also brought it to the brink of civil war. During his era, he was both the most loved and the most despised man in Greece.

In this chapter, we return to a more conventional narrative mode in order to tell the story of how Greece rebounded from the disasters that occurred at the end of the nineteenth century and then went on to score some of its greatest domestic and international successes a few short years after that, only to be plunged back into chaos by an event that is still referred to simply as the 'Catastrophe.' Since Venizelos played so prominent and important a role in the events that first united Greece and then divided it, our story centres first on the Cretan leader.

National malaise and Venizelos's rise to power

Eleftherios Venizelos was born in the village of Mournies near the city of Hania in the western part of the island of Crete in 1864. He was one of the six surviving children born to Kyriakos and Styliani Ploumidaki Venizelos. Eleftherios was born healthy and hardy, much to his parents' joy as three of their infants had died and their eldest son had become severely handicapped after contracting typhoid fever. Kyriakos was a store owner and a prominent member of respectable Cretan society. He was active in philanthropic and educational organizations in his community, and he was a strong supporter of Cretan unification with Greece. Nonetheless, as discontent at the so-far unfulfilled promises of the Ottoman reforms grew and, as a consequence, so did talk of rebellion, Kyriakos was among those who urged caution. In spite of his moderate stance, when the rebellion broke out in 1866, he feared that he would be among those blamed for it. Consequently, he packed up his family, including the then two-year-old Eleftherios and fled. The family eventually settled on the island of Syros where they remained until 1872. During his formative years growing up in the city of Hermoupolis, Eleftherios acquired a proper Greek national education as well as Greek citizenship. After a brief period back in Crete, in 1877 he left for Athens to continue his secondary education. It was really only after he entered university that he began to shine intellectually. His quick mind and even quicker tongue earned him a reputation as a brilliant but arrogant student. In spite of his father's wishes that he take over the family business, he opted to study law, and received his degree from the University of Athens in 1887. His law school days politicized him and gave him an opportunity to become acquainted with prominent scions of Greece's political class. Upon graduation, he returned to Hania and hung out his shingle. In addition to his career as a lawyer, he went on to become a journalist and a politician. Possessing an agile mind, a deep intellect and a charismatic personality, in the words of one of his biographers, 'he was alternately an audacious revolutionary and a thorough constitutionalist, liberal by education and principles but intolerant by temperament, a popular agitator and a sober statesmen, an outlaw and a prime minister.'[1]

We examined in Chapter 5 the story of the Cretan Question from 1832 onwards, and we saw that though the ultimate goal of some Orthodox Cretans (union with Greece) remained unfulfilled, their actions caused the European powers to pressure the Porte into granting greater autonomy to the island's Christian population. Given his natural aptitude and his ardent patriotism, not surprisingly, the young Venizelos quickly became a leading figure in the Cretan liberation movements. At approximately the same time that he returned to Crete, the Pact of Halepa (discussed earlier) was amended to allow for greater freedom of the press. When this promise remained empty, he penned a scathing editorial, liking the current policy to the Spanish Inquisition. This opinion piece earned him enemies in government but elevated his political stock. Thus, he entered politics in 1889 as an assemblyman in the short-lived Cretan assembly.

Between that date and the second Cretan revolution of 1896–7, Venizelos was very active writing articles and making fiery speeches in favour of unification. While the goal, the liberation of Crete and its union (*enosis*) with

Greece, was always clear, his views on the means for achieving it was not. He opted for a strategy of 'guns and negotiations' (*doufeki kai pazari*), though how these two were to be balanced and carried out was never really clear. His initial inclination was to be cautious and to avoid an outright confrontation with the Ottoman authorities; this position mirrored that of the Greek government of Prime Minister Harilaos Trikoupis, but it also put him at odds with many members of his own political faction. His credibility as a leader rose when the brief insurrection of 1890 was easily suppressed, thus proving him correct in his cautious approach. The outcome of the war of 1897, however, changed his mind.

The settlement between Greece and the Ottoman Empire in the aftermath of the April 1897 war seemingly granted major concessions to Greece regarding Crete, in spite of the fact that Greece had been soundly defeated. As we saw earlier, it had been the developments in Crete that had caused the war and so in the deliberations that ended it, the great powers sought to resolve the Cretan Question once and for all. The Treaty of Constantinople was signed by the Kingdom of Greece and the Ottoman Empire on 4 December 1897. Among other things, it modified the status of Crete within the Ottoman Empire. It would still be under Ottoman sovereignty, but it would be governed as an autonomous province under the rule of a high commissioner selected by the great powers. The treaty also allowed for local participation in government by establishing a Cretan assembly composed of 138 Christians and 50 Muslims. To keep the peace, the accord created a locally devised and operated judicial and criminal justice system, also calling for the deployment of a multinational military contingent. European powers selected King George I's son and namesake, Prince George, as the High Commissioner, a choice that the Porte objected to but could do nothing about. Crete had achieved quasi-independence and was governed by three political entities: the office of the High Commissioner, the Consuls of the Great Powers and the Cretan Assembly representing the various indigenous political parties. Venizelos emerged as the leader of the Cretan liberal faction. He helped to draft the constitution and became the first Minister of Justice, and by all accounts, he did a tremendous job in that capacity. More broadly, however, in spite of the concessions made to the islanders, their ardent desire for unification was not dampened. If anything, the bestowal of autonomy and the appointment of a member of the Greek royal family only stoked the fires of nationalism and elevated the Cretans' hopes that unification was imminent.

Many Cretans found Prince George high-handed and overbearing, and even though he was an advocate for unification, they believed that he was not doing all he could to push the process forward. The reality was that the great powers had no intention of altering the status quo on the island. After a series of confrontations with the High Commissioner, Venizelos resigned from the government and in 1905, at the head of a small band of armed followers, he raised the banner of revolt. From his mountain stronghold at Therisso, he declared unification of Crete with the Kingdom of Greece. A few days later, the Cretan assembly followed suit and demanded that Prince George bring the issue before the representatives of the European powers. George was caught in a dilemma. He knew that it was futile to press the powers, but he would lose the support of the moderates if he did not pursue the matter. He also realized that Venizelos's actions directly challenged his authority, but he was loath to order the Greek gendarmerie to fire on other Greeks. Finally, the great powers intervened and Venizelos was forced to capitulate, but he did so on terms that were fairly favourable to his position and which had not been cleared with Prince George. The settlement made it obvious to all that Cretan unification was only a matter of time.

The results of this episode were long lasting and important. First, the Prince had lost face and his position on the island became untenable. Accordingly, he resigned. Thus began a lifelong antipathy between the royal family and Venizelos. Second, the Cretan leader emerged as a national hero in the wider Greek world. 'As a politician he was viewed as a man who was trying to introduce a novel political methodology and bold thinking, a young leader willing to advance new positions and new solutions to old problems. In short, a man competent to settle not only the problems of Crete but perhaps those of mainland Greece as well.'[2] It was, then, because of the reputation he had earned as a nationalist leader in Crete that Venizelos was able to enter the stage of Greek politics on a national level in 1910 when he answered the call of the military coup that had taken place in Athens in 1909. He would stay in the limelight for over two decades.

The so-called 'Goudi coup' of 1909 had deep and multi-stranded roots. We have already touched on some of the more important ones, like the financial collapse of 1893–5, the military debacle of 1897 and the vacillating fortunes of the national struggle in Macedonia and Crete. Together, they helped to create an ongoing crisis of the entire political system and they fostered a *fin-de-siècle* malaise that infected much of Greek society. Following Harilaos Trikoupis's departure from politics and his death in Paris in 1896, there was a void in the leadership of the pro-Western reformist faction. The conservative Deliyiannis had been discredited by defeat at the hands of the Ottoman military and, after he was stabbed to death on 13 June 1905 by a gambling-house bouncer upset at his proposals to crack down on public gambling, his party also plunged into disarray.

A new generation of political leadership was developing, but there was no unifying force equivalent to Trikoupis's reform-mindedness and Deliyiannis's populist conservatism. Instead, four figures emerged from the older parties, but none of them proved able to fill their predecessor's shoes. Giorgios Theotokis took over control of the Modernist party, but he lacked the dynamism to control the party's old guard and his cautious moderation alienated the younger, more reform-minded newcomers. Kyriakoulis Mavromichalis and Dimitrios Rallis split the Deliyannis party, and Alexander Zaïmes, Deliyannis's nephew and a moderate centrist, was able on occasion to siphon off enough members of the two main parties to form a viable third party. In the end, neither of the two traditional parties nor any of the old guard among the political leadership proved able to mobilize sufficient support among the people or to gain the steadfast backing of the palace to rule the country effectively.

The result was a political gridlock, the nature of which historian Victor Papacosma captures well:

> Party propaganda, extravagant promises, bribery and patronage flourished. Since party discipline was nonexistent and individualism rampant, deputies continued to shift parties for politically selfish reasons. Parliamentary obstructionism remained standard practice with politicians, generally adept in oratory, often filibustering up to three days to block legislation. At other times sizeable groups of deputies absented themselves from the *Boule* so that quorum requirements necessary for business could not be met.[3]

Government was almost at a standstill.

Fragmenting the political scene even further was the emergence of new political groupings based on a variety of ideologies ranging from anarchism to popular radicalism to agrarian conservatism. Turned off by the nature of the old parties, many men who once would have formed the parties' new cadres, now looked elsewhere. Some, like Stefanos Dragoumis, Dimitrios Gounaris and their colleagues, eschewed partisanship and argued instead for political, economic and social modernization in order to achieve the nation's goals. They were dubbed the Japan Party, or the Team of the Japanese, because they aimed to reform Greece in a manner reminiscent of what the Meiji dynasty had recently accomplished in Japan. Others argued that it was, in fact, modernization and the importation of 'Western' ideas that were creating Greece's problems. They urged that society should return to one in which the Orthodox Church was the dominant institution.

At the same time, political parties and movements began to develop that were both secular and opposed to the old guard. In those regions where an industrial workforce had come into existence, workers' centres were founded. These helped to create class-consciousness among labourers and they provided a forum in which workers were exposed to the writings of leading socialists and Marxists. Even in the countryside, radical organizations began to take root among the poor sharecroppers and rural labourers. Established in 1902, the Sociological Movement rapidly emerged as the leading voice of a new socialist movement in Greece. Trade unions had also made significant strides in organizing Greek workers. Labour confederations, for example, united working men in most of the major cities and towns, and especially in Volos. An organization called the Radical Movement led by Yiorgos Skleros started to gain momentum as a political movement, especially after it combined with the Sociological Movement to form the Panhellenic Labour Confederation. The spectre of socialism was rising and it terrified the old political order. Finally, a last cultural response to the national malaise that cut across boundaries of class and political ideologies was the continuing spell that romantic nationalism cast over many. The struggles in Macedonia and Crete continued to exert an almost mystical hold on large segments of the Greek population. The vacuum in public life created by the collapse of the old parties was quickly filled by an odd assortment of new movements, almost all of which challenged the status quo.

Just as important as the rise of ideological opposition to the old order were the numerous episodes of actual disorder in the streets. Periodically, this manifested itself in mass, violent actions. On 5 November 1901, for example, perhaps as many as 50,000 people took to the streets of Athens to protest; the demonstrations soon led to clashes with the police and the military, during which at least eight people were killed and scores more wounded. The cause of the riot was the publication of the Bible in demotic, or popular, Greek.

We saw earlier how important the language question was in regard to Greek national identity, and the so-called 'Gospel' riots indicate the strength of feeling over this issue. But there were other factors involved as well and they speak to the issue of the national crises of the early twentieth century that interests us here. Advocates of Katharevousa saw the translation of the Bible into popular Greek as a betrayal of Hellenism and as part of a Pan-Slavist plot, led by no less a figure than Queen Olga. Those who supported the translation argued that it was only demotic Greek that could unite the entirety of the nation, both those within the kingdom and those who had yet to be redeemed. Thus nationalism, Hellenism, the Megali Idea, cultural identity and the Macedonian issue all came together at a time when many believed that their government was impotent to protect the national struggle, and the result was mass violence over an issue that seemed trivial to the rest of Europe.

Numerous other violent public demonstrations that occurred over the next years only served to heighten the sense of national crises. There was, for example, the 'sanidika' demonstration (so called because of the planks or sanides torn from kiosks and used by the rioters as weapons) in December 1902 in which members of various artisan and merchant guilds rioted in protest at the failure of the November elections to produce a working government. A few months later, uprisings by tens of thousands of peasants protesting against the deplorable state of the rural economy rocked the Peloponnesos and required the intervention of the army before order could be restored. Even the royal family was not spared in 1905, when guild members besieged the palace demanding an audience with the King to protest against the government's recent tax hikes.

Contributing to this unrest was the poor state of the economy. New international loans and ever-increasing taxes were required to pay the bills, but Greece was frozen out of the financial markets and poverty had eroded the tax base. Migration to the cities, especially to Athens and Piraeus, and emigration to the United States, as we saw in the last section, were creating social dislocation on a massive scale. Finally, there was a widespread and pervasive sense among the people that none of the existing political parties could deal with all of these problems. Nor did they believe that the monarchy could.

Politically, in addition to the void created by the absence of a strong party or leader, there was also a crisis of legitimacy regarding the monarchy. Crown-Prince Konstantinos partly bore responsibility for the national humiliation in Thessaly, and by extension, his father also had to share in the blame. The reign of the Glücksburg dynasty was at its lowest point ever. After an unsuccessful attempt on his life and the ever-increasing evidence that he had lost the support of much of the population, King George even considered abdication. The military was angry over what it saw as unfair criticism. The high command believed that blunders by the politicians had forced them to fight a war for which they were ill-prepared and under-equipped. The relationship between the monarchy and the military had for some time been a cause for concern. As commander-in-chief of the military, the King could play a very active role. Thus, favourites of King George and his sons often had a fast track to promotions while other, more qualified officers did not. Disgruntlement spread in the officers' corps because of favouritism and the consequent lack of mobility for qualified men, the absence of good leadership in the armed forces, the vacuum of political direction and cuts in military spending.

The result of this situation was the formation of clandestine societies within the military. The most important of these was the *Stratiotikos Sindesmos*, or the Military League. A series of events beginning in 1907 led to the decision of the League's leadership that the intervention of the military into politics was required. The first of these was the situation regarding Macedonia. Britain was continuing to put pressure on Greece to stop the activities of the Greek bands. When during the summer of 1907 Britain entered into a pact with Russia, fears were raised that a solution unfavourable to Greece would be forthcoming. The following year, the Young Turk Revolution brought into power a reform-minded Ottoman government that promised major modifications to the administration of the region. This held out the promise of ending the troubles that plagued the region and could lead to Macedonia remaining as an integral part of the Empire. The radical nationalist turn of the Young Turk government in the spring of 1909 threatened to plunge the region back into sectarian violence at a time when it was clear to the Greek military leadership that the current government in Athens was unprepared to deal with it.

These events came on the heels of another disastrous year economically and the consequent increase in civil unrest. Finally, the impending trials in a court martial of some of their colleagues in the military for having presented the government of Prime Minister Dimitrios Rallis with a list of demands provided the final pretext for action. Rebuffed yet again by the government, Colonel Nikolaos Zorbas and First Lieutenant Theodore Pangalos, prominent members of the League, gathered 5,500 troops at the garrison at Goudi and, on 28 August 1909, used them to stage a *coup d'etat*.

After bloodlessly overthrowing the government, the Military League issued four demands:

1   A written acknowledgement from the government that it had received and accepted the memorandum of reforms which they had issued;

2   Formal assurance that the parliament would not be dissolved;

3   Amnesty for all those who had taken part in the coup or who had been dismissed for political reasons in the months leading up to it;

4   The dismissal from the military of those officers who had opposed the League.

Rallis refused to accept these terms and resigned. King George appointed a caretaker government and did the best that he could to keep up the appearance that the monarchy was still in charge, but the Military League held the reins of power.

The Military League had a very narrow agenda, limited primarily to issues involving the armed forces and the National Question. The coup initially met with wide support, not because the Military League furthered the interests of a single class but rather because they symbolized action at a time of national malaise. Once in power, it became apparent that the League leaders were unsure how to proceed. King George was very concerned about his position; the European powers had never supported the coup and reiterated their firm support of the monarchy. Moreover, the coup imperilled Greece's relationship to the international financial community. As a consequence of these developments, the leadership of the Military League finally recognized that it needed to return the reins of power to civilian politicians. The dilemma for them was who would best be able to step in and not lead the nation back into the 'politics as usual' of the previous period. Who could command popular support, could rally the nation in the name of reform, and could further the national cause?

The League chose Eleftherios Venizelos for three primary reasons: (1) he had demonstrated his bona fides as a nationalist leader through his recent activities in Crete; (2) those activities had resulted in the resignation of Prince George as High Commissioner of Crete and so Venizelos was seen as an opponent of the monarchy; (3) he was not associated with any of the old political parties and the old political system, known as the *palaiokommatismos*, and thus was seen as someone who could break the gridlock of pre-coup politics.

Once he became the spokesman for the military, Venizelos engineered the dissolution of the caretaker parliament and called for an election to obtain a mandate for a new government. The so-called 'revisionary' parliament was returned in August 1910 with no clear victor. While this was occurring, elections were held in Crete and Venizelos was elected première there. Having established himself in Athens as a force to be reckoned with and having been the driving force behind Cretan unification, his prestige in the Greek world soared. Venizelos returned to Athens in September and was greeted by enthusiastic crowds and wary politicians. No one was quite sure what to expect from the Cretan. Rather than fire, he breathed the language of moderation. Seeing that Venizelos was the only politician who could control the military, King George gave him his support. The monarchy was thus saved and Venizelos's stature grew even more.

The first golden age of Venizelism

Eleftherios Venizelos became the focal point of a new party – the *komma ton Fileftheron*, or the Liberal Party. It would be the dominant political force in Greece for twenty years with a legacy that would persist long after that. After some initial political machinations, Venizelos won two resounding victories in national elections, garnering 260 out of 346 (75 per cent) seats in the election of December 1910 and 145 of 181 (80 per cent) in a second election fourteen months later. The period from 1911 to 1916 is often referred to as the 'First Golden Age' because of the striking successes that Venizelos and the Liberals would achieve both domestically and abroad.

The popular base of the Liberal Party was diverse. It drew on younger, educated professionals seeking advancement. Trikoupists, who saw the party as a continuation of their old movement, flocked to the Liberal banner. For a variety of different reasons, urban merchants and artisans, industrial workers and factory owners also gave their support to the new regime. The party's evident nationalist orientation helped to solidify support across the board. Unlike the conservative parties that refused to recognize that class divisions had developed in Greece during the previous twenty years and the various parties of the Left that had adopted explicitly class-based orientations, the Liberal Party recognized class differences but endeavoured in some way to address the needs of all of them. Thus, in the period between 1910 and 1912, Venizelos and the Liberals passed a bevy of legislation at a frantic pace.

During the first six months of 1911, for example, no less than fifty-three constitutional amendments were passed dealing with the procedures and powers of the judiciary, the legislature and even the monarchy. New bureaucratic organizations, most importantly a new council of state and a consultative committee for drafting legislation, were established. The eligibility requirements for parliament were altered; the age of qualification was lowered; commissioned officers in the armed forces were barred from holding office, as were civil servants and directors of banks and public companies. The powers of the state were expanded. The administration of public education was taken out of the hands of local authorities and placed under central control. The state's ability to confiscate private property was eased, requiring only that the state show 'public benefit' rather than compelling 'public need'. One amendment rendered to the state the capacity to suspend fundamental civil rights, such as protection from arbitrary seizure, the right to a trial by jury, the need to show cause for a search of a person's body or premises, the freedom of the press and the right to public assembly. These latter amendments show the autocratic side of the charismatic Cretan.

In the months that followed, Venizelos demonstrated his populist side by pushing through an impressive array of legislation, over 330 separate laws. Many of the new regulations dealt with social issues. He passed a variety of new laws dealing with work place conditions and the delineation of workers' rights. For example, legislation was passed that fixed wages for women and children, regulated child labour, established the six-day working week and created a labour relations board. Trade unions were legalized and joint trade associations (these were management-controlled workers unions, which employees had to join as a condition of employment) were outlawed. 'Feudalism' and the archaic law of summary seizure for debt were abolished. A law was passed for the creation of a national health insurance system. Land reform and land redistribution schemes were passed and implemented. An attempt was made to simplify the Byzantine tax system by introducing a graduated income tax; many of the most onerous and regressive indirect taxes were removed from the books. Seen as a whole, this was the single most comprehensive agenda of social reform legislation in Greek history. Moreover, it had something for everybody, and so stole the thunder of the parties both to the Left and the Right.

Recognizing the circumstances that had brought him to power, Venizelos was careful to address the needs of the armed forces. Not only was he cognizant of the potential interference of the military, but he also saw clearly that Greece needed strong armed forces both to achieve his own dream of Cretan unification and to further the cause of Greek irredentism elsewhere. Consequently, he embarked on a programme of reform and restructuring of the military. He introduced compulsory military service and increased the size of the army to 150,000. Massive expenditures were made on the latest armaments from Germany and elsewhere. French advisors had been brought in to staff the new officers' training college he founded. The monarchy was allowed its traditional connection to the army, but its role became more ceremonial than real. The Greek fleet was expanded and modernized and its officers sent to study with British Royal Navy experts. Paying for the reforms and the military expansion was made possible through the financial management skills of Stefanos Dragoumis. He managed to raise revenues through tax reform, which, when combined with new loans and re-negotiated terms on existing loans alongside higher revenues, led to cash surpluses in the treasury by 1912. The nation had been re-armed and Venizelos would soon put the refurbished military to use.

In his first years of office, Venizelos oversaw the re-invigoration of Greece after the financial collapse of the 1890s, the national humiliation of the Greek military on the plains and hills of Thessaly, and the malaise and discontent of the 1900s. His social reforms addressed fundamental questions and problems that, if left unanswered, threatened to erupt in massive unrest – as had occurred in many other parts of Europe. His fiscal reforms brought a semblance of financial stability in the wake of the chaos of the previous decade. His military reforms had re-armed the nation and set it on a footing to compete for power in the Balkans.

The Balkan Wars

The Balkan Wars of 1912–13 ushered in a decade of conflict and violence that would completely transform the region. By the wars' end, after almost 600 years, the Ottoman Empire in Europe, to a large extent, no longer existed. The Balkan Christian states had completed the 100-year-long process of partitioning the Empire in Europe and creating their own exclusivist nation-states, while managing to stifle the nationalist ambitions of smaller groups. The Greek world, not surprisingly, was also completely transformed.

The Kingdom of Greece experienced both incredible highs, like almost fulfilling the Megali Idea in 1919, and catastrophic lows, such as its humiliating defeat at the hands of the Turkish National Army in 1922. Greek Russia was profoundly impacted by the First World War and the Russian Revolution and would never be the same. Ethnic cleansing and population exchanges had caused one of the largest forced migrations of people in human history. The Rum population of the Ottoman Empire largely ceased to exist, with only a few pockets of them remaining in what was now the Turkish Republic, the rest having been reduced to refugee status in Greece. Migration and massacres decimated the large Muslim population that had for centuries dwelt all across the Balkans to a fraction of its pre-war size. In sum, by 1923, southeastern Europe was a very different place. What caused these conflicts and why did they have such horrendous consequences?

The Balkan Wars were caused by a number of factors, some internal to the region and some that emanated from outside. Internally, the driving forces behind the conflict were the unresolved irredentist ambitions of Montenegro, Bulgaria, Greece and Serbia that produced interstate tensions between them and the Ottoman Empire and among themselves.

Through the first decade of the twentieth century, the problem of Macedonia had remained an issue of national and international significance. As discussed previously, during the late nineteenth and early twentieth centuries, rival factions, in particular IMRO and the *Ethniki Etaireia*, which continued to be active even after its formal disbandment in 1897, struggled to define the ethnic and cultural identity of the region. Language, religion and education were for a time the chosen battleground, but soon the conflict took on a more violent aspect. The situation was complex: some wanted total unification with Greece, others wanted a separate Macedonian state, and still others wanted Macedonia to be included in a Serbian, Albanian or Bulgarian state. Villages and even households were split, and deciding which cause one espoused was increasingly a matter of life or death. *Makedonomaxoi*, guerrilla warriors from all around the Greek world, flocked to Macedonia to join the fighting. Matching them were fighters from all the other sides. In spite of the hyperbolic propaganda produced by the various factions, it is clear that atrocities were being committed and that no one group was any guiltier than the others.

Athens was actively supporting the irredentist movement in Macedonia. Money, materials and men were being surreptitiously sent northwards. The Metropolitan of Kastoria, Germanos Karavangelis, spearheaded the Hellenic cause in Macedonia. Greek bands totalling approximately 2,000 men waged constant guerrilla war against IMRO and other exarchist bands. Terror was a tactic used by both sides against non-combatants. An economic war was also waged. In Salonika, for example, exarchist shop owners found themselves facing boycotts aimed at compelling them to sell out, or even worse, they became subject to terror tactics intent on the same goal. The result was that the city was starting to become more of a Greek city. To be sure, Jews and

Muslims still outnumbered Greeks, but the Slavic population was decreasing and, consequently, the exarchist forces were losing access to the main port of the northern Aegean. The situation was becoming increasingly tense.

The great powers became more involved in the Macedonian problem through the first decade of the twentieth century. Britain, in particular, endeavoured to find a workable solution to the question. Russia had expressed continued interest in the Slavic cause, which in turn caused concern in Austria. Pressure was brought to bear on Greece to curb the activities of the *Makedonomaxoi*. British Foreign Secretary Sir Edward Grey, in a series of speeches in the British Parliament, began to explore the idea of an independent Macedonian state. The Young Turks Revolution of 1908 changed the situation dramatically. The initial response to the Young Turks was very favourable. Their promise to decentralize rule, to create a true multi-ethnic state and to hold elections, which included the Christian population, generated great enthusiasm. Bands from all sides came forward and surrendered their arms. Negotiations between Athens and Istanbul were cordial and held the promise of success. The respite in the conflict was short-lived. After a failed counter-coup in 1909, a nationalist faction of the Young Turk movement came to power and they reverted to an older, authoritarian model of rule. Gone was the promise of decentralization; gone was the pledge of self-rule; gone was the guarantee of multinationalism. In Macedonia and in Crete, the new regime was even more intransigent than the Hamidan dynasty it had overthrown. War clouds loomed.

The Cretan problem also continued to stew through the first decade of this century. The autonomous/protectorate status of the island was simply unacceptable to the nationalists who wanted *enosis* at any cost. The matter came to a head with the accession to power of Venizelos. The Ottoman Empire threatened war when he took up the office of prime minister. Tensions increased further when the assembly in Crete voted to send representatives to the new parliament of 1912. The British fleet intervened to stop them from reaching Athens, and after they were released, Venizelos forbade their admission into the session. Nonetheless, the response from the Porte was clear: the issue of Crete could lead to war yet again.

The final cause of the Balkan Wars was the nationalist issue in the Balkans. Bulgarians, Albanians, Serbs and Montenegrins all sought to advance their respective nationalist causes. The rallying cry of the day was 'the Balkans for the Balkan states'. The way forward seemed to be through a form of Pan-Slavic movement, or failing that, at least through some configurations of bilateral cooperation. Such an arrangement of major importance was signed on 13 March 1912, between Serbia and Bulgaria. It was a mutual defence pact, obligating each to assist the other in case of war. The treaty also divided northern Macedonia between them. It assumed that the fate of southern Macedonia would be decided between Bulgaria and Greece.

The response in Athens to this development was the signing of a bilateral agreement with Bulgaria and the opening of negotiations with Serbia. Venizelos, however, was cautious about these developments. He feared that Greece was at that moment the least prepared to go to war and that it was the one with the most to lose; he was thinking here of the massive Greek population in Asia Minor. But Macedonia was very much on his mind as well. This made the Bulgarian treaty particularly important because, in spite of lengthy negotiations and general agreement on numerous other issues, no consensus could be reached on the fate of the region. Essentially, the three Balkan powers agreed to cooperate militarily against the Porte, but after that each was expected to grab what it could, any way it could. While the treaties set the stage for war against Turkey, they also left too many vital issues unresolved for peace to endure.

The Balkan Wars lasted from October 1912 until August 1913. The three powers declared war on the Ottoman Empire on 18 October 1912, having marshalled combined forces of over 1,290,000 men. Venizelos's modernization plan paid rich dividends. The Greek military forces were larger, better equipped and well trained. Within a matter of weeks, the Greek army pushed back the Ottoman army, taking Katerini, Elassona and Kozani by October 25. Along the northwestern front, Greece successfully moved deep into Epiros. Bulgarian and Serbian forces were also successful and by early November, the Ottoman forces were faltering on all fronts.

The war effort went incredibly well. By early November, the Bulgarian army in Thrace had driven back Ottoman forces and were besieging the city of Edirne. In a short time they hoped to threaten Istanbul itself. Inclement weather that rendered the roads impassable and an outbreak of cholera stopped the Bulgarian army in its tracks. The Ottomans dug in for a last ditch effort to protect the capital, and a form of trench warfare that would later characterize the campaigns of the First World War commenced. Neither side could gain a strategic advantage, and by early December there was a gridlock and stalemate. The Bulgarian invasion of Macedonia was a complete success and by early November, the advancing forces were rapidly closing in on Salonika. The path to the city was now open and the race was on with the Bulgarians to see who could get there first. The commander of the Ottoman forces, Hassan Tahsin Paşa, saw that his position was hopeless and so he commenced negotiations with both sides. The Greeks offered more favourable capitulation terms and so on 8 November, he agreed to surrender the city to them. Shortly after the Greeks took control of the city, the Bulgarian army arrived. Its commander claimed that the city was under his control, going so far as to telegraph Tsar Ferdinand that the city was his. A tense standoff ensued, but the

Greeks clearly had the upper hand. In the West, Greek forces laid siege to Ioannina. But the Ottoman garrison put up a stiff resistance and the city held out. It would take a long campaign before the city surrendered.

It is fair to say that by the end of November 1912, the armies of the Balkan League had attained almost all of their strategic goals. But it had taken an enormous effort, and all sides were near exhaustion. Negotiations commenced that ended with the declaration of an armistice on 3 December. Two weeks later in London, a conference began to hammer out the peace treaty, with Venizelos representing Greece. Bulgaria and Serbia were ready to sue for peace. Greece, however, was reluctant to do so because Ioannina had yet to capitulate. Negotiations dragged on through January, but then broke down and the fighting recommenced. Of the three Balkan powers, Bulgaria was faring the worst in this second phase of the conflict. It had overextended its forces to the southeast and so had lost a valuable opportunity to stake a claim to Macedonia. Greece's stock soared when its fleet scored stunning victories over the Ottoman navy in January 1913. Greece controlled the Aegean. This meant that the Porte was unable to move its forces from the Levant or North Africa to assist in the Balkan campaigns. In addition, the Greek navy could even threaten to blockade the Dardanelles. The Greek success at sea more than any other factor perhaps compelled the Empire to capitulate. A few weeks later, Greece gained the other prize that it sought. On 6 March 1913, the Ottoman commander of Ioannina surrendered the great city to Prince Konstantinos. Greece could now go back to the negotiating table with a much stronger hand to play.

On 30 May, the Treaty of London was signed and Ottoman Europe largely ceased to exist. The big winner at the peace table was Bulgaria. Its re-drawn borders now encompassed almost all of Thrace, placing the border with the Ottoman Empire only a few miles away from Istanbul. It also received much of Eastern Macedonia and drew the boundary with Greece only a few miles north of Salonika, which had gone to Greece as part of the negotiations. Northwestern Macedonia and Albania were divided between Serbia and Montenegro. The treaty also established a minuscule independent Albania. No one was particularly pleased with the treaty. Serbia and Greece thought that their national ambitions had been thwarted and that Bulgaria had received far too much. Bulgaria, on the other hand, felt aggrieved because Salonika had gone to Greece. Tensions rose in the region, especially after Greece and Serbia negotiated a bilateral agreement in which they proposed to re-draw the map of Macedonia.

The Bulgarian response was to go on the offensive, with disastrous consequences. On the night of 29–30 June, Bulgaria attacked Serbia and Greece and triggered the Second Balkan War. It would not last long. Greece and Romania entered the fray, invading Bulgaria from the south and the north, respectively. The Ottoman Empire, now under the leadership of a military dictatorship, launched a counterattack of its own, driving back the Bulgarian army. By the end of July, the Bulgarian situation was hopeless and it capitulated. Three agreements, the Treaty of Bucharest (10 August), the Treaty of Istanbul (30 September) and the Treaty of Athens (14 November) ended the Balkan Wars and re-drew the map of the Balkans. Bulgaria lost significant territories, and correspondingly, Greece, Serbia, the Ottoman Empire and Romania gained them. The boundaries of Albania were expanded. In sum, the map of the Balkans took on a more recognizable form.

The Balkan Wars were a watershed moment in the history of the region and they had manifold consequences – both good and bad. Across the board, the war was a humanitarian nightmare. The military forces of all the combatant states, through deaths in battle and disease, had suffered horrendous casualties. Bulgarian losses alone totalled 66,000 dead and 110,000 wounded. More appalling but less susceptible to quantification were civilian deaths. During the war, each side mobilized paramilitary groups whose task it was to ethnically cleanse the territory seized by the national armies. They hoped to strengthen their claims to an area by proving that it was occupied predominantly by their co-nationals, and removing all others was the most straightforward way to do so. People of all ethnicities and faiths suffered, but the axe fell especially heavily on the Muslim population. Thousands were massacred and tens of thousands fled the region to be resettled as refugees elsewhere in the Ottoman Empire. Traumatized and eager for revenge, they would become a powerful destabilizing factor in the Empire.

Under Venizelos's skilful guidance, Greece scored some notable successes in the international arena. With the addition of southern Epiros, Macedonia, Crete and some of the Aegean Islands, the size of the country was increased by 68 per cent, including some of the richest agricultural land on the peninsula. The population rose from 2,700,000 to 4,800,000. The great cities of Ioannina and Salonika (now called Thessaloniki, its ancient name) were incorporated into the kingdom. Indeed, the Balkan Wars had brought the Megali Idea closer to realization than ever before. Territorial expansion, however, brought with it new challenges. First and foremost was the humanitarian challenge of dealing with huge numbers of people who had been left destitute and homeless by the war. Second, for the first time in its history, the Greek state had to confront the issue of how to incorporate into the nation-state very large numbers of people who did not possess a consciousness or a national identity that was Greek. In the new territories, there were still substantial populations of Muslims, Jews, Vlachs, Bulgarians, Albanians and others. Some, like the Jews of Salonika, manifestly did not want to be incorporated into the Greek state and, in fact, were terrified at the prospect. Others, like the sizable

Slavic-speaking population, looked on Greece as the enemy, while still others, like the Albanians and Vlachs, sought either inclusion in another state or a country of their own.

For the more than three million 'Greeks' outside the kingdom's boundaries, the war was a disaster. While no one could have predicted that within a decade after the Balkan Wars the Rum presence in the Ottoman Empire would be virtually nil, many communal and religious leaders feared dark days ahead. Defeat in war and the loss of its European territories unleashed a wave of anger and dismay that shook the Empire to its foundations. For the Ottoman political elite, most of whom originated from the European provinces, it was as if the beating heart of the Empire had been ripped out. Mustafa Kemal, a prominent militaryman and future founder of the Turkish Republic, for example, broke down into tears when he was informed that his home city of Salonika had fallen to Greece. Psychological trauma turned to outrage. The military dictatorship now in control of the CUP declared the experiment in democratic pluralism a failure, concluding that the non-Muslim populations had made it clear that their loyalties lay elsewhere.

Turkish nationalism replaced Ottomanism as the dominant ideology of political discourse. Stoked by the reports of persecution, massacres and forced evictions, Ottoman Muslims looked to take revenge against non-Muslims, especially the Ottoman Greeks (Rum) – now increasingly castigated as being 'Greeks' (Yunani) – and Armenians. Balkan Muslim refugees who were settled in areas where there was a significant Rum population, like the region along the coast of the southern Marmara (the Vilayet of Hüdavendigar), sought revenge. The decade after 1913 saw widespread and horrendous violence against the non-Muslim population of the Empire, culminating with the genocide of the Armenians. From a Greek Ottoman perspective, then, the future looked bleak.

That was assuredly not the case in Athens. The dark days of the fin-de-siècle seemed to be over. Even the assassination of King George I could not dampen the public's enthusiasm and unbridled optimism. In the late afternoon of 18 March 1913, the aged monarch went out on his daily afternoon walk along the waterfront in Salonika. As he passed a seaside café, a man named Alexandros Schinas stepped up behind him and shot him in the back. The assassin said he had killed the King because he would not give him some money, but most Greeks believe that the killer was a Bulgarian agent. The *New York Times*, however, labelled him an 'educated anarchist' and a socialist who had killed the king because the Greek government had closed the Greek school in New York City where Schinas had been employed.[4] Historically, then, there is a great deal of conflicting information about the killer and his motives. The result, though, was that the longest-reigning monarch in all of Europe was dead. Ironically, just before he was slain, George had decided that he would take the opportunity of the forthcoming Jubilee celebration of his coronation to abdicate in favour of his eldest son, Crown-Prince Konstantinos.

While mournful on the death of their old king, Greeks greeted the coronation of Konstantinos with special enthusiasm, seeing in it momentous portends for the success of the Megali Idea. With the coronation of King Konstantinos, a new rallying cry was heard: 'A Konstantinos founded it [the Byzantine Empire]. A Konstantinos lost it [Constantinople]. And a Konstantinos will get it back.' The 'it' referred to in this slogan is, of course, the great city of Constantinople/ Istanbul. Unfortunately for Greece, this was not to be.

The National Schism and the Great War

The outbreak of the First World War shattered the internal stability that had been achieved and left in its place bitter divisions that would last for generations. In the summer of 1914, Europe was divided into competing alliance groups, with the Triple Entente (Britain, France and Russia) on one side and the Triple Alliance (Germany and Austria) on the other. Of the states of southeastern Europe, only one was involved at the start of the war, and that, of course, was Serbia. Within days of Austria declaring war on it on 28 July 1914, all of the countries listed above would be in a state of war. But since it was obvious from the start that the Balkans would be directly implicated in the conflict, a critically important question was what the other states in the region would do, and that included Greece.

To answer that question we need to get a sense of what was happening in each country. The Ottoman Empire was a changed place after the Balkan Wars. The democratic experiment had failed and the Empire was now ruled by a three-man ruling council, consisting of Enver Paşa, Talaat Paşa and Djamal Paşa. The reality was that they formed a dictatorship with strong ties to the Ottoman military. For the first time in its history, it was a non-Eurocentric empire, and reflecting this new reality was the emergence of Turkish nationalism and a greater emphasis on the Islamic character of the state. The Ottomans had a long-standing friendship with the German Empire and so it is particularly surprising that they entered the war so quickly. In October 1914, at the behest of the dictatorship, Sultan Mehmed V declared jihad against Great Britain, France and Russia. The Ottoman entry into the war changed the spatial geography of the situation, threatening the lifeline of the British Empire through the Mediterranean and the southern flank of the Russian Empire. This made it even more imperative that the Entente find allies in the region. Their efforts, however, were matched by those of the Triple Alliance. Enticed by the promise of the Austrian Balkan territories and many of the Greek islands, Italy joined the Entente in May 1915. A few months later (October 1915), Bulgaria responded favourably to German overtures and promises of massive territorial expansion at the war's end. In August 1916, Romania joined the fray on the side of the Entente. This left only one country on the sidelines: Greece.

Greece found itself in a difficult situation. It had a number of reasons for opposing the Triple Alliance. First, Ottoman participation on the side of the Alliance threatened to kill the Megali Idea, which still sought ways to incorporate the remaining areas that constituted Greece's imaginary national space, Asia Minor in particular. It also posed an existential threat to the still massive Ottoman Greek population. Second, Bulgaria's alignment with the Central Powers meant that should that side win, Macedonia and Thrace, at a minimum, would be lost. Third, Greece had treaty obligations that bound it to Serbia, and the Serbs were at war with the Central Powers. Finally, the Entente Powers had been the ones who had most consistently supported Greece in the past and so could make a claim on past friendships.

On the other side of the ledger sheet were the close connections between the royal house of Greece and the German monarchy. The reigning Queen of Greece, Sofia, was the sister of Kaiser Wilhelm. In addition, there were close connections between the German military establishment and the Greek leadership, many of whom, including King Konstantinos, had been trained in Germany. As the other countries in the region picked sides, the pressure for Greece to do so became even stronger. There were only three choices: join the Entente, join the Triple Alliance or remain neutral.

In July 1915, Kaiser Wilhelm made the case for joining with him. According to a contemporary, the German ruler laid out the case in a lengthy letter, at the end of which he wrote: 'I have spoken frankly, and I beg you to let me know your decision without delay and with the same absolute frankness.' Konstantinos replied, 'It seems to me that the interest of Greece demands an absolute neutrality and the maintenance of the status quo in the Balkans. This way of thinking is shared by the whole of my people.' Privately, the Kaiser's response to this assessment was curt and pointed: 'Rubbish!' Publicly, his official response was a threat: 'I will treat Greece as an enemy if she does not adhere at once.'[5] King Konstantinos, in spite of his brother-in-law's best efforts, then, sought to keep Greece neutral. His sympathies were clearly with the Triple Alliance but he also realized that Greece's interests could be best served by remaining outside the fray. His most frequently and publicly stated argument was that only neutrality would keep his people safe. Venizelos, on the other hand, was staunchly pro-Entente. He was by inclination more sympathetic to Britain and France. Moreover, British promises made shortly before hostilities broke out completely convinced him that Greece's interest lay with the Entente. As he noted during secret talks with David Lloyd George, Winston Churchill and John Stavridi, Greece '... with the friendship of England

and France would become a power in the East which no one could ignore.'[6] In January 1915, Britain made the following offer: if Greece would enter the war and send troops to assist the hard-pressed Serbs and contribute to the invasion at Gallipoli that was to take place in February, at the end of the war, Greece would agree to give Kavala, Drama and Serres to Bulgaria (which Britain was still wooing) and would receive in exchange territorial compensation in Asia Minor. Calculating that the Entente would win the war, Venizelos saw this as an offer he could not refuse.

A royal council consisting of Venizelos and a number of previous prime ministers, the members of the general staff of the armed forces and the King was convened to craft the country's response to the various offers being floated to Greece by Britain. The Greek people, meanwhile, were making their feelings known with massive public rallies in support of the Entente. Initially, Konstantinos agreed with those politicians who urged acceptance of the British offer. After the resignation of some military commanders and at the urging of other members of his staff, he changed his mind.

This was a very difficult time for the King. In addition to the growing crisis within his government, he was also extremely ill. Already suffering from pleurisy and pneumonia, he contracted blood poisoning after surgery to remove some of his ribs. It took the miraculous healing powers of the holy icon of the Virgin Mary from the island of Tinos to bring Konstantinos back from death's door. Faced with an intransigent monarch backed by the General Staff, on 6 March Venizelos resigned as prime minister. The King appointed Dimitrios Gounaris as the new one, but the real power in Parliament still belonged to Venizelos. So began the constitutional crisis that came to be called the *Ethnikos Dikhasmos*, or the National Schism.

In June of 1915, the Greeks went to the polls and there was really only one issue at hand: war or neutrality. The broader context, however, included the following: the Gallipoli campaign was not going well; Serbia was fighting for its life and losing; the Armenian genocide was in full swing; and the persecution of Ottoman Greeks was moving apace. Much hinged on this critical election. Six parties fielded candidates and the Liberals easily carried the day, winning the popular vote and garnering 187 out of 316 seats in Parliament. The people had voted for war. The King, however, refused to accept the result and, claiming ill health, stalled for time. Thus, it was not until August that he allowed the new government to be formed. Machinations had gone on through the summer with the result that by early autumn, Bulgaria had decided to capitalize on Serbia's seemingly imminent defeat and so declared war on it. Sofia also claimed Macedonia and Thessaloniki as its own. Venizelos demanded that the army be mobilized in compliance with the treaty with Serbia. Konstantinos reluctantly agreed on the stipulation that the army would fight only if Greece, not Serbia, was attacked. In response, Venizelos allowed French and British troops to be landed in Macedonia in order to assist the campaign on Gallipoli and to potentially establish a northern front. He had moved so quickly that Konstantinos had little time to react. Venizelos escalated tensions further by requesting a parliamentary vote on a declaration of war on Bulgaria, and, by extension, against the Triple Alliance. The motion was carried by a 37-vote margin. The next day the King called Venizelos to the palace and demanded his resignation. A constitutional crisis had erupted.

Having just won a major victory at the polls, the Liberals and their followers refused to accept the King's order. Technically, the Greek constitution did give the monarch the right to dismiss a government unilaterally; in this case, the King felt that he was better qualified to make the crucial decisions about war and peace. Be that as it may, the spirit of the constitution was that he should only do so when the popular will of the nation was in doubt. In this case it was not.

The June election had been fought precisely on the issue of war or neutrality. New elections were called for December. The Liberals, along with the vast majority of the electorate, boycotted them, with the result that the newly elected government had no base of popular support. Relations between Venizelos and the Liberals and Konstantinos and the monarchists continued to deteriorate as each staked out a harder line. Popular opinion vacillated depending on circumstances.

For example, when French and British troops landed in Macedonia in October 1915 over the protests of the King, popular sentiment was with him as most Greeks saw the Allied manoeuvre as a breach of Greece's sovereignty. But the tide of public opinion soon shifted. After Konstantinos balked at allowing the Allies to transport Serbian troops over land from Epiros to the Macedonian front, the Allies started to grow increasingly impatient with the royalist government. When pro-monarchist military leaders, in May 1916, surrendered Fort Rupel in Eastern Macedonia, one of Greece's most important northern fortifications, to the Bulgarians and so allowed the region to fall to the Triple Alliance, public opinion was outraged. The Allies were now convinced that the King and his government were untrustworthy and that Venizelos was their only hope for getting Greece behind the war effort. Also outraged by the surrender were numerous members of the officers' corps, who now threw their support behind the Venizelists. The crisis was becoming critical and there was widespread uncertainty as to who actually spoke for the nation.

In the autumn of 1916, Greece stood on the brink of civil war. Venizelos had previously withdrawn to Crete where he waited for an opportunity to re-assert himself. It was not slow in coming. Simultaneously, military officers loyal to him formed a clandestine organization, the National Defence (*Ethniki Amina*), based in Thessaloniki and aimed at bringing down the King and restoring the government of June 1915. They staged a coup and called on Venizelos, who was in Athens at the time, to join them. Escorted by a French cruiser, he went first to Crete where he officially announced his support for the coup and then he visited many of the Aegean Islands to gauge the level of support he enjoyed on them. Finally, in late September 1916, he arrived in Thessaloniki and formed a 'provisional' government. Greece now had two competing governments.

The Allies meanwhile were putting great pressure on the King to capitulate. After much equivocation, they recognized the provisional government. When Allied troops were fired on at Piraeus, France and England set up a blockade of all ports under Konstantinos's control. The King, however, remained firm. Text-box 22 reproduces an interview that Konstantinos gave to a Greek reporter for the *New York Times*, in which he laid out his position. From this it is clear that up until the moment that he lost his throne, see below, he remained defiant and convinced about the correctness of his position. But now he had to face the wrath of Britain and France. Beginning on 7 December 1916 and continuing for 106 days, no goods were imported or exported at central and southern Greek ports. 'During the dark months that followed thousands of unemployed Greeks were thrown into the streets to beg for food. Even in the villages there was starvation...'.[7] Many people became more sympathetic to Konstantinos's position because of the hardships created by the Allied blockade. The rupture within the political system also took on a geographical dimension and inaugurated a division between 'Old' Greece to the south and 'New' Greece in the north. The significance of this north–south division would only increase in the decades ahead.

The political division also led to partisan violence. Under the leadership of Ioannis Metaxas, former acting Chief of the General Staff, aide de campe of Konstantinos and future dictator of Greece, a reactionary paramilitary unit, the 'League of Reservists', was founded and it embarked on a systematic campaign of terror and repression against Venizelists who had remained in Athens and against anyone who did not support the monarchy. To kill a Venizelist, they believed, was a sacred duty. The pro-monarchy Archbishop of Athens excommunicated Venizelos and his supporters from the Orthodox Church. Mobs gathered in downtown Athens and hung effigies of the Cretan leader. Elsewhere, equally virulent demonstrations against the monarchy erupted. The rift between Royalists and Venizelists was polarizing society and starting to tear it apart, and this was happening not just in Greece but in the Diaspora as well. In many Greek-American communities, like the one in Manchester, New Hampshire, where my family lived, for example, the Orthodox Church split, with one faction breaking away from the other to form its own place of worship. Moreover, Greece's stance in the war was generating powerful anti-Greek sentiments around the world, culminating in the atrocious anti-Greek riots in Toronto in August 1918. Over a five-day span,

Text-box 22 King Konstantinos on the National Schism (1917)

'Germany will not be defeated, and the Entente will not be defeated. This thing is bound to drag on for years, and peace will only be signed when all the belligerents reach the end of their resources. This peace will not take into account the small nationalities: neither will it establish permanent rules of righteousness and justice. He who at the end of the war will be stronger than the others will get the best terms, and the weak and small will have to pay, as it has been the case always since the world existed.

I am not saying this for Greece alone: the rule applies to every little country that can neither get free nor live by itself. Belgium and Serbia, when freed, will owe their liberty to someone else, and will get the best of their freedom, as is the case with Navarino and Greece. This is the reason why I wanted Greece to stay out of the war, and the Greek people are clever enough to view the situation in the same light. Another thing that I want you to have always in mind is that the Entente powers have always been, they are today, and they will be in the future, more pro-Bulgar then they have ever been pro-Greek. And this is another reason why I want neutrality at this time. Bulgaria today, even when fighting against the Allies, has more friends in London and Paris than Greece has had since the days of Hugo and Beranger. It is a case of incurable Bulgaritis, from which all the Entente Powers are suffering. Unfortunately, I can do nothing in this case,' the King concluded laughing.

He kept me nearly an hour: the Minister of war, General Kallaris, was waiting to see him; the Serbian minister was also announced; I rose to take leave of his Majesty. He likewise rose, a towering figure over 6 feet tall.

'When do you expect to sail for America?' he asked me.

'In 2 days,' I answered.

'Do you want to ask me any other questions?'

'Yes, Your Majesty,' I replied and my question was this: 'What shall I tell people when they ask me why the fort of Rupel was delivered to the Germans and the Bulgars?'

'Tell them,' His Majesty said gravely, 'that the salvation of Greece is immensely more precious than all the Rupels of the world. In fact, the salvation of Greece is more precious than the Greek throne, and the life itself of Constantine.'

Excerpts from an interview that King Konstantinos gave to Adamants Th. Polyzoides and published in the *New York Times* (9 January 1917).

50,000 Anglo-Canadians went on a rampage, 'hunting Greeks' as they put it, and destroyed every Greek business in the city.[8] The war issue was creating a schism in Greek society that set loose a pattern of violent, partisan reprisals that once begun would prove very hard to stop.

By late spring 1917, matters were coming to a head. The provisional government in Thessaloniki had grown in strength and enjoyed a considerable degree of legitimacy both at home and abroad. The French and British blockade rendered the King's position precarious. Newspapers that previously extolled his principled stance against foreign interference now began to question the wisdom of his obduracy in the face of his people's suffering. Allied leaders, still concerned that their projected invasion of the Balkans could be jeopardized as long as Konstantinos was on the throne, began openly to call for his abdication. The French leadership, in particular, was outspoken in its support of the provisional government and its opposition to the King. British Prime Minister David Lloyd George, who had come to power in December 1916, joined them in calling for the Greek monarch's departure. The King's position in Athens was also becoming less certain. According to a confidential report sent to the British Foreign Office from an operative in Athens: 'The King is steadily losing followers. Fifty-seven officers recently left Athens in one day for Salonika and the stream is continuing. Since the Provisional government declared that the population of any territory seceding hereafter to the National government will not be mobilized the last plank was pulled from under the King's feet, and it is at least most doubtful if any of the rank-and-file will be found to stand between him and his fate.'[9] And that fate came to pass on 11 June 1917, when the High Commissioner of the Protecting Powers, Auguste-Charles Jonnart, delivered an ultimatum to the pro-monarchy government in Athens: if Konstantinos agreed to leave Athens and appoint his son Alexander as king, he would be allowed to return to the throne when the war was over; if he did not, then Athens would be attacked and the monarchy as an institution would be abolished. Jonnart's justification for making these demands was that Konstantinos had violated the Greek Constitution and that as its guarantors, Great Britain, France and Russia had the legal right to intervene in order to protect it. As flimsy as this pretext was, it left Konstantinos with little choice but to leave. Three days later, he announced to his bewildered followers, many of whom still declared their unshakable resolve to die on his behalf: 'It is necessary to obey, and I must leave. I am fulfilling my duty to my *patrida* (fatherland). I am leaving you Alexander and beg you to resign yourselves and accept my decision; trust in God, whose blessings I invoke on you.'[10] He, along with other members of the royal family, most prominently his eldest son and heir George, then left aboard a British warship that conveyed them to Italy from whence they would make their way to Switzerland.

Venizelos now had a much more amenable partner to work with. Alexander was cut from a different cloth than his father or elder brother. He was by nature out-going, adventurous, athletic and good-looking. Over the years he had earned a reputation as a bit of a bad boy who liked fast cars and even faster women. The 23-year-old monarch was also pro-Entente and a supporter of Venizelos's position; this did not mean, however, that the two got along especially well. It was absolutely clear who was in charge and the headstrong young king had trouble reconciling himself to that reality. He had no choice. As Venizelos once told the Russian ambassador, 'If the new King turns out not to be a Constitutionalist, we'll deal with him the way you did in Russia.'[11] When Alexander called on him to form a new government, Venizelos reconvened the parliament that had been elected in the June 1915 elections, arguing that it was still the legitimate governing body because all of the subsequent elections had been unconstitutional. Known thereafter as the Lazarus Parliament, because like him it had risen from the dead, with Venizelos at its head, the new government led its people to war.

Under the leadership of Lieutenant-General Pandelis Danglis, ten divisions of the Greek army joined with their French and British colleagues and fought with great valour in the1918 autumn campaign along the Macedonian front. They routed German and Bulgarian positions and pushed the front line northwards at a great human cost. The hard fighting was soon rewarded as Germany and its allies capitulated. Then came the reward as Greek troops triumphantly marched into Constantinople/Istanbul. At the cost of splitting the nation, Venizelos had brought the nation into the war on the victorious side. In order to justify the cost, he now had to win the peace: the wounds of war would only be healed with the fulfilment of the Megali Idea. But even then, the deep cleavages wrought by the National Schism could not be undone. The legacy of sectarian violence would endure.

8

The inter-war period, 1919–1940:
A time of turmoil

With the cessation of the 'Great War,' Greece could have known peace for the first time in years, but it did not. Instead, more war, catastrophic defeat and an enduring legacy of social and political instability would mark the inter-war era in Greece. The combination of the Balkan Wars and the First World War had exacted a heavy toll on Greek society. The key question in 1919 was this: Could Eleftherios Venizelos and the Liberals gain enough from the Allies at the Paris Peace Conference to compensate for the country's sufferings? At first, it appeared that they had. Soon after the conference, Greece would come as close as it ever would to achieving the dream of the Great Idea. But the dream would soon turn into a nightmare. Military defeat at the hands of the Turkish nationalist forces would all but bring to an end the millennial-long Hellenic presence in Asia Minor. Consequent upon this military debacle would be a decade of social unrest, political chaos and economic disaster. Then Greece, like so many other places in Europe, would fall prey to the sickness of the inter-war period: authoritarianism.

Peace and war

Prime Minister Eleftherios Venizelos went to the Paris peace talks armed with the vague assurances made to his government by the Allies during the war, all of which focused exclusively on the issue of territorial aggrandizement for Greece. The task before him was daunting and the stakes were high. Internally, political stability hinged on his coming away from the negotiations with a settlement favourable to Greece. As a politician who had risen and stayed in power largely through his successful pursuance of the irredentist cause, he had to ensure that the cause of Hellenism in Asia was advanced. Representatives of the Greeks of Asia Minor specifically were lobbying him to ensure that the sufferings visited upon them during the war were recompensed. And their sufferings had been substantial. While nowhere close to the horrors perpetrated on the Armenians, the persecution suffered by the Greeks of Trebizond and Asia Minor during the war had been considerable. In lieu of military service, the Ottoman government had enrolled over 200,000 Greek men in labour battalions. Forced to work long hours repairing road and rail lines or in other sorts of arduous tasks while being housed in squalid conditions and fed starvation rations, tens of thousands of them had perished. Text-box 23 recounts what conditions were like in the camps. Though fictional, the sufferings it describes were very real. Thousands of others, including women and children, were driven from their homes or fled on their own, with over 80,000 migrating to Russia alone. Those who stayed behind faced various travails, including land confiscations and the physical destruction of their homes. The slate of issues, then, that Venizelos had to address at the Paris Conference was long and formidable.

Text-box 23 Life in the Ottoman labour camps (1916)

On 14 September 1916, I once again shipped out for Ankara. My battalion, the Second Amele Taburu, was now stationed at a village called Yavsan, near the Kizilirmak River. The welcoming ceremony this time was different. Three gallows had been set up and from each dangled a man with a sign on his chest that read: 'I am a deserter'.

The conscripts stared at the hanged men but their faces betrayed no emotion. The gallows, the neck-irons, the torture – nothing could stem the tide of desertion. It was a kind of war against the war …

However, life in the camps had improved. Our tents were bearable. Every Friday was housecleaning day. Lice were eradicated. Whoever fell sick was sent to hospital. Now hunger became our most dire tormentor. The Turkish camp guards took from us whatever we had, our clothing, foodstuffs, money; they opened the packages from our parents. We worked fifteen hours every day, breaking rocks, digging tunnels, building roads. Day and night, we yearned crazily for food. Like lunatics we waited for the moment when the bread was distributed. We ripped into enormous chunks and bolted it down without chewing. … Many could not stand the hunger, and sold their clothing, their shoes. Then, naked and barefoot, they fell victim to pneumonia and frostbite, and perished.

D. Sotiriou (1991), *Farewell Anatolia*, Athens: Kedros Publishing, 110–12.

The wily Cretan was up to the task. In short order, Venizelos had earned a reputation for moderation, wisdom and statesmanship. Using his considerable diplomatic skills, personal charm and powers of persuasion, he pressed Greece's claim to the utmost. He wooed leaders like Woodrow Wilson and Lloyd George. He cajoled some and threatened others. For all of his best efforts, and they were considerable, Venizelos could not escape one fundamental truth: Greece could not achieve its goals without the active assistance of the major powers and such cooperation would be forthcoming *only if* the powers perceived it to be in their best interest. But in the rapidly changing circumstances of the Paris talks, such interests were often in flux. Furthermore, in the context of the truly momentous issues that confronted the leaders of war-ravaged Europe, the affairs of the Eastern Mediterranean were little more than a sideshow.

Even while the talks were in progress, military forces were required to act as policing agents and as peacekeepers in various occupied zones. Venizelos was quick to offer the services of the Greek military. At one point, for example, Greek troops assisted French forces in an operation in the Black Sea region. This paid international dividends, as foreign leaders became more indebted to him and began to see Greece as a stabilizing force in an unstable region. Working with Lloyd George, he was able to take advantage of Woodrow Wilson's anger at Italy over the disposition of Fiume in the Adriatic and George Clemenceau's ambivalence about the region to obtain permission to occupy specified regions of Asia Minor. 'But from the start the French were halfhearted, the Italians opposed and the Americans distracted. Greece was never to have firm inter-Allied support.'[1]

Over lunch on 6 May 1919, Lloyd George, Wilson and Clemenceau decided that, acting as a proxy for the Allies, Greek troops should occupy Smyrna. When the British leader informed Venizelos of their decision and inquired as to Greece's preparedness, the Cretan curtly replied, 'We are ready'. Widespread euphoria greeted the announcement in Greece. The newspaper *Nea Chios,* for example, exclaimed 'Glory to God. The Nation has risen . . . Greece has found herself again!'[2] Not everyone was as pleased with this decision. Italy, for example, saw it as a direct threat to its interests in the region. Some members of the British general staff warned that the Greek military presence would be seen by the Ottoman leadership and the Muslim population more generally as an invasion and an act of war. Venizelos, in his speech announcing the expedition, tried to allay the fears of the latter while placing blame on the former: 'Greece is not making war against Islam, but against the anachronistic Ottoman Government, and its corrupt, ignominious, and bloody administration, with a view to expelling it from those territories where the majority of the population consists of Greeks.'[3] His words, however, largely fell on deaf ears.

On the morning of 15 May, Smyrna's quayside was packed with members of the city's Orthodox Greek community. Greek flags were draped everywhere. At 7.30, the first ship carrying Greek troops arrived to a hero's welcome. Archbishop Chrysostomos blessed them. Liberation and unification were at last becoming reality. On the previous day, Allied troops had landed and were deployed around the city in an effort to forestall any incidents between the Greek troops and the Ottoman garrison still stationed there. They were unsuccessful. Within hours of their arrival, the Greek forces were involved in a shootout with the Ottoman troops. From the start, then, there were ominous indications that the dire warnings uttered by many of the military advisors to the Supreme Council that allowing the Greeks to occupy Smyrna was a major mistake were correct. But in the spring of 1919, nothing it seemed could stand in the way of the realization of the Megali Idea. All that remained, many believed, was the signing of the treaties that would finalize the occupation. But before discussing that issue, we need first to examine the domestic situation in Greece in the aftermath of the Great War.

Greece had not suffered to the extent that so many other countries in Europe had during the First World War. The figures of casualties suffered by Germany, France, Britain and Russia are too well known to need repeating here. It is enough to note that Greece did not experience anywhere near the manpower losses that the other countries of the region did. Greece's loss of approximately 175,000 pales in comparison to the 725,000 war casualties that Serbia sustained, let alone the 3.2 million that the Ottoman Empire did. Neither did Greece experience anywhere near the same magnitude of destruction that they did. Most of the fighting had been restricted to Macedonia and Thrace, and the rest of the country was largely spared from direct attack. Nonetheless, the war had had a deep impact on Greek society and its economy. We must bear in mind, for example, that the armed forces had been mobilized almost continuously since the Balkan Wars and so the losses during the Great War must be added to the earlier casualty figures. Also, these losses have to be placed in the context of the massive out-migration of young men that had been occurring since the turn of the century (see Chapter 6); granted, many men returned to Greece from the United States to fight, but their numbers did not offset the numbers of those who continued to leave. Second, the nation was becoming war-weary and even the call of nationalism was starting to fall on increasingly deaf ears.

The economic situation was also dire. The agrarian sector, which was still the backbone of the economy, emerged from the war years in a depressed condition. The addition of the new lands in Epiros and Macedonia after the Balkan Wars and the high prices that appeared at the start of the First World War led to an initial upswing in the rural economy. The combination, however, of manpower shortages, protectionism, government requisitioning, the devastation of Macedonia and the Allied blockade soon created a crisis. Some of Greece's most important industries, such as mining, went into decline at the start of the war and never recovered; according to one estimate, the size of the labour force involved in mining was halved between 1912 and 1922.

Manufacturing output and profits rose because of a combination of protectionism and wartime demand, but were hard hit by the Allied blockade on account of Greece's dependency on foreign imports of coal and other vital raw materials. This led to a large and increasing trade deficit. Fiscally, the situation was grim, but it could have been managed if not for the Asia Minor campaign. Greece had emerged from the Balkan Wars in debt but was well on the way to paying them off, mainly through public subscription at home and through additional foreign loans. It was, however, unprepared to foot the massive expenses the First World War generated. Loans were contracted, and the Allies pledged millions of pounds in credits, against which the National Bank of Greece issued banknotes.

Nonetheless, Greece emerged from the war deeply in debt. The war years witnessed another emerging crisis: the rise and spread of labour unrest and class division. We saw in the last chapter that workers and peasants were prepared to take direct action in order to get their grievances heard. This trend of public unrest continued but with two additional dimensions. The first was that workers' movements became more organized. Trade unions and workers' associations spread through many sectors of the economy, and they grew in scale, culminating in 1918 with the foundation of the General Confederation of Greek Workers. The second development was the emergence of specifically class-based political parties, often themselves tied to the trade union movement. In 1915, for example, an all-Greece conference of socialists was convened and three years later, the Socialist Labour Party of Greece was formed. As working-class movements became more organized, they became more powerful and could exert greater pressure on the Liberal government.

The lengthy war years had taken a great toll on the Greek people, and even while the negotiations were going on in Paris, serious problems on the home front threatened to jeopardize the grand plans being devised there. Moreover, the Liberal administration that Venizelos had left behind in Greece was growing increasingly unpopular. Since the summer of 1917 (see above pp. 186–7), the Venizelists had wrought a terrible retribution against their political opponents. Royalists were purged from the military and the civil service. Prominent anti-Venizelists were imprisoned or exiled. These actions simply drove the wedge of division that was the National Schism even deeper into the body politic. Rifts even began to develop within the Liberal Party. Thus, even as he scored successes abroad, the Venizelists' mismanagement of domestic affairs was costing Venizelos popularity at home. Finally, Venizelos put all of his energies into winning the peace talks and neglected matters back in Greece. He would eventually pay for this neglect.

After two years of intense negotiations, peace was achieved, for a short time at least. The Treaty of Sèvres was signed on 10 August 1920 by representatives of the Sultan's government in Istanbul and the leaders of the delegations from Great Britain, Italy and France. The treaty dealt a harsh, and ultimately fatal, blow to the Empire. Like the other defeated powers, it had to massively reduce its armed forces and it had to pay a huge war indemnity. In order to ensure that this penalty was paid, the Allies took control of the major Ottoman financial institutions. Moreover, it lost most of its territory and even control over its own capital city: Istanbul and the Dardanelles were converted into an international zone under the administration of the Allies. New countries, like Armenia and Hejaz, were created; large swathes of territory in the Levant were established as protectorates under French or British control. Italy got the Dodecanese islands. The Ottoman Empire was reduced to just Anatolia, but even then not all of it, as considerable territories were designated as zones of Allied occupation. While disastrous for the Ottomans, Sèvres was a boon for Greece and with it the country stood on the verge of fulfilling the Megali Idea.

Greece received the Aegean Islands, including Imbros and Tenedos, and all of Thrace. More significantly, a new territory around the city of Smyrna (see Map 1) was established and placed under the protection of the Greek government, and, in accordance with the principle of national self-determination, all Greeks in Asia Minor were encouraged to move there. The Smyrna Protectorate was still under the aegis of Turkey but was administered by Greece – at least temporarily, as Article 83 of the treaty made clear (Text-box 24).

Since May 1919, Greek troops had been stationed at Smyrna and so the treaty merely formalized and made the occupation legitimate. The presence

---

Text-box 24 Article 83 of the Treaty of Sèvres (1920)

When a period of five years shall have elapsed after the coming into force of the present Treaty, the local Parliament referred to in Article 72 may, by a majority of votes, ask the Council of the League of Nations for the definitive incorporation in the Kingdom of Greece of the city of Smyrna and the territory defined in Article 66. The Council may require as a preliminary, a plebiscite under conditions which it will lay down.

Treaty of Peace with Turkey signed at Sèvres, 10 August 1920, London: His Majesty's Stationary Office, 1920.

of the Greek military had attracted many Orthodox Christians from the countryside, who feared Turkish reprisals or bandit attacks. The massive shift in population was extremely important because, as Article 72 of the treaty made clear, representation in the local parliament was to be based on 'an electoral system calculated to ensure proportional representation of all sections of the population, including racial, linguistic and religious minorities.' Thus, as the number of Greek-speaking Orthodox people grew, so too would the number of their members in the elected assembly, making it all but certain that within five years' time, Smyrna would become a permanent part of Greece. Venizelos could, then, announce triumphantly that there was now a Greece of two continents (Europe and Asia) and five seas (Black, Aegean, Mediterranean, Ionian and Marmara). The irredentist dream seemed to be coming true, as the wildly popular lithograph shown in Figure 12 demonstrates.

FIGURE 12 *Venizelos and the triumph of Hellenism (1919). This widely circulated drawing celebrates the seeming fulfilment of the Megali Idea by Eleftherios Venizelos at the Paris Peace Conference. Led by an angel waving the Greek flag, Venizelos descends from heaven on a chariot like a conquering Roman hero. Standing beside him is an allegorical figure representing war. Meanwhile, depicted as comely young maidens are the various regions of Greece, which had now been united with the Motherland. From left to right, they are Crete, Thrace, Macedonia, Ionia, Epiros, the Aegean Islands and the Dodecanese. Finally, looming in the lower left-hand corner is the greatest prize of all: Constantinople.*

Sotirios Chrisides (1919). GallantGraphics all rights reserved.

The moment of triumph, however, was to be short-lived, and the nightmare was about to begin.

Right from the start, the Smyrna Protectorate was a powder keg waiting to explode. To head the Greek administration that along with the elected assembly would govern the protectorate, Venizelos selected Aristeides Stergiadis. He became, in fact, its de facto governor. In many ways, he was an ideal choice. In addition to being a close friend of Venizelos, he was also an expert in Islamic law. 'Stergiadis quickly got on the wrong side of the local leadership. He was determined to establish an administration impartial as between Muslim and Christian and willing to offend Greek susceptibilities in doing so.'[4] He introduced many progressive reforms, establishing schools which students of all faiths would attend, he built hospitals and other facilities that were a-religious in nature, and he introduced many economic reforms, particularly in the area of land ownership and agriculture. Many of his initiatives were opposed and even blunted by Greek nationalists who wanted to homogenize the population. In addition to compelling Muslims to leave the protectorate, close to a quarter of a million Greeks from the kingdom were brought in as colonists, lured by the promise of land and subsidies. Inter-communal tensions ran high, and there were numerous attacks and massacres perpetrated by Greek troops. As reports of the violence became known, international pressure began to be put on Greece to restrain its forces; the US Senate went so far as to pass a resolution demanding that the violence against the Turkish population be stopped. From the start, then, Greece's Anatolian adventure was fraught with difficulties. Developments at home and abroad would only exacerbate them.

At 8.20 on the evening of 12 August 1920, Venizelos entered the Gare de Lyon train station in Paris, intending to catch the evening train to Marseille where he would board a ship to Athens. He never made it. Two monarchist military officers, Apostolos Tserapis, formerly a lieutenant in the Greek Marines, and Yiorgos Kyrikis, a reserve lieutenant in the Greek Engineers, stepped out from behind a pile of luggage and opened fire on the premier. Two of their seven shots found their mark. His wounds, however, were not life threatening, but nonetheless, they incapacitated him at a time when he needed all of his vigour and energies. Already out of touch with the developments in Greece, his extended convalescence isolated him even further from the domestic scene. In addition, the response in Greece demonstrated that the deep divisions created by the earlier political rift were still present. Upon hearing of the shooting, pro-Venizelist mobs attacked and even destroyed buildings that housed pro-monarchy newspapers. Prominent opponents of the Liberal Party leader were assassinated in the streets. In a society in which the ethos of vengeance runs so deep, each drop of blood spilt demanded repayment in kind. The slide to anarchy, moreover, was just beginning.

Two months later, an untoward event shattered the uneasy compromise regarding the monarchy. On the afternoon of 2 October, King Alexander took his favourite dog, Fritz, for a walk in the gardens at the royal estate of Tatoi. Startled by the barking dog, two Spanish monkeys jumped out of a tree and attacked. Alexander stepped forward to save his pet and was himself savaged, suffering severe bites on his legs and abdomen. By evening, septicaemia had set in. Racked by fever and beset by delirium, he clung to his life for over three weeks before succumbing. A crisis over the succession quickly developed. His brother refused to ascend to the throne, leaving his father, the exiled Konstantinos, as its primary claimant. A war-weary and nervous electorate brought down the curtain on Venizelos's term of office in the elections of November 1920.

A coalition of pro-monarchy parties, called the United Opposition, led by his old nemeses, Dimitrios Gounaris and Dimitrios Rallis, won 260 of the 370 parliamentary seats contested – even though the Liberals won 52 per cent of the total vote. The United Opposition had made three campaign promises: first, they pledged to end the 'tyranny' of the Venizelists by restoring the civil liberties and freedoms that the Liberals had abridged, first on the pretext of wartime necessity and then on the grounds of public order; second, they promised to restore Konstantinos to the throne; and third, using the rallying cry 'peace now!' they promised to bring an end to Greece's military ventures, meaning demobilization and the withdrawal of troops from Asia Minor. They also sought to assure the European powers that Greece would live up to its commitments. If that meant adherence to the Treaty of Sèvres, then could they realistically pull back militarily from Asia Minor? And could they be a nationalist movement and not support the Great Idea? On this last point, however, there was no complete unanimity within the coalition; some voices from the centre-right spoke out in favour of a small but stable Greece rather than a large but unstable one. Like modern-day Kassandras, their prophecies of doom in Asia Minor went largely unheeded. Repudiated by the nation at the moment of his greatest triumph, Venizelos went into self-imposed exile. Under the leadership of Gounaris, the United Opposition formed a government and took up office. One of their first actions was to schedule a plebiscite regarding the restoration of Konstantinos. Following a landslide victory (999,960 in favour and only 10,383 against) in what was clearly a rigged ballot, on 19 December 1920, Konstantinos returned to the throne of Greece.

There were four major consequences to these developments. First, after years in the political wilderness, royalist supporters let loose counter-purges against Venizelists in the provincial administration, the judiciary, higher education, the civil service and the military. This acted only to perpetuate the wounds of the National Schism. In many ways, the most important effects of this development were felt in the military. Almost all of the leading command posts were given to Royalist officers. Though many of these officers were competent military commanders, the change in command did have a deleterious impact on the armed forces, especially in Asia Minor, as we shall see shortly. Second, the election of a conservative government, by a minority vote at that, drove even more members of the working class, including many poverty-stricken peasants, into the folds of leftist parties. The Socialist Labour Party of Greece's membership, for example, increased considerably. This added a new and important dimension to the National Schism. In addition to the monarchist–Venizelist cleavage, there was now a growing Left versus Right division. Third, some of the conservatives attempted to be even more fervent in their nationalism than the Venizelists had been and so adopted a more aggressive, radical line in regard to Turkey. Fourth, since many of the commitments made to Greece were personal ones between Allied leaders, like Lloyd George and Wilson – who themselves would fall from power – and Venizelos, after the removal of the Cretan statesman from power, these obligations also lapsed. The result was that Allied support, especially that of Great Britain and France, waned, while that of Italy vanished completely.

Most importantly, the Allies made good on their threat to punish Greece if Konstantinos returned: they refused to make available the millions of dollars in credit that they had promised at the Paris peace table. When that happened, the Royalist government also found the European financial markets closed to it. Greece alone would have to foot the bill for the irredentist struggle, and it was going to be very steep indeed.

The Asia Minor catastrophe

While these developments were taking place in Greece, the situation in Anatolia was also changing dramatically. By the summer of 1919, the Ottoman authorities had by and large become resigned to the dismantling of their empire, but what they had not become reconciled to was the invasion by a foreign army and the occupation of a vital region of their homeland. A new movement, Turkish nationalism, and a new leader, Mustapha Kemal, emerged from the ashes of defeat and they both posed a direct threat to Greek irredentism. Kemal was a Muslim from Salonika who had risen through the ranks of the Ottoman army. During the war, he had distinguished himself at Gallipoli, on the Russian front and in the Middle East campaign. At the end of the war, he became one of the most vocal of the many military officers who felt betrayed by the actions of the Ottoman government in Istanbul. In order to remove him from the scene, the government assigned him the military inspectorate of the Eastern districts. Shortly after his arrival in Samsun on the

Black Sea in May 1919, he launched the Nationalist Movement. It quickly grew in strength and power, until just under a year later (23 April 1920), it participated in the Grand National Assembly, which declared itself the legitimate sovereign Turkish administration, known as the Ankara government. There were now two Turkish governments – one in Istanbul headed by Mehmed VI and one in Ankara whose president was Mustafa Kemal. The Ankara government refused to recognize the Treaty of Sèvres and so considered all Allied occupation of Turkey and, in particular, the Greek occupation of Smyrna as illegitimate. Ankara announced its intention to reclaim the sacred and inalienable territory of Turkey from the foreign invaders. There would be a Turkish war of independence. By autumn of 1920, at the same time that the changing of the guard was taking place in Athens, the Ankara government had developed into a force to be reckoned with. Turkish national liberation and Greek irredentism were on a collision course.

During the winter of 1921, the Gounaris government in Athens had decided to confront the Turkish nationalist movement more aggressively. In an effort to avert a conflict, Lloyd George and his Foreign Minister, Lord Curzon, met with representatives of the Greek government in February. Already piqued that Konstantinos had been restored over their objections, the British warned the Greeks that they should be prepared to make compromises because British support would not be as staunch as it had been in the past and because the French were now willing to support the Turkish demands. Paris's warning to Greece was brief and blunt: Greece would stand down or it would stand alone. At the subsequent London Conference, however, it quickly became apparent that compromise between the various parties was impossible. Upon returning to Athens in March, the Greek delegation recommended that the time for talking was over. Greece essentially had three options: (1) evacuate Smyrna; (2) establish a defensive perimeter along the borders of the Protectorate to ward off an attack by the Turkish nationalist army; or (3) bring the war to it by attacking the Kemalist government in Ankara. The Gounaris government chose the third option and so the order was given, and on 23 March 1921, the Greek military launched a major offensive that would drive deep into the Anatolian hinterland. The invasion proved to be a disaster.

Under the command of Royalist supporters, first General Anastasios Papoulias and then General Giorgios Hadjianestis, the Greek army pushed eastwards along two fronts, one to the north and another in the south. The military high command aimed to employ a pincer movement to bottle up the Turkish nationalist forces in central Anatolia. On the political side of the military equation was the idea of isolating Istanbul and by so doing, putting pressure on the Allies to grant even greater concessions to the Greeks. The southern front advanced more easily than the northern one, which encountered fierce resistance. Attacking along two fronts and across such a broad area was a strategy that entailed taking some very serious risks, the most important of which were spreading the Greek forces too thin and over-extending the supply lines. At one point, the Greek line extended across much of Anatolia. Yet the advance continued.

Through 1921, the Greek army met mostly with success and this encouraged the strategic command to persist with their high-risk gamble. The campaign seemed to be going so well that Konstantinos himself visited the front line and his son George remained there as a member of the high command. But there were warning signs that all was not well. Greece was finding itself isolated from the Allies. Britain and the United States urged caution and offered to mediate a solution. France and Italy openly supported the Turkish nationalists, supplying them with arms and material. The nation's cash resources were running out as the Allies withdrew their loans in protest at the continued hostilities. Internally, the Greek army was fraught with divisions between Venizelists and Royalists that impaired almost every aspect of the conduct of the campaign. After one defeat snatched out of the mouth of victory because of poor planning and inadequate logistical support, Arnold Toynbee, a reporter for the *Manchester Guardian,* noted that the Greek troops 'were angry – angry at spending so much blood and labour in vain, but even more humiliated at a defeat which broke a long record of victory of which they had been intensely proud.'[5] Finally, ammunition and supplies were beginning to run out, and there was no money to purchase more.

Kemal enticed the Greek army to progress even deeper into the rugged heartland of Anatolia. Historian Michael Llewelyn Smith reproduces the memorandum in which the strategy was laid out. After proposing that his forces retreat, the nationalist leader understatedly observed, 'If the enemy should pursue us without coming to a halt, he would be getting farther away from his base of operations. ... Thus our army will be able to rally and meet the enemy under more favourable conditions.'[6] This was truly an understatement. The Greek forces did, in fact, follow the retreating nationalist forces and the consequent over-extension of the Greek line proved disastrous.

By late August of 1922, Kemal judged that the Greek position was untenable and so he launched his carefully planned counter-offensive. By concentrating all of his firepower at a few strategic points, he was able to gain an overwhelming superiority. The assaults by the Turkish nationalist forces were fierce and the results swift. The Greek line was shattered. Through a series of coordinated north–south pincer movements, Kemal isolated and destroyed numerous sectors of the Greek army. A rout turned into a race as the ragtag remnants of the Greek forces retreated to Smyrna with the Turkish forces at their heels.

The scene became chaotic as tens of thousands of Greek troops joined by legions of civilians fled before the Turkish cavalry. All sought an escape, but exits were scarce. Most headed for the main point of departure out of Anatolia under Greek control: Smyrna. A contemporary witness, George Horton, vividly captured the scene as troops and refugees converged on the city (Text-box 25).

Nothing stood between the Turkish forces and the great city of Smyrna. Ships from the naval fleets of the great powers arrived to evacuate foreign nationals and diplomats. Greek ships arrived disembarking troops whose assigned task was to keep order in the city. Their stay was a brief, and ineffective, one. As the Turkish forces approached, the scene on the waterfront became more chaotic as people sought any means possible to flee. For most, however, it was too late.

'The Turks are coming!' This cry rang through the streets of Smyrna on the morning of 9 September 1922. The cavalry arrived first. Armed to the teeth and seemingly well rested, they swept through the city spreading panic before them. Later that evening, the looting and killing commenced. Initially, the violence was fiercest and bloodiest in the Armenian quarter, but it soon spread. After Archbishop Chrysostomos was humiliated and butchered by a Turkish mob, the massacre began in earnest. Then on the evening of Wednesday 13 September, a fire broke out in the Armenian quarter, and quickly spread. As soldiers, sailors and journalists from around the world watched from ships anchored in the bay, the city burned. Flames rose up behind them forming a fiery wall of death as mobs of people ran to the waterfront, hoping to be conveyed to one of the ships lying in the harbour. But it was an impossible task. In addition to the paucity of conveyances, strict orders not to interfere had been issued to the captains of the foreign warships. The results were horrendous. Tens of thousands of Greeks and Armenians died during the

Text-box 25 The Greek army returning to Smyrna (1922)

Then the defeated, dusty, ragged Greek soldiers began to arrive [in Smyrna], looking straight ahead, like men walking in their sleep.... In a never-ending stream they poured through the town towards the point on the coast at which the Greek fleet had withdrawn. Silently as ghosts they went, looking neither to the right nor the left. From time to time, some soldier, his strength entirely spent, collapsed on the side-walk or by a door.

G. Horton (1926), *The Blight of Asia. An Account of the Systematic Extermination of Christian Populations by Mohammedans and of the Culpability of Certain Great Powers; With the True Story of the Burning of Smyrna*, Indianapolis: The Bobbs-Merrill Company, 119.

destruction of Smyrna. For all intents and purposes, the Megali Idea went up in smoke on the shores of Asia Minor.

The war, however, was not over with the devastation of Smyrna. After regrouping the remnants of the forces that had escaped from Asia with newly mobilized reserves, the Greek army prepared to make one last stand in Eastern Thrace. An eyewitness to the events there, Ernest Hemingway, captured well the ignominious end to the Greek adventure in Asia Minor (Text-box 26).

The catastrophe compounded

The Asia Minor catastrophe had serious and lasting consequences. Two problems immediately faced Greece. The first concerned the internal political situation: Who would rule Greece? Related to this was the question of who was to blame for the disaster. The second was how to achieve peace in Asia Minor and how to cope with the flood of refugees who were pouring into Greece daily.

The first dilemma was quickly addressed. A small, dedicated band of military officers gathered on the battleship *Limnos* after the debacle and formed a Revolutionary Committee. At its head were Colonels Nikolaos Plastiras and Stilianos Gonatas, and naval Captain Dimitrios Fokas, all Venizelists of long standing. Given the chaotic conditions of the time, it was relatively easy for a small, organized and armed group to take control, and this they did.

Text-box 26 Description of the defeated Greek army (1922)

Greece looked on Thrace as a Marne where she must fight and make a final stand or perish. Troops were rushed in. Everybody was in a white heat. Then the Allies at [the negotiations to arrange a truce at] Mudanya handed Eastern Thrace over to the Turks and gave the Greek army three days to start getting out. The army waited, not believing that their government would sign the Mudanya convention, but it did, and the army, being soldiers, are getting out. All day I have seen passing them, dirty, tired, unshaven, wind-bitten soldiers hiking along the trails across the brown, rolling, barren Thracian countryside. No bands, no relief organizations, no leave areas, nothing but lice, dirty blankets, and mosquitoes at night. They are the last of the glory that was Greece. This is the end of their second siege of Troy.

E. Hemingway (1985), *Dateline Toronto: The Complete Toronto Star Dispatches, 1920-1924*, New York: Schribner's, 232.

On 11 September 1922, they landed at the port of Lavrion on the coast of Attica with a force of 12,000 men and sent an ultimatum to the government in Athens. A group of officers went to the King and offered to muster a force to defend the monarchy and there were scattered public gatherings of royalist supporters, but for the most part, there was little opposition to the putschists. In a letter of 26 September, the Revolutionary Committee demanded the resignation of the government and the abdication of King Konstantinos. After hasty deliberations with his closest advisors, the King agreed that both demands would be met.

Shortly after Konstantinos left the country, his eldest son George was sworn in as king. The Committee set about establishing a government and purging the bureaucracy and the military of royalists. Their next major move was to assign blame for the catastrophe. A show trial of the leaders in charge of the Asia Minor campaign was conducted by a military tribunal. At what became known as the Trial of the Six (even though there were eight defendants), General Giorgios Hatjianestis, former Prime Minister Dimtrios Gounaris, Petros Protopapadakis, Giorgios Baltazzis, Nikolaos Stratos and Nikolaos Theotokis, together with Xenophon Stratigos and Michael Gouadas, were charged with high treason. This was an act of political retaliation and scapegoating. These men were certainly guilty of ineptitude and gross incompetence, but not of treason. All eight were found guilty: six were sentenced to die, two to life in prison. On 27 November 1922, the Six were executed by a firing squad. With their deaths, the Venizelist–anti-Venizelist rift grew wider and more ferocious. The politicization of the military was furthered, and the militarization of politics ensured. Moreover, the episode cost the Revolutionary movement a great deal internationally, with two of Greece's most valuable allies, Great Britain and the United States, withdrawing support; the former actually recalled its ambassador, while the latter threatened to do so. The Trial of the Six would cast a long shadow over inter-war Greece.

To address the other pressing problem, negotiating an acceptable peace with Turkey, the Revolutionary Committee led by General Plastiras turned to Venizelos and asked him to represent Greece at the upcoming treaty negotiations. He agreed to do so but only under certain conditions. One very important one was that the government evacuate the Greek army from Eastern Thrace, which was still under its control at the time of the armistice. This was necessary in order to ensure the goodwill of important allies, and in particular Great Britain and the United States, both of whom had been estranged with Athens since the Trial of the Six. Reluctantly, the Revolutionary government agreed to do so. Venizelos put together a team of advisors and arrived in the city of Lausanne, Switzerland, on 20 November 1920. The conference was a huge affair: since the Ankara government had never accepted the terms of the Treaty of Sèvres, technically Turkey was still at war with the Allies, and, consequently, delegations from all of them were present. The main players at the conference, however, were Great Britain, United States, France, Italy, Japan, Greece and Turkey. After lengthy talks and countless hours of meetings and deliberations, an agreement was finally reached and a document produced. On 24 July 1923, the representatives of the various participants signed the Treaty of Lausanne, which would be ratified by all of the participating countries over the next ten months. The document contained 143 articles. The most important ones for our purposes are these: first, the treaty formally ended the First World War between Turkey and the Allies. Second, Turkey relinquished all claims to the territories that had formerly been part of the Ottoman Empire. Third, in return the Allies recognized Turkey's independence and its borders. Regarding borders, Greece agreed to cede Imbros and Tenedos to Turkey. Thrace was divided into two sections with Greece receiving the western sector. In addition, Greece also obtained the Aegean Islands running along the coast of Turkey, but they were included in a demilitarized zone. In exchange for these territorial acquisitions, Greece relinquished all claims to Asia Minor.

Within the framework of the Lausanne Conference, a bilateral agreement called 'The Convention Concerning the Exchange of Greek and Turkish Populations' was negotiated and signed by Greece and Turkey on 30 January 1923. The idea of two countries agreeing to a mutual exchange of populations had been around for a while and, indeed, had been conducted; Venizelos himself had been involved in one such exchange between Greece and Bulgaria. But the one agreed to in this convention was different from anything that had gone before because of the sheer size of the numbers of people involved and by the fact that this was to be a compulsory exchange. Article 1 laid out the heart of the agreement: 'As from the 1st May, 1923, there shall take place a compulsory exchange of Turkish nationals of the Greek Orthodox religion established in Turkish territory, and of Greek nationals of the Muslim [sic.] religion established in Greek territory. These persons shall not return to live in Turkey or Greece respectively without the authorization of the Turkish government or of the Greek government respectively.' Article 2 identified the only two populations that would be exempt from the exchange: the Greek inhabitants of Constantinople and the Muslim inhabitants of Western Thrace. Article 3 of the convention broadened the scope of the exchange to include all Greeks who had fled the territory of Turkey and all Muslims who had fled the territory of Greece between 18 October 1912 and 30 January 1923. Altogether, 1,300,000 Orthodox Christians were exchanged for 585,000 Muslims; by the end of January 1923, approximately 850,000 of the former were already in Greece while 389,000 Muslims remained there. They, along with the remaining Orthodox Christian population in Turkey, would be relocated in the coming months. Even while the two countries were negotiating the convention, then, Greece was already confronted with having to deal with huge numbers of destitute and desperate refugees. Also included in the Convention were certain provisions for the protection of Orthodox Greeks and Muslims who were granted special status and allowed to remain where they were: the Thracian Muslims or the Greeks of Constantinople, for example. Lastly, the Convention set forth the administrative mechanism by which the exchange would be conducted.

The Treaty of Lausanne established for the most part the boundaries of Greece, which obtain to this day, and it ended once and for all the Megali Idea. The convention that mandated the exchange of populations, in theory at least, turned Greece into an ethnically homogenous nation-state by removing the major minority group. It also created a massive problem: what was to be done with almost one and a half million refugees?

The exchange of populations and its cost

Even before the Treaty of Lausanne had been signed, a torrent of refugees from Asia Minor and Eastern Thrace was making its way to Greece. The torrent soon turned into a flood of destitute and despairing humanity. Given their condition, not surprisingly the arrival of the first wave of refugees created immediate and huge problems. First and foremost was the difficulty of finding food and shelter for them. Initially, families were settled wherever space permitted. During the autumn of 1922, 'tin towns' and tent villages sprang up around Athens and Thessaloniki. The situation of the refugees was desperate. Most had had to flee with only the few items that they could carry. Many had nothing at all. There were a disproportionate number of women, children and elderly men because of the systematic arrest and detention in labour camps of able-bodied young men by the Turks before the exchange. In the refugee settlements around Athens, for example, women over sixteen outnumbered men by almost two to one. Only a major, concerted relief effort could forestall a human disaster.

The Greek fiscal situation was already dire and the state simply did not have the funds needed to deal with the situation. Various international relief organizations, like the American Red Cross and the League of Nations Refugee Treasury Fund, stepped in with food, supplies and medicines. The Red Cross, for example, expended over $3,000,000 between October 1922 and June 1923, and the organization's timely efforts stopped at least one major outbreak of typhus and prevented others from spreading across the country. But the international humanitarian relief efforts served only as a temporary solution to the much greater problem. The exchange of populations agreed to in the treaty was about to present Greece with close to one and a half million displaced persons.

The wave of immigrants who arrived in Greece through the organized exchange of populations was different from the previous wartime influx. More families arrived intact, though overall there was still a gender and age imbalance. They were able to bring with them personal property, portable wealth and cash, and so were not destitute like those who had fled for their lives during the darkest days of 1922. That they were forced out of their homeland with more than the clothes on their backs did not minimize the trauma that this second wave of migrants experienced.

The Greeks from Asia Minor were a very heterogeneous group. Some were wealthy, educated and sophisticated merchants, lawyers and professionals who had called the Ottoman urban centres home. Others were agriculturalists who had owned vast tracts of land in one of the rich riverine valleys or wide upland plains of Asia Minor. In addition to class and occupational differences, there were cultural ones as well. The people called *karamanlides*, for example, spoke only Turkish but because they were Orthodox Christians, they were included in the exchange of populations. They found themselves, then, enmeshed in a new country where they could not even speak the language. Settling and incorporating such a huge and diverse refugee population was an enormous challenge.

There were two primary strategies for accomplishing this Herculean task. One focused on establishing the refugees on farms in the countryside and the other on creating an urban labour force. The majority of the Anatolian Greeks were settled in the areas of Macedonia and Thrace left vacant by the departing Muslim population; smaller numbers were settled in Thessaly and Crete. The international Refugee Settlement Commission provided families with a plot of land, some farm equipment and supplies. Before the war, Greek farmers in Asia Minor had been remarkably successful in growing tobacco, and this soon became the dominant cash crop in some regions. In addition, there was an appreciable increase in the production of wheat and other cereals for domestic consumption.

But the agrarian resettlement programme cannot be deemed a complete success. Some settlers refused to become farmers and gravitated to the cities. Others, dissatisfied with the plots of land they had been given, abandoned them and moved elsewhere. In some areas this problem was especially acute because wealthier members of the indigenous Greek population had already purchased or usurped the better parcels of land previously owned by Muslims. Finally, the most widespread and acute problem faced by the rural settlers was debt. Unable to sustain their families on the lands provided, many Anatolian agriculturalists had to borrow from the local Greek rural elite. Caught in the nexus of debt, many found themselves reduced to the status of sharecroppers or landless hired labourers compelled to eke out a living working for others.

In the cities, refugee neighbourhoods developed around the makeshift camps in Athens (e.g. Kaisariani, Vyrona, Nea Ionia), Piraeus (e.g. Nea Kokkinia, Drapetsona and Keratsini) and Thessaloniki. The Refugee Settlement Commission devoted considerably fewer resources to dealing with the urban migrants, and so conditions for them remained difficult for longer than they did for the rural settlers. Some state and commission-funded housing was provided, but many people had to make do with hastily constructed shanties (see Figure 13 and Text-box 27). The male refugees provided a skilled and relatively cheap work force.

Women refugee workers entered the labour force in large numbers out of the need to supplement their household incomes or to compensate for the lack of male wage earners. Many of those who settled in the cities had been professionals or entrepreneurs before the exchange, and they helped to invigorate the industrial sector of Greece. Cigarette and cigar rolling, carpet weaving and textile manufacturing grew dramatically, primarily because of the Asia Minor Greeks. The Greek economy between 1924 and 1930 witnessed its highest level of industrialization up to that time. Nonetheless, for many years, the economic condition of the refugee population was grim. Low

FIGURE 13 *Inner City Blues (1938). This cartoon captures vividly the dark side of the Athenian underworld in the aftermath of rapid urbanization, the influx of the Asia Minor refugees and the economic turmoil of the 1930s.*

Alexandros Koroyiannakis (1938), National Gallery and Alexandros Soutzos Museum, with permission.

Text-box 27 Refugee housing conditions in Athens (1922)

Almost all public housing is squalid even when from time to time the houses appear whitewashed from the outside, because they are all badly built, with roofs through which you can often see the sky, damp earth for a floor, doors leaving huge openings and windows without glass panes. In the old quarters of both cities [Athens and Piraeus], the situation is horrible. ... Narrow streets. Old houses, many ready to crumble. Staircases the planks of which slip underneath the feet of anyone who steps on them. Dry rotted floors, dirty and uneven from the planks that cover the holes one on top of the other, together with pieces of tin that lacerate the feet of barefoot children. Grey walls on which mould and humidity draw bizarre patterns. Narrow courts, humid and dirty. Small rooms like holes. Rooms that used to be warehouses, kitchens or wash-houses. Basements without light, without air, deep basements, some without windows. ... From every door emerge children, pale, yellow, sickly, with drawn faces, eyes red from trachomas, with reed-like legs that make them look like old people as they slowly move their wrinkled little bodies. Filth reigns supreme there.

This excerpt is taken from the conclusions of Employment Supervisors Maria Desypri and Anna Makropoulou concerning the issue of popular housing; although they refer to the first years of the period under examination, they are nonetheless relevant. http://www.ime.gr/chronos/14/en/1923_1940/society/sources/05.html.

wages, nagging poverty and prejudice made life extremely difficult for the urban refugee population.

The refugees faced other problems as well. For many Anatolians both in the city and in the country, there was a culture shock. Torn from their homeland and thrust into a largely alien society, where, as we shall see shortly, they were not particularly welcome, their sense of alienation and psychological dislocation was profound. The plaintive voice and poignant lyrics of the Anatolian singer Antonis Dalgas in his song 'Soútsa Polítiki' captured well the sense of loss and longing that his compatriots felt:

The City [Constantinople] and the Bosphorous
Are my dream
There where my love lives
There is my beloved.

Within a short period of time, the rich cultures of the Asia Minor Greeks began to assert themselves, especially in music, which helped to keep alive a specifically Asia Minor identity. Many refugees were also less than impressed with their new home.

> Their [the refugees] initial impressions of mainland Greek life were disappointing. By contrast with the towns and villages of their homeland, metropolitan Greece could not be viewed in a favorable light. This small country was backward, and parochial, and its people unsophisticated.[7]

To many of those in Old Greece, however, the Asia Minor and Pontic Greeks were different and inferior, and a process of cultural integration was required before they could be fully assimilated into mainstream Greek society. This proved to be very difficult and for some time they faced prejudices bordering on racism. The writer I. M. Panayotopoulos vividly captures this sentiment in the following passage from his novel *Astrofengia* [*Starlight*]. In the midst of a heated debate about the refugees, a royalist protagonist launches into this diatribe:

> Should a person leave his house to give it to one of them? Forget the fact that all of them smell, that they're sick and penniless. One and a half million people! What can poor Greece do for them? . . . There isn't a school, a shed, or a tent left unused. [They are in] theaters, cinemas, churches, coffeehouses – all over Greece. Everywhere! And what people! God protect you from them! ... Let them stay in their homelands.[8]

So, regardless of their previous situation, many refugees faced prejudice and were often denigrated as 'Turkish seed' or 'Turkish-born,' or 'baptized in yogurt' by the native population who considered them dirty, smelly, lazy, ignorant and sexually licentious. On a number of occasions during the 1920s, there were violent clashes between the locals and the refugees in the cities of Athens and Piraeus and in the countrysides of Macedonia and Thrace. The cultural cleavage that divided indigenous and refugee Greeks would take on other dimensions, mainly political, that only served to further rigidify the demarcation between the two groups. In short, the class dynamic of Greek society was altered forever.

In the long term, however, the incorporation of the refugee population into the mainstream of Greek culture and life brought certain benefits; in the short term, there were numerous difficulties and challenges. Greece was now a land polarized along a number of axes. In addition to the political one based on the National Schism, there was now a rupture based on identity – indigenous (*dopii*) versus foreign/refugee Greeks; related to that was another based on geography – Old Greece (south) versus New Greece (north); and yet another based on class and wealth distribution. These ruptures, not surprisingly, translated into profound political instability.

Counting coups

For much of the 'Roaring Twenties', Greece was racked by political turmoil. The old political division between Venizelists and anti-Venizelists ran deeper than ever before, and added to them was an equally deep division between those who wanted to keep the monarchy and those who favoured its replacement with a republic. Moreover, once unleashed, the military found it hard to stay its hand from grabbing the levers of power. In July 1923, a staunch anti-monarchy group within the armed forces formed a group called the Military League; it grew quickly in membership and was led by a number of prominent commanders such as Generals Theodoros Pangalos, Alexandros Othonaios, Giorgios Kondylis and Admiral Konstantinos Hatzikyriakos. The extremism of the Military League soon led to the formation of opposing factions of monarchist officers and of officers who were neither republicans nor monarchists but who simply wanted to bring the schism to an end. One of these latter groups attempted rebellion in October 1923. The Plastiras government quickly suppressed it and, with its suppression, the republican movement gained further momentum. The elections for a national assembly in December were boycotted by the anti-Venizelist parties and so the new chamber was dominated by Venizelists, but the majority of them were opposed to altering the constitution. Nonetheless, because of the growing power of the Military League and the emergence of a numerically significant political party, the Republican Union, the die was cast: the monarchy had to go. Venizelos, even though he was not an avid supporter of abolition, agreed to become leader of the new government in the vain hope that he could keep the ship of state aright.

After less than one month, however, he realized that he was mistaken. The intransigent factions in his own ranks, ranging from the rabid pro-militarists on the right to the socialists on the left, made it impossible for him to command effectively. So once more he went into exile. In the wake of his departure, the Liberal movement split into a number of factions, each of which competed to gain support among the military. After a brief interlude, the Republican Union under the leadership of Alexandros Papanastasiou came to power. He appointed to his cabinet two prominent members of the Military League. Judging the time to be ripe, he brought a resolution calling for the establishment of a republic before the assembly. Some of the other Venizelist parties abstained and so the vote in favour was overwhelming (259 to 3). A few months later, the resolution was ratified in a public referendum by a vote of 69 to 31 per cent. On 13 April 1924, Greece became a republic for the second time. King George II and the royal family left Greece; for the King, this was the second time that he had been forced to leave his homeland, and his bitterness grew even greater. The constitutional questions, however, would not go away, beginning with the fact that many Royalist politicians and supporters refused to accept the abolition of the monarchy and refused to recognize the Republic as legitimate. So, even the change from monarchy to republic did not stem the tide of unrest but, in fact, exacerbated it. In truth, however, many in the general public evinced little enthusiasm one way or another. For government civil servants and for members of the military officers' corps, on the other hand, it was an issue of enormous importance – indeed, possibly even one of life or death. Political instability through the 1920s, then, was in many ways a continuation of the National Schism, only in a different form. Between 1924 and 1928, there were ten prime ministers, two presidents were deposed and one resigned, and numerous military coups occurred. The most brutal of these was that of Theodoros Pangalos in the middle years of the decade.

Pangalos was a career military officer who had begun his climb up the ranks during the Balkan Wars. During the First World War, as the National Schism emerged, he was firmly in the Venizelist camp, serving as military staff of the Provisional Government of National Defence. When Greece entered the war, he commanded an infantry division on the Macedonian front. His real skill, however, was in administration, and in late 1918 he was appointed chief of staff of the General Headquarters. When the Liberals fell from power in November 1920, he was among the Venizelist military officers dismissed from the army. He remained active politically and joined the Venizelist opposition to the Royalist campaign in Asia Minor. He supported the 1922 coup that overthrew King Konstantinos, and played a critically important role in the revolution. His stock rose further when he took on the duties of prosecutor in the Trial of the Six. His disillusionment with parliamentary democracy was driven by his hatred of the Treaty of Lausanne. He felt that Greece had been betrayed at the negotiating table and had given away territories when he felt certain that the national army could defend them. He continued to support Liberal governments, even participating in the cabinet of one in 1924, but he was increasingly disillusioned with the political chaos that seemed to be engulfing the country. And so he joined and then soon led a cabal in the army and the navy aimed at overthrowing the civilian government.

They struck on 24 June 1925. By threatening to attack the main government buildings, Pangalos forced the president of the Republic to appoint him as prime minister. Immediately upon taking up the post, he suspended the Constitution and introduced a series of draconian acts, such as curtailing freedom of the press, as well as a number of others intended to maintain public order. Some of them were substantive, like his ban on public gatherings, while others were purely superfluous but indicative of his conservative bent, like the one that mandated the length of women's skirts. In early 1926, he began ruling as a dictator, modelling his new regime on that of Benito Mussolini in Italy. His dictatorship was a disaster both domestically and internationally. Internally, his actions not only drove deeper the wedge between Royalists and Venizelists, but alienated other sectors of society as well. His disastrous foreign policy damaged Greece's credibility and relations with the Allied powers. A good example of his political blundering was the ill-fated War of the Dog fought with Bulgaria in October 1925. The conflict began when a Greek border guard ran into the frontier zone with Bulgaria to retrieve his dog and was shot by a Bulgarian soldier. Rather than treating this as a minor misunderstanding because of the tensions between Greece and Bulgaria over IMRO's frequent raids into Greece (and Yugoslavia), Pangalos used the incident as a pretext for war. The strategy backfired and the European powers intervened. Greece was penalized for the episode and humiliated. The dictator's support even within his own government fell away, culminating in a counter-coup led by General Giorgios Kondylis on 29 August 1926.

After a brief hiatus, popular elections were held on 7 November 1926. No less than twenty-seven parties put forward candidates. The Venizelist Liberal Union faction won 31.6 per cent of the popular vote and garnered 108 of the 286 seats in Parliament; in the second place was the conservative People's Party (in Greek it was the Λαϊκό Κόμμα; it is sometimes translated as the Populist Party) – they won approximately 20 per cent of the vote and 60 seats. Surprisingly, in third place was the Freethinkers' Party; this fascist movement had been founded in 1922 and was led by King Konstantinos's former chief of staff, a military officer called Ioannis Metaxas. If we aggregate the popular vote not by party but by Venizelists versus anti-Venizelists, then the former won 47 per cent of the vote while the latter won 42 per cent. No one party, or faction, received a majority. And so, after rounds of intense negotiations, a broad coalition representing all of the major parties was formed and the ensuing government was known as the 'Ecumenical government.'

The new government included party leaders across the political spectrum, ranging from the left wing of the Venizelists to the fascist Metaxas. Four major issues faced the all-party government: (1) the regime issue – republic or monarchy; (2) the military question – how to remove the military from politics; (3) the restoration of economic stability; and (4) normalization of relations with neighbouring countries and with the Allies. Venizelos continued to reside abroad but he made known that he supported the Ecumenical government. Given how divisive the issues were and how far apart politically the different parties and the government were, it is surprising that it lasted as long as it did. However, the fragile coalition was collapsing in the summer of 1928. The Liberal coalition was splintering once again and there were rumours of an impending Royalist military coup. In this climate of uncertainty, many in Athens reached out to Venizelos and the severity of the situation, as he put it, 'obliges me to reconsider my former decision not to return to the political stage.'[9] Upon his return, he united the liberal factions and confronted the Royalists, by demanding that they formally and publicly declare whether or not they accepted the Republic. By design, then, the coalition government was brought down and new elections declared.

Venizelos redux

In 1928 Venizelos once more stepped on to centre stage in Greek history. In the August election, the Venizelists captured 63.5 per cent of the popular vote and 90.4 per cent of the seats in Parliament (223 out of 250). Text-box 28 reproduces the widely held views expressed by the novelist Giorgios Theotokas. One Royalist supporter saw Venizelos quite differently. So returned, in his view, 'a real rascal, a true traitor, a real Caligostro of politics, a Cretan liar, who, unfortunately for Greece still lives.'[10]

Weaving together an electoral coalition consisting of the old liberal base and the refugees, 91 per cent of whom supported him, Venizelos crafted an overwhelming majority in Parliament, while the political opposition was thrown into disarray. Many prominent opposition party leaders, in fact, lost their own seats. Metaxas's Freethinkers party saw its support shrink from 16 to 6 per cent and only one seat in Parliament, and the General himself lost in his constituency on the island of Kefalonia. Venizelos was firmly in command and he remained in power until 1932. During these years, he oversaw a period of political stability and economic growth. Under his banner, he brought together an array of interests, including those on the left who found the Balkan policies emanating from the COMINTERN, particularly its support for

Text-box 28 Return of Venizelos (1928)

Chief, saviour, symbol of half of Greece, Satan to the other half, he was certainly for all the President of Greek affairs, the axis around which the Nation was starting to whirl again. Nobody understood what he had in mind, but his presence was enough to upset everything as if this presence emitted some mysterious current, which shook all at once all the forces of the national organism, the forces of faith and heroism, of adventure and plunder, of creation and dissolution, of malice and envy. All the vital instincts which slept unused, awoke again and boiled forcefully on the rosy coasts of the Eastern Mediterranean: Venizelos! Venizelos!

G. Theotokas (1951), *Argo*, London: Methuen, 101.

the establishment of an independent Macedonian state, as sufficient grounds for repudiating the only true leftist party in Greece, the Communist Party. The leftist populist Agrarian Party had grown in numbers but was still a minor presence. The conservative Populist Party provided the main opposition and the central issue separating the two major parties, above all else, was the constitutional question. In spite of a strong parliamentary base, Venizelos had to negotiate his way through treacherous waters. On the one hand, he needed to keep the hardline anti-Royalists in line, most of whom were conservative in other respects; on the other, he had to address the issues held most dear by old-style liberals, leftists and the refugees, a group that, increasingly, was leaning to the left.

Venizelos was able to implement a number of changes, most of them funded by external loans. He introduced numerous reforms aimed at improving Greek agriculture, such as land reclamation schemes, agricultural credit programmes, cooperatives and price supports for agricultural produce. In 1929, for example, the Agricultural Bank of Greece was established with its primary goal being to supply low-interest loans to farmers so as to alleviate the debt crisis. The road and rail networks were improved and expanded. Protective tariffs were raised to make indigenous products more competitive in the marketplace. Public housing projects were erected and made available to poor Greeks. A loan of over £1,000,000 was contracted for the building of public schools. The success of this programme can be gauged even today by the frequency with which one finds 'Venizelist' schools in even the most remote reaches of the country. All of these were sound measures that led to some notable progress. But all too often, in their implementation, these initiatives fell prey to sectarian struggles and political patronage. Typical was the case of the village of Karpofora in Messenia, where two rival cooperatives developed, one for the royalist faction and the other for the supporters of the republic. The schism had become deeply embedded into the fabric of Greek life and the distribution of state resources became integrally tied to political allegiance.

Venizelos also scored some notable successes in foreign policy. He successfully took part in the establishment of the Balkan Pact, a move aimed at lessening its members' reliance on the European powers. In like vein, he signed a treaty restoring cordial relations between Italy and Greece. The most important of his foreign policy initiatives, however, was his rapprochement with Atatürk, culminating with the Ankara Convention of October 1930 by which Greece and Turkey officially recognized the existing territorial boundaries and accepted naval equality in the Eastern Mediterranean.

While this agreement did achieve a workable *modus vivendi* with Turkey, it proved to be a domestic disaster for the Liberals. The treaty stipulated that the lands abandoned by Greeks and Muslims were to be considered as a commensurate exchange and so no compensation would be paid to refugees on either side. This was a bitter blow to the Anatolian Greeks and it led to their turning away from their Cretan champion. Disillusioned and angry, debt-ridden and despondent, many refugees looked to parties on the Left for support.

The 'second golden age of Venizelism' also witnessed an ominous extension of the policing powers of the central state. Even in his first administration, Venizelos had been a firm believer in the need for large and well-trained police forces, and he had taken steps at the time to develop them. Like the military, both the rural and the urban police forces soon became caught up in the mutual recriminations that followed in the wake of the National Schism. The rise of the Communist and the Agrarian Parties during the 1920s led to an even greater emphasis on 'law and order' issues. During the dictatorship of General Pangalos in 1925–6, in particular, the police were given *carte blanche* to break strikes and to combat the increasingly leftist labour movement.

In his second term (1929), pressed by the right wing of his party, the Venizelos government passed the *Idionym* (Special) Law. This legislation gave the state far-reaching powers to crack down on any form of protest. For example, it made it a 'criminal offence to agitate for an overthrow of the existing socio-political order.' Moreover, it became illegal even to propagate ideas that could be construed as threatening the social order. The law also placed very tight restrictions on the activities of trade unions, especially on their legal rights to strike. Under the new law, thousands of labour leaders, trade unionists and Communists were arrested or deported to remote Greek islands. A new fissure, Left versus Right, emerged in inter-war Greece, and the mechanisms of order designed to combat the 'Bolshevik' menace greased the slippery slide to authoritarianism.

The financial crises of 1930 and 1931 initiated a period of political chaos and pushed Greece even further into civil conflict. Venizelos was unable to address the economic dilemma effectively, and so his fragile political coalition began to unravel. The refugee vote splintered as some became disillusioned with the lack of improvement in their lot and so they turned to the more militant parties of the Left, while others abandoned the Venizelist banner because of the diplomatic overtures to Turkey that they perceived as a betrayal. Within the Liberal coalition, splits became evident as men like Papanastasiou, Kondylis, Kaphandaris and Zavitsianos broke ranks and asserted themselves, each seeking to succeed the aged Cretan.

Casting a pall over all political discourse was the constitutional issue, in the latest manifestation of the National Schism. In one parliamentary debate, Panayis Tsaldaris, the leader of the Populists, proclaimed that there would be no crisis in Greece if only the nation could call on the talents of the Martyred Six (referring to the six leaders executed in 1922). Some Royalists even proposed that a public monument be erected to commemorate the slain Six. Venizelos responded by stating that the nation would be solvent but for the 40 million gold pounds of credit promised by the Allies but lost when Konstantinos was returned to the throne.

More significant than the parliamentary posturing was the very real threat of reprisals and purges felt in the military in the event of a change in leadership. Unable to maintain control, Venizelos relinquished power, and elections in the autumn of 1932 produced a hung parliament (Liberals 98 seats, Populists 95 seats, Communists 10 seats and the Agrarians 11 seats). Tsaldaris and the Populists were, after many negotiations, allowed to form a government. When it fell, elections were held once more. On 5 March 1933, in an election contested by nine political parties, the Populists won a clear majority, receiving 38 per cent of the popular vote and 100 of the 248 parliamentary seats. The Liberal vote fell to 33 per cent and its number of seats totalled only 80. The remaining parties shared what was left of the vote, and only one of them got more than 5 per cent of the vote. Plastiras would not accept this outcome and so he attempted a *coup d'etat* in March 1933. The day after the election, Athenians awoke to find fluttering down from the sky leaflets announcing that democracy was suspended and that Plastiras had been appointed as the military dictator. After a series of meetings between the political leaders, including Venizelos, it was agreed that Plastiras would stand down once the new parliament convened on 27 March. Plastiras's attempt to keep the Populists out of power failed miserably. The bitterness of the old disputes rose to the surface of public life.

A few months later, things went from bad to worse. Aggravating an already tense situation was a bungled assassination attempt on Venizelos during the summer of 1933. On the morning of 6 June, Venizelos and his wife were in their car, and along with a police escort, they were making the drive from the affluent suburb of Kifissia to the city centre. When they were about 5 miles from the capital, suddenly their car was overtaken by another one containing five or six men. The assassins suddenly swung their car in between the police vehicle and Venizelos's. They then opened fire on the Cretan's vehicle. Venizelos and his wife flung themselves to the floor of the car as the killers' vehicle overtook them. Over forty bullet holes were found in his car. Miraculously, Venizelos was unscathed. His wife, however, was hit four times and his driver once.

The attempt on his life exacerbated the tensions in the country and created an even greater polarization, particularly after it became known that the assassins had connections to the police and the Populist Party. Tensions remained high and in March 1935, another unsuccessful attempt to topple the conservative government took place, ostensibly to pre-empt a pro-Royalist coup that would abolish the Republic, and this time Venizelos was directly implicated in the military intervention: 'Encouraged by close associates to believe that the Republic was in danger, himself encouraging other associates to believe that the danger was real, the elderly statesman allowed himself to become part of a conspiracy against the elected government of the country, believing all the time that the defence of the Republic against real or imaginary dangers justified the unconstitutional activities of his political and military associates.'[11] Venizelist military personnel were tried and executed, in a move that many say as payback for the Six. Venizelos himself was convicted in absentia of sedition. On 9 June 1935, in an election boycotted by the Liberals, the Populist Party won in a landslide: 65 per cent of the vote and 96 per cent of the seats in Parliament.

The Populists now held power, but still stability proved elusive. The monarchists in his own party toppled Tsaldaris. Led by Kondylis and General Papagos, a rump parliament declared the restoration of the monarchy and in a rigged plebiscite, in which 97 per cent of the electorate supposedly agreed, a bitter and vindictive King George II was restored to the throne. He returned to Greece on 25 November 1935. From Paris, up until his death on 18 March 1936, Venizelos continued to make his voice heard in Greece, but to little avail. The new government scheduled elections for January; these were intended to legitimize and validate its actions. The government had, however, miscalculated the mood of the people. The Royalists won 143 seats, but the Republicans captured 141; with its largest vote ever, the Communist Party won 15 seats and so held the balance of power.

This development was unacceptable to the King and the Right. The political balance was precarious. Labour unrest and massive strikes in May raised the issue of public order. After the strikes were bloodily put down, the Communists were blamed for them. Emerging as a presence in government was Ioannis Metaxas. As one study observed:

> Greek politicians now seemed only too ready to give Metaxas enough rope to hang the Left, a convenient scapegoat, as it has often been in Greece; only they were soon to discover that the aspiring dictator was reserving the other end for them.[12]

When General Papagos seemed unable to maintain order, the King replaced him with Metaxas as Secretary of War. Metaxas consolidated his power base, placing men loyal to him in key positions in the military. Using as a pretext the threat of general strikes planned for 5 August 1936, Metaxas staged a coup. On 4 August he seized control, dismissing what remained of the government and with the King's blessing, he suspended the constitution. Metaxas had become dictator of Greece.

The Metaxas dictatorship

Ioannis Metaxas was born in 1871. After studying at the Prussian Military Academy in Berlin, he became a lifelong soldier. He greatly admired the Germanic qualities of regimentation and seriousness, which he contrasted with the individualism and lack of discipline he saw in Greeks. He rose through the ranks and became a staff member during the Balkan Wars. He established at that time close connections with the royal family, and in particular with the then Crown-Prince Konstantinos. A royal favourite, he soon became acting Chief of Staff. He resigned in 1915 as the schism between the King and Venizelos developed, and he spent much of the war in exile on Corsica. He rose to the rank of general after the restoration but resigned his commission in 1920 in protest over the Asia Minor adventure.

From then on, he was a persistent but minor voice emanating from the far-right fringes of Greek politics. His various forays into electoral contests were mostly unsuccessful; his monarchist parties never received more than a handful of votes. His rise to power was linked completely to his connection to the royal family. Thus, when George took the throne in 1935 and looked for a strong man who could hold the situation together, his gaze fell on his family's old and trusted friend.

Metaxas's 'Third Hellenic Civilization' (the first being ancient Greece and the second the Byzantine Empire) was a curious blend of elements borrowed from the fascist regimes in Italy and Germany and his own idiosyncratic notions about corporatism. Unlike Hitler or Mussolini, Metaxas had no broad base of popular support; Greek fascism was not a mass movement. Also, unlike them, it was not based on any coherent ideology or racist dogma. At best, his rule can be described as authoritarian paternalism. For the most part, the Greek public neither actively resisted nor supported his regime. The type of royalist monarcho-authoritarian regime that Metaxas established with King George II was not too dissimilar from the other fascist regimes that King Alexander had established in Yugoslavia or King Boris in Bulgaria.

Metaxas styled himself as the 'First Peasant' or 'First Worker' of the state. The virtues he extolled were hard work, selfless commitment to the state and self-sacrifice for the public good. His goal was to reshape the national character. Pragmatically, he addressed a number of issues of importance to the working classes. He instituted a coherent programme of public works and drainage projects. He declared a moratorium on debt in the countryside. Price supports for produce were introduced. There were new regulations for the collection and distribution of subsistence grains. For industrial workers, he set wage rates, regulated working hours, guaranteed the five-day working week and passed other measures aimed at making the workplace safer. The bureaucracy was revamped and made more efficient. The military forces were purged and expenditures on men and material increased. He established a variety of national organizations, like the National Youth Organization (EON), aimed at instilling those virtues that the diminutive dictator held dear.

All of this, of course, came at a price: deprivation of freedom. Strikes were outlawed, unions suppressed. Civil liberties and personal freedoms were curtailed. Opposition and obstruction of the public good became treasonable. There was one major uprising against the Metaxas regime, and it took place in August 1938. The insurrection erupted in Crete and Aristomenis Mitsotakis, Venizelos's son-in-law, led it. In the aftermath of its suppression, Metaxas had himself proclaimed 'Premier for Life.' His regime became even more brutal. Under the direction of Konstantinos Maniadakis, the secret police became all-powerful. Communists and other leftists in particular were subjected to systematic repression. Over 30,000 of them were arrested and detained in prisons and concentration camps or sent into exile on remote Greek islands. Torture was routinely used to extract confessions or to make people sign documents that branded others as 'communists' or 'obstructionists'. The new National Schism of Left versus Right was on track to develop into a civil war. But that fight would be delayed for a few years as international affairs intruded into the life of the nation.

The main dilemma for Metaxas was in foreign affairs. By temperament and inclination, he looked to Germany and Italy as his closest friends. And there was certainly a major increase in German economic penetration into Greece. But he also realized that Greece's fortunes were closely connected to Great Britain whose fleet would always pose a threat to his maritime nation. Moreover, throughout the 1930s, it became evident that Greece's national interests in the Eastern Mediterranean (concerning control of the Aegean islands and the Dodecanese, for example) and in the Balkans (especially Albania) clashed directly with Mussolini's plans for his 'new Rome'. Italian expansionism in the region placed Metaxas and Mussolini on a collision course. As war approached in Europe, Metaxas found it increasingly hard to walk the fine line between the Allies and the Axis powers. Mussolini's persistent provocations settled the issue. First came his announcement of the annexation of Albania in April. Then, as his impatience increased at Germany's continued overtures into the Balkans, he decided to assert his independence and so he turned his attention to Greece. Italian aircraft persistently violated Greek national airspace, some even dropped bombs in the proximity of Greek warships, and then on 15 August 1940, torpedoes launched from Italian aircraft sank the Greek cruiser *Elli* in the harbour of the island of Tinos. When he learnt that the Nazis had occupied Romania, Mussolini decided it was time to act: 'Hitler always faces me with a fait accompli. This time I am going to pay him back in his own coin. He will find out from the papers that I have occupied Greece.'[13]

At 3.00 am on 28 October 1940, the Italian ambassador, Emanuele Grazzi came to the dictator's house and delivered an ultimatum: Greece must allow Italian forces to occupy strategic locations in northwestern Greece along the border with Albania or else Italy would invade and occupy them. According to Lela Metaxas, his wife, who was in their room above his office where the meeting was taking place, their conversation began calmly. But soon, she recalled, their conversation became more animated. Her husband responded in an angry tone and at the same time, she heard a loud bang on his desk as he shouted *Oxi!* (No!) Shortly thereafter, he returned to their bedroom and told her that the country was at war and that he must dress quickly. Greece was plunged into war. This was one of the dictator's last acts – he died three months later – and this one act did more to restore Greece's national pride than all of his other actions combined.

9

The terrible decade: Occupation and civil war, 1940–1950

The decade of the 1940s was the most devastating and deadly in Greek history. The horrors of foreign military occupation were combined with the peculiar ravages that only a civil war can bring. The events of this decade left scars that even seventy years later have yet to heal. The literature on this period is vast and growing, as more sources, government documents, personal accounts and oral histories become more accessible. Ideology continues to shape historical interpretations as well. The brief account that follows makes no attempt at completeness, but like the rest of this book, it aims at providing the reader with a general overview of events and developments, and their consequences in shaping modern Greece.

The 'good' war

'GREEKS TO ARMS!' screamed the headline of the popular newspaper *Asyrmatos* on 29 October 1940. Just below it, the sub-headline was 'The Enemy Has Come.' Then in an offset text-box, the paper's editor-in-chief declared on behalf of all Greeks, 'Our Lives in the Service of the Fatherland!'[1] So began the Italo-Greek War of 1940–1.

The Italian forces seized the initiative, and even though they were inadequately prepared, they launched a massive invasion from Albania into Epiros along three fronts. Because of the mountainous terrain, their superiority in armoured vehicles was obviated and because of poor weather, they could not fully capitalize on their superior air power, though they managed to launch some sorties, one of which bombed the city of Patras. By 5 November, the Italian forces had reached the farthest point of their incursion into Greece. Along the coast, they marched south and captured the city of Igoumenitsa, from where they had planned to invade the island of Corfu; rough seas, however, washed out their plans. They had made their greatest gains in central Epiros, pushing deep into the interior and capturing the area around Mount Smolikas, including the town of Konitsa and the large villages of Kerasovo and Samarina. Altogether, over 80,000 Italian troops participated in this initial invasion of Greece.

On the morning after Metaxas's strident declaration of Greece's resistance to Italian aggression, tens of thousands of Athenians took to the streets to show their support for the dictator. The nation as a whole rallied behind him, and men of all political persuasions ran to join the fray. While beneficial to the nation, this development spelt trouble for the diminutive dictator. 'The danger to [Metaxas] was that his liberal and socialist opponents were even more ardently opposed to the Axis than his supporters. . . .'[2] The leadership of the Communist Party, for example, sent out a letter calling on its members to join the war against the fascist invaders, arguing that the class war against the Greek Right could only be waged once the nation was safe from foreign invaders. Many of those who had escaped incarceration by signing a declaration of renunciation saw the Italian conflict as a chance for them to redeem themselves. The war became a struggle for national liberation that cut across old political divisions and current ideological divides.

There were, however, warning signs. The first was that, hidden behind the zeal of the officers' corps to defeat the Italians, there still remained sympathy for fascism as a political system in general and for National Socialism in particular. Second, the very high levels of German investment in Greece made some financiers and industrialists reluctant to support any moves that could alienate the Third Reich. These rifts, however, would only become evident later. At the start of the war, unity was the cry.

Under the leadership of General Giorgios Tsolakoglou, commander of the III Army Corps, the Greek forces in Epiros had by early December driven the Italian army out of Greece, through most of Albania, and were on the verge of pushing forward even possibly to the sea. Many Greeks saw this campaign not only as a war against the Italian invader but also as an opportunity to liberate the Greeks of 'northern' Epiros. Had it not been for the onset of a very severe winter that literally froze the army in place, the campaign would have been successful (see Text-box 29 for some accounts of conditions along the front during the frigid winter months).

Great Britain at this time had no other active ally except for Greece, and Churchill was determined to stand firm with Greece; consequently, he offered Metaxas air support and troops. The dictator accepted the former but not the

Text-box 29 Epirote front during the winter of 1940–1

The arm cracked like glass

One night a soldier, the son of a general, died of cold. He had been on guard and had fallen into a torpor in the cold and when they changed duties, they found him frozen. They took him by the arm to lift him up, but his arm cracked and fell off like glass. The major was scared lest other lads die in the night and decided to have fewer duties, to keep only the vanguards with sub-machine-guns, in order that fewer soldiers would be exposed to the snow-storm. ... One dawn, the major heard the sub-machine-guns firing and rushed to see what was going on. It wasn't an Italian attack, as he thought, but a soldier had again frozen and his companions were shooting their machine guns to heat their barrels and warm his frozen body with them.

Christos Zalokostas. http://www.ime.gr/chronos/14/en/1940_1945/war/pigi04.html.

The march to the front

Night after night, we would walk without stop, one after the other, like the blind, with difficulty ungluing our feet from the mud where at times they sank knee-deep. More often it was drizzling in the streets outside as it was drizzling in our souls. And the few times we stopped to relax, we wouldn't say a word, staying grave and taciturn. Shining a small torch, we would share raisins one by one. Or there were times, if it was convenient, when we would quickly undo our clothes and scratch ourselves with rage for hours on end, till the blood started dripping. For the lice had reached our necks, and this was more insufferable than tiredness. Then sometimes a whistle was heard in the dark, a sign that we were starting, and again like beasts we shuffled forward to gain time, before it was dawn and we became the target of aeroplanes. For God didn't know of targets and such stuff, and as is his custom, he always made the light of day dawn at the same time. Then hidden in the gullies, we would lean our heads towards the heavy side, where no dreams came out. Even the birds were angry with us, because we didn't pay any attention to their words – and maybe because we made the world ugly for no reason.

Odysseus Elytis. http://www.ime.gr/chronos/14/en/1940_1945/war/pigi04.html.

latter for fear of provoking Hitler into intervening. If Britain were to provide troops, the forces would have to be large enough to defend Greece from a German attack. Otherwise, a large British presence in Greece would be counter-productive. When Metaxas died of septicaemia on 29 January 1941, his successor, Alexandros Koryzis, changed course and accepted London's offer, and in March, a British Commonwealth expeditionary force of 63,000 men landed in Greece and on Crete. But the fate of Greece hung on decisions made not in London but in Berlin. As early as December 1940, because the Italian advance had faltered so badly and was edging towards failure, Adolf Hitler and the German High Command had determined that German military intervention would almost certainly be needed, and so they started to plan for it. Operation Barbarossa, the German invasion of the Soviet Union, was on course for the spring of 1941 and, for two reasons, the Balkan front had to be secured. First, history had shown Germany that its underbelly to the south could be exposed, and the idea of simultaneously having to fight a three-front war was very unattractive. Second, the vital oil supplies to the Middle East and North Africa had to be safeguarded. Since Mussolini did not seem up to the task, the Germans decided on a joint invasion with their Bulgarian allies against Yugoslavia and Greece. The invasion plan was called Operation Marita (Map 5).

The British expeditionary force that had landed in March proved of little help as a result of confusion between the various military commanders, and so, because of poor coordination, the forward Greco–British line was established too far south for it to be defensible. During the inter-war period, Greece had constructed a number of artillery fortresses near the Bulgarian border known as the Metaxas Line. When the German blitzkrieg was launched on 6 April 1941, the Greek and British forces quickly fell. One part of the German expeditionary force moved westwards through Macedonia, and captured the city of Florina. By 19 April, this force had pushed forward to Grevena and then Metsovo, thus isolating the army of Tsolakoglou from the rest of Greece. Trapped between the Italian army to its north and the German army to its south, without even putting up a fight, it capitulated to the Germans on 20 April. To add insult to injury, Tsolakoglou offered to serve in a government of occupation, if that were the Führer's wish.

Meanwhile, the other part of the German invasion force rapidly rushed south. As had happened in France with the Maginot Line, rather than assaulting the Metaxas Line head-on, the Wehrmacht used their greater mobility and just went around it. The advancing Nazi forces demonstrated overwhelming tactical and technical superiority against the Anglo–Greek forces, which continued to fall back before the German assault. Once the Metaxas Line fell, they retreated to the Aliakmon Line, which held out for three days; the next defensible point was the pass of Tempe near Mount Olympus, but it also had to be abandoned in a matter of days. The next stand was made on the spot where many times in the past Greeks had stood against an invader from the north: Thermopylae. This time, however, the men defending the pass were mostly non-Greeks: they were New Zealanders and Australians.

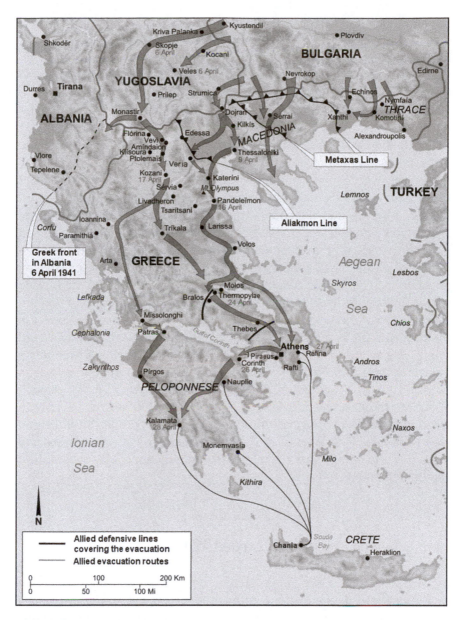

MAP 5 *Operation Marita, 1941.*

The Germans mounted a frontal assault on the pass, hoping to break through quickly, catch up, and then force a battle that would completely destroy the retreating Anglo–Greek army. But numerous small detachments put up a stiff rearguard resistance, sometimes holding their position with just a few men and a single gun. They held on as long as they could, firing until they had exhausted their ammunition. From 18 April onwards, this was the story: rearguards holding the German advance just long enough to allow the main forces to retreat to Athens, until eventually there was nowhere to retreat to. Then the Greek leadership had to choose between fighting a battle impossible to win, or evacuation. The government and the military abandoned Athens. It would be years later and after much suffering that Allied troops would re-enter the city.

On 26 April, Axis forces entered Athens without encountering resistance. Athenians had been told in advance not to put up a fight but to bear the occupation with courage and patience. Over German opposition and at Mussolini's insistence, the Axis military paraded through the city's sullen streets. King George II and the civilian government under the newly appointed Prime Minister Emmanouil Tsouderos fled and eventually settled in Egypt. It would be a government-in-exile for some time to come. The remnants of the Greek army and the British expeditionary forces crossed over into the Peloponnesos determined to make a stand at the other place where Greeks had traditionally defended their land: the Isthmus of Corinth. Within sight of the great medieval walls that had defended the region in the past, the Greek forces dug in, but before doing so they blew up both the railway and the road bridges across the Corinth Canal. But even these measures failed to halt the Wehrmacht's advance. German warplanes pounded the Greek positions, while German army engineers built makeshift bridges at the east end of the canal, thus allowing mechanized vehicles to cross into the Peloponnesos. Yet again, resistance had proven futile and what was left of the Anglo–Greek army evacuated to Crete. It remained there until the brutal invasion by German paratroopers in May successfully captured the island.

Occupation

By June 1941 Greece was a defeated country. The German authorities were then confronted by the question of how to control this crucial part of the world. They established a puppet government under the leadership of General Tsolakoglou so that some semblance of a legitimate Greek government with which they could deal would exist. Tsolakoglou had a very difficult time convincing members of the old political order (who had not fled) to join his government and so he had to rely on inexperienced military men like himself. In the end, he also had to draw on the support of a number of far-right Greek parties, such as the Greek Fascist Party, the National Union of Greece and the Nationalist-Socialist Political Organization of Greece.

The primary duties of his quisling administration were to maintain law and order, to oversee the economic takeover of the country and to liaise with the occupying powers. Shortly after the fall of Athens, the SS, working with the Greek police and using the infamous files kept from the days when Maniadkis was head of security, began to round up known Communists, Venizelists and anyone else whom they considered to be an enemy of the Reich. Germany and its other Axis allies met with the quisling government to divide the country into zones of occupation over which Axis powers would have administrative control. The way that people experienced the occupation varied significantly depending on which zone of occupation they were in and their proximity to their region's administrative centre.

The Germans retained control of Athens, Thessaloniki, Crete, the Thracian border zone with Turkey and a number of the Aegean Islands. The Bulgarians were given Thrace and Eastern Macedonia, which they proceeded to rule with an iron hand. The Italians occupied the rest of the country. The loss of Macedonia and Thrace to the Bulgarians was especially humiliating to the Greeks. The barely healed wounds from the Macedonian struggle and the inter-war period (the War of the Dog) were opened again as the Bulgarian army of occupation let loose a reign of ethnic terror that caused over 100,000 Greeks to leave the Bulgarian zone of occupation. They also actively encouraged and provided material inducements to Slav Macedonians who were Greek citizens to sign Bulgarian identity cards.

The Italians also used ethnicity as a means of dividing the rural Greek population, especially among the Slav Macedonians and the Vlachs. In the region of Thessaly, for example, they formed a paramilitary force called the Roman Legion that consisted almost exclusively of Vlachs. Though this strategy of divide and rule met with only limited success, the impact of foreign occupation on local society was, nonetheless, devastating, as the passage in Text-box 30 shows.

In addition to predations by the occupation forces and their local surrogates, the systematic plundering of the nation's economic resources was also overseen by the Germans. It was akin to a systematic rape of the Greek economy. Key commodities like bauxite and other minerals were either seized or purchased at a fraction of their true value. The bulk of the harvests of the major food crops – wheat, olives, vines, citrus and other fruits – were confiscated for the provisioning of the occupying troops. Moreover, the Greek people were to underwrite the costs of the foreign forces. As Mussolini ruefully put it, 'The Germans have taken from the Greeks even their shoelaces and now they pretend to place blame for the economic situation on our shoulders.'[3]

This ransacking of the Greek economy combined with the naval blockade, which the British put in place in order to prevent supplies from falling into Axis

> ## Text-box 30 Description of collaborationist forces (1941)
>
> This [1941] was indeed a thrice-accursed winter... . Black, black as pitch, was the night that this unbearable slavery had cast over them! And in this night of horror, the [Roman] Legion, greatest blight of all, lightened and thundered! In very truth, the Legion stormed through the night. Its army now amounted to more than three thousand men and was made up of a collection of the most impudent adventurers and worst vagrants in the area. Most of them were criminals who had managed to escape from the prisons when the Germans invaded the country. They wore arm-bands on the sleeves, carried truncheons in their hands, pistols in their belts, and, occasionally, light Italian rifles on their shoulders. They strutted, well-fed and clothed, among the starving and ragged population and spread terror around the plain. Reports came in from every village of brutality, insults, beatings and torture; of people being hung by the arms or legs from trees in the public squares so that whole villages might witness the tyranny and humiliation. There was nowhere to turn for protection. No one dared to ask for protection for if a court decision was issued against the offenders, they would pay the victims back with more beatings and with even more ferocious persecution
>
> E. Averoff-Tossizza (1981), *The Call of the Earth*, New Rochelle, NY: Pella, 195.

hands, quickly produced massive food shortages. By May 1941, there was only twenty-one days' worth of wheat left in the national stores. Through the summer, peasant farmers began to hoard food, refusing to send anything to the urban markets. The German leadership turned a deaf ear to the warning calls, and the Italian authorities responded that they were simply unable to help. By October, the first bodies began to appear on the streets of Athens. Famine soon spread to other regions and cities as well. Some perished from lack of sustenance and many others from malnutrition-related illnesses. Accurate statistics are not available and so the numbers of deaths related to the famine are estimates. Also, the impact of food shortages varied across the country, with some regions suffering more than others. Perhaps as many as 50,000 people perished during January and February, and all together, by the end of the Occupation, approximately 300,000 people had died as a consequence of famine and malnutrition (Chart 5).[4] Hard hit were infants and children, with diphtheria in particular taking a gruesome toll on them. Over the course of January 1942, 700–800 children were dying daily from the disease; this mortality rate was exacerbated by the fact that Athenian hospitals had exhausted their supply of the diphtheria antitoxin. At that point, anywhere from 400 to 1,000 people were dying every day in Athens and

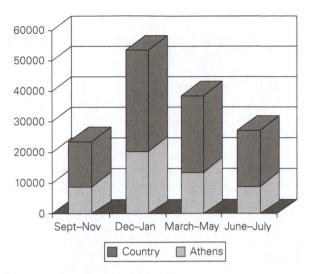

CHART 5 *Famine deaths in Greece, 1941–2.*

Piraeus (see Text-box 31).[5] Eventually, the British government agreed to lift the blockade and allow humanitarian aid to enter the country. During the darkest days of winter, the Turkish Red Crescent acted as a conduit through which supplies purchased with funding from abroad (see below) were conveyed (Figure 14). Soon the Swedish-run Joint Relief Commission took the leading role in coordinating the supply and distribution of aid.

Greece's valiant stand against the Italian invasion and then its horrific suffering under the occupation forces did more to rehabilitate the image of Greeks and Greek-Americans in the eyes of mainstream American society, but it also mobilized Greek-American communities like nothing before. In many communities, it was through their collective relief efforts that the wounds of the National Schism were healed. One organization more than any other played a critically important role. The Greek War Relief Association was co-founded in 1940 by Spyros P. Skouras, a Greek immigrant who was CEO of 20th Century Fox. Using his Hollywood connections, the organization sponsored fundraising events starring some of the biggest celebrities of the day, such as Bob Hope, Judy Garland, Bing Crosby and Frank Sinatra. Skouras used his studio's resources to produce short films to be shown in movie cinemas. Altogether, the organization eventually raised over $7 million to purchase supplies to be sent to Greece (Figure 15). By February 1942, for example, it had already sent over $1 million to Turkey for the purchase of food supplies for Greece.[6] In addition to sending supplies, the Association also funded the construction and supplying of over 150 medical clinics. The Greek Orthodox Church of North America, and especially the charitable organization, the Ladies Philoptochos Society, mobilized at the community level. The church,

Text-box 31 The famine: First-hand experiences (1941)

13 December 1941 [Diary Entry]

Starvation and misery in the streets and houses. People get swollen. They die in the streets. Germans take everything. The price of food is inconceivable. The spectacle of people unconscious from starvation on the pavements of Panepistimiou Avenue becomes more frequent daily. ... At the station a woman collapses before my eyes as if thunder-struck. She is helped up, people crowd around her and give her money. What's the use of it though?

A. Panselinos (1941), http://www.ime.gr/chronos/14/en/1940_1945/occupation/pigi02.html.

Long sad queues

Queues are long, pathetic, with sad people following a strict discipline of their own – that of a herd. ... Mother offered to join the queue at the bakery. I left home at nine in the morning. She had woken up at six thirty. She believed that she would be among the first. She found two hundred people waiting. I came home at nine in the evening and she was still there, at the same spot waiting for flour to be brought, kneaded, baked and distributed: thirty grammes per person. I held and supported her on the return home. That's why I bought bread from the driver. You buy it with a British gold sovereign.

G. Karagiorgas (1941), http://www.ime.gr/chronos/14/en/1940_1945/occupation/pigi02.html.

I'm hungry [Diary Entry]

Occupation. At street corners the rubbish bins don't expect the car or rather the cart to empty them. They expect hungry people to look in them for something edible: lemon rinds, onion leaves. ... The grocers' shops are empty. The only thing we could find was mustard. Mr Vangelis – our grocer – wonders why everybody buys mustard. ... One day I answered his question: 'Great food', I tell him. ... The words 'I am hungry' echoed constantly in our ears. Children wandered pale and skeleton-like along the pavement shouting 'I'm hungry' so that residents in the ground floors who could hear them would be moved to give them something, if they had anything ... . Sometimes the bakeries gave us bread on ration. It was from sorghum seeds. If you held it in your hands to take home, somebody might have snatched it from you without shame.

Eri Melekou (1941), http://www.ime.gr/chronos/14/en/1940_1945/occupation/pigi02.html.

FIGURE 14 *Famine in Athens (1941). The first to feel the effects of the food shortages of the winter of 1941 were the very young and the elderly. The photograph shows one of the many soup kitchens that were set up to provide basic sustenance to the famished population of Athens.*

Voula Papaioannou and the Photographic Archives of the Benaki Museum, with permission.

for example, mobilized Greek-American children to collect food, clothing and shoes to be compiled into care packages and sent to Greece. Among other things, the Ladies Philoptochos Society conducted sewing bees under the slogan 'knit a sweater, save a soldier.' The activities of the Greek-American community proved instrumental in helping their homeland during its darkest days beginning with the Italian invasion.

By the summer of 1942, the worst of the famine was over; shortages still existed, but a new catastrophe made the situation even worse: hyperinflation (Table 5). The prices of almost every commodity skyrocketed, completing the devastation of the Greek economy. A loaf of bread, for example, that cost 10 drachmas in 1940, by September 1944 cost 34 million. A kilo of olives went from 50 drachmas to 4 billion over the same year span. A pair of typical adult shoes increased in price from 450 drachmas to over 22 billion, perhaps explaining why, according to the author's mother who was active in the relief effort in the Greek community of Manchester, New Hampshire, the most frequently requested item from our relatives back in Epiros was shoes. The Greek drachma was for all intents and purposes worthless, and the only reliable currency in the country was the British gold sovereign. Black markets

FIGURE 15 *'Don't Let Them Starve' (1941). Thousands of posters like this one were produced by the Greek War Relief Fund and distributed all across the United States. They were meant to help mobilize support in America for Greece during the height of the famine. Accordingly, foregrounded in the poster is a depiction of an emaciated mother holding her clearly distressed child. In the background lurks the Greek flag and beneath it, a dying fighter and a desolate landscape.*

GallantGraphics all rights reserved.

flourished and profiteers and collaborators benefited from the sufferings of others. Memories of these dark days would be indelibly etched in the minds of many and the thirst for revenge against those who had exploited the situation would only widen the already yawning divisions within Greek society.

The brutality of foreign occupation did not stifle the will to resist. Shortly after Greece's capitulation, in the spring of 1941 sporadic acts of resistance occurred, the most audacious of which took place on the night of 30 May when two youths, Apostles Santas and Manolis Glezos, scaled the sheer slopes of the Acropolis and tore down the Nazi swastika flag from its flagpole. Their daring and heroic act of defiance gave the people of Athens much-needed

TABLE 5 Hyper-inflation in Greece during the Axis occupation (October 1943–September 1944)

	1940	October 1943	April 1944	September 1944
Bread	10	13,000	46,000	34,000,000
Cheese	60	120,000	6,000,000	11,600,000,000
Olive Oil	50	80,000	28,000,000	4,000,000,000
Olives	26	22,000	12,000,000	4,000,000,000
Shoes	450	8,000,000		22,040,000,000

Text-box 32   Resistance and liberation organizations (1944)

All Party

PEEA: The Political Committee for National Liberation

Leftist National Liberation Groups

EAM: The National Liberation Front
ELAS: The National People's Liberation Army
EPON: The National Panhellenic Youth Organization
OPLA: The Organization of Political Popular Defence
EEAM: The National Workers' Liberation Front

Centre-Right Groups

EKKA: The National and Social Liberation Front
EDES: The National Republican Greek League

Pro-Axist/Monarchist

ED: National Action

hope at a critically important time. To this day, Glazos is venerated and his act of defiance still celebrated. Other sporadic acts of sabotage that caused real as opposed to symbolic damage were conducted in various parts of the country. On 29 May, for example, two Bulgarian ships were blown up in the harbour of Piraeus; two days later, a Wehrmacht arms depot in Thessaloniki was destroyed. These were for the most part sporadic and uncoordinated actions.

During the summer of 1941, however, more organized resistance movements began to form (there would eventually be many of them, and Text-box 32 gives a list of the major ones with their full names in English and their Greek acronyms). Workers and trade union leaders in Athens, for example, created the National Workers' Liberation Front (EEAM). Other groups also started to organize. In September, an organization was formed to direct resistance activities: EAM – the National Liberation Front (EAM, the *Ethnikon Apeleftherotikon Metopon*). Text-box 33 reproduces excerpts from the organization's foundational statement. While its primary goal was to drive the Axis forces out of Greece, an ancillary aim soon emerged: to ensure that there would be a free choice regarding the nature of the government that would be formed when the country was liberated. The old constitutional issue raised its head once more.

From the onset, members of the Communist Party of Greece (KKE) held dominant positions in EAM and in the other resistance organizations it created, like ELAS and EPON (about which more will be said shortly). They

---

Text-box 33 The statutes of EAM (1941)

By the representatives of the undersigned parties the National Liberation Front (EAM) is founded. Every other party or organization that accepts the principles of the statutes and wishes to work for the implementation of the objectives of EAM is equally accepted by it. In order for any organization to be accepted into EAM, the past or its ideas concerning the future reconstruction of the free and independent Greece are not examined, but simply its belief in the necessity of the National Liberation Front, its honesty towards it and the acceptance of the principles of EAM included in the statutes.

The objective of the National Front is:

a) To liberate our Nation from the present foreign yoke and to acquire full independence for our country.

b) To form a provisional government of EAM immediately after the expulsion of foreign conquerors, the sole objective of which will be the proclamation of elections for a constitutional assembly, under a system of proportional representation, in order for people to express their view as sovereign on the way they want to be governed.

c) To consolidate this sovereign right of the Greek people to express their views on the way they want to be governed, protecting them from every reactionary attempt that may try to impose on people solutions against their will, and to eliminate any such attempt by all the means of EAM and the instruments forming it.

27 September 1941

From the text of the statutes of EAM. http://www.ime.gr/chronos/14/en/1940_1945/resistance/pigi02.html.

were able to do so for a number of reasons. First, the persecutions during the Metaxas years had forged an identity and a unity that gave the organization coherence. It also gave many party cadres a powerful incentive for revenge against members of the Right, some of whom were now actively collaborating with the occupation forces. Second, it possessed an organizational structure and experience at clandestine activities that meant it was the one group ready and able to undertake resistance activities. Third, with its slogans about social justice, people's power and economic prosperity, the Communist Party projected a vision of a better future that resonated with the impoverished peasants and destitute workers at a time of great suffering. Fourth, they were standing firmly with the people in Greece in contrast to the old politicians and the king who had fled to the safety of London or Cairo. From shared suffering came unity of purpose.

EAM and ELAS were without a doubt the most important resistance organizations and they were simply different branches of the same one. EAM was the political arm of the resistance. Its role was to coordinate civilian opposition to the occupiers. In addition, it was to constitute an alternative Greek government to the quisling, collaborationist one in Athens or the monarchical one abroad. EAM would govern at the head of the people's democracy in Free Greece. The vast majority of members of EAM and ELAS, however, were not Communists, even though the leadership clearly was. Instead, it drew on a wide spectrum of Greek society, and it attracted, in particular, many men and women who had been largely unempowered under the old style of elite politics that had dominated Greece since its inception. In resistance to the Axis occupation and in the space provided by EAM, many experienced personal freedom for the first time. This was especially the case for women, as the excerpts in Text-box 34 make clear. For the reasons set out here, then, the majority of people were ready to follow EAM, even though

Text-box 34 Women in the resistance (1945)

We just wanted some freedom as women, the right to speak up, not to be the subjects of men … working and getting beaten. We wanted some freedom for ourselves. Here we went out to the mountains, carried ammunition on our backs, built pillboxes for machine guns, worked day and night – we even became liaisons, even though we were women. And all we wanted was some good to come to us. Some freedom, not slavery, how would you call it? To have the right to open our mouths.

R. Van Boeschoten (1997), *Αναποδα χρόνια. Συλλογική μνήμη και ιστορία στο Ζιάκα Γρεβενών (1900-1950)*, Athens: Plevron, 102.

many did not support the KKE's political vision of a Communist post-war Greece. There were other resistance groups, the most important of which was the National Republican Greek League (EDES). But EAM/ELAS remained the dominant formation.

The government-in-exile and the monarchy had little contact with the forces in occupied Greece. King George II was active in lobbying the Western allies on behalf of Greece. During 1942 and 1943, he visited the United Kingdom, the United States and Canada, making speeches and meeting with government officials. During the summer of 1942, for example, he spent nearly two weeks visiting with President Franklin D. Roosevelt. As the First Lady noted in her diary: 'We sat on the South Porch, had tea and talked for a little while. The dinner in the evening was entirely official. The President, both last night and this morning, had an opportunity to get to know this ruler of a country which is today undergoing such terrible hardships. Of all the countries in Europe, Greece seems to be suffering more from lack of food than any other.'[7] Using these venues, he launched appeals for aid for his country, he reminded the Allies of the great sufferings that Greece was undergoing, and he emphasized the role of the regular Greek army in fighting the Axis. Rarely did he mention the activities of the resistance movement inside occupied Greece. There were contingents of the Greek armed forces that continued fighting alongside their British and American allies. But even within the regular military, men were becoming dissatisfied with the old political leadership, and, indeed, on a number of occasions mutinies did take place. Already tainted by his role in the Metaxas regime, the King's position at home was made even more suspect by his absence. Already deeply fractured by the cleavages that divided them since 1915, the old political parties found themselves out of touch with the Greek people as well. Moreover, many new faces were emerging through the vehicle of the resistance movements.

> Patriots! I am Aris Velouchiotis, Colonel of Artillery. Starting today, I am raising the banner of revolt against the forces occupying our beloved country. The handful of men you see before you will soon become an army of thousands. We are just a nucleus.[8]

So spoke Athanasios Klaras to the villagers of Domnitsa in central Greece in June 1942. Standing behind him were 300 armed men who more closely resembled bandits than they did an army. But men and women from Dominitsa and hundreds of other villages and towns soon proved his words true as the ranks of ELAS swelled. Under his nom du guerre, Aris Velouchiotis, Klaras emerged as one of the leading *Kapetanioi* (Captains) in ELAS. Born in the town of Lamia in 1905, he came from a modest background. While a teen, he joined the Communist Party and became so active a member that he was arrested by the Metaxas regime. Like many others, in order to secure his release from custody, he signed a declaration of repentance, a move that alienated him from many in the party and raised suspicions about him with others. These tensions persisted during the years of the resistance. He was both charismatic and brutal: known for his fits of anger as well as his common touch. From the moment of ELAS's inception in February 1942 onwards, Aris played a role in it and participated in its greatest successes. Even after professional soldiers, like General Stefanos Sarafis, joined the movement and took on leadership positions, Aris continued to be, as it were, the face of armed resistance.

By late 1942, ELAS contingents had been formed in central Greece, under the command of Aris, as well as in the Peloponnesos, Macedonia, Thessaly and Thrace. The number of guerrilla warriors in its ranks grew from 2,000 in February 1942 to 45,000–50,000 by September 1944. ELAS became by far the largest of the resistance forces, but in order for it to succeed, it needed support from Western Europe, and that meant Great Britain.

The Special Operations Executive (SOE) of the British military provided arms and experts to the Greek resistance. The SOE, operating together with Aris and other fighters from ELAS and EDES, struck a serious blow against the German war efforts in the Mediterranean, when on 25 November 1942, they destroyed the railway bridge over the Gorgopotamos gorge in central Greece. The result of this was that the supply line to the German forces in North Africa was severed for six weeks. This came at a critically important time because with the Allied victory in Operation Torch (8–11 November) and the subsequent defection of the Vichy French troops, the German High Command was desperate to get replacement troops and supplies to the Wermacht forces in Tunisia. ELAS was forging a resistance movement against the Axis powers that would become the most effective one in Europe.

Through 1943 and into 1944, the Greek resistance movements, and especially ELAS, conducted numerous successful operations against the Axis Powers. According to an SOE operative, Eddie Myers, between 1941 and 1944, they damaged or destroyed over 150 steam locomotive engines, blew up over 100 bridges, and sank well over 250 ships. This was in addition to the ongoing and recurrent destruction of roads and telegraph lines, as well as the ambush attacks on occupation and collaborationist patrols.[9] So successful was the resistance that during 1943, Mussolini diverted thirteen Italian divisions to Greece. Then, after Italy withdrew from the war and Germany took over the task of occupying the former Italian territories, it also had to send six divisions to reinforce its military mission to the country. But ELAS was not the only branch of EAM that was making Greece difficult to rule.

Two of them, in particular, stand out: EPON and OPLA. EPON was the organization responsible for mobilizing the country's youth to oppose the occupation. Similar such movements had, of course, been around before the war. Most notably in the case of Greece was the Metaxas youth organization, whereas the most famous was the Hitler Youth Movement. EPON tended to be most active in the cities and larger towns where the occupation forces were most concentrated. It organized strikes, public protests and marches in order to provoke them. A frequently employed tactic was to have young girls deployed in the forefront of protest marches, defying the collaborationist police to use violence against them. Because children were almost always out and about in public, playing, they could get into places and observe what was going on without provoking the same suspicions as would happen if an adult was doing it. Children could be a valuable source of intelligence. The same freedom of mobility made them ideally suited to act as messengers.

Another effective arm of the resistance movement was OPLA. Its goal was to terrorize the occupation forces and their collaborationist colleagues through assassination and intimidation. Only unmarried men between the ages of eighteen and twenty-two were permitted to join OPLA. Then, after receiving training as assassins, they set about their work. One operative, for example, blew up the police station in the city of Volos in a suicide mission. OPLA forced over 4,000 collaborationist civil servants and teachers to resign by issuing death threats; that so many men found the threats credible speaks volumes about OPLA's efficiency. They also targeted Nazi officers, and at one point even managed to kill a senior officer in the Wehrmacht. It is estimated that during the early months of 1944, OPLA was killing German officers on a daily basis.

ELAS's success had important consequences. First, as it grew in size, its composition changed. Many of the men who flocked to the banner of resistance did so because ELAS was the only organization winning in the struggle with the forces of occupation. This meant that the percentage of fighters who were not Communists increased dramatically. Second, the larger the size of the army, the more challenging was the task of seeing to its logistical needs. Getting sufficient armaments and ammunition remained a real problem throughout the war. In addition to the issue of quantity, there was also the matter of compatibility. In some areas, they were able to get ammunition but the bullets did not fit the guns that they had. And the even more pressing logistical problem was food. Throughout the war, the Greek population was confronted with the daunting task of finding sufficient food to feed their families. While most attention focuses, as it should, on the famine, putting food on the table remained a problem even after the hunger had abated. ELAS and its forces competed with the occupation authorities to get access to the food that was coming in from foreign relief agencies.[10] Because the currency was worthless, almost all commerce and trade was conducted via the barter system. ELAS and EAM increasingly found themselves in the position of having to commandeer food from local farmers with the promise of compensation later, if at all. This policy threatened to alienate the allegiance of the local population, without which the resistance stood no chance of success. Third, ELAS's military success led to the liberation of considerable parts of the country. The single largest contiguous area under EAM's control stretched from northern Attica through central Greece and then up to and including Epiros and Western Macedonia. This was the core of Free Greece, and EAM had the task of governing it, in ways we will discuss shortly.

So, paralleling the successes of its military wing, EAM grew both in size and strength, and became a major political force. But the resistance movement as a whole started to dissolve because of internal pressures. British attempts to coordinate all resistance activities foundered because of Winston Churchill's steadfast support for the Greek monarchy in the face of the widespread resistance to restoration by people of all political persuasions in Greece. It was not long before fighting broke out between ELAS/EAM and the non-Communist resistance groups, especially EDES. This was the largest of the other resistance organizations. Led by a Venizelist, anti-Monarchist military officer named Napoleon Zervas, this organization had split from ELAS. EDES cast itself as the only viable non-Communist-controlled resistance organization and it soon became the favoured resistance unit for the British. So, some of the animosity was based on the virulent anti-Communist feelings among some Greeks, but, by and large, the sectarian violence at this point was based on specific, localized disagreements and antagonisms rather than being part of a concerted effort by the Communist Party to eliminate opposition groups. The struggle over the future course once the occupiers had been driven from the land was yet to come.

One source of antagonism between the resistance movements in the countryside and the old political leadership in the cities was related to the advisability of there being any resistance movements because of the brutal reprisals being visited on the civilian population. As acts of sabotage and resistance increased, so too did reprisals by the occupation forces.

> There were bodies everywhere – in front of the houses and inside them ... there was a church or small chapel in the main square ... and in front of this church lay a large heap of bodies. So far as I could see from the tangled mass of humanity there were more women and children than men there.[11]

This description of the massacre at the village of Komeno in Western Greece in the summer of 1943 could be multiplied many times over.

As ELAS expanded its activities and as the occupation powers started to lose their tight grip on the country, the German Wehrmacht started to play a greater role in maintaining order and security. Then, with Mussolini's fall in the summer of 1943, the Wehrmacht and SS took responsibility for nearly the entire country. There was also a change in policy towards the greater use of violence and fear against the Greek people. The Germans implemented a policy of taking hostages in a vain attempt to undercut local support for the *andartes*. When this proved largely unsuccessful, they decreed that fifty Greeks would be killed for every German soldier lost; as a consequence of this policy, entire villages were destroyed. In some cases, in order to heighten the terror among the populace, groups of people would be randomly selected, marched to a public place and shot. Finally, the German authorities in conjunction with the quisling government of Ioannis Rallis began to utilize gangs of thugs and collaborators whom they organized into units called Security Battalions. Some of those who joined were simply hardened criminals and bad men; the majority were die-hard royalist military officers and policemen, who were opposed to the resistance movements because of the constitutional issue. All told, the security battalions numbered approximately 18,000 men. Divided into ten units, the Greek-manned battalions unleashed a wave of violence and terror that surpassed the actions of the SS.

In October 1943 alone, German and collaborationist forces razed 28 villages, took 839 people hostage and executed another 918. In retribution for resistance activities, on 31 December 1943, 696 men and boys were massacred in the village of Kalavryta in the Peloponnesos. As the war continued to go badly, the revenge exacted on the civilian population increased. In May 1944, for example, 37 villages were destroyed, 671 people were taken hostage and 1,149 were publicly executed. In order to terrorize the population even further, it was common practice after mass executions to string up the bodies along the streets of the towns and the villages where the massacres had taken place. The activities of the Greek security battalions brought terror and destruction that would leave lasting scars on the Greek population for decades to come.

One of the war's other great tragedies was the destruction of the Greek Jewish population. Before the war, there had been vibrant and sizeable Jewish populations in cities like Thessaloniki, Athens and Ioannina. Almost immediately after the occupation began, the German authorities in Thessaloniki began the persecution of the city's large Jewish population. Initially, those efforts took the form of confiscating books and manuscripts. Then, Jewish men were compelled to perform labour service building roads. The ancient Jewish necropolis was destroyed and the headstones used as building material. On one occasion in the summer of 1942, thousands of Jewish men were herded into one of the city's main squares where they had to endure hours of physical torture and public humiliation. Finally, in the spring of 1943, the decision was made to implement the final solution. In the short span of two and a half months, close to 50,000 people from the Macedonian capital alone were sent to Auschwitz and Treblinka; few returned. The communities from the rest of Greece were not spared either. The ravaging of the Greek Jewish communities would have been worse but for the actions of some Christian Greeks who helped their Jewish neighbours to elude detention and deportation. By the time of the last deportation in August 1944, the long history of Jews in Greece had largely come to an end.

In the summer of 1943, events took a new course. British policy underwent a change in direction. In order to pave the way for the Allied invasion of Normandy, it was necessary to convince Hitler that the main theatre of operation was to be elsewhere, for example in Greece. The policy had merit because of the Gallipoli campaign of the First World War. The cooperation of all the resistance movements was required if the plan was to succeed. ELAS, in particular, was needed because it controlled the largest army and occupied the most territory; in fact, by 1943, it had liberated significant parts of the countryside. Increasingly, the occupiers held only the towns and cities.

The so-called 'National Bands' agreement was made in July 1943 and it gave EAM/ELAS primacy in exchange for a cessation of violence against the other groups. The dubious prospects for long-term cooperation between the various resistance groups and the British were shattered in August 1943 as a consequence of a disastrous series of meetings between guerrilla leaders, the government-in-exile and the King in Cairo. The leaders of the resistance had two demands. The first was that the King agree not to return to Greece until a plebiscite had been held. The second was the assurance that EAM/ELAS representatives be given the portfolios of interior, justice and war in the post-war government. Both demands were refused. The guerrilla representatives returned convinced more than ever that the British intended to force King George on the nation.

The immediate result of the Cairo conference was the onset of fighting between ELAS and EDES in October. Forced to choose, the British opted for EDES and so it stepped up arms shipments to them while cutting off the supply to ELAS. This proved ineffective because the surrender of the Italian forces in September had left ELAS much better equipped. Having stabilized its position militarily, EAM declared the formation of a Political Committee of National Liberation (PEEA) on 10 March 1944 with its capital in the heart of 'Mountain', that is, liberated Greece. The PEEA enjoyed a good deal of popularity, in part because it counted among its members prominent non-Communists. To be sure, the KKE was firmly in control, but even the semblance of political ecumenicalism gave it a degree of legitimacy it would not otherwise enjoy. Moreover, with its formation, for the first time since the war had broken out there was an alternative to the government-in-exile. Support for the government of Free Greece only increased when it held elections for a national council. On 25 April 1944, somewhere between 1.5 and 1.8 million Greeks, including, for the first time, women, voted for representatives to sit on the council. In fact, more Greeks voted in this election than in the last free election before the dictatorship.[12] Backed now by a popular mandate, the PEEA set about creating a state including a constitution, a legal system and a financial organization. Not surprisingly, numerous people rallied to its banner. For many in the liberated areas of Greece, the experience of PEEA rule had been an uplifting one, as the following quote suggests:

> The benefits of civilization and culture trickled into the mountains for the first time. Schools, local government, law-courts and public utilities, which the war had ended, worked again. Theatres, factories, parliamentary assemblies began for the first time. Communal life was organized in place of the traditional individualism of the Greek peasant ... EAM/ELAS set the pace in the creation of something that the governments of Greece had neglected: an organized state in the Greek mountains.[13]

For many women, in particular, the experience of the resistance movement was one of personal liberation; they became empowered as never before. Many women echoed those sentiments. Women took part as warriors and workers. Peasants and working-class men also found the prospect of going back to the old ways unacceptable.

Another group also rallied to the call of the PEEA. The only arm of the Greek military that had escaped from the Germans largely intact was the navy. During the years of occupation, it had been forced to play no active role. Many bridled at this inactivity while occupied Greece suffered. The formation of an alternative government provided an impetus for action. Mutinies erupted in the military forces stationed in the Middle East as men clamoured for the formation of a government of national unity that would carry the fight to Greece. The British resolve to resist such a move was bolstered in October 1944 when Churchill and Stalin agreed that Greece was to be in the British sphere of influence and that the USSR would not interfere.

The mutinies led to a change in the Greek leadership. George Papandreou was appointed as the new prime minister. As a loyal liberal supporter of Venizelos and a Republican, he, it was hoped, would woo away non-Communist, anti-Monarchist EAM supporters; as a staunch anti-Communist, he, it was expected, would toe the British line. His appointment was like waving a red flag, as it were, at the guerrilla forces. It nearly guaranteed a deadlock. In an attempt to form a workable government, Papandreou convened in May a conference in Lebanon, the goal of which was to devise a structure for the restored government. Twenty-five PEEA delegates attended the conference, but only two of them were Communists. The affair was stage-managed by the British. After intense debate, an agreement was drafted, but in the course of the conference, the Communist members found themselves isolated, even from the other members of their own delegation. Though the final pact assured EAM of participation in the government, the Communists did not gain control of the key ministries they sought, those relating to the military and the police. Initially, they refused to accept the agreement. But under pressure from Moscow, they finally acceded. Elevating tensions even higher was the impact of the agreement arranged at Caserta in September between Communist representatives, the government and the British authorities whereby ELAS agreed to allow British troops to land in Greece to support the Papandreou government, to place ELAS troops under the command of British General Ronald Scobie, and to keep ELAS forces out of the major metropolitan areas and out of those few regions controlled by EDES, and finally they accepted that only the Government of National Unity would have the right to try and punish collaborators.

The Germans began to withdraw from Greece in October 1944. For the previous five months, Greece had witnessed a vicious three-sided war between the German forces and those of Occupied Greece, and those of Free Greece. As the Wehrmacht marched northwards towards the Bulgarian border, it left a swathe of destruction in its wake. Villages were burnt, bridges destroyed and roads and railways blown up. The resistance forces harassed the retreating German army at every turn. They also turned their wrath on the garrisons manned by the Security Battalions that the Germans had left behind. In an orgy of revenge, collaborationist forces in the Peloponnesos, Macedonia and Thessaly were slaughtered. With the Third Reich's forces removed from the equation and the Security Battalions in disarray, ELAS was left as the paramount military presence in the country. Yet, the PEEA made no concerted attempt to seize power – something it could easily have done. Why the Communist Party, whose members occupied most of the key posts in the government, did not seize this moment when they still possessed a formidable fighting force and enjoyed a broad base of support with the general populace is still the topic of intense debate. They would soon lose both, and with that passing, the opportunity for a Communist seizure of power had come and gone.

Civil war

October 1944 was a fateful month for Greece. On the 18th, George Papandreou and the Government of National Unity entered Athens. He did not come alone. With him were the Greek armed forces that had been in exile and a small British expeditionary force under the leadership of General Ronald Scobie. Papandreou appeared to be the right man for the job because he was more or less acceptable to most of the key players. A lifelong Liberal, he had been a strong supporter of Venizelos and during the National Schism he was a hardline opponent of King Konstantinos. From then on, he was against the institution of monarchy and a supporter of Republicanism. During the Metaxas dictatorship, he had been exiled and so was out of Greece when the Italian war began. Shortly thereafter, he joined the government-in-exile in Egypt. Many on the Left felt that he was acceptable because he was a Republican; to many centrists and to the British, his ties to Venizelos gave him credibility; to non-collaborationist conservatives, he was acceptable because of his well-known anti-Communist stance. With tepid support from the major Greek factions, Papandreou had to rely largely on British support to undertake the Herculean task of rehabilitating occupied Greece.

Initially, the euphoria of liberation swept all before it. Rejoicing in the streets went on for days as people tried to forget, for however brief a time, the horrible travails of the last four years and the daunting task of reconstruction that loomed before them. But fear and mistrust abounded. Too many key issues remained unresolved; prominent among them was the constitutional question. Should the monarchy be allowed to return? And, if so, under what conditions? Was a referendum required? Or should the country become a republic once more? The constitutional question was, however, not the only one. In a culture where the ethos of vengeance runs deep, retribution against those who had cooperated with the Axis Powers was on many people's minds. Would Papandreou aggressively pursue and punish the collaborators? On the other side, the new government laid down conditions for the participation of the government of Free Greece in the new liberation coalition government. They were that ELAS had to disarm and the political wing had to dissociate itself from international communism. Given the climate of distrust and suspicion that pervaded Greece at the time, not surprisingly, tensions between the liberation National Unity government and Free Greece increased.

Meanwhile, thousands of miles away, an event was taking place that would play a critically important role in determining Greece's future. At some point during the Second Moscow Conference of the Allied leadership (9–19 October), Winston Churchill and Josef Stalin came to an agreement known as the Percentages Agreement (Text-box 35 reproduces Churchill's recollection of the event). As the agreement made clear, Greece, or 90 per cent of it at least, was to be under British influence.

When, therefore, Papandreou and the British showed little interest in pursuing and punishing collaborators and members of the Security Battalions, suspicions on the Left were raised further. As part of the agreement reluctantly agreed to earlier, on 10 December, the 60,000 armed men and women of ELAS were to lay down their arms, with the exception of one elite unit equal in size to the government's Sacred Battalion and Mountain Brigade. In late

Text-box 35 The percentages agreement (1944)

'Let us settle about our affairs in the Balkans. Your armies are in Romania and Bulgaria. We have interests, missions and agents there. Don't let us get at cross-purposes in small ways. So far as Britain and Russia are concerned, how would it do for you to have 90% predominance in Romania, for us to have 90% of the say in Greece, and go 50–50 about Yugoslavia?'

While this was being translated, I wrote out on a half-sheet of paper:

Romania – Russia 90%, The Others 10%
Greece – Great Britain (in accord with USA) 90%, Russia 10%
Yugoslavia – 50–50%
Hungary – 50–50%
Bulgaria – Russia 75%, The Others 25%

I pushed this across to Stalin, who by then had heard the translation. There was a slight pause. Then he took his blue pencil and made a large tick upon it, and passed it back to us. It was all settled in no more time than it takes to sit down.

Then, there was a long silence while the pencil and paper lay on the centre of the table. At length I said, 'Might it not be thought rather cynical if it seemed to dispose of these issues, so fateful to millions of people, in such an off-hand manner? Let us burn the paper.'

'No, you keep it,' said Stalin.

(Churchill)

November, however, Papandreou demanded a total demobilization of ELAS's forces, and this the leadership would not do. The question was which side would relent.

In a move designed to put greater pressure on the government, EAM called for a massive rally on 3 December as a prelude to a general strike in protest over the government's high-handedness. Thousands of men, women and children gathered in the Sintagma Square in the heart of Athens. Their banners proclaimed: 'Everyone and everything for the struggle and victory of Democracy.' Three young girls carried a sign with a more ominous message: 'When the people are in danger of tyranny they choose Freedom and the Arms of ELAS.' Tensions ran high. Shortly before the demonstration, an explosion near Papandreou's house had resulted in a policeman's death. For reasons still unknown, and seemingly without provocation, a policeman fired into the large and largely passive crowd. Before the world's press corps, his colleagues joined in. Sixteen people were killed and many more wounded. Open fighting exploded in the streets of Athens between the police, British troops and ELAS fighters. ELAS forces captured a number of police stations, prisons and the security force's headquarters. EAM was not, however, attempting to seize power. Indeed, in cities outside of Athens where ELAS forces far outnumbered British troops, there was no fighting. It would seem that once the fighting against the British had commenced, the aim was to bring down Papandreou. However, ELAS forces outside of the metropolitan areas did seize on the opportunity of the '*Dekemvriana* [December event]' to settle old scores. Napoleon Zervas and his EDES troops in Epiros were attacked and demolished, and elsewhere ELAS fighters went after known collaborators. The potential for escalation of the fighting all across the country was clear.

The situation was extremely tense. Churchill and his Foreign Secretary Anthony Eden flew to Athens in order to gain a first-hand assessment of the situation. They came away convinced that the constitutional issue had to be resolved as expeditiously as possible. Under strong pressure, King George II agreed to stay out of Greece and to appoint Archbishop Damaskinos as Regent. In a concession to the opposition, Papandreou was removed from office and replaced by the old Liberal warhorse General Plastiras. In addition to these concessions, the Communist leadership was leaning towards compromise because it was becoming evident to them that, in spite of their limited successes in December and January, they lacked the supplies to carry on fighting and if they still did so, they would risk losing their greatest asset, the support of the rural populace.

The Greek people had suffered greatly during the war and they wanted peace in order to rebuild their lives. The battles on the streets of Athens had devastated much of the city, as the moving account in Text-box 36 conveys. Reconstruction was going to be a long and costly process, and could only proceed if there was peace. But could a lasting accord be forged out of the ashes of the war? Also, as we saw earlier, during the Dekemvriana, ELAS forces had struck out at anyone who did not actively support them. Both sides committed atrocities. Innocents were killed. The firm support that ELAS and EAM had enjoyed in the liberated zones had started to dissipate. The Communist leadership sought compromise and so a conference was convened to try and stop the conflict.

On 12 February 1945, the Varkiza peace agreement was signed. It ended the fighting of December 1944 and aimed to reconcile the opposing blocs of the country. The Minister of Foreign Affairs Ioannis Sophianopoulos, the Minister of the Interior Periklis Rallis and the Minister of Agriculture Ioannis Makropoulos participated in the talks, authorized by the government of Plastiras, while the EAM delegation consisted of Georgios Siantos, secretary of the central committee of the KKE, Dimitrios Partsalidis, secretary of the central committee of EAM and Ilias Tsirimokos, general secretary of ELD.

Text-box 36   The battle of Athens (1944)

I go up to the big street that begins at Omonia Square, I look, I look, and I cannot take it, my eyes fill with tears. … I keep going up and even though I want to arrive quickly, I stop now and then. The houses that have the most damage shout at me and summon me to mourn for them, to mourn with them for their misfortune … the way is still long. And as no tram or car is to be seen, I will have to walk all the way. In this way I will see a big part of the wounded body of Athens, in neighbourhoods and central streets, and I will grasp what a wild war took place in the thirty-three days that we were shut up and isolated, receiving only the echo of the battle.

I stop now and then, I look and look again as if I want to record the disaster, and here and there I forget where I am. Two in three houses in a row have collapsed, have been blown up, the street is changed, it's not the street I used to know. Athens is like a face so disfigured by wounds that it is hardly recognizable … from one street to the next I get used to the misfortune and I don't look for those responsible and guilty anymore.

I walk down, I keep on walking down the streets, where the hatred became the greatest calamity. Whole houses are missing and the street looks like an open, toothless mouth. Here is where most blood has been shed. A bit further down, in the small square, which is close to our house, I see the first crosses. Among the flowerbeds of the square, in their meagre grass and their much dug earth, three crosses and three names. A few days ago they were three very popular cypresses and now they are three poor wooden crosses a few inches above the earth, in one of the patchy cemeteries, in one of the cemeteries of war and necessity.

P. Haris (1992), *Ημέρες όργες (Δεκέμβρις 1944)*, Athens: Esti, 402–5.

Each side had with it three military experts, while the proceedings were closely supervised by British dignitaries in Athens.

The agreement included nine articles on the basis of which civil liberties, and especially the freedom of the press and union freedoms, were reinstated. It also granted a general extended amnesty, with the exception of offences in common law against life and property, while the government pledged to purge the civil service, the gendarmerie, the Security Police and the police. In return, EAM/ELAS were committed to the liberation of their prisoners and the disarmament of their armed sections. Finally, the Greek coalition government promised to form a national army into which the members of ELAS would be accepted, and undertook to conduct a genuine, free plebiscite as soon as possible during 1945. The agreement was made even more significant by the fact that its text was published in the Official

Gazette, a fact that conferred on its contents the force of law. Nevertheless, the breach of its terms by both sides led to fresh political polarization and the commencement of the civil war.

The Varkiza Agreement initiated what became known on the Left as the 'White Terror'. Rather than prosecuting the collaborators, the Ministry of Justice and the security apparatus, itself still rife with far-right supporters and men appointed during the Metaxas dictatorship, went after leftist resistance fighters. For example, in March 1945, Mihalis Monidas and two compatriots, who had fought valiantly against the Nazis in the liberation of Piraeus in 1944, were sentenced to death for the killing of collaborators during the occupation. The amnesty on 'political crimes' seemed to apply only to members of the Right, like the infamous Security Battalions. Judges of the Popular Justice Tribunals that had flourished in Free Greece were charged with murder. Tax collectors for the PEEA were charged with theft because they were not acting at the time as officially recognized agents of the government, that is, the government-in-exile. Even the young members of EPON were not spared from Rightist persecution (see Text-box 37). Granted, this report by the American Youth for the Youth of Greece, which was after all a communist organization, is extremely biased; nevertheless, the episodes that it recounts are accurate and supported by other source materials.

Right-wing death squads and paramilitary groups, like the *Chi*(X) organization in the Peloponessos, embarked on a campaign of terror and assassination against leftists. Aris was one of those who refused to accept the Varkiza Agreement and so he took to the mountains of Central Greece to once more raise an army of resistance. Alienated from his former political allies, he was easy prey for the national government's forces. In June 1945, he was cornered in his mountain hideout, and rather than surrendering, he committed suicide. The X squad that found his body decapitated it and displayed his severed head on a lamp-post in the Thessalian city of Trikala. Not surprisingly, given the wave of terror that had been unleashed against them, many EAM/ELAS members, Communists and non-Communists alike, went underground for their own safety. Through 1945, a series of weak governments proved incapable of stemming the escalating sectarian violence.

Themistoklis Sophoulis, yet another of the Liberal old guard, formed a government at the end of 1945, and he announced that there would be a national election on 31 March 1946 that would be followed immediately by a plebiscite on the monarchy. This inverted the order stipulated in the Varkiza Agreement. The Left claimed that fair and impartial elections were impossible in the climate of violence and repression overlying the land. The leftist parties, including the KKE, decided to abstain. So a war-weary people went to the polls in what the Allied Mission for Observing the Greek Election (AMFOGE) called 'on the whole' free and fair elections. Without the Left, the choices were

Text-box 37 Treatment of resistance youth during the civil war (1948)

The Greek traitors – the rulers and reactionaries of the country – attacked with particular fury the youth who had created the EPON organization. They did this because they felt that the youth, liberated from their fascist influence, had gone over to the side of the people and democracy. They centred their attacks on the heroic EPON in order to shatter it and disperse it with blows, slanders and lies, they tried to represent it as a terrorist anti-national organization. They hindered its legitimate work, they arrested, demolished and set fire to the premises and institutes of EPON. They arrested thousands of its members, tortured and killed them. They tried to humiliate the girls by cutting off their hair and keeping them away from EPON. They helped the resuscitation of fascist youth organizations by every possible means. EPON, and the whole progressive movement of our youth, were threatened with great danger from these quarters, as a result of this policy of the fascist reaction. The basic duty in these circumstances was thus formulated by the presidency of EPON: 'We must tackle all the new specific problems created for us by the foreign intervention, in order to preserve, in this new storm, the mass character of our organization.'

Excerpt from a report by the socialist organization American Youth for the Youth of Greece entitled the *Youth of Greece is Fighting for Freedom, Independence and Democracy; the Heroic Struggle of Epon* (1948), New York: American Youth for the Youth of Greece. Marxists Internet Archive. https://www.marxists.org/subject/greek-civil-war/1948/x01/youth-greece.htm.

between the United Order of Patriotic Thinkers, a loose grouping of the old Populist Party with Metaxasists, monarchists and anti-Communists, a centre-right coalition, the National Political Union, aged Liberals, and the National Party led by the old EDES warrior, Napoleon Zervas. Even an avowedly fascist party ran in the election. Clearly, the abstention of the Left had a major impact on the balloting and in the final analysis was probably most responsible for putting the United Order in power with 56 per cent of the popular vote that equated to 206 of the 354 seats in Parliament. The leader of the government became Konstantinos (Dino) Tsaldaris, the nephew of the pre-war Populist leader.

The Tsaldaris regime renewed the persecution of the Left, removing civil servants and university professors from their posts because of their politics; head hunting by right-wing bands was stepped up. Arrests were renewed, and soon over 46,000 men and women were interned in concentration camps or sent to island exiles. The country drifted ever closer to civil war.

Far ahead of schedule, Tsaldaris demanded a plebiscite on the monarchy. Rather than waiting until 1948, as had been agreed, he called for the referendum in September 1946. The following excerpts from campaign posters that plastered the walls all around Athens give a sense of how the conservative government presented the case for restoration of the monarchy. In one, a personification of Greece holds up a sign with one word: YIORGIOS (George). Meanwhile, two figures, one symbolizing the USSR and the other the Greek communists, flee in the face of the monarch, and the caption at the bottom of the poster reads: 'Him they fear. Vote for the Monarchy!' Another very popular one was less visually striking but carried a more detailed message. 'The Cross is in danger! The religion of our ancestors is in danger! Patriots beware! Only the return of the King will save Greece. Only the Bulgarians don't want the King to return!!'

By a majority of 68 to 32 per cent, the monarchy was restored. So it was that on 28 September 1946, to the roar of a 101-gun salute, George II ascended to the Greek throne for a third time. The plebiscite was suspect. If not outright rigging, there was certainly coercion. For many Greeks, the restoration represented a betrayal of everything they had fought for. As best we can judge, there was definitively widespread opposition to the idea of a Communist government, but we can be equally certain that there was also widely and deeply felt antipathy to the monarchy in general and to King George II in particular, tainted as he was by his cosy relationship with Metaxas. Others joined the hardcore former ELAS warriors who had fled once again to the mountains of Greece for safety. War clouds gathered on the horizon.

In October 1946, Markos Vafiadis announced the formation of the People's Democratic Army of Greece (PDA). Many came forward and offered to fight. The reason for many was simple, as one partisan put it: 'For a whole year I was tortured, imprisoned, persecuted. I gritted my teeth. But eventually I could stand it no longer, I went to the mountains.'[14] Others more towards the middle of the political spectrum, as well as moderates and rightists who had fought with ELAS against the occupation forces, refused to join the new force. Consequently, the size of the PDA fell from its previous wartime level of approximately 50,000 and now fluctuated between a high of 28,000 fighters to a low of approximately 13,000.

Fighting the foreign occupiers and their collaborationist lackeys was one thing, picking up arms for a Communist revolution was quite another. Atrocities and other assorted acts of violence against those who opposed or who would not join them drove many who had previously been supporters of ELAS into the opposition's camp.

The civil war commenced in earnest during the winter of 1946–7. Markos adopted a strategy of guerrilla war, utilizing hit-and-run tactics to harass the National Army and its ancillary groups like the police and the paramilitary bands. PDA forces scored some notable successes but they were unable to capture any of the major towns. At one point, Markos attacked Konitsa in Epiros, aiming to make it the capital of the Provisional Democratic Government. The assault failed.

The civil war was, like all internecine conflicts, marked by brutality on both sides. Villages were destroyed and civilians killed. Partisans from the Left and soldiers from the Right fought and the majority of the people were caught in between. As one victim of the war recalled, 'Each side [was] as bad as the other.' In addition to the havoc wrought by the armed forces, people used the civil war to fight out personal animosities and hostilities – that was the worst. People who didn't like each other before, or had some long-standing complaint or quarrel with another, used this as a basis for killing and fighting each other.[15] The atrocities of the war would leave lasting scars on the consciousness of the nation.

By the spring of 1947, Britain was reaching a point of exhaustion; it simply could not meet the increasingly high demands for money and supplies. In a memo, the British Foreign Secretary, Ernest Bevan, informed the US State Department that as of 31 March, Great Britain would no longer be able to provide further assistance to Greece. The role of external patron would have to be assumed by the United States, and this was a role that it was willing to play. Increasingly, the State Department had come to see Greece as a place of great strategic importance. George Kennan of the European Desk articulated what became known as the domino theory. He argued that if Greece were to fall to the Communists, then so too would Turkey, and after that, all the states of the Middle East. The containment of communism would begin in the Balkans. With the Greek case specifically in mind, President Harry S. Truman set out in March 1947 a policy of global containment of Communist expansion, pledging US support to all free peoples under the threat of Communist takeover: $400,000,000 in aid and military assistance were made available to Greece. US advisors and military personnel under General James van Fleet came to Greece to train and supply the National Army and the security forces, which grew in time to over 250,000 men.

The outcome was inevitable. But PDA's mistakes hastened its fall. Nikos Zahariadis, who favoured a more conventional approach to war, ousted Markos. Shifting from guerrilla tactics to set piece battles proved a disaster. Outgunned and outmanned, the PDA found itself being pushed further northwards and deeper into the mountains. The closure of the supply routes through Yugoslavia after Tito was expelled from Cominform only hastened the end. As the situation deteriorated, the forced conscription of men and women and the forced evacuation of children to the Communist bloc only eroded the PDA's popular base of support.

The issue would be settled in the summer of 1949. In late August, General Alexandros Papagos, commander-in-chief of the Greek National Army launched Operation Torch, the goal of which was to capture Konitsa and destroy the PDA. In a brutal campaign, the National Army routed the PDA in a series of battles on the slopes of Vitsi and Grammos in Western Macedonia. Finally, on the brink of total defeat, Nikos Zachariadis announced a ceasefire. The PDA had given up. And so on 16 October 1949, the civil war came to an end. Greece would endure its legacy for decades to come.

10

Reconstruction and retribution, 1950–1967

After nearly ten years of fighting, the terrible decade had come to an end. All wars leave in their wake death, devastation and suffering, but because of their nature, civil wars tend to inflict even deeper, more lasting psychological wounds as well. Such was certainly the case in Greece. It would take years for the wounds of war to heal, and indeed, some scars remain to this day. What had the wars of resistance and civil strife accomplished? For one thing, the political conflict between the Left and Right that had emerged in the inter-war period was settled, for the time being at least. The Right had won. Greece's destiny would henceforth lie with the Western capitalist bloc. The monarchy was restored, but the constitutional question that had beset Greece since its founding refused to go away. Foreign dependency continued but with a changed orientation. The United States supplanted the former great powers of Europe as Greece's patron. Because of the influence that the United States exerted on Greece, some have gone so far as to label the early days of the Cold War as a period of *Amerikanikokratía*. While this is an overstatement, it accurately conveys the sense that from the end of the civil war onwards, Greece's fortunes were tied to the Western bloc.

In addition to that development, a number of other themes dominate the history of Greece from 1950 until 1967. We have already touched on one – the ongoing constitutional question. In the realm of politics, others included the rise of the Cyprus question as a major foreign policy concern. The period also witnessed an economic boom of sorts that left an indelible imprint on the country. The process of reconstruction and the uneven pace of economic development that it created inaugurated some far-reaching social, political and economic changes that shape the story of Greece even to this day.

Reconstruction

The losses incurred during the civil war were horrendous. At least 80,000 people had died; 20,000 more were detained in government prisons and concentration camps; approximately 5,000 others had been executed. The many years of fighting had made 700,000 people refugees in their own country. The Ministry of Welfare listed as indigent 1,617,132 men, women and children. Destitute, despondent and directionless they looked to Athens for assistance. Another 80,000–100,000 had fled their homeland to be resettled in various parts of the Communist world; the largest such settlement was in Tashkent in Central Asia. Furthermore, the ravages of both the occupation and civil war had crippled the economy of Greece. The countryside lay in ruins, the nation's industrial infrastructure was largely rubble and the government was broke. The most pressing need, then, was the material reconstruction of the country, and massive amounts of US aid were required to accomplish this task. Re-invigorating Greece was given a priority in the early days of the Cold War because of its strategic location as a frontline state in the emerging conflict. In a bipolar world, Greece's options were extremely limited and, in large part, its orientation was chosen for it.

Related to the Marshall Plan for the reconstruction of Europe, an American Mission of Aid to Greece (AMAG) was established on 22 May 1947. A few months before this event, Great Britain had informed the US State Department that as of 31 March, it would cease providing monetary assistance to Greece and Turkey. The British Foreign Office made the case as to why the United States should agree to put on the mantle and provide the resources needed to restore stability in the region. This was the context for President Harry S. Truman's address to Congress in which he articulated what came to be called the Truman Doctrine. In that well-known speech, the American president laid out a foreign policy agenda aimed at containing the spread of Soviet communism. His Secretary of State, Dean Acheson, succinctly explained why Greece was so crucial: 'Like apples in a barrel infected by one rotten one, the corruption of Greece would affect Iran and all the East'. Greece was seen as the first domino in the row, and should it be allowed to fall, it would topple the other fragile regimes in the Middle East and Africa. AMAG's function, then, was to prevent the 'corruption' of Greece by overseeing its military victory over the Communists and then by assisting in its economic and fiscal recovery.

Millions of American dollars poured into Greece. According to one estimate, between 1947 and 1950, $1,237,500,000 in foreign aid was sent to Greece. An additional $181,000,000 was allocated in the fiscal year 1951–2 and $21,300,000 in the following year, by which time the US government had already cancelled the reconstruction programme. Even before the Mission had been established, various 'Greek experts' in the State Department and at the US Embassy in Athens were expressing grave reservations about the ability of the Greek government to administer the aid effectively. Ambassador Paul Porter, in particular, was adamant in his view that without stringent US control of the distribution and utilization of resources, the aid programme would fail. Consequently, the bilateral agreement that established AMAG gave the Mission officials great influence, and in some areas even direct control, over governance. US officials could veto Greek governmental decisions and their approval was required before policies could be implemented. One newspaper reporter's description of AMAG chief Elliot Griswold as the most powerful man in Greece was not far off the mark. At times, AMAG came close to being a shadow government. Greece had become, for all intents and purposes, a client state to the United States.

Initially the bulk of foreign aid went into military expenditures, and so, while other countries in Europe were using American dollars to rebuild the infrastructure of their industrial economies, Greece was forging a military apparatus whose sole function was to contain Communist expansion. Facing the threat of aggression to its north, Greece became a frontline state in the emerging Cold War. Nonetheless, it was widely recognized that if the Soviet Union and its Balkan allies launched an invasion of Greece, the Greek forces would be unable to stop them, regardless of the level of material support the United States provided them with. In reconstructing the Greek National Army, then, the aim was to create a force capable of defeating the internal enemy of the government in Athens. Though the issue was raised repeatedly, the Truman administration decided not to deploy US troops in Greece. Instead, it established a military section within the framework of AMAG. American military advisors working in conjunction with their Greek counterparts devised the strategy that would eventually vanquish the Peoples' Democratic Army; thus began a long relationship between the United States and Greek armed forces.

In addition, the American Mission played a direct role in altering the relationship between the Greek military and the civilian government. Motivated by the long and chequered history of the military's involvement in Greek politics, the military leadership was awarded control of the administration of the armed forces and the role of the civilian authorities in it greatly diminished. This institutional autonomy of the military would later have serious repercussions. Expanded in size, equipped with US supplies and arms, and directed by Greek and US officers, the revamped National Army, as we saw in the last chapter, soon crushed their Communist foe.

With the cessation of the civil war in 1949, the focus of aid spending shifted more towards civilian needs, and there were many of these. The drachma, for example, needed stabilization because of the horrendous bouts of hyperinflation during the war years that had rendered it valueless. Faith had to be restored in the monetary system. The balance of trade had to be brought in line. One move in this direction was the decision to devalue the drachma in order to make Greek products more competitive in international markets. Other measures were taken to attract foreign capital to Greece. In addition to these financial reforms, the heart and soul of Greek agriculture and industry required reconstruction.

All of the major cities had suffered severe damage during the wars. The devastation of the countryside during the Axis occupation had been compounded by the policy implemented during the civil war of forced relocation of peasants from their homes to temporary camps. These people had to be resettled and their villages rebuilt, in a process we will examine in more detail shortly. Greece quickly came to resemble a giant work site with building construction going on everywhere. Efforts were also made to establish a material infrastructure on which the modernization of the economy could be based. As a consequence, over 1,000 miles of new roads were built and scores of old ones refurbished; dams were built in order to produce hydroelectricity. These policies had a major impact, and the Greek economy grew. But as we shall see, it remained fragile. Moreover, economic assistance came at a price: foreign dependence in politics.

Political restoration

The political situation in Greece during the late 1940s, not surprisingly, was tense. In 1947, the official Communist Party of Greece (KKE), as well as all other Communist parties, was outlawed, and it would remain legally proscribed for twenty-seven years. And this was only a minor element in the systematic repression of the Left. 'In the countryside, right-wing mobs lynched prominent leftists and the occupants of village prisons, while home guard units, anxious to claim the official bounty for the killing of "bandits", exhibited severed heads.'[1] Thousands more were rounded up and sent to concentration camps on remote islands. Tens of thousands were charged before military courts-martial and many of them detained even before facing any criminal charges. Others were confronted with bogus charges, some of which bordered on the absurd – as in the case of a man who was called on twice to testify in the trials of men who had been accused of having murdered him. Apparently, his physical presence in the courtroom was insufficient evidence for the charges to be dropped. The arrests, detentions and the deportations of Leftists, trade unionists and others who were less than forceful in support of the victors continued unabated, even after the Democratic Army was defeated.

One of the few ways for former resistance fighters, their supporters and their families to escape prison and all that went with it was to sign a declaration of repentance. To do so, however, was to shamefully buy one's safety by selling out the ideas and beliefs that so many comrades had fought and died for. Signing the declaration left a different kind of scar, but a scar nonetheless. The wounds that these persecutions inflicted could not easily be healed, especially when at the same time many of those who had collaborated with the occupation forces not only eluded punishment but were, in fact, now occupying similar jobs under the post-civil war governments. The schism in Greek society that had begun in the 1910s was destined to continue through much of the Cold War era.

In addition, another hoary issue from the past re-emerged – the constitutional question. The issue *seemed* to have been solved with the plebiscite of September 1946 in which a two-thirds majority voted in favour of restoration. To be sure, the political atmosphere in which the election was held leads us to be suspicious of the vote. The position of the monarchy as an institution was placed on firmer ground with the accession of King Paul following the death of his brother George in 1947. Paul was not as tainted as his brother by association with the brutality and repression of the Metaxas years and by his conduct during the dark days of the occupation. The fact that his wife was a descendant of the old German royal family, however, did little to add to the couple's popularity. Though he was more palatable than his brother, popular support for the monarchy was thin and many among the political elite had serious reservations regarding the constitutional powers still vested in the King.

On 5 March 1950, the first general election since 1946 was held. No less than 44 parties contested the 250 seats. Konstantinos Tsaldaris and the Populists won 62 seats, and so the balance of power was held by a number of centre-right parties: the Liberals, led by Sophokles Venizelos (son of Eleftherios), the National Progressive Centre Union under General Nicholaos Plastiras and the modestly named George Papandreou Party. These three parties agreed to form a coalition government with Plastiras at the helm. The fragile alliance soon split, primarily over the issue of the degree of leniency to be shown to rank-and-file members of the Democratic Army. When the alliance collapsed in August, Venizelos was able to cobble together enough support to obtain the post of prime minister, but his thirteen-month-long administration was relatively ineffective.

In the general election of 9 September 1951, a new political party appeared on the scene: the Greek Rally. Founded by Field-Marshal Alexandros Papagos, who was still basking in the light of his successful stint as commander of the victorious National Army, and modelled after Charles De Gaulle's Rassemblement du Peuple Français, the Greek Rally stole the thunder from the Populists, garnering 114 seats to the Populists' 2. The United Democratic Left, a front for the banned KKE, won 10 seats even though many of its candidates were in prison. The Liberals and the Centre Union won a combined 131. With no one faction gathering a clear majority, yet another shaky centrist coalition was formed. At this point, the sharp edge of US dependency made itself felt. Utilizing the 'club', as Dwight Griswold once referred to American aid,[2] Ambassador John Peurifoy compelled politicians to amend the Greek constitution. He threatened to withdraw aid unless the Greeks changed the electoral system from proportional representation to simple majority, arguing that, with so many different political parties fielding candidates, unstable coalition governments would almost always be the result. Politicians grumbled, but made the change. The shift in electoral systems, however, tipped the balance in favour of the Greek Rally.

The election of 19 November 1952 swept the Right into power. The Greek Rally received 47 per cent of the vote and occupied 247 out of 300 parliamentary seats. This election was especially important for two reasons. First, it consolidated the position of Papagos and the Greek Rally in power and it ushered in a period of political stability. Second, it represented a return to the old game practised so often in the inter-war period of political parties altering the electoral laws while in office in ways aimed at ensuring electoral success. The former of these developments was a positive one because it established a stable political climate, which was needed for reconstruction. The latter, however, re-invigorated a very dangerous practice, and one that, as we shall see, would come back to haunt parties of both the Left and the Right.

Papagos's tenure as prime minister lasted until his death on 4 October 1955. The last months of his life were difficult ones. Personally, he had become quite ill and his health was failing; politically, the Cyprus issue had exploded on the scene and dealing with it, and especially Greece's rapidly deteriorating relationship with Turkey, had cast a deep pall over his final days. Upon his death, a heretofore relatively minor politician, Konstantinos Karamanlis, took his place, and he, more than anyone else, came to dominate Greek politics of the post-war era. Karamanlis was born in 1907 in Macedonia, the son of a schoolmaster turned tobacco merchant. A man of dynamism and drive, he rose quickly in local politics. He was elected as a Populist Party deputy in 1936, but his term was cut short when Metaxas seized power. Unlike some of his peers, he did not come out in open opposition to the dictatorship. Knowing that he was under surveillance, he chose the path of silent non-cooperation.

When fascist Italy invaded Greece in 1940, though he was thirty-three years old and so a member of one of the last age groups to be mobilized, he came forward voluntarily to join the armed forces but was rejected as being medically unfit. During the gloomy days of the Axis occupation, he remained in Athens and tried to eke out a living as a lawyer, trying as best he could to keep a low profile. Towards the war's end, however, he joined a circle of politicians and intellectuals of various stripes that met surreptitiously to discuss the country's post-liberation future. As a group, they, of course, opposed the Axis powers but they distrusted EAM as well.

Karamanlis's feelings about the KKE were well known and as a consequence when the civil war broke out, the Communists detained him for some time. He managed to escape and made his way to Egypt where he joined the government-in-exile. After the restoration of Greek civilian rule, Karamanlis's stock rose. He was well connected personally and he had solid conservative credentials. Moreover, his actions since the overthrow of the republic in 1935 had made him a popular figure. He had abstained from having any dealings with the Metaxas dictatorship, had stayed in Greece and opposed the occupation – albeit in a low-key fashion – and he was a committed anti-Communist. In the conservative Greek Rally government of 1952–5, he held the post of Minister of Public Works, a role in which he was very effective, though many bridled at his autocratic style of leadership. When Papagos died in October 1955, much to the surprise of many on the political scene, King Paul chose Karamanlis to form a new government rather than either Panagiotis Kanellopoulos or Stefanos Stefanopoulos, both of whom were more senior than Karamanlis and both of whom had been deputy prime ministers during the regime's previous ten months. The 48-year-old Macedonian reconstituted the Greek Rally as the National Radical Union and he developed a political machine that proceeded to hold on to power until 1963.

Economic recovery

The economy during the Karamanlis years continued to expand but did not fully modernize. Gross national product grew at a robust annual average rate of 7.3 per cent. The standard of living improved, and the average per capita income rose from $112 in 1951 to $500 in 1964. Industrial output also rose dramatically. If we use the level of output from 1939 as our base and set it at 100, then the magnitude of the recovery becomes clear. Output during the 1940s fell to 54 and had risen to only 87 by 1949. It then began to climb, reaching 110 by 1951, 172 in 1954 and, finally, 325 by 1962. Prices remained stable, and in some years even fell, while wages rose only slightly.

Shipping was greatly increased, and Greek-owned ships constituted the largest merchant marine in the world. By 1955, merchant shipping generated $28,000,000 in revenue and employed over 35,000 men. Construction continued at a rapid pace, and the building trade came to absorb ever larger numbers of labourers. Faster, cheaper means of travel and a low cost of living started to attract tourists to visit Greece's splendid antiquities, as well as to experience the sun and sea. The tourist business would soon become a major industry in Greece.

In spite of these developments, there were signs of fragility in the economy. Agriculture was becoming more mechanized and efficient but on a per capita basis, it remained the least profitable sector of the economy. The trade balance was still a serious problem. Greece imported far more than it exported. Also, there continued to be a 'capital crisis' in that most of the capital that fuelled the economy came from foreign loans and was distributed through state agencies. Indeed, by and large, the economy was still under state control, and restrictive legislation on, for example, trade unions showed the negative side of government paternalism.

The state bureaucracy was the fastest growing employer in the nation. By 1963, 33 per cent of those not directly involved in agriculture were employed by the state. The bureaucracy was becoming bloated and inefficient, but politically entrenched. The service sector was the fastest growing element in the Greek economy. Nonetheless, for many Greeks, the 1950s saw a marked improvement in their standard of living, especially when contrasted with the sufferings of the previous years.

Society in the 1950s and 1960s

Domestically, the period 1950–67 witnessed some major changes in Greek society. There are three especially important ones that we need to discuss, and as will become clear during our discussion, all three are interrelated. The first area we need to examine is the social and economic reconstruction of the Greek countryside. Developments in the countryside shaped in fundamental ways the other two major aspects of note – urbanization and emigration.

Unlike for our discussion of rural society during the nineteenth century, for the post-war era we have an abundance of sources. Foreign-aid officers and government bureaucrats who had been sent out to assess the situation in the countryside have left us contemporary reports and *post hoc* memoirs. Most importantly, during the 1950s and 1960s, rural Greece emerged as a site for ethnographic studies by anthropologists. The village studies produced by them help us to examine in detail the impact that reconstruction had at the local level. In addition to these studies, the fieldwork for which was conducted then, there are also many more recent studies that examine people's memory of the period. Augmenting these anthropological works are the sociological studies that Greek and foreign scholars began to carry out during the 1960s.

The richness and the diversity of the sources available for the post-war era, however, present some difficulties. When we tried to analyse rural society in the past, the paucity of materials meant that we had to draw broad generalizations from a slender base; for the modern period, the problem is how to draw generalizations from such a wide array of local studies.

First, we need to appreciate just how devastated the Greek countryside was in the aftermath of the wars. According to one estimate, by 1948, over 5,000 villages had been razed. Large swaths of the landscape lay uncultivated. Two-thirds of the rural population was suffering from malaria. The sheep, goat and cattle populations had been severely depleted. Approximately one-third of the country's forests had been destroyed. All of these figures increased during the civil war that followed the occupation. Because of the fighting and the forced evacuations, close to two million people were indigent refugees by 1947.[3]

In addition to the physical devastation, the wars left deep psychological scars. William McNeill, for example, observed:

When first I arrived in the village [of Nea Eleftherochori in 1947], no one was sure of his neighbour. Food was scant. Even an ordinary meal had become a furtive occasion. A knock at the door meant a scurry to put bread and cheese out of sight lest a stranger see what the family had to eat... . Cold darkness enveloped the village at night; fear was close at hand all the time. Hopelessness about the future daunted almost every spirit.[4]

Rekindling the spirit took longer than rebuilding the villages.

The Herculean task of reconstructing the countryside was begun in 1948, and by the winter of 1950, some form of shelter had been found for most of the refugees. Initially, the focus was on repairing those salvageable houses in villages that were geographically distant from the fighting. Heads of families were provided with funds, some of which were in the form of a grant and the rest as a low-interest loan, to rebuild their houses. By the end of 1953, over 175,000 new houses had been constructed. In addition to housing, AMAG and its associated agencies undertook a number of other rural initiatives.

If the agrarian economy was to recover, then, farming families had to be supplied with a great deal more than just houses. They also needed seeds, tools, fertilizer, livestock and equipment. Agricultural advisors were dispatched to work with them to help improve the yields of wheat, rice, tobacco and cotton. Lowland areas where mosquitoes bred were drained. Irrigation works were constructed in other areas. After the mission ceased to operate, Greek national agencies like the National Bank of Greece and the Agricultural Bank made low-interest loans available to farmers for the purchase of tractors and combines, for the installation of irrigation systems, for the introduction of new crops or the expansion of the production of hitherto under-utilized crops (like citrus fruits and rice), and for the development of marketing co-operatives. Farming families in those parts of the country where arable lowlands were available, like Boiotia, Thessaly, Macedonia and some parts of the Peloponnesos, were able to modernize agricultural production through mechanization.

In mountainous and hilly regions of the country, such modernization was not possible. In broad terms, then, two very different rural landscapes developed – a potentially vibrant lowland sector and an antiquated upland sector where older patterns of life continued to predominate. We see in operation the process of social change and the growing division in rural society reflected in the anthropological and sociological studies of the 1950s and early 1960s.

We can catch a glimpse of one part of this process in Ernestine Friedl's study of the village of Vasilika in Boiotia. By the late 1950s, the households in this modestly sized farming village had recovered from the wars and were experiencing the changes initiated by reconstruction. Some had been able to purchase tractors and other machines. Combine harvesters, hired or rented from professional operators, were employed to do the grain harvesting, and gangs of hired labourers were called on to pick the other crops, like cotton. While subsistence was still an element of their production strategy, households were now producing cash crops in greater quantities than before the war. Elements of the old – small plots producing a variety of foodstuffs for domestic consumption with the same tools and technologies that had been used for centuries – were thus combined with the new. The construction of a paved highway nearby now more easily connected the small world of the village to the rest of the country.[5]

Much the same story appears in Irwin Sanders's accounts of the villages he visited that were located on Greece's best farmland.[6] We see the hand of change having an impact even on groups, like the shepherding Sarakatsanoi, whose way of life would seem to still be rooted in the past. But as John Campbell's study of this group showed, their lifeways were also changing.[7] I am not, of course, arguing that Greek agriculture was totally modernized during the 1950s and 1960s. It was not, and there are aspects of it that are still troublesome to this day. Nonetheless, it was certainly the case that farming families in some areas were able to take advantage of the opportunities presented by the various initiatives at that time, and that as a consequence they witnessed an improvement in their material well-being. Though the introduction of new technologies clearly improved overall incomes for farming households, it may also have had deleterious implications for some sectors of society. People in other regions of the country, however, were less fortunate.

Many aspects of modern, mechanized agriculture were simply inapplicable to upland, mountainous terrain, and since so much of the country falls into this category, the rural economy of hundreds of villages remained rooted in the traditional technologies and production strategies. In places like many of the Aegean islands, Epiros, Evrytania and central Greece, upland areas on Evvoia, and the mountainous districts of Peloponnesos, households continued to practise a type of agriculture very similar to the one that existed in the nineteenth century and which we discussed in Chapter 6. Families worked small plots, often perched on terraces and scattered over a large area, on which they grew a variety of crops that were intended primarily to meet the household's subsistence needs. Some cash crops were also cultivated, but their production was ancillary. Each family would possess a few heads of livestock, again aimed at meeting the family's needs.

As in the past, a variety of extra-household sources of income (gathering herbs, seasonal wage labour, making charcoal) were required for the household to make ends meet. This does not mean that the winds of change did not extend to the uplands. They did, and so elements, like the construction of roads, had an important impact on people's lives. The pace and magnitude of change, however, did not keep up with the people's expectations, especially those of the young, for a betterment of their way of life. And so, they began to abandon the countryside, leaving in their wake villages inhabited disproportionately by the elderly or by no one at all.

One of the most important consequences of the wars and the post-war recovery in the countryside was a very high level of mobility. Young Greeks were on the move. There was, however, more than one emigration stream. One flowed from the countryside to the cities, and especially Athens. Another reached out to distant parts of the globe like Canada and Australia. And yet a third projected northwards to the more industrialized areas of Europe. Let us focus first on the rural–urban migration inside of Greece. People flocked to Athens in numbers unheard of since the late nineteenth century (Table 6).

TABLE 6 Urbanization in Greece, 1941–71: Population distribution (percentage)

	Athens	Thessaloniki	Other cities	Rural
1941	15.3	3.7	13.0	68.0
1951	18.6	4.0	14.9	63.1
1961	22.1	4.5	16.1	57.3
1971	29.0	6.4	17.4	47.2

Some of the movement towards the capital city began during the civil war. People fleeing the unrest, or forced out by government policies, settled as best they could in slums around the city. As one newspaper reporter observed at the time:

> ... in some of the left-wing areas of Piraeus, ... one-room shacks cluster around mud swamps infested by sewerage from the town drains. Equal squalor can be found, often concealed behind the presentable façade, in the heart of Athens. Close to Omonia Square a small shed without sanitation or furniture, except for broken planks covered in filthy rags used as a bed, was ... the home of an old woman, her consumptive son, his wife, and ailing children.[8]

The horrendous housing situation was one of the first problems to be addressed during the period of reconstruction. Athens came to resemble a huge construction site as young people in search of a better life flocked there by the thousands during the 1950s and early 1960s.

The growth rate per annum for Athens between 1951 and 1961 was 3 per cent; broken down into five-year segments, the rate rises to 4.13 per cent per year between 1951 and 1956 and 2.25 per cent between 1956 and 1961. A 1960 survey conducted by the Greek Statistical Service found that 56 per cent of the inhabitants of the Greater Athens area, approximately 1,300,000 people, were post-war migrants. After the period of subsidized housing, families built accommodations out of cement and brick wherever they could. Many housing projects were illegal and hundreds of dwellings remained unfinished as people strived to save the money to foot the costs of financing them. The reason why so many chose to relocate is clear.

According to Susan Sutton, 'The move from village to city enables individual migrants to leave low-cash-producing, low-power situations and enter ones with more possibilities for earning money and being close to the decision makers in Greek society.'[9] Parents increasingly wanted education for their sons so that they could obtain a job in the city; grooms sought brides whose dowry included an apartment in the city. Chain migration linked families in the city with those that remained in the countryside. Once one person had established himself, he then provided support for others to follow. Athens became populated by 'urban villagers', and neighbourhoods developed that replicated village life.

In the countryside as well, there were rising expectations of material betterment. The Bishop of Messinia told sociologist Irwin Sanders:

> People have now raised their standard of living well above their possibility to pay. They want running water in their homes, city clothes, and modern

furniture. They don't necessarily go into debt to obtain these things, but they have stopped saving as they used to... . They all want a road right up to their village so automobiles can reach them; they all want electricity. The changes which would have normally taken fifty years are now compressed into ten.[10]

High expectations of a better life elsewhere, then, led to internal migration and urbanization.

People's chances of fulfilling their dreams were much better in Athens than anywhere else in the country. Athens, and to a lesser extent Thessaloniki, experienced a rapid and quantitatively significant bout of industrial growth. Industrial production grew in Greece at a rate of 10 per cent per year – the highest growth rate in all of Europe. Foreign investment in industry fuelled the development of capital-intensive industries (Figure 16). The result of these developments was that in the early 1960s, for the first time in Greek history, exports of manufactured goods exceeded agricultural exports. The prospect of jobs then was the magnet attracting rural dwellers to the city.

The move to the city inaugurated a process of transition in the role of women and gender relations in Greek society. Women in very large numbers

FIGURE 16 *The American Express office in Athens (shown as it appeared in the 1950s) has been a potent symbol of the tensions in Greece during the post-war era. To some, it epitomized the benefits of the economic miracle of the 1950s. To others, it represented the continuing foreign dependency of Greece and the conquest of global capitalism, and so it has often been the target of protest.*

streamed into Athens; some were young and unmarried, others joined their spouses in the journey to the capital. Once established in the city, women took on wage labour outside of the household. A large percentage of working-class women laboured as non-live-in domestic servants. Others took jobs in manufacturing, especially in the textile and food service industries. In increasing numbers, daughters went to work outside of the household as well. But the old ways of patriarchal control were not completely overthrown. Instead, we see elements of the old and new combined.

Women and girls could work in only a relatively few occupations; all of them were traditional 'female' activities, and in most cases they laboured alongside other women, thus perpetuating the idea of gender segregation in public. Women's extra-household work, unlike men's, was seen as life-cycle dependent, meaning that a woman was supposed to work only until she married, at which time she was to revert to the more traditional lifestyle that centred on domestic duties. Married women were to stay at home and care for the children. In fact, women in the city contributed less to the household economy than did their rural sisters. What we see in the 1950s and 1960s in the city, then, is the beginning of a transition in gender as new aspects were introduced while old ones, rooted in the rural past, persisted.

The dream of Greeks for an improvement in their lives led also to external migration. Two different migration streams developed in the post-war era. The first predominated during the 1950s and continued through the 1960s and it was characterized by the permanent migration of Greeks, often in families, to distant lands. Some who had relatives in the United States were able to move there, but the changes in US immigration laws meant that many Greeks had to look elsewhere. The destination they chose was either Canada or Australia (see Table 7). Some of the emigrants were Greeks from the diaspora, like those of Egypt who were compelled to leave after Nasser's revolution; others, like many of the Ionian islanders, left when an earthquake destroyed their homes in 1954. Most, however, emigrated for the same reason that many of their compatriots moved to Athens.

TABLE 7 Post-1949 emigration

	1955–9	1960–4	1965–9	Total
Australia	32,484	57,451	59,371	285,026
USA	24,083	18,946	49,308	92,337
Canada	21,003	20,857	27,041	161,238
Total	77,570	97,254	135,720	699,839

The second migration stream of the post-war era consisted of Greeks who moved to some other region of Europe in search of work. These 'guest-workers' migrated on a temporary basis only; their goal was to work in one of the more industrialized countries to the north, save their earnings and then return to Greece. The countries of choice were Belgium, Italy, Sweden, and especially the Federal Republic of Germany. Between 1960 and 1969, approximately 500,000 Greeks worked in West Germany as guest workers. As in the past, the massive emigration of Greeks abroad was a mixed blessing. On the one hand, it provided a safety valve for draining off the pressures of a surplus rural population. And as in the past, the remittances sent home by emigrants or workers abroad helped to sustain the Greek economy. But it also impaired the development of a fully developed industrial economy by draining off surplus labour.

By the mid-1960s, then, Greece looked rather different than it had in 1950. Athens had grown tremendously and came to exert an even greater influence over the country – politically, socially, economically and culturally – than it ever had before. Some areas of the countryside had experienced remarkable economic growth and social change, while others seemed to have been frozen into a timeless 'traditional' past. Finally, Greeks, in greater numbers than ever before, migrated abroad. Some extended the diaspora to even more distant reaches, like Australia, while others moved a much shorter distance to industrialized Europe. In so many ways, then, the age of reconstruction left an indelible mark on how Greek society would develop during the latter part of the twentieth century.

NATO and Cyprus

Turning away momentarily from domestic politics and social issues, in terms of foreign policy, two issues dominated the immediate post-war era: the Cold War and Cyprus. Konstantinos Karamanlis was firmly convinced that Greece's fortunes lay with the West and that Greece had to become 'European', thus, presumably, bringing to a close the long and tortured history of Greek identity. The dictates of Cold War needs led to Greece's inclusion in the North Atlantic Treaty Organization (NATO). He also saw NATO membership as a means to better deal with the Cyprus situation. But Karamanlis wanted to go even further in solidifying Greece's position in the Western bloc. He pushed for a relationship with the European Economic Community, and he won for Greece 'associate' status beginning in 1962 and the promise of full membership in 1984. He also established a close relationship with Washington and at one point hosted a visit by Dwight D. Eisenhower; he followed that up a few years later with an official state visit to meet with his successor, John F. Kennedy (see Figure 17). Text-box 38 reproduces excerpts from the meeting between Karamanlis and Kennedy and gives us a very clear indication of how Karamanlis endeavoured to make the argument as to the importance of Greece to the West. After all of his efforts, Greece was thus firmly ensconced in the Western camp.

The other overriding issue of the day was Cyprus. The island housed the last significant population of unredeemed Greeks. Since the Treaty of Berlin in 1878, it had been controlled by Great Britain. The history of the British in Cyprus is a long and storied one. For centuries, the Christian and Muslim communities had coexisted on the island. This is not to say that there had not been bouts of unrest and tension. There had, but it was only with the advent of modern nationalism – the Megali Idea on the Greek side and Atatürk's Turkish nationalism on the other – that inter-communal tensions really developed. However, most of the open unrest involved the Greek community, and their

FIGURE 17 *President John F. Kennedy and Prime Minister Konstantinos Karamanlis (1961). While on an official visit to the United States in April 1961, Konstaninos Karamanlis hosted a dinner at the Greek Embassy for President Kennedy and his wife, Jacqueline Kennedy. The scene here shows the 'first couple' with various dignitaries. The visit was part of Karamanlis's efforts to get US support on a variety of issues, but most importantly on Cyprus and NATO.*

John F. Kennedy Presidential Library and Museum. Public Domain. Digital Identifier: JFKWHP-AR6521-B.

Text-box 38 A conversation between Karamanlis and JFK (1961)

Caramanlis [sic.] said that it was essential to the success of NATO that equilibrium be preserved in the south of NATO. Greece for the past ten years had been endeavouring to achieve this. However, the NATO allies displayed a remarkable lack of willingness to make NATO strong. Disagreements existed. There was no disposition to make sacrifices in the interest of the whole as Greece had done in connection with the Cyprus question. The NATO members were too selfish.

Caramanlis said that among the NATO allies Greece was the only country ready and willing to have a larger army. Geography might account in part for this, but the fact remained that Greece was the poorest of the NATO allies and was always pressed to find ways and means to make ends meet. ...

Caramanlis said that he wished to draw to the President's attention the special Greek interest in the Balkans and the Middle East. Greece was European, but rather far away. For centuries it had been subjected to pressures from its neighbours to the north. These pressures are greater today since Greece's neighbours are Communists and determined to push to the Aegean. He said that Greece was in a delicate and even 'critical' situation. It was trying to preserve equilibrium in the Balkans and was sacrificing to do this. Caramanlis went on to say that Greece is the link between Turkey and Yugoslavia. So far as the latter country was concerned, Greece would be satisfied if it stuck to its neutral policy.

Department of State, Conference Files: Lot 65 D 336, CF 1836. Confidential. Washington, 19 April 1961, 10.30 am.

https://history.state.gov/historicaldocuments/frus1961-63v16/d312.

target was the British. In October 1931, for example, five days of vicious fighting between Greek Cypriots and government forces left many dead and thousands were arrested. Severe restrictions on civil liberties were imposed as British rule took on an authoritarian edge. Throughout the war years, British control of the island remained firm and forceful.

In the post-war climate of British decolonization, however, expectations in the Greek community were rising that Cyprus too might be set free from the grip of the British Colonial Office, and thus be able to join with Greece. There were two enormous issues that had to be dealt with before that could happen: whether Britain would agree to relinquish the island in spite of its strategic importance and what would become of the Turkish population on the island.

For Britain, Cyprus had special significance. As Anthony Eden put it: 'No Cyprus, no certain facilities to protect our supply of oil. No oil, unemployment and hunger in Britain. It is as simple as that. We shall never relinquish Cyprus.'[11] Many other prominent members of the British government echoed this strident pronouncement. The sizeable Turkish population on the island meant that Turkey also had a stake in the future disposition of the island, if Britain were to agree to any change in its status. But the rising tide of sentiment for unification of Cyprus and Greece would soon introduce violence in its wake.

On 1 April 1955, a series of bomb explosions rocked the island. Leaflets were circulated announcing that 'with God's help and the support of all the forces of Hellenism the struggle to throw off the British yoke had now begun'. A terrorist organization called EOKA (National Organization of Cypriot Fighters) led by Colonel George Grivas, a former member of the *Chi* death squads during the 1940s, embarked on a campaign of violence aimed at disrupting British rule. The situation began to spiral out of control. In an attempt to stop the escalation of violence, the British government invited Greek and Turkish representatives to a conference in London. After some equivocation, the meeting began in August 1955. While the Tripartite Conference was in session, with the compliance of the Turkish government, mobs of rioters attacked the Greek communities in Istanbul and Izmir (Smyrna). The talks broke down without resolution.

The Greek Cypriots under the leadership of Archbishop Makarios took their case to the United Nations. Violence continued on the island. Greek elections on 11 May 1958 returned Karamanlis's National Radical Union party to power with a sizeable majority. From a stronger position internally, Karamanlis pressed the case for Cypriot self-determination, obliquely suggesting to Western representatives that failure to support the Greek case could lead his government to reassess its commitment to NATO and the West.

After years of conflict and delicate negotiations, a settlement was finally reached in 1959. On 16 February 1959, the London–Zurich Agreement was finalized. The island would be independent and ruled by a joint Helleno-Turkish government based on a complex formula according to each group's size. The Turkish minority had veto power. Britain got military bases. Greece and Turkey were able to station military advisors on the island. The three powers, Britain, Greece and Turkey, jointly guaranteed the security of the island, and each had the right to intervene to defend it. The establishment of even temporary peace on Cyprus was a major accomplishment, but domestically in Greece, the solution arrived at was not a popular one.

The slide to chaos

Seeking validation of his pro-Europe policies and the Cyprus treaty, Karamanlis went to the polls in 1961. His Radical Union Party obtained 51 per cent of the vote and held 176 seats. George Papandreou and his Centre Union Party, in association with some smaller centrist parties, gathered 34 per cent of the vote and won 100 seats. The United Democratic Left finished third with 15 per cent and 24 seats.

The election was marred by widespread allegations of tampering and corruption. Pre-election fears of a fall in the vote on the Right brought out paramilitary groups and the security forces, which openly intimidated voters, especially in areas known for their left-wing sympathies. Papandreou found an issue to rally the people: he charged electoral fraud and demanded that the elections be declared void. When they were not, he announced his 'relentless struggle' to ensure free and fair elections in Greece.

Many people had grown weary of the stifling of the Left that had continued since the end of the war. Many leftists were still in prison; the security forces continued to wield great influence; advancement in the civil service and the military was directly linked to one's politics. In short, after a decade, people were tired of the stifling of personal freedoms. As political violence increased, exemplified by the assassination of the left-wing deputy Dr Grigorios Lambrakis in 1963 by right-wing thugs connected to the security forces, so too did the sentiment for change.

Karamanlis felt the ground slipping out from under him both to the Left and to the Right. He clashed with King Paul and Queen Fredericka (the Greek nickname for her, 'Friki' – the horrible one – captures the public's opinion of her) on a number of issues, and in particular, on the relationship between the monarch and the military. In a speech in 1962 to the army of Macedonia, King Paul proclaimed, 'God has united us – I belong to you and you belong to me.'[12] Furthermore, Karamanlis also became convinced that the military was exerting an unacceptable amount of power for a democratic state. And, indeed, it was the case that the military had become a powerful institution within the state, with its own vested interests that often were at odds with those articulated by politicians on behalf of the nation.

Once more the constitutional question regarding the role of the monarchy was rising to the surface of Greek political life, and as in the past, it inevitably drew the armed forces in as well. Finally, in early 1963, Karamanlis found the situation unacceptable. His relationship with King Paul was strained; open hostility better captures the nature of his relationship with Queen Fredericka, a very powerful figure in her own right, and Crown-Prince Konstantinos. On 17 June 1963, Karamanlis tendered his resignation. Upon its acceptance, he went into self-imposed exile in Paris.

After 1963, a number of developments came together that led to the military coup in 1967. The first development was the decline in the economy. The economic bubble had burst. Inflation began to rise while wages remained stagnant. Unemployment and under-employment increased. As people's expectations of material betterment evaporated, some responded by migrating (452,300 left Greece during these four years alone), others turned to labour unions and went on strike more frequently and in greater numbers than ever before, and still others looked for political alternatives at the ballot box. Street protests and workers' strikes often led to clashes with the state's security forces.

Another development centred on Cyprus. The 1959 treaty was proving unworkable and fighting broke out on the island. At one point, Turkey threatened to invade the island to 'protect' the Turkish Cypriots. Only the forceful intervention of US President Lyndon B. Johnson prevented it. A number of American-brokered peace plans were proposed, but all failed. The Cyprus conflict convinced many in the military of the need to step up war readiness.

Third, King Paul died and was succeeded by his young, untried son, Konstantinos, in March 1964. Just one month before this, the Centre Union had won a resounding victory, garnering 52.7 per cent of the popular vote, which translated into 171 seats in a parliament of 300. The Right was out of power. The military had lost its royal patron. 'Public order', in the eyes of the Right at least, was deteriorating. And the likelihood of war with Turkey seemed high.

The Papandreou government enacted a number of far-reaching social and political reforms, prominent among which was the releasing of most political prisoners. To deal with the economic crises, George Papandreou appointed his son Andreas as Minister to the Prime Minister and then as the alternate Minister of Coordination. Andreas was literally the prodigal son who had returned home. While receiving an education appropriate for someone with his family background, he had become active in student politics as a leftist, a stance that got him arrested and detained by the Metaxas regime. Upon his release in the spring of 1940, he migrated to the United States, where he soon entered Harvard University. He became an American citizen. In 1943, he earned a doctorate in economics, and shortly after receiving his degree, he entered the US Navy and served in various posts between 1944 and 1946. After he left the armed forces, he took up a number of academic posts beginning at Harvard and then moving on to the University of Minnesota. While in the Midwest, he would meet and then marry Margaret Chant from Chicago. For most of the 1950s, he held academic positions, including chairmanship of the economics department, and then Dean, at the University of California, Berkeley. His prize-winning works in economics brought him into contact with some of the best and brightest minds in the United States and he became close to the inner circle of advisors to John F. Kennedy. As the recipient of a J.S. Guggenheim Fellowship, he returned to Greece to help set up an economic think-tank. He and his family made their relocation to

Athens permanent in 1963, just as his father's political party was rising to prominence. In 1964, he renounced his US citizenship and was elected to parliament in the February election. He then joined his father's cabinet as First Minister of State.

Many in the CU resented Andreas's rapid rise to a top spot in the party and in government. While he was clearly a brilliant man, many felt that nepotism and not merit was behind his advancement. Especially galling to some was that he rose so quickly without having to have served his time in the party. In particular, rising stars in the party, like Konstantinos Mitsotakis, the future conservative party leader, felt slighted by the appointment. The younger Papandreou held far more radical views than his father and his leftist leanings were now augmented by nationalist ones in response to the situation in Cyprus. At the same time, his father began to implement aggressive measures to reform the post-civil war security apparatus, and this raised very serious concerns among conservatives, the military and the palace. In January 1965, Papandreou passed a law purging the urban and rural police. This sparked open rumours that King Konstantinos, upon the advice of advisors who counselled him that this was a move by Papandreou to seize power, sought to oust the premier. According to a February CIA report, 'The Team considers this another move by Papandreou to consolidate his power by installing his own men. If the government lasts many more months, the King will be unable to force the resignation because Papandreou will attain sufficient strength by placing his own people in key positions in the military, police, and throughout the government.'[13]

Shortly thereafter, in May 1965, a government report written by Papandreou's opponents in his own party charged that Andreas had become involved with a group of left-leaning military officers known as *Aspida*, and this organization sought to overthrow the monarchy and replace it with a left-wing military dictatorship. The Right viewed these developments suspiciously and their anxieties rose when in June, George Papandreou proposed a purge of the military. In response to these developments, cabals formed as once again Right-wing military men set themselves up as the 'protectors' of the nation. When George Papandreou confronted the King with the demand that he be allowed to hold the portfolio of defence as well as being prime minister and the King refused, the constitutional question came to the forefront. In this case, it was over who governed the country: the king or the prime minister, the Monarchy or the People?

In disgust, Papandreou resigned on 15 July 1965. He had, in fact, been ousted by what many considered to be a royal coup. As Dreanos notes, 'The King had finally managed to topple the country's popularly elected Prime Minister, igniting a crisis that would turn the country's politics upside down.'[14] The Centre Union still had a majority in Parliament, as well as a popular

Text-box 39 The manipulation of democracy (1965)

King [Konstantinos II] recognized that even if [Stefanos] Stephanopoulos were to receive a vote of confidence, one could not predict how long his govt [sic.] would last. It is of greatest importance that new govt not be formed on the basis of a commitment to hold elections notwithstanding fact elections must eventually be held. It would be most unfortunate if elections were held now on the basis of who is right and who is wrong. Important thing is to form govt of ostensibly indefinite duration thereby eliminating prospects of early election which provide [George] Papandreou with hold over substantial number of his deputies. When activities of the Left have been controlled, electoral system changed, and appropriate situation had been created, quick decision could be taken to hold new elections. King expressed opinion elections should be held under proportional system. Although proportional system might strengthen hands of Communists, Communists would be clearly visible and power of Papandreou would also be reduced.

Telegram from Norbert Anscheutz, Deputy Chief of Mission at the US Embassy in Greece to the Department of State, Athens, 17 September 1965, 1525Z, reporting a conversation with King Konstantine II. Department of State, Central Files, POL 15 GREECE. Secert; Limdis.

https://history.state.gov/historicaldocuments/frus1964-68v16/d206.

mandate to continue its term of office. And so the faction in the party that opposed the Papandreous stepped in. In September, in a blatant manipulation of the democratic system, the King asked Stefanos Stefanopoulos to form a government and he was able to win a vote of confidence in Parliament by the slenderest of margins (see Text-box 39). For breaking with the elected leadership of their party, he and his followers became known as the Apostates. A series of caretaker governments came and went in the succeeding months. The ship of state was adrift and chaos dominated the political scene. King Konstantinos finally called for elections in May of 1967, and an overwhelming Centre Union victory with the Papandreous in charge seemed certain. Fearful of the consequences, especially a likely purge of the military of hardline right-wingers, a group of junior officers acted. On 21 April 1967, Operation Prometheus was put into action and the government of Greece fell into the hands of the junta of the Colonels.

11

Dictatorship, democratic restoration and Europeanization, 1967–1990

The period from 1967 when the banal but brutal regime of the Colonels stole Greek democracy until the fall of the Socialist government in 1989 was one of the momentous epochs in Greek history. The period is divided into two parts: 1967–74, when the Junta was in power, and from 1974 to 1989, an era referred to in Greek as Μεταπολιτεύσης (*Metapolitefsis* – political transformation). Socially, economically and culturally, the Greece of 1967 would bear only a passing resemblance to the Greece of 1989. Politically, many of the key issues that had shaped the history and development of the nation – the constitutional question, Greece's place in the world, etc. – would either be resolved or move closer to resolution. In this chapter, then, we trace the development of Greek society over these two important decades. The period did not begin well.

The dictatorship of the Colonels

The leaders of the self-styled 'Glorious Revolution' were Colonels Georgios Papadopoulos, Nikolaos Makarezos and Brigadier General Stilianos Pattakos. Their regime came to be called the Junta or simply the Regime of the Colonels. The leading members of the junta were mostly officers from lower-class backgrounds who had achieved career advancement through the armed forces. Many of them had previously served or were actively serving in the intelligence services, and some of them had received training in the United States. Moreover, most of them had been active in the right-wing machinations of the parastate for some time. Papadopoulos, for example, had been the leader of the National Union of Young Officers, a group that was fervently nationalistic and anti-communist, and had nothing but contempt for parliamentary democracy. A number of groups within the military were conspiring with King Konstantinos II to overthrow or temporarily suspend democracy. The primary one that we know about involved General Giorgios Spandidakis and other high-ranking officers. The Colonels were part of that group. But fearful of losing their posts because of their involvement in right-wing conspiracies, a worry that was exacerbated when the generals kept postponing the date of the coup, the Colonels struck first.

In the early hours of 21 April 1967, tanks rolled through the streets of Athens. Some of them entered Sintagma Square and trained their weapons on the parliament. Others shut down the main arteries into and out of the city. The key communications facilities were commandeered, giving the coup leaders control of the airwaves. Within a matter of hours, all of the major political figures had been either detained or placed under house arrest 'for their own protection'. The CIA-trained Hellenic Raiding Force seized the headquarters of the Greek armed forces.

The people of Athens awoke that morning to news broadcasts announcing the takeover. 'The revolution, carried out bloodlessly, marches forward to fulfillment of its manifest destiny! Greeks, pure and of a superb race, let the flowers of regeneration bloom out of the debris of the regime of falsehood.'[1] The Colonels' claims that they had staged the coup in order to forestall a Communist takeover are simply not credible. No such threat existed. They were able to succeed because of the vacuum of leadership that existed in political life at the time and because they were able to strike quickly and effectively. By seizing all of the major defence and communications facilities, they presented an unsuspecting nation with a fait accompli.

As Thanos Veremis scathingly notes, 'The Colonels came to power with no clear policies, no coherent ideology of their own, and no consistent views on the shape of the regime or the nature of its future options.'[2] Initially, the junta's main problem was legitimacy and so it tried to rule through the King and the existing political system. They could find, however, very few politicians who would cooperate with them and immediately began to arrest prominent centrist and left-wing politicians, and anyone else who showed any signs of resisting the takeover. Within a matter of days, 10,000 people were arrested, including all of the major politicians. Prime Minister Kanellopoulos, George Papandreou and Andreas Papandreou, for example, were arrested in night-time raids during the coup. Finding a paucity of notable politicians who would work with them, the junta looked to the King to prevent the regime from becoming an international pariah. In the days immediately after 21 April, Konstantinos had been approached by a number of military officers who urged him to oppose the junta by force. But his equivocation gave the coup leaders time to remove those officers from their posts, and the opportunity to nip the dictatorship in the bud was lost.

After that unfortunate development, Konstantinos cautiously agreed to cooperate. The pretence of parliamentary democracy was maintained and Konstantinos Kollias, former prosecutor to the Supreme Court, became prime minister. But power lay with the Colonels who were given ministerial appointments in the Kollias government. Once sworn into office, the new administration suspended the relevant articles of the constitution that protected civil liberties, until all of the radical elements had been purged from society. Based upon the principle of 'guided democracy,' in May 1968, the junta appointed a Constitutional Commission to draft a new constitution; displeased by the document drafted by this group, the Colonels cobbled together their own version, which was ratified in a rigged plebiscite in November 1968. These moves, plus the increasing use of violence and torture to quell all opposition, were too much for the young king to tolerate, and by summer he was openly disavowing the regime. As he told US President Lyndon B. Johnson at a meeting in September, 'This is not my government!'

While abroad, he contacted many of the leading politicians, like Konstantinos Karamanlis, who either were already in exile or who had fled when the Colonels came to power, seeking their support. Emboldened by the responses he received from leaders abroad, when he returned to Athens in the autumn, the King organized a counter-coup. Calling on some pro-Monarchy generals to mobilize a few small forces with which to seize key facilities, the King planned on making a broadcast urging the Greek people to rise up and join him. The counter-coup of December 1967 was poorly planned and even more poorly executed. It failed miserably. Konstantinos fled into exile. In absentia, he was deposed and, after a period of time during which a regency was imposed, the monarchy was eventually abolished in 1974. How ironic it was that the slide towards the final demise of royal rule was commenced not by bourgeois republicans or Communist cadres, but by forces of the Right – the monarchy's previous bastion of support.

With the King removed, Papadopoulos rose to the top of the regime and remained there until November 1973. The junta's aims and policies were a curious mix of populist reforms and paternalistic authoritarianism backed up by propaganda and terror. The overarching, proclaimed intent of the Colonels was to purge Greek society of the moral sickness that had developed since the war. The symptoms of this disease were the supposed spread of Communism and the failure of liberal democracy to achieve the union of Cyprus with Greece. The Colonels sought to create a new 'Helleno-Christian' state and this goal shaped their domestic agenda. Like the phoenix, which they deployed as a symbol for their regime, they would raise Greece out of the ashes (Figure 18).

Some of their more ludicrous policies were the banning of miniskirts and the imposition of a mandatory hair length for men. Most of their domestic initiatives were aimed at removing anyone whose loyalty to the regime was suspect and at forcibly indoctrinating society with their peculiar brand of messianic nationalism. The civil service was revamped and anyone who did not pass the loyalty litmus test was removed. The judiciary and the legal profession likewise were stripped of independent thinkers.

FIGURE 18 *Phoenix rising (1967). The Dictatorship of the Colonels adopted the phoenix as the emblem of their regime because it symbolized Greece's rising from the ashes of failed democracy. Posters like this were plastered on walls all around Greece as part of the Junta's propaganda campaign.*

Special emphasis was placed on reforming the education system. In addition to removing teachers and professors who did not toe the party line, the entire curriculum and the textbooks used in classes were revamped to reflect the Colonels' politically correct view of Greece's past. While recognizing the importance of controlling the flow of information and propaganda, 'the junta's media "philosophy" was so simple as to defy analysis'. Their sloganeering was simplistic and provided Greeks with a source of satire and jokes. Though they were by and large ineffectual in getting out their own message, the dictators were more efficient in silencing, with their usual brutality, the opposition press.

The Colonels inherited a fairly sound economy and that, more than anything that they actually did, accounted for the continuing growth of the Greek economy from 1967 to 1972. The junta endeavoured to attract foreign capital and industry to Greece, and it tried to wean back the major Greek ship owners by offering them very generous concessions. This worked to some extent, though the benefits of these policies to the Greek economy were negligible. The Colonels borrowed heavily to finance their economic programme, and that fiscal irresponsibility would leave a lasting mark. One result at the time was inflation. But because they had muzzled the trade unions and other workers' associations through brutal repression, they were able to keep wages stable. More than anything else, it was remittances from emigrants abroad and tourism that kept the fragile economy growing under the inept control of the military regime. The only major economic 'achievement' of the junta was to exacerbate even further the maldistribution of wealth in Greek society.

Like so much else about it, the junta's foreign policy reflects a curious mixture of ideologies and intentions. Shortly after seizing power, the regime found itself a pariah among European states. A group of northern Europe states filed complaints with the Council of Europe over the widespread use of torture and the rampant trampling of individual civil liberties by the dictatorship. The Colonels resigned from their membership in the Council only days before their regime was to be kicked out of the organization. Many European nations remained steadfast in withholding their recognition of what they considered to be a rogue regime.

Greece's relationship with NATO, however, was complicated, even though many of the same countries that belonged to the Council of Europe were in NATO. The primary reason was the United States, which was the first country to accord official recognition to the Colonels' government (Turkey and Great Britain did shortly thereafter). Even so, President Lyndon Johnson openly expressed his disquiet over the regime. It was under his successor, Richard Nixon, that relationships between the two countries became more cordial. This was partly due to personal factors, in particular, the friendship between Vice President Spiro Agnew and a number of prominent members of the powerful

Greek-American business community, which supported the dictatorship. Partly it was due to geostrategic factors. The Mediterranean had become a hot spot in the late 1960s. The seizure of power by Muammar al Gadhafi in Libya and the election of Dom Mintoff in Malta had deprived NATO of some key naval bases. At the same time, the continuing Arab–Israeli conflict and the increased Soviet naval presence in the region called for NATO and the United States to expand their forces in the region. More than ever, in the Cold War era that meant that the West needed Greece. And so, though at times relations became testy, the junta maintained Greece's position in NATO and developed a working relationship with the Republican Nixon administration. But because it was outcast from so much of Europe, the Colonels reached out to some unexpected places, like many of the Balkan members of the Eastern bloc, Albania and Romania in particular, and some of the new states in what came to be called the Third World.

The regime of the Colonels never developed a broad base of popular support and remained in power largely through terror, intimidation and coercion. They constructed a formidable secret police apparatus, which undertook the systematic persecution of, at first, leftists and then anyone suspected of opposing the regime. Torture and other human rights violations were legion and widely reported by international organizations like Amnesty International. Indeed, the brutality of the regime surpassed even the banality of its domestic policies.

The campaign of terror at home was effective, and so it was abroad that resistance movements to the Colonels formed. This is not to say that there were not resistance movements inside of Greece. As during the dark days of Nazi occupation, leftist parties provided a popular front within Greece. While they proved more effective than other movements because of their greater expertise at clandestine activities, their radical political agenda drove off many moderates and anti-junta centrists, thus preventing the formation of a united opposition. But resistance activities did take place. A group called Democratic Defence formed very shortly after the coup, and they succeeded on a number of occasions in embarrassing the regime. Even after some of its leaders were arrested and sent into internal exile to one of the Aegean islands, the group continued to resist. On one occasion, for example, an assassination attempt was made on the life of Papadopoulos, and just barely failed in its mission.

Nonetheless, the wholesale use of terror, repression and exile effectively hamstrung all concerted attempts at open resistance at home. Strict censorship of the press and other media also made it very difficult for opposition to be expressed in public. Instead, Greeks found clever ways to couch their opposition to the dictatorship by, for example, revitalizing traditional protest songs that had been incorporated into the national discourse and thus providing a veiled cover to the songs' real intent. Art and literature were also employed as poignant weapons of the weak to challenge the police state.

Also very active at the time were various groups that formed abroad in London, Paris, New York and elsewhere. Prominent among the overseas anti-junta groups was the Panhellenic Liberation Movement (PAK) led by Andreas Papandreou. It and organizations like it were instrumental in keeping the issue of the junta and its actions before the eyes of the international community. But it was the junta's own ineptitude and lack of legitimacy that led eventually to its downfall.

Three developments, more than all of the others, brought down the Colonels. The first was the student movement, the second was the global economic crisis of the early 1970s that plunged the Greek economy into turmoil and the third was Cyprus. In January 1973, university students began to challenge the authority of the dictators. At the Law School and Medical School in Athens, at universities in Thessaloniki and Ioannina, students held protests, boycotted classes and in other ways disrupted the higher education system. On one occasion, Papadopoulos himself called for meetings with both academics and students, and made clear to them that he would never allow 'Communists' to bring down the universities. Large-scale student demonstrations that openly defied the junta's ban on public assemblies began in October 1973. When the students occupied the Polytechnic University in Athens in November and began to broadcast on clandestine radios calling for the people of Athens to rise up against the tyranny, the junta had to respond. They did so brutally by calling in the army. The streets of Athens ran with blood as tanks crushed the gathering on the night of 17 November 1973.

The Polytechnic incident showed the bankruptcy of the regime and it demonstrated that resistance was not futile. Papadopoulos was toppled from power by a coup from his own right-wing. Dimitirios Ioannides, former head of the secret police, replaced him and the junta lurched even further to the right. With this change in power, the issue of Cyprus once more took centre stage. During the first six years of the junta, the relationship between the Greek leadership and Archbishop Makarios III, the president of Cyprus, had become severely strained. The Cypriot leader repeatedly called for a gradual, diplomatic solution to the island's bitter troubles. And so he was no supporter of the junta's hard line on unification. Moreover, the island had become, with his tacit support, a haven for opponents of the dictatorship at the same time that its president was pushing for the recall of the Greek National Guard. At least one assassination attempt was made upon Makarios and many others were plotted, and the junta was complicit in all of them.

Believing that a major nationalist cause would rally the people behind him, Ioannides ordered yet another assassination attempt on Makarios. It failed, but it provided Turkey with a pretext to intervene. On 20 July 1974 (five days after the failed assassination attempt), Turkey invaded Cyprus. Turkish forces swept across the northern part of the island. Ioannides called immediately for a full mobilization of the Greek military, but nothing happened. The regime had lost whatever base of support it had previously enjoyed.

The Colonels had to go. Military leaders, some of whom had escaped the earlier purges and others who, in fact, owed their positions to the Colonels, made it clear that they would no longer support the regime, and that they were prepared to use force if necessary to expedite their removal. At home and abroad, politicians from the pre-junta parties met and debated the country's future. Two men, one in Paris and one in London, anxiously awaited the results of the various deliberations.

King Konstantinos and Konstantinos Karamanlis had been two of the leading figures in exile who had presented the Greek case to the wider world, though they had done so in very different ways. The two had met in June and decided to cooperate when the time came. The King's position, however, was tenuous since the constitution of 1968, which, as we saw earlier, had been ratified by a popular, albeit suspect, referendum, and had severely curtailed the powers of the monarchy. The hastily convened committee of military commanders and politicians in Athens decided that only Konstantinos Karamanlis possessed the ability and the level of popular support needed to dismantle the dictatorship and to restore democracy to Greece. On 24 July, the phone rang in his Paris apartment and Karamanlis received the call to return to his homeland and to save it from chaos. The other Konstantinos sat in his London suite, waiting by a phone that did not ring. The restoration of democratic rule would proceed without a king.

Karamanlis and the restoration of democracy

Konstantinos Karamanlis faced the formidable task of clearing the wreckage left by the seven years of military rule. There were two major domestic missions: the restoration of a full range of political parties and re-establishing the military as a positive force. Having been sworn into the office of prime minister, Karamanlis formed a council of ministers drawn from the leading politicians of the old centrist parties in order to establish a Government of National Unity. Shortly thereafter, the council issued the 'Constitutional Act of August 1st'. This act restored the Constitution of 1952 until such time as a new constitution could be drafted and ratified. The Act, however, stipulated one important change to the old charter: it left the issue of the monarchy in limbo until a popular referendum could be held. The 1952 Constitution, following the model of the 1864 charter, created a 'crowned democracy' that invested sovereign power in the people. The Act restored democracy, but not the Crown. The immediate political goals of the Government of National Unity were the drafting of a new constitution and a legitimate referendum on the monarchy, but crafting a new role for the military remained a controversial and imperative objective as well. In the late summer of 1974, the army still presented a clear and present danger to the restoration of democracy. As Karamanlis's Minister of Defence, Evangelos Averoff, noted, the government was still the 'prisoner of the army'. On 11 August, Karamanlis had a showdown with military leaders at the Greek Pentagon and issued an ultimatum: 'Either me or the tanks'. He carried the day, but the future was still in doubt.

In this uncertain climate, Karamanlis scheduled elections for November. But even before that, he had legalized the KKE, a symbolic step towards finally ending the tensions that had simmered under the surface of Greek politics since the Metaxas regime. Karamanlis's newly formed party, New Democracy (*Nea Demokratia*, ND), swept into power with 54 per cent of the vote and 220 seats in Parliament (Chart 6 shows the results of all the legislative elections between 1974 and 1989, and shows, among other things, the development of the two-party system from 1977 onwards). Surprisingly, the Panhellenic Socialist Movement (*Panhellinion Socialistiko Kinima*, PASOK), which Andreas Papandreou founded on the basis of his anti-junta resistance group, the Panhellenic Liberation Movement, received nearly 14 per cent of the popular vote with a platform opposing Western alliances and the monarchy. The Centre Union, the only major pre-coup party to appear on the 1974 ballot, gained 21 per cent of the vote, but it was soon to be a

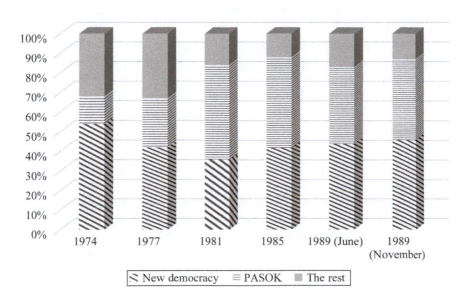

CHART 6 *Greek election results, 1974–89.*

spent force. The United Left Party (*Enomeni Aristera*), a coalition of the pro-Moscow and anti-Moscow Communist factions that had separated in 1968, received 9 per cent of the vote. Now other political questions loomed; most important of these were the fate of the monarchy and the disposition of the junta and its followers.

Karamanlis staged yet another referendum on the monarchy (the sixth since 1920), in an effort to settle finally the rancorous debate that had poisoned Greek politics throughout the twentieth century. In December 1974, a majority of 70 per cent of Greek voters opted to abolish the monarchy. Not coincidentally, this margin was nearly identical to the figure attained in the only other legitimate vote on the monarchy, that of 1924, which had established the inter-war republic. The Third Greek Republic thus came into existence. King Konstantinos remained in exile, still hoping that someday the call beckoning him to his homeland would come.

Punishing the junta and reforming the military and the civil service were more delicate operations. Karamanlis wanted to avoid a repetition of the military retributions of the 1920s and to preserve relations between the civilian government and the military. Nonetheless, the leadership had to be made accountable. Accordingly, the three top leaders of the junta, Papadopoulos, Makarezos and Pattakos, were charged with a bevy of crimes, including high treason, murder, conspiracy to commit murder and obstruction of justice. Ioannides was charged with many of the same offences. Over the course of two years, all were tried and convicted. During the proceedings, the Colonels made abundantly clear the contempt they had for democratic society. Each received the death sentence, which was later commuted. None of the more than 100 civilian ministers who had served the junta were convicted of a criminal offence. Many people serving in the military and the police were tried and convicted of criminal offences, and universities were purged of junta sympathizers.

On 8 June 1975, the revisionary parliament completed the new constitution that established Greece as a republic with a political structure modelled on that of France. The constitution vested great power in the president, who was obligated to choose as prime minister the leader of the party gaining the most seats in parliamentary elections. Until the constitution was amended in 1986, the president could veto legislation, dissolve parliament and call for a direct vote of no confidence in parliament. The sharp escalation of executive authority was controversial, but Karamanlis declared that strong presidential powers were necessary to deal with the extraordinary episodes of Greece's political conflict. The five-year administration of Konstantinos Tsatsos, the first president under the new constitution, passed without his using the considerable powers that had been given to his office. The legislative branch consisted of a 300-person assembly elected by direct, universal and secret ballot. The constitution also protected fundamental civil liberties such as freedom of assembly, speech and association and it ensured the freedom of the press. The Orthodox Church was recognized as the 'established' rather than the 'state' church of Greece, thus allowing for the free practice of other religions. Nonetheless, the question of the rights of religious and other minorities still presents this largely homogenous culture with problems. By and large, however, the 1975 Constitution, still in force with some modifications today, established the framework of a modern liberal polity.

Cyprus continued to dominate Greek foreign policy in the mid-1970s. From the Greek standpoint, the unresolved status of the island was chiefly the doing of the United States, and a substantial anti-Western backlash coloured Greek foreign policy during that period. Since the invasion of 1974, Turkish troops had remained on the island. Although a ceasefire was negotiated in Geneva in August, talks broke off almost immediately, and the Turkish army began to expand its zone of occupation to a line that included 37 per cent of Cypriot territory. Karamanlis, however, was intent on avoiding armed conflict, for which Greece was unprepared, and talks resumed shortly thereafter. In many ways, then, the new administration had at its disposal a relatively limited range of options. In 1975, a Turkish Federated State of Cyprus was declared in the northern part of the island, and negotiations continued intermittently for another two years. A 1977 agreement divided the island provisionally, but no lasting, workable solution was achieved. Even now, the fate of Cyprus remains a pressing issue that continues to impair relations between Greece and Turkey.

The Greek public reacted to the Turkish presence on Cyprus with resentment towards NATO and the United States. In the view of many Greeks, the benefits of membership in a West European security organization were meaningless if the alliance could not stop a NATO ally from invading a country such as Cyprus. In protest, Karamanlis withdrew Greece from the military structures of NATO, a status that remained until 1980. Greece held the United States and its foreign policy establishment particularly responsible for the Cyprus invasions because of its failure to prevent Turkish action or to compel Turkey's withdrawal after the fact. In 1975, the US Central Intelligence Agency was still widely held responsible for aiding the junta's accession and supporting its regime. This hostility was partly a backlash against the dependent relationship of post-war Greece to the United States, and partly the result of resentment for the US support of the junta.

In blaming the United States for events in Cyprus, Greece also overestimated its leverage over Turkey. Tension increased in 1976 when the United States, having partially repealed its arms embargo, exchanged $1 billion in military equipment for military installations in Turkey. Greek protests resulted in a similar agreement with Greece, worth $700 million, and the establishment of a seven-to-ten ratio that became the standard formula for US aid apportionment between the two countries.

In the late 1970s, two new issues exacerbated animosities between Greece and Turkey. The first involved the control of the northern Aegean. Each side claimed (and still claims) large areas of the region on the basis of offshore territorial rights. Because the boundaries between mainland Turkey and the Greek islands in the Aegean are so close, the six-mile offshore limits often overlap. Control of the continental shelf became much more critical with the discovery of oil in the region. On three occasions since the late 1970s, Greece and Turkey have nearly gone to war over this issue. Other sources of irritation were the question of air control over the Aegean, Greece's attempts to extend its six-mile limit to the 12-mile limit used elsewhere and the two countries' treatment of their respective Greek and Turkish minorities. The end of the Cold War greatly diminished the incentive for cooperation against Communist neighbours, emboldening both countries to take more independent stands over regional issues.

The period of domination by the ND included concerted attempts at national reconciliation. Economically, Karamanlis pushed for closer integration with Europe, a policy rewarded in 1981 with full membership in the EC. The ND government practised statist capitalism, meaning that the state had an intrusive and direct role in determining economic policy at the same time that it tried to foster a free-market system. The primacy of the state in economic affairs was evident in all areas, from prices and wages to labour law. In post-junta Greece, the debate has centred on the degree, rather than the existence, of government intervention in the economy.

Karamanlis called an election in 1977, a year earlier than required by the constitution. A particular goal of this strategy was to obtain validation of his government's foreign policy initiatives. The major surprise of the 1977 election results was the rise of Andreas Papandreou and PASOK. ND's share of the vote fell to 42 per cent (171 seats) while PASOK's share rose to 25 per cent (93 seats). The Centre Union dropped to a distant third place (12 per cent and 16 seats), barely ahead of the KKE (10 per cent, 11 seats). PASOK's success came largely at the expense of the declining Centre Union, which split into factions shortly thereafter. ND's losses had multiple causes. Some ND supporters moved to a new far-right party, and the political equilibrium that Karamanlis had achieved since 1974 removed some of the urgency with which the Greeks had supported him in the previous election. ND lacked a clear ideology; instead, the gravitas of its leader was its chief rallying point.

At the same time, PASOK's message had an increasing resonance with the people. From the very foundation of the party, it was clearly different from the rest. Text-box 40 contains excerpts from the party's founding manifesto.

Text-box 40 Foundation of PASOK (1974)

We are announcing today the inauguration of a new political movement, a movement that we believe represents the desires and needs of the average Greek: the farmer, the worker, the craftsman, the salaried worker, and our courageous and enlightened youth. The movement belongs to them, and we will call on every exploited Greek to strengthen our ranks, to form categories and participate in the moulding of the movement in order to promote our national independence, popular sovereignty, social liberation, and democracy in all phases of public life.

Andreas Papandreou, 3 September 1974.

http://agp.archeio.gr/archive.php?action=list&sub=subject&lang=en&value=Speeches.

PASOK was a grassroots party that was predicated not just on popular support but also on mass participation. It was new; it was radical; it captured the tone of the time. Thus, in his rhetoric, Papandreou crafted a skilful mix of nationalism ('Greece for the Greeks') and socialism ('PASOK in government, the people in power'). PASOK promised a 'third road' to socialism and a middle way in foreign policy, restoring national pride by breaking the bonds of foreign dependency and re-orienting Greece with the non-aligned countries. PASOK's structure also gave it a base of grassroots support that other parties lacked. Besides its strong central committee, PASOK had local party offices and cadres in towns and villages across Greece. This system proved very effective in organizing support and validating the claim that the party was not based, like the others, on networks of patronage. And, perhaps most importantly, PASOK's slogan of 'change' (αλλαγή) struck a chord with the Greek people's search for a new way forward after forty years of conservative rule. Lastly, we cannot gainsay the impact of Papandreou himself; he was a powerful speaker and some have attributed to him that greatest political gift of all – charisma (Figure 19).

Changing times: Andreas Papandreou and PASOK in the 1980s

By the elections of 1981, the electoral momentum had shifted away from an uninspired ND to the promise of change offered by a newly moderate PASOK. For the next eight years, Papandreou applied his programmes to society and

FIGURE 19 *Andreas Papandreou and PASOK (1981). This composite illustrations shows Papandreou, in his orator's pose, superimposed on the PASOK party logo. The party and its leader radically changed the way elections in Greece were conducted.*

GallantGraphics all rights reserved.

the economy, with mixed results. In 1980, Karamanlis decided to step down as leader of the ND and to seek presidency. Two weeks after informing his cabinet of his decision, he was elected on the third ballot. Three days later, on 8 May 1981, the ND elected the lacklustre Giorgios Rallis as its new leader, and thus the incumbent prime minister in the following year's elections. In the elections of October 1981, PASOK and Papandreou swept into power with 48 per cent of the popular vote and 172 seats in Parliament. The ND, which could not match Papandreou's charisma or the novelty of PASOK's programme, finished a distant second with 36 per cent of the vote and 115 seats, and the KKE came in third with 11 per cent and 13 seats.

Between the 1977 and 1981 elections, PASOK and its leader had continued the move away from an initial image as a Marxism-based, class-oriented party, in order to reassure centrist voters. The 'privileged' class against which Papandreou ran in 1981 had shrunk considerably to a small number of Greece's wealthiest citizens. The societal results of the 'change' were left deliberately vague. The election result meant that, for the first time in Greek history, an explicitly left-wing party held the reins of government. The transformation from authoritarian rule to democracy was finally complete.

As it exercised power for the next eight years, PASOK did oversee considerable change in some areas. The new government brought in a sweeping domestic reform programme under Papandreou's 'Contract with the People'. Many initial reforms were long overdue and cost little. New laws legalized civil marriage, abolished (in theory) the dowry system, eased the process for obtaining a divorce and decriminalized adultery. Another law enhanced the legal status of women by dissolving the long-held notion that family and not the individual constituted the central unit in society, and that women, as the legally subordinate partners in marriage, were subsumed under the legal control of their husbands. In marriage, and in a number of other areas, the PASOK government passed legislation that endowed women with rights as autonomous individuals. Taken together, these legal reforms represented a revolution in women's rights.

The university system was overhauled, giving more power to staff and students. In 1983, a comprehensive national health service was introduced. Under the control of the newly established Ministry of Health, Welfare and Social Security, the service made modern medical procedures available in rural areas for the first time. It also ensured equality of health care delivery across the country. It established nationally supervised training programmes for nurses. The programme dramatically changed the quality and level of health care for the average person, but was expensive. By 1985, Greece was spending 5 per cent of its gross domestic product on the health service.

Some of PASOK's initiatives met with considerably less success, especially its attempts to reform the civil service and to manage the economy. The pervasive blanket of smog over Athens, instead of being banished as promised, became thicker during the early 1980s. Endeavours to deal with this and other serious environmental issues have at times exposed the administrative incapacity of the central state. Papandreou vowed to slay one of the great shibboleths of modern Greece: the bureaucracy and civil service. The only thing greater than the size and inefficiency of the civil service was the low esteem in which the vast majority of the population held it. 'Professionalization' and administrative streamlining were the cries of the day. In spite of a promising beginning, PASOK succumbed to the temptation that had ensnared so many governments before it: of stocking the bureaucracy with the party faithful. 'These two goals, the professionalization of the bureaucracy and its transformation from a conservative bastion into a socialist battering ram, were inherently contradictory.' In the end, the Socialists' reform programme met with mixed results.

Lastly, after PASOK reforms initially gave trade unions greater freedom of action and improved labour relations, circumstances soon caused Papandreou's labour policy to reaffirm state control over labour-union activity. The selective socialization of key means of production, which was to emphasize worker participation and improve productivity, led, instead, to increased state patronage for inept companies and continued state control of unions. Papandreou also attempted to further national reconciliation by officially recognizing the role of the resistance during the Second World War, by granting rights of residence in Greece to those who had fled to Communist countries after the civil war, and by ending all public ceremonies that celebrated the victories of the National Army over the Democratic Army of Greece. Only Greek refugees were allowed to return, however, excluding a large number of Macedonian Slav members of the PDA (see p. 250).

The greatest challenge to PASOK in the 1980s was managing the economy, and by almost any measure, they did not do it well. To be fair, PASOK inherited an economy that was already showing signs of weakness. Greece had never fully recovered from the 1972 oil crisis, and throughout the 1970s, the economy grew at a very slow rate of only 1.8 per cent of the gross domestic product. Wages had increased dramatically after the restoration of democratic rule and the inflation rate stood at 24.5 per cent when PASOK came to power. The main problem facing Papandreou, then, was how to pay for PASOK's ambitious social programmes while keeping Greece militarily strong in such a bleak economic environment. In keeping with his campaign promise, Papandreou initially raised middle and low incomes, instituted price controls and introduced tax incentives on investments, giving the state an even larger role than it had had under the ND regime. But by 1985, the annual inflation rate had risen to 25 per cent, which led to devaluation of the drachma in what was presented as an austerity plan. The operating budget deficit still grew, eventually reaching 10 per cent of the gross national product. The public debt that spiralled out of control in the late 1980s continued to be a serious deterrent to economic growth in Greece into the 1990s.

In foreign policy, PASOK proved far more moderate in power than it had been as an opposition party. Part of the PASOK platform on 1981 had called for a radical departure from anything that had come before regarding Greece's foreign relations. As we have seen throughout this book, foreign dependency has been a recurrent feature in the history of modern Greece. PASOK called for a break with the past: '... our opponents pretentiously ask us whether we are with the West or the East, and our reply is: We are for peace and support only Greece's interests.'[3] Although Papandreou's strident anti-American rhetoric caused friction with the administration of US President Ronald Reagan, PASOK was willing to compromise on specific issues such as continuation of US bases in Greece, after vigorous negotiations. Despite his theoretical non-alignment and conciliation of *bêtes noires* of the West such as Muammar al Gadhafi of Libya, Saddam Hussein of Iraq and Yasser Arafat of the Palestine Liberation Organization, Papandreou balanced Greece's international position by keeping Greece in

NATO. With regard to membership in the European Community, here again the strident hard line of opposition was ameliorated once PASOK came into power. Certainly, during Papandreou's second term of office from 1985 to 1989, Greece became fully integrated into the organization that it had once denigrated as an evil entity.

In its policy towards Turkey, the PASOK government stood firm. In 1982, Papandreou became the first Greek prime minister to visit Cyprus, which signalled strong support for the Greek population of the divided island. In 1984 he mobilized the Greek military for war when Turkish batteries opened fire on a Greek destroyer. And in 1987, he once again brought Greece to the brink of war when Turkey threatened to send an oil exploration vessel into Greek territorial waters. In 1988, a thaw resulted from a meeting between Papandreou and Turkey's President Turgut Özal in Davos, Switzerland, where new avenues of bilateral communication and consultation were arranged. Soon thereafter, however, the 'spirit of Davos' was strained again by disputes over the treatment of minorities, air space and access to Aegean oil.

Papandreou's fortunes began to turn during the summer of 1988. In August, he underwent a major heart surgery, but he refused to yield the reins of power. The opposition mocked his technique as 'government by fax'. A further complication was the announcement that Papandreou intended to divorce his American wife of thirty-seven years – a very popular figure in Greece – in order to marry a 34-year-old airline stewardess who had gained influence in Papandreou's entourage. The family rift caused by this announcement damaged the cohesion within PASOK because Papandreou's sons occupied key positions in the party.

But it was a financial scandal that rocked the political world of Greece most violently. In November 1987, George Koskotas, the owner of the Bank of Crete, whom Doyle McManus of the *New York Times* referred to in a 16 April 1989 report as the 'Donald Trump of Greece', was in Washington DC to attend a fund-raiser for the then Vice-President George H. W. Bush. As was their standard practice, the American Secret Service ran background checks on all of the guests, and they discovered that there was an outstanding federal warrant for Koskotas's arrest on charges of fraud and tax evasion. After posting a bond and obtaining a fake passport, he fled the country. One year later, on 24 November 1988, he was arrested while trying to re-enter the United States in New Bedford, Massachusetts. Greece sought his extradition, which he fought, arguing that his life would be in peril if he was returned. While in custody, he revealed financial shenanigans that if proven true would bring down the Greek government. Text-box 41 contains excerpts from a story written by Robert Ajemian in *Time* magazine. In a narrative that reads like it came from a spy novel, Koskotas told of how over $210 million was embezzled from the Bank of Crete. He recalled that on a regular basis blue briefcases stuffed with cash were delivered to high-ranking officials in the Greek government and in PASOK. The corruption, he asserted, went all the way to the top, explaining that on one occasion he had delivered to Papandreou himself $600,000 stuffed in a Pampers Diapers box. The prime minister vehemently denied the story and even sued *Time*. Nonetheless, Koskotas's accusations gained traction, leading to the resignations of several ministers and demands for a vote of no confidence against the government. Papandreou, whose second four-year term was to expire within months, held on to power, but not for long.

Text-box 41 Scandals: The looting of Greece (1989)

Greeks were exhilarated in 1981 when Andreas Papandreou and his Socialist Party swept to power. Their enthusiasm has long since turned to bitterness and disbelief as the worst financial and political scandal in four decades engulfs Greece. The press, the Bank of Greece, a magistrate and Parliament are delving into charges of corruption, seeking to uncover how more than $210 million disappeared from the Bank of Crete. Charges of embezzlement, kickbacks and bribery, of banknotes stuffed into briefcases, have been levelled against high officials.

The scandal has scorched the Socialist Party (PASOK), and public cynicism has increasingly focused on the party's leader, Papandreou himself. The Prime Minister last September was already the target of snickering and outrage as he conducted a highly public extramarital liaison with airline flight steward Dimitra Liani, 34. As the parliamentary investigations dug through the testimony, the question loomed: Was the Prime Minister aware of the crime all along?

Papandreou has not testified before investigators, though he vehemently denies any involvement in what he calls a 'conspiracy aiming to hurt Greece.' But investigators have yet to hear from the central figure in the case, George Koskotas, 34, a one-time New York house painter who vaulted to power as the multimillionaire owner of the Bank of Crete. Now jailed in Massachusetts on a variety of charges levelled just before he fled Greece last November, Koskotas is facing extradition to answer accusations of looting his own bank ...

The Koskotas's accusations are extraordinary, though difficult to verify. In six lengthy prison interviews with *Time*, the banker describes a Socialist government riddled by extortion and criminality. Koskotas charges that millions of dollars missing from his bank were actually payoffs that went directly to the head of the government, Andreas Papandreou, and PASOK officials. The Prime Minister, says the banker, personally authorized the plan to bleed the Bank of Crete.

Robert Ajemian, *Time*, 13 March 1989.

As he awaited PASOK's inevitable losses in the elections of June 1989, Papandreou adjusted the electoral system to make it more proportional and to hinder formation of a majority by a rival party. The strategy succeeded in part. Under the leadership of Papandreou's old rival Konstantinos Mitsotakis, the ND won 44 per cent of the vote, but it fell six seats short of a majority. A short-lived conservative–communist coalition government was formed. In a matter of months, a second election also failed to produce a clear victor who could form an effective government. For many, these two elections, indecisive as they were, marked a watershed in Greek political history and signified the end of Metapolitefsis. The reason is that, even though the Communist Party became a coalition party in government, there was not even a hint of any opposition from the armed forces. In other words, these elections suggested that the demilitarization of politics and the stabilization of democracy had been achieved at last. Finally, in April 1990, the ND won a narrow majority of seats and formed the government. Papandreou and the Socialists were finally out of power after almost ten years. With their fall, a very important chapter in the history of modern Greece had come to a close.

Greek society during the era of restoration and socialism

I want now to return to the arena of social history and examine the momentous developments that took place in Greek society during the period from the fall of the junta to the collapse of the Berlin Wall. We can pick up the threads of the analysis where we left off earlier and explore the following areas: urbanization and the changes in urban lifeways, the continuing impact of migration on Greek society and, finally, the way that society and economy developed in the Greek countryside.

By the time of the census of 1991, Athens had become a megalopolis. In a country of approximately 10.2 million people, 3.1 million (or 31 per cent) of them lived in the greater Athens area. The rate of population growth of Athens and its suburbs had slowed considerably from the heyday of the 1960s, but it was still a not inconsequential 27 per cent during the 1970s, and 21 per cent in the 1980s. The massive transference of population from the countryside to Athens had abated and the city's growth in the post-junta era was driven by a combination of in-migration from the countryside, the return of Greeks who had migrated abroad and the natural demographic growth among the city's population. Along with the continued expansion of Athens, most of the other cities and large towns of Greece also grew. As Table 8 demonstrates, by 1991, almost two-thirds of the entire population lived in urban areas. Only fifty years

TABLE 8 Percentage of population in Greece from 1940 to 1991
            based on category of settlement

	Urban	Semi-urban	Rural
1940	33	15	52
1951	38	15	47
1961	43	13	44
1971	53	12	35
1981	58	12	30
1991	62	18	20

Note: Urban: >10,000; semi-urban: 10,000–5,000; rural: <5,000.

before, the situation was the reverse, as the majority of the population resided in villages.

Attracting newcomers to the city between 1974 and 1989 was the prospect of work in the building trades and the service industries, or even higher-paying jobs in manufacturing. These prospects were not as bright, however, as they had been during the halcyon days of the 1950s and early 1960s. As second- or third-generation working-class urbanites grew in number, they competed for the same types of work that attracted outsiders. Athens and Thessaloniki were still the locations for a significant portion of the Greek industries. But, drawn by the prospect of higher profits, lower competition and reduced labour costs, by the mid-1980s, the locus of dynamic growth in manufacturing had shifted away from the major cities to the smaller towns and the countryside. This not only put a brake on urban migration but it also had an impact on lifeways in the countryside, as we shall see shortly. Another pattern of population movement was emerging, however. Increasingly, those coming to the city were professionals or people seeking professional training, especially students.

In addition to changes in size, during the 1970s and 1980s, there were radical changes in the character and quality of life in the city also. In spite of the very rapid in-migration of rural folk, Athens did not experience many of the social problems that so commonly accompany urbanization. Crime and violence, poverty and destitution, unemployment, class conflict and other such social ills did not manifest themselves in Athens during the 1950s and 1960s. This was partly due to the pattern of migration, whereby large numbers of women and children were also part of the migrating population, and partly to the economic boom conditions. It appears that many of the maladies associated with the modern city only appeared in Athens in the post-junta era.

From 1975 onwards, the crime rate in Athens, and the rest of Greece, increased dramatically. Moreover, the types of crimes committed also shifted to a pattern more like urban areas elsewhere and less like the one found in rural areas. Evasion of market regulations and other laws pertaining to the economy, motor vehicle violations and public offences (vagrancy, brawling, etc.) accounted for a large percentage of Athens' crime. Charges for drug possession increased considerably as well. Violence and homicide did occur, but only in very modest numbers.

One of the biggest changes in criminal activity involved the people who committed crimes. During the 1970s, and especially during the 1980s, Athenian women and juveniles were charged with criminal offences in numbers unheard of before this time. In the post-junta period then, Greece experienced a modernization of crime, and thus the pattern of criminal activity in Athens came to resemble more closely that of other major cities around the world.

Another social development in Athens was the increasing segregation of neighbourhoods according to class. The 'urban village' phenomenon faded over time as second- and third-generation urbanites established neighbourhoods that centred more on class than a regional identity. There was also a change in women's roles in the city. The process that had begun during the 1960s developed further during the post-junta era, and especially after the social reforms, discussed earlier. Women's participation in the workplace expanded greatly, and many women remained in the workforce even after marriage. More than ever, class also shaped women's life experiences. More women received higher education, including university degrees, than ever before, and this opened the door to careers that had previously been closed to women. In addition, the women's movement developed in Greece and drew its strength especially from educated urban women. New forms of inter-gender sociability developed between unmarried men and women, and married women demonstrated a greater autonomy of action, including over their reproductive behaviour, than ever before. In short, Greek society came increasingly to resemble other European societies with regard to social structural complexity, gender relations and education.

Greek rural society also continued to develop and change. The dimorphism of agricultural systems we discussed in Chapter 10 continued through the late 1970s and 1980s. When Greece became a full member of the European Community in 1981, the agrarian sector became subject to the EC's Common Agricultural Policy (CAP). CAP's aim was to solve the chronic agricultural problems of the community by supplying price-trading support and by providing capital to member states to address structural deficiencies; the latter in the Greek case were deemed to be the persistent problem of minifundia and the underdeveloped marketing system. Greek agriculture received additional EC support after the implementation of the Integrated Mediterranean Programmes. The aims of the IMPs were 'to improve incomes and the employment situation, by helping agriculture to modernize and by creating opportunities for jobs or sources of income on the non-farm sector, both for those who remain[ed] in agriculture and for those who desert[ed] it.'[4] The results of those programmes were that large amounts of capital in the form of investments and subsidies flowed into the countryside. It was, however, primarily in those regions that had already modernized to some extent that they had their greatest impact. Producers of commercial and cash crops such as tobacco, fruits and vegetables (especially, citrus fruits, tomatoes and the like), cotton and rice received the lion's share of the subsidies (over 79 per cent of the total input). Only one part of rural society was effectively assisted by these programmes. Nonetheless, that sector did well.

Two other dynamics, however, marked the development of the Greek countryside. During the 1980s, rural manufacturing started to take off. Entrepreneurs, often returning Greek migrants, found it more profitable to establish industrial plants in the countryside or in small towns rather than in the major cities (see above, p. 294). Using capital saved from years of working abroad, in conjunction with finances obtained through the IMPs, Greek merchants established textile mills and food processing plants. We have already seen that there was a long tradition of pluriactivity among Greek farming families, and so the establishment of industrial concerns neatly tapped into a long-held economic strategy among agricultural families. Men could supplement the income of their farms by working part-time in industry, and female members of the household could add to the family's total income by working full- or part-time. Interestingly, young women dominated the labour force, especially of the textile mills, and the opening up of the labour market to women altered gender roles in much the same way that women's work had in industrializing Athens during the 1950s and 1960s.

Another important development in the countryside has been the advent of tourism. Villages and small towns adjacent to the major archaeological sites or along coastal zones were transformed by the great increase in tourism. In 1987, for example, the receipts from tourism accounted for nearly 5 per cent of Greece's gross national product as over six and a half million foreign tourists came to visit a land that itself had a population of just over 10 million. In addition, during the 1980s internal tourism took off, as urban Greeks left the cities during the hot summer months to visit the villages from which their grandparents or great-grandparents had come or simply to play tourist in their own land. By adding on a room or converting one to a guest bedroom, households could take in boarders. 'Rooms to let' signs appeared along village streets like flowers in springtime. Providing food, snacks, ice cream and soft drinks to guests became very lucrative.

The influx of revenue from tourism had a profound impact on rural society. It gave families a non-agricultural income that could, in many cases, surpass the income earned off the land. As a number of recent anthropological studies have shown, it dramatically changed gender roles and class relations. Because many of the activities related to servicing tourists fell into the categories of 'women's work', it was women who controlled this new source of revenue. The combination of rural industries and tourism changed the face of the countryside significantly. Those areas that in the past had dwelt in a delicate balance between natural resources, agriculture and population could now develop, and perhaps even flourish, with the aid of the new sources of income. The engine that had driven so many Greeks abroad for so long had at last been turned off. In fact, it started to operate in reverse, as we will discuss in the next chapter. What we can conclude here, however, is that the policies followed by Papandreou and PASOK had a profound, and mostly positive, impact on Greek society. Incomes for average Greeks were higher than ever before; social and legal modernization transformed people's lives, and the establishment of national education and health systems made them better. But all this came at a cost. The economy remained fragile and it was probably the most pressing issue facing the country as it entered the *fin-de-siècle*.

12

From boom to bust in the age of globalization, 1990–2015

The year 1990 raised the curtain on Greece's second *fin-de-siècle* as an independent country and like the first, it is a time of incredible highs and devastating lows. What is also quite remarkable is how similar many of the developments that Greece experienced during the first *fin-de-siècle* are to those of its second. To start with the high point – in both periods, 1896 and 2004, Athens hosted what were by most accounts exceptionally successful Summer Olympic Games. On both occasions, the Games put Greece front and centre on the world stage, and each time the country proved the naysayers, who up until the games began had foretold disaster, wrong. Politically, both eras saw the collapse of the two-party system and the demise of the two leaders who dominated those parties: these being Trikoupis and Deliyannis the last time and Papandreou and Karamanlis during this one. On both occasions, the collapse of the old parties resulted in political fragmentation and the emergence of far-right parties, which enjoyed considerable popular support for a time. In 1897, Greece went to war with the Ottoman Empire, with disastrous consequences; almost one hundred years later, it nearly did so again, except that this time it was with the Empire's successor state, Turkey. Each *fin-de-siècle* also saw Greece experience massive population shifts. The last time, it witnessed the emigration of almost one-fifth of its population, whereas this time it saw the immigration of hundreds of thousands of foreign nationals. Lastly, there are remarkable parallels between Greece's financial woes then and now. In the 1890s, the country went bankrupt; it has not yet this time, though that remains a stark and terrifying possibility. Both times, its financial future was placed largely in the hands of organizations representing Greece's major creditors: then it was the International Commission, representing Great Britain, France and Germany, whereas now it is the Troika, representing the European Commission, the International Monetary Fund and the European

Central Bank. We examined in Chapters 3 and 7 Greece's last *fin-de-siècle*; in this chapter, we explore the current one. The last time, Greece eventually emerged from its crisis stronger and more prosperous than before; we can only hope that it will do so this time as well.

Changing of the guard, 1990–1996

The 8 April 1990 election saw New Democracy win 47 per cent of the popular vote, as opposed to PASOK's 38 per cent; nonetheless, because of the changes to the electoral laws passed by the previous government, the conservatives only controlled 150 seats in Parliament, and thus needed a coalition partner to rule. This they obtained but the move only gave them one additional vote. Konstantinos Mitsotakis, then, faced the daunting task of having to govern with only the slimmest of majorities (Chart 7 shows the results of all the legislative elections between 1990 and 2015).

One of his first priorities was to rehabilitate Greece's relationship with the United States. As we saw, throughout the 1980s, Papandreou had relished his testy engagement with Washington, and, if anything, it got worse because of the Koskotas scandal. Andreas publicly and frequently denounced the entire affair as a US plot against him. Not surprisingly, one of Mitsotakis's first major

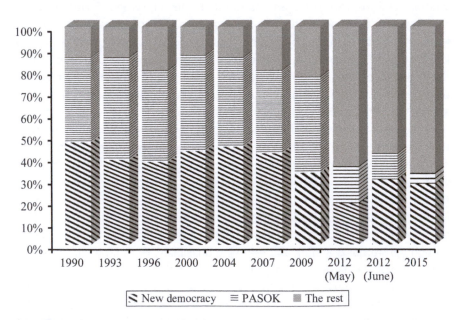

CHART 7 *Greek election results, 1990–2015.*

acts was a ten-day visit to America in June 1990. In addition to visiting with leading Greek-Americans and spending time in New York at the United Nations, he also went to Washington to consult with President George H. W. Bush. The following summer, their initial discussions were followed up by an official state visit to Greece by Bush on 18–20 July 1991. As Mitostakis made clear, his goals in these meetings included (1) restoring cordial relations between Athens and Washington, (2) negotiating a new military alliance with the United States regarding bases in Greece, (3) reassuring the United States about Greece's unwavering commitment to NATO, (4) asserting Athens's intention to play a leading role in the Balkans after the fall of Communism and (5) seeking from the United States military and financial assistance. Bush responded positively to all of this in his speech to Parliament on 18 July 1991, even speaking of the special relationship that existed between Greece and the United States; a relationship, Bush proclaimed, that had been built by Venizelos and Karamanlis and that now would be deepened and strengthened by Mitsotakis.

Besides mending fences with the United States, the other big foreign policy issue that the ND confronted related to developments in the region after the fall of Communism, and in particular, the breakup of Yugoslavia. On 21 June 1991, the first group of Yugoslav republics declared their independence and this had two results: it triggered the onset of war in the region, particularly in Croatia and Bosnia, and it led to other republics doing so as well. It was particularly troubling for Greece when the Yugoslav Republic of Macedonia did so. From its founding in 1944, the constitution of the Communist republic had laid claim to territories within Greece's borders as being part of its national homeland; the government even produced official maps showing Greek Macedonia as part of it. Fearful that the new state would perpetuate these irredentist sentiments, tensions developed between Athens and Skopje on a variety of issues; prominent among them would be what the new state would be officially named. From October 1991 onwards, the name issue has bedevilled relations between the two countries, with Greece insisting that the new country be forbidden from using any name that suggested a claim to Greek Macedonia. Officially, since then, the new country has been known as the Former Yugoslav Republic of Macedonia. The name issue touched a nerve in Greek society. The memories of when large areas of northern Greece had been under foreign control were fresh, specifically the Bulgarian zone of occupation during the Second World War. Huge public rallies, bordering on hysteria, proclaimed that 'Macedonia is Greek.'

Another important development related to the collapse of the Communist world was a massive population shift in Greece. For the first time in its history, Greece became more of a receiver than a giver of migrants. One important migrant stream emanated from the former Soviet Union. Over the course of the 1990s, close to 150,000 people of Greek descent entered the country, with the vast majority of them (83 per cent) coming between 1990 and 1996. Hailing primarily from Georgia and Kazakhstan, these repatriated (παλιννοστούντες) Greeks were welcomed into their 'ancestral' homeland. Arriving in much greater numbers, and certainly not as welcome, were close to 500,000 illegal immigrants from Albania. Text-box 42 reproduces excerpts from a report by Helsinki Watch, a human rights group, regarding Greece's treatment of Albanian illegal immigrants. In spite of the fact that the Greek economy benefitted by this influx of cheap manual labour, Albanian immigration generated a strongly adverse reaction in Greece that bordered on being a moral panic. For a time, every crime in the country was attributed to an Albanian. Anti-Albanian sentiments eventually abated, not because of their acceptance but because new immigrants from other parts of the world replaced them as the new bogymen. The migrant, as we will discuss late in this chapter, remains a critically important issue in Greece.

Domestically, the ND faced two major challenges, one political and the other economic. Politically, the issue of the day related to the Koskotas scandal, and, in particular, to what was to be done with Papandreou. On 11 March 1991, he and a number close associates went on trial before a special tribunal made up of thirteen leading jurists. The trial lasted for ten months and on 17 January 1992, he was acquitted of all four charges (the vote on three of them was 7–6 and 10–3 on the fourth). Throughout the proceedings, Papandreou insisted that the entire affair was a vendetta against him by his political opponents and the United States, and he refused to participate in any way, and that included boycotting the trial. Indeed, he was not even present when the verdicts were handed down. The septuagenarian showed once again his knack for political survival.

The other great issue of the day was the economy. The ND had inherited one that was beset by high levels of public debt, persistently elevated rates of inflation (20 per cent the year they came to office), chronic primary budget deficits and huge government expenditures, including expended public funds to keep afloat failed companies. Beginning with his first budget, Mitsotakis introduced a programme of austerity. He cut government spending across the board and raised taxes on a variety of goods, including fuel oil. He froze public-sector salaries and pensions. In order to attract capital, deregulation of certain areas, such as banking, were introduced. None of these steps met with much popularity, but the most unpopular measure of all was his repeal of the wage price index, which had kept people's incomes high but which had also fuelled inflation. In the end, the ND's economic policies began to turn the economy around, but the pace at which it was doing so could not keep up with the rising public discontent.

The 10th of October 1993 raised the curtain on Andrea's final appearance on the public stage. In April of the previous year, Mitsotakis had removed Antonis

Text-box 42 Greece and Albanian immigration (1996)

In late August 1996, more than 7,000 illegal, mainly Albanian, immigrants were apprehended in their homes or workplaces and summarily expelled from Greece, some visibly abused by the police. Although that piece of information was available in Athens, hardly any media chose to mention it; they were all too busy covering, sometimes at length, the simultaneous expulsion of some 300 African immigrants from the St. Bernard church in Paris ... . The near-silence persisted, even after the Albanian government officially protested to its Greek counterpart, the Greek and Albanian Helsinki committees denounced the mass expulsions, and the embarrassed Greek government spokesperson was refusing to comment on the event in the daily briefing.

There was nothing new in these expulsions per se. In the 1990s, Greece had seen the number of mainly Albanian – but also Polish, Filipino, Egyptian, etc.– illegal immigrants rise to – even according to official estimates – 500–700,000 (for a legal population of 10.5 million). Naturally, the police is regularly expelling such foreigners; nevertheless, the only mass expulsions have been those of Albanians and they were never related to their illegal status in the country, but to strains in the Greek–Albanian relations. ... The 1996 wave of expulsions though was a surprise. ... This is why many suspect that the expulsions were this time motivated by intra-Greece disagreements over the Greek–Albanian rapprochement ...

Luckily for the Albanian immigrant community in Greece, the so-eager-for-international contacts Albanian government and the very pragmatic Greek foreign minister (who reflects the prime minister's realism and modernism) managed to forget the incident and Mr Pangalos' one-day visit (31/8) ran smoothly. ... This long-awaited normalization of the status of Albanian and other immigrants in Greece is supported by all NGOs and left-wing opposition parties, but also by a large fraction of socialist PASOK government members. However, it has been increasingly opposed by the right-wing opposition and the corresponding media, which have been blaming the immigrants for the rising unemployment and criminality, though they have absolutely no data to support their arguments ...

The fact that so many foreign immigrants have been in Greece for many years indicates that the Greek economy today, like other Western economies in the past, needs such a labour force. Unlike the latter countries though – many of which were hosts to millions of Greek immigrants – Greece has hitherto refused to admit that reality and adopt accordingly a consistent policy on the matter, as if the present situation, which leads to the worst kind of exploitation of these workers by their employees and also gives leverage to Greek authorities in the Greek–Albanian relations, suits them well.

P. E. Dimitras, 'Helsinki Watch', 1996. http://www.greekhelsinki.gr/english/articles/albanians.html.

Samaras as his Minister of Foreign Affairs over their disagreement on how to handle the Macedonian name question. Eventually, Samaras broke from the party and created his own, called Political Spring. Some members of the ND followed suit, and when two of them resigned from the party in September, it triggered the October election. PASOK was swept back into power, winning 47 per cent of the popular vote and claiming 170 seats in the new parliament, compared to the ND, which got 39 per cent of the vote and 111 seats. Mitsotakis resigned as party leader and was replaced by Miltiades Evert. Papandreou's final term of office was his least memorable as he was in poor health, and was long past his firebrand days. Largely restricted to his home because of illness, he stopped being a hands-on premier, and access to him was largely controlled by his wife, Dimitra Liani, who herself accumulated considerable political power because of her role as gatekeeper. Andreas had to confront the same problems as his predecessor, and his policies hewed fairly close to his. He modified the economic policies of austerity but not to any great extent. In foreign policy, he proved even more hawkish, especially regarding the Macedonian name issue, instituting in 1994 an embargo against the small landlocked Balkan country. Eventually, he was unable to continue in the job and so resigned as leader of the party. On 18 January 1996, his successor was chosen: Kostas Simitis. Andreas lived for another six months, passing away on 23 June. His old political rival, Konstantinos Karamanlis, outlived him but not by much (he died on 23 April 1998). With the passing of these two figures who had dominated the Greek political scene since the 1950s, there was a fundamental changing of the guard.

Modernization and Europeanization, 1996–2008

Kostas Simitis had very little in common with his predecessor except for their academic training as professional economists. Simitis lacked Papandreou's charisma and oratorical skills but he made up for them in other areas. He was a careful and deliberative thinker, unlike his mercurial predecessor. His strengths as a leader included his willingness to delegate and to foster a climate of collaboration. 'Manager' was a word often used to describe him; some meant it as a criticism, while for others it had positive connotations. Simitis was born in the year democracy in Greece had failed: 1936. He studied economics in Germany and the United Kingdom before relocating to Athens. During the years of the Dictatorship, he was an active opponent of the regime until forced to leave the country, and while abroad, he joined PAK. After the restoration of democracy, he entered politics as a founding member of PASOK.

During the Papandreou administrations of the 1980s and the 1990s, he held numerous posts, most of which dealt, not surprisingly, with the economy. Even though he had earned a good reputation among the party members, he was never particularly close to Papandreou and so he was not the favourite to replace the ailing premier in 1996. But he beat out his rivals by a slender margin and took up the premiership on 18 January. He assumed leadership of the party in June and then led PASOK to a clear victory on 22 September. In an election contested by 29 parties, the socialists won 42 per cent of the vote and got 162 seats in Parliament, while the ND earned 38 per cent of the vote and 108 seats (as Chart 7 shows, the other 26 parties shared the remaining 20 per cent of the vote). He would follow up this victory by winning a second term in office in the election of 9 April 2004, albeit by a much smaller margin – 43.79 per cent to the ND's 41.49. Ruling with a reduced parliamentary majority, Simitis would remain in power until 2004.

Two connected and overarching goals shaped his years in power, and they were modernization and European integration. Both of them placed important emphasis on economic development. For some time, there had been a growing movement towards greater European economic integration, which came to be called the Economic and Monetary Union of the European Union. The movement picked up pace in 1990 and then started to take a concrete form in 1992 with the signing of the Treaty of Maastricht. It set forth the criteria for membership and defined the conditions for membership in the union, especially with regard to inflation rates, levels of public debt, interest rates and exchange rate stability, among others. A second phase in the development of the union took place between 1994 and 1998, and it witnessed the establishment of the financial institutions that would undergird the EMU. The most important of these organizations was the European Central Bank, founded in 1998. The third phase began the following year with the introduction of the euro. Simitis's economic policies, then, between 1996 and 1 January 2001, when Greece joined the EMU and adopted the euro, were driven by the need to ensure that Greece met the Maastricht criteria for inclusion in the Eurozone.

The linchpins to PASOK's economic programme were (1) reining in inflation, (2) attracting investment, (3) stimulating the economy with infrastructure projects and (4) generating economic growth while maintaining control over foreign debt. In all areas, he was relatively successful. Through a combination of borrowing and investment, he undertook an ambitious programme aimed at modernizing Greece's infrastructure. Under his leadership, the Metro, the Athens subway system, was completed in 2000 (work on it had begun in 1992). Shortly after taking office, his government oversaw the construction of a new airport, the Eleftherios Venizelos International Airport (work began in 1996 and was completed in 2001). Another incredibly costly and ambitious undertaking was the construction of the Rios-Antirrios Bridge that connected the Peloponnesos and Central Greece (started in 1998 and completed in 2004). Lastly, while not in and of itself an infrastructure project, Athens being awarded the 2004 Summer Olympic Games in 1997 certainly spurred investment and massive government expenditures on building projects. At times during the early 2000s, Greece resembled a huge construction site once again.

Simitis's policies stabilized prices and wages, cut labour costs, and increased, generally, the country's economic competitiveness, while attracting investment. Between 1999 and 2004, the rate of fixed investment in Greece was 7.3 per cent, almost double the rate in the other EMU countries. At the same time, inflation fell to 3 per cent. The result of these policies was a sustained period of economic growth. Chart 8 shows the country's annual GDP (Gross Domestic Product) growth rate from 1990 to 2013; as it shows, under Simitis, GDP grew annually at a rate greater than 4 per cent and even reached 6 per cent in 2003. In the next section of this chapter on the crisis years (2008–15), I will refer to this chart as well as Charts 8 and 9. At this point, what we need to appreciate is that Greece was one of the fastest growing economies in Europe. Chart 9 shows roughly the same thing but gives an impression of what those growth rates really meant for the people. It shows the change in GDP per capita, and what we can see is that under PASOK, it went from approximately $11,000 per person in 1995 to almost double that amount by 2006. This is not to argue, of course, that everyone in society benefited equally from the economic growth. Income inequality was and is a persistent problem in Greece, and that was certainly true even during the growth years. In fact, one of the criticisms of Simitis's policies was that under him, the rich got richer and the poor got by. Lastly, PASOK was able to achieve this growth without substantially increasing public indebtedness. This is not to say that the government did not borrow heavily in international financial markets. It did, but, as Chart 10 shows, GDP growth and public-sector borrowing grew apace. As we can see, the debt to the GDP ratio between

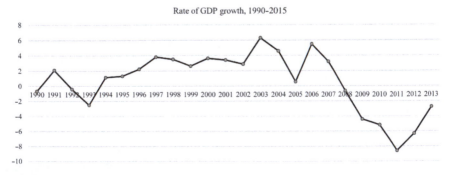

CHART 8 *GDP growth, 1990–2015.*

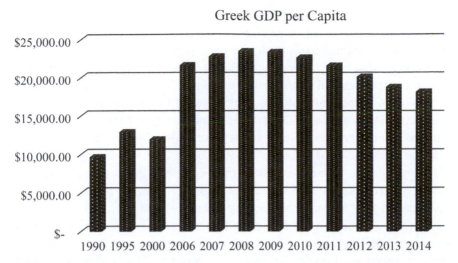

CHART 9 *GDP per capita, 1990–2014.*

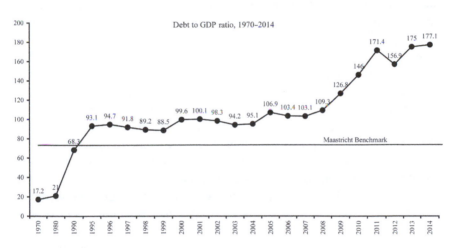

CHART 10 *Sovereign debt to GDP ratio, 1970–2015.*

1996 and 2004 remained roughly constant at rates between 90 and 100 percent. In sum, Simitis's economic policies qualified Greece for inclusion in the Eurozone and once it became a full member in the EMU, the full benefits of inclusion became clear: economic growth. But there were warning signs of possible troubles ahead. The public sector remained horribly bloated and the funding for some of the key social welfare programmes, especially the social security system, was greatly imbalanced: more monies were being paid out than were being taken in. In the short term, growth and prosperity overshadowed these looming problems, and there was no political will to address them.

In regard to foreign policy, the two most important issues Simitis faced were the same ones that his predecessor had: Turkey and Cyprus. Regarding the former, confrontation with it in the Aegean was the first major crisis that he faced in office. On 31 January 1996, Greece and Turkey stood at the brink of war over possession of an uninhabited island in the eastern Aegean called Imia. Whose national territory the island belonged to was in and of itself not the issue. Being able to claim the area between it and the coast as one's national territory was. War was averted but Greek–Turkish relations took a turn for the worse after it. One of Simitis's goals then was to improve them. He sought to use Greece's position in the European Union as leverage with Turkey, which was itself seeking admission to the Union. But the biggest boost towards amiable formulations took place between August and September 1999. Both Greece and Turkey were hit by devastating earthquakes, and on each occasion, one came to the other's aid. This inaugurated a phase of what became called 'earthquake diplomacy.'[1] In regard to Cyprus, Greece pushed hard for its admission into the European Union and this happened on 1 May 2004. Regarding Greece's place in the world, under Simitis, it achieved full integration into Europe and became a leading political and economic power in the region.

Domestically, probably the high points of the *fin-de-siècle* were the 2004 Summer Olympics and the destruction of the domestic terrorist group 17 November. In the run-up to the games, there was a great deal of anxiety expressed, primarily in the world's media, about whether or not the venues would be completed, whether the infrastructure of Athens could handle the influx of people coming to the games, and about security concerns. All of these proved baseless. The Olympic Games went off smoothly and actually proved to be an incredible showcase for Greece. In many ways, it highlighted the economic development that Greece had undergone since the mid-1990s. Of course, this came at a cost. It is estimated that the games cost Greece close to $11 billion, much of which had to be borrowed.

17 November (17 N, as they abbreviated their name) was the oldest and most successful domestic terrorist group in Greece. It took its name from the Polytechnic episode in 1973 that helped bring down the military dictatorship. The group had been active, carrying out attacks beginning in 1975. Over the years, it carried out a number of assassinations of Greek politicians and foreigners, including CIA agent Richard Welch and some other US military personnel. It was also responsible for numerous bombings of buildings and government ministries in the country. For decades, the group had eluded capture. However, in 2002, a member of the organization was wounded while carrying out a bombing attack against a company in Piraeus. Based on intelligence that he provided, the authorities identified and then arrested much of the organization's leadership. At the end of a trial that ran from March until

December 2003, all of the defendants were found guilty and the verdicts were upheld on appeal. The dismantling of 17 November marked a singular success in the war on terrorism.

Over time, however, there developed domestic opposition to Simitis and PASOK's modernization programme. In the summer of 2000, the government announced a programme to revamp the identity card that all Greeks have to carry so that it would conform to European norms. This meant that religion would not be listed on the new cards. For the Orthodox Church leadership, in particular for Archbishop Christodoulos of Athens, and for conservatives, this was seen as an assault on Greek identity. For them, being Orthodox was synonymous with being Greek, and so the removal of religious identification on state-issued IDs, in their view, threatened the essential fabric of society. After a number of very large public rallies, the issue faded in significance, but it certainly had an impact on the government's popularity. Even more important in this regard was the impact of PASOK's economic policies. As I mentioned earlier, the fruits of economic growth were not being equally distributed across society. Wages and benefits had in some instances gone down and in others they were static, and so people's real purchasing power actually went down. What compensated for this was the flood of cheap consumer capital, particularly credit cards that now became available to the average Greek. Banks were literally throwing credit cards at people, and practically anyone who applied for a card got one. So while incomes remained relatively static, per capita consumption increased dramatically, but it did so through debt spending. Beginning in 2003, Greece was hit by numerous strikes, some of which, like the one on 10 October, attracted huge numbers of protesters. In the face of this increasing domestic opposition, and grown weary after almost a decade in power, Simitis decided to step down. On 7 January 2004, he announced that he was resigning from leadership of the party and he would not participate in the forthcoming March election. The figure who had provided the bridge between the old guard and the new post-war generation of Greek politicians thus left the political stage.

On 4 March 2007, PASOK and ND faced off once again and, as had been the case so often in the previous half-century, leading the former was a Papandreou while at the helm of the latter was a Karamanlis. In this case, however, it was not Andreas and Konstantinos who were at the respective helms but the son of one, George Papandreou, and the nephew of the other, Kostas Karamanlis. After a heated campaign, the result was a victory for the conservatives, who won 45.4 per cent of the vote and 165 seats to PASOK's 40.5 per cent (117 seats). Among the smaller parties that fielded candidates in this election was one called SYRIZA; the Alliance of the Radical Left was not really a fully formed party, but, instead, was the amalgamation of numerous small, left-wing parties. And in this, its first, election, it got 3.3 per cent of the vote and six seats in Parliament.

The day, however, belonged to the ND. Since Simitis had moved PASOK much closer to the political centre, and had really transformed it from a socialist into a neoliberal democratic party, Karamanlis's policies did not differ significantly. After basking in the Olympic afterglow, the ND settled in to be a rather unadventurous administration. By 2006, economic growth was slowing, while borrowing and deficit spending remained robust; as a result, the critically important debt to the GDP ratio began to creep up, remaining above 100 per cent (see Chart 8). Karamanlis and the ND were re-elected in 2007 but with a smaller majority and an increasingly restive public. This was especially the case after the wave of riots that rocked the country in response to the slaying of a teenage boy, Alexandros Grigoropoulos, by the police in December 2008. This was the situation when the financial tsunami that began on Wall Street in 2008 and spread around the world hit Greece and started the Crisis that would bring Greece to the verge of bankruptcy and unleash a humanitarian disaster.

The Crisis, 2008–2015

In mid-September 2008, the world's financial markets started getting nervous. The housing bubble that had pushed stock prices to new highs began to show troubling signs that suggested that it was about to burst. Credit markets, in anticipation of this event, began to tighten up. By early October, the financial system seemed to be on the verge of a systemic breakdown, and the situation just became worse over the course of the month. The crash that then took place inaugurated what is probably the largest financial crisis in human history. It triggered a banking, and then a sovereign debt, crisis the consequences of which are still to be fully felt. While the Greek economy was not severely impacted by the 2008 collapse, it was to be one of the worst-hit places in the world in the aftermath. By the summer of 2009, Greece was feeling the effects of the financial crisis – the economy was contracting quickly (see Chart 8) – and so, even though he did not need to, Karamanlis called for a snap election in October. His reasoning was that the crisis had grown to such a proportion that his government needed a new, clear and unambiguous mandate to lead the country. And that was forthcoming. Just not for him and his party.

The election on 4 October produced a landslide victory for Papandreou and PASOK, as they won 44 per cent of the popular vote and 160 seats in Parliament, while the ND saw its share of the popular vote fall to 34 per cent, which equated to a loss of 61 seats in Parliament. A few weeks after being in office, the new finance minister, George Papakonstantinou, made a chilling announcement. Greece's sovereign debt was much greater than the previous government had reported and the country had a number of bond issues and debt repayments becoming due over the next few months. And the government, he reported, did not have the cash on hand to pay them. Greece would have to depend on selling debt on the financial markets at precisely the time that no one was buying. Moreover, the revelations about the Greek debt led to the country's credit worthiness being questioned. The major rating agencies, Fitch, Standard and Poor's and Moody's all downgraded Greece's credit rating, meaning that Greece would have to pay more to borrow, that is if anyone would lend to them. The critical issue over the winter months of 2009–10, then, was whether Greece could repay its debts.

Papandreou and PASOK had to act quickly and aggressively to stop the slide into fiscal chaos. But there were few options available. In February and March, the government passed legislation introducing a variety of austerity measures that included cutting the salaries of all government employees, freezing pensions and introducing spending cuts. Along with these cuts in expenditures, the government sought to raise revenue by raising taxes; VAT was raised from 19 to 21 per cent; and the rate of tax on fuel, cigarettes and alcohol were all raised substantially. But these measures were inadequate. Greece did not have the funds on hand to meet its outstanding debt repayments. Consequently, on 23 April, Papandreou formally requested an international bailout that would be organized and administered by the European Union (under the control of the European Commission), the European Central Bank and the International Monetary Fund. A few weeks later (2 May), the Troika, as they came to be called, announced a bailout package worth $143 billion, but in exchange the Greek government had to enact even more draconian austerity measures in addition to undertaking fundamental restructuring of Greek public finances. A few days later, the Greek Parliament passed the new austerity package, while outside the chamber's doors, Greeks were protesting, demonstrating and even rioting in the street. In one demonstration, three people were killed by a firebomb. The Greek Crisis was now well and truly underway.

The remainder of 2010 into 2011 saw the government largely trying to implement the austerity measures amid growing public unrest. On 25 March 2011, for example, the Greek Indignant Citizens Movement occupied Sintagma, vowing to stay until the policies of austerity were ended (Figure 20). Nonetheless, the economic situation continued to deteriorate, and Greece's credit worthiness continued to sink. In June, under increasing pressure from the Troika, Papandreou announced new and even more debilitating austerity measures, which passed in Parliament by only 17 votes. Popular unrest and protests grew as the economic conditions worsened and the humanitarian crisis grew more severe. With the country's future in the balance, Papandreou stepped down and a coalition government consisting of PASOK, ND and the

FIGURE 20 *Protesting Austerity (2011). Over the course of 2010 and 2011, tens of thousands of Greeks took to the streets to protest against the Memorandum and the politics of austerity, for a while even occupying Sintagma Square. This picture shows a selection of the banners and posters that they posted during the protests. Notice the way that they drew on the repertoire of symbols and slogans from past protest movements. One large banner, for example, proclaims that 'The Junta did not end in '73.' Nearby is another that points the finger at who was to blame for the Crisis: it shows the Finance Minister of the then PASOK government, George Papakonstantinou, being recognized by Goldman Sachs as its 'employee of the decade'.*

right-wing party LAOS took over, with Loukas Papadimos, an economics professor and former governor of the Bank of Greece, at the helm. This caretaker government remained in office for only six months.

In May, the Greeks went to the polls once again and the election failed to produce a clear victor. Consequently, a second round of polling was held shortly thereafter. On 17 June 2012, the New Democracy under the leadership of Antonis Samaras won 29.7 per cent of the votes, but not enough parliamentary seats to form a government. It had, therefore, to form a coalition with PASOK and a party called the Democratic Left. These two elections marked a watershed in Greek political history, marking for the first time since 1974 that PASOK and New Democracy did not enjoy the support of the overwhelming majority of Greek people. We will talk about this political fragmentation shortly.

In order to hit the fiscal targets set forth in the Memorandum of Understanding between Greece and the Troika, additional austerity measures were imposed, with disastrous consequences as we will see. Increasingly, Samaras found himself caught between a rock, the Troika's demand for more reforms and budget cuts, and a hard place, the burgeoning public unrest. By the end of 2014, social and economic conditions in Greece had deteriorated to beyond crisis level. We can now look at some of the consequences of the policies of austerity.

First, and most importantly, austerity triggered a catastrophic contraction of the economy. As Chart 8 shows, the total GDP fell by an average of 4 per cent annually, while in 2011 alone, the economy lost 8 per cent of its value. Economic contraction led to an increase in unemployment. Chart 11 presents the unemployment data. For a decade before the crash, the rate had varied between 8 and 11 per cent, a rate on par with much of the rest of Europe. Beginning in 2010, however, it began to skyrocket, rising into the 20s by 2012 and then peaking at 27 per cent in 2014; as bad as they are, these figures pale in comparison to youth unemployment, the rates for which rose to over 60 per cent. A vicious cycle was forming. As unemployment rose, consumer spending fell, lessening demand for goods and services, which led to more firms firing employees or going out of business. A total of 40 per cent of retail stores in Athens had gone under by 2013. As millions of people saw either a dramatic drop in their income or its loss altogether, they had to bear an ever-increasing tax burden, including levies on necessities like food and fuel, at the same time that the safety net that was designed to protect them was being torn to tatters. The result has been a humanitarian disaster.

According to the OECD, as of the end of 2014, 30 per cent of the Greek population lived below the poverty level and Greece had the highest poverty

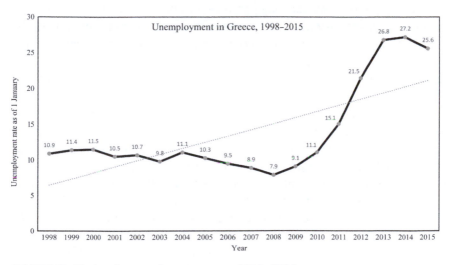

CHART 11 *National unemployment rates, 1990–2015.*

rate of any of the core Eurozone countries. The same study concluded that 17 per cent of the population did not receive enough food to meet people's daily nutritional needs. Homelessness had reached crisis proportions after a 25 per cent increase since 2010. Athens now had the twelfth largest homeless population among the world's major cities. At the same time, government spending cuts imposed by the Memorandum of Understanding had had a major impact on the health care system.

In 2006, Greece expended 13.2 per cent of GDP on public health; by 2012 it had fallen to 11.2 per cent, placing Greece well below the EU average. Certainly, even before the Crisis the health care service, both health insurance and the care delivery system, needed major structural reforms. As a recent study has noted, 'The old social health insurance (SHI) system suffered from a large number of funds and providers with varying organizational and administrative structures offering services that were not coordinated. This resulted in different population coverage and contribution rates, different benefit packages and inefficient operation; all led to large accumulated debts.'[2] Consequently, health care was a major focus for reform and for budget cuts. Between 2009 and 2013, the total health care budget was cut by 23.7 per cent, and that of the public hospital system by 8 per cent. The cuts in subsidies for pharmaceuticals were slashed by 32 per cent in hospitals and by 43 per cent for public pharmacies. Up until 2011, the SHI, which was linked to employment status and type of employment, had provided coverage for the entire population. In 2011, the SHI was merged with various other funds to create the National Health Services Organization (EOPYY). As with its predecessor, health insurance entitlement status was dependent on a person's employment, but as we have seen, unemployment skyrocketed to above 25 per cent, and has stubbornly stayed there. The unemployed continued to receive health insurance for only two years, after which they lost their coverage. There are, consequently, close to 2.5 million people who do not have health insurance now. The health system, then, has drastically reduced in scale, scope and funding.

And the results of the cuts to the health care system are manifestly evident. To take just one measure among many possibilities, the infant mortality rate has risen by 40 per cent since 2008, and the rate looks more like what one finds in underdeveloped countries rather than in a developed European one. No sector of public life has been spared. Education, for example, has been devastated by budget cuts amounting to 35–40 per cent of pre-Crisis levels. All of this has generated social malaise and abject hopelessness. Not coincidently, the suicide rate in Greece has risen dramatically since 2010.

There have been other debilitating consequences to the Crisis as well. A political one has been the shattering of the two-party system that has governed the country since the restoration of democracy in 1974. Both New Democracy and, especially, PASOK saw their core levels of support collapse as the political spectrum broadened. One of the most ominous developments has been the emergence of a far-right fascist party, Golden Dawn. For a long time, Greece has had its share of right-wing nationalist movements, including Golden Dawn as well as a smaller hyper-nationalist party, LAOS, that it has largely eclipsed. Chart 12 shows the electoral performances of the two parties from 2004. Golden Dawn only made its presence felt in 2009, but after that it emerged as a major political force, becoming the country's third largest political party. Its popularity was based upon its anti-austerity, hyper-nationalist and anti-immigrant stances that, along with its skilful manipulation of public opinion through its supposedly philanthropic activities, led to its gaining considerable support in some parts of the country. Because of its propensity for violence, many of its party leaders have been arrested and face charges on a variety of offences (as I write this, their trials have just got underway).

Just as there was a shift among the Greek electorate to the Right, so was there an even more important one to the Left. Because of their participation in the coalition government that imposed austerity, PASOK fell out of favour with a large sector of the public. A new political movement, SYRIZA, which then became a party in 2012, emerged to take its place. Its rise to ascendancy has been nothing short of remarkable (Chart 13). As we saw, it was only in the 2004 campaign that it first put forward candidates. And in the pre-Crisis years, it remained a minor, fringe movement. In 2009, it received only 4.6 per cent of the vote, far less than LAOS did. By 2012, however, it had emerged as

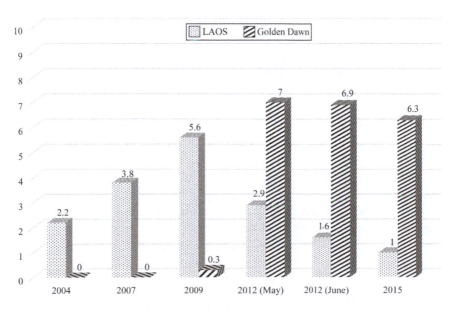

CHART 12 *Electoral performance of right-wing parties, 2004–15.*

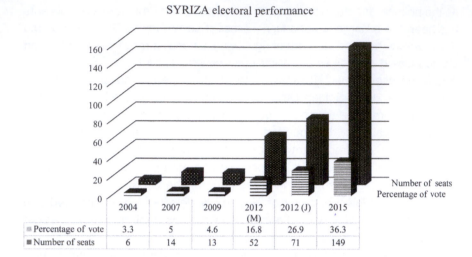

CHART 13 *Rise of SYRIZA.*

the second largest party in the country, winning 26.9 per cent of the popular vote in the June election and that equated to 71 seats in Parliament. The crisis, then, has ended the two-party system that had ruled the country since the 1970s.

Another chilling consequence of the Crisis has been the emergence of virulent anti-immigrant sentiments in the country. Beginning in the mid-2000s, ever-increasing numbers of immigrants, many of them illegal, immigrated to Greece. They came from places different from those of the migrants during the 1990s. These people were coming from the Middle East and Africa, most of them Muslims and people of colour. As often happens in times of crisis, mainstream society looks for scapegoats to blame. And in this case, public ire was directed to these new alien others. There have been numerous episodes of attacks against immigrants, and even when there is no physical violence, devoid of any legal protections, immigrants face a variety of other forms of abuse and discrimination. Some, like the detention camps, have come at the hands of the government. Immigration is a controversial and exceptionally important issue in contemporary Greece, and looks to remain so for some time to come.

At the end of December 2014, the term of President Karolos Papoulias was coming to an end and the Samaras government had to oversee the election of his successor. According to the Greek Constitution, the party in power gets to nominate a candidate to be the new president, and then they have three opportunities to get their nominee elected by the parliament. New Democracy failed in this task and so elections were called for 25 January 2015. Led by its rising young leader, Alex Tsipras, SYRIZA rode a wave of anti-austerity support to a stunning victory, winning 36 per cent of the popular vote and 149 seats in Parliament (ND came in second with 28 per cent and 76 seats). After agreeing to an alliance with one of the smaller right-wing parties, Tsipras and his party came to power, promising to re-negotiate the terms of Greece's financial arrangements with the Troika.

Casting the current financial crisis not as a Greek but as a European problem and emphasizing that the ravages of austerity cannot be continued, SYRIZA is attempting to re-negotiate the terms of relationship with its creditors. The current policy clearly has not worked. Austerity and the savage budget cuts that went along with it have shrunk the economy faster than the debt could be paid down, and the result is, as Chart 13 clearly shows, the magnitude of Greece's sovereign has ballooned to an incredibly high 177 per cent of the GDP. Tsipras and SYRIZA face the daunting task of convincing the fiscally conservative guardians of European neoliberalism that a new way forward must be found that will allow Greece to repay its debts while addressing the humanitarian crisis and economic catastrophe that the current policies have caused. At this point, whether or not they will succeed, and whether or not Greece will, in fact, go bankrupt and have to leave the Eurozone are open questions. But what is clear is that the clock is ticking.

Notes

Chapter 1

1 Greene 2015: 1–22.
2 Greene 2015: 29–36; see also Papademetriou 2015 and Konortas 1998.
3 Zarinebaf, Bennet and Davis 2005: 21–8.
4 Greene 2015: 8.
5 J. Bintliff 2012: 438–52.
6 A. K. Vionis 2013: 45–56.
7 White 2011: 125.
8 Tezcan 2010: 225.
9 Historians dispute the exact meaning of these key clauses in the treaty. The best discussion of the document is: R. Davison (1976), '"Russian Skill and Turkish Imbecility": The Treaty of Kuchuk Kainardji Reconsidered', *Slavic Review*, 463–83 and (1979), 'The "Dosografa" Church in the Treaty of Küçük Kaynarca', *Bulletin of the School of Oriental and African Studies*, University of London, 42(1), 46–52.

Chapter 2

1 Gourgouris 1996: 53.
2 There has been published recently a great deal of new scholarship on the Greek War of Independence that is revising in numerous and important ways how we understand the conflict; some of the best of these new works are cited in the 'Suggestions for Further Reading' section; for a fuller discussion of the war based on this revisionist scholarship, see Gallant 2015: 51–107.
3 T. Gordon (1832), *History of the Greek Revolution*, W. Blackwood: London, vol. I, 183.
4 I. Makriyannis (1966), *The Memoirs of General Makriyannis, 1797–1864*, London: Oxford University Press, 48.
5 Gallant 2015: 105.

Chapter 3

1 Papageorgiou 2005: 401–8.
2 T. W. Gallant (2008), '"When Men of Honor" Met "Men of Law": Violence, the Unwritten Law and Modern Justice', in S. d'Cruze, E. Avdela and J. Rowbotham (eds), *Crime, Violence and the Modern State, 1780–2000*, London: Edwin Mellen, 1–25; for the situation with civil law, see Doxiades 2012.
3 Cited in Koliopoulos 1987: 85.
4 G. Finlay (1877 [1971]), *History of Greece from its Conquest by the Romans to the Present Time, B.C. 146–A.D. 1864. 7 vols*, London: Zeno, vol. 7, 197.

Chapter 4

1 R. Just (1992), 'Ethnicity and the Village: The "Them" and "Us" in Rural Greece', in J. Burke and S. Gauntlett (eds), *Neohellenism*, Melbourne: Australian National University, 114.
2 Spyridon P. Lambros, 1905: in his inaugural lecture as Rector of the National and Kapodistrian University of Athens. Cited in Gazi 2000: 84.
3 *Athena*, 11 November 1861, p. 1. cols. 2–3.
4 Gallant 2002: 15–55.

Chapter 5

1 L. Sergeant (1897), *Greece in the Nineteenth Century: A Record of Hellenic Emancipation and Progress, 1821–1897*, London: T. Fisher Unwin, 41.
2 W. Miller (1925), 'Finlay's "History of the Insurrection in Crete,"' *Annual of the British School at Athens*, 27, 108.

Chapter 6

1 T. Bent (1886), 'Greek Peasant Life', *The Fortnightly Review*, August: 214.
2 T. Kolokotronis (1851 [1977]), Απομνημονεύματα, Athens: Tolmidi, 144.
3 See Gallant 2015: 249–51, and especially Map 7.2 for more about transhumant pastoralism.
4 *Evrydiki*, 21 November 1871, cited in Sant Cassia 2006: 223–4.
5 E. Bastea (1999), *The Creation of Modern Athens: Planning the Myth*, New York: Cambridge University Press, 131.
6 *Avgi*, 13 January 1895, p. 2, col. 3, para. 4.

Chapter 7

1 A. L. Macrakis (1982), 'Eleftherios Venizelos in Crete, 1864–1910: The Main Problems', in Nikiforos Diamandouros and A. Lilly Macrakis (eds), *New Trends in Modern Greek Historiography*, New Haven: Modern Greek Studies Association, 82.

2 Macrakis 2006: 75.

3 Papacosma 1977: 16.

4 *The New York Times*, 19 March 1913, p. 1, col. 2.

5 G. A. Abbott (1922), *Greece and the Allies, 1914–1922*, London: Methuen & Co. Ltd, 8–11.

6 Quoted in Llewellyn-Smith 1998: xiii.

7 Dakin 1972: 215.

8 Gallant et al. 2005: 14.

9 Dispatch dated 2 May 1917 and reproduced in *The New York Times*, 13 June 1917, p. 2, col. 1.

10 Quoted in Dakin 1972: 216.

11 Quoted in Dalby 2010: 71.

Chapter 8

1 Llewellyn-Smith 1998: xvi.

2 Quoted in M. Mazower (1992), 'The Messiah and the Bourgeoisie: Venizelos and Politics in Greece, 1909–1922', *Historical Journal*, 35, 904.

3 E. Venizelos (1920), 'Not War Against Islam – Statement by Greek Prime Minister', *The Scotsman*, 29 June, p. 5.

4 Llewellyn-Smith 2006: 166.

5 A. J. Toynbee (1922), *The Western Question in Greece and Turkey*, New York: Houghton Mifflin Company, 252.

6 Llewellyn-Smith 1998: 227.

7 Hirschon 1989: 31.

8 Quoted in Doulis 1977: 64–5.

9 T. J. C. Martyn (1928), 'Venizelos Comes back to the Helm in Greece', *New York Times*, 17 June, p. 125, col. 1.

10 Xenophon Hatzisarandos, quoted in Mavrogordatos 1983: 62.

11 Koliopoulos 2006: 240–1.

12 Koliopoulos 2006: 243.

13 G. Cianos (1947), *Cianos Diary, 1939–1943*, London: Heinemann, 297.

Chapter 9

1 *Asyrmatos*, 29 October 1940, p. 1, cols. 1–2.

2 Close 2015: 54.

3 Quoted in Mazower 1993: 32.

4 P. Voglis (2006), 'Surviving Hunger: Life in the Cities and the Countryside during the Occupation', in Robert Gildea, Olivier Wievorka and Anette Warring (eds), *Surviving Hitler and Mussolini: Daily Life in Occupied Europe*, Oxford: Berg, 23.

5 Bruno De Wever, Herman van Goethem and Nico Wouters (2006), *Local Government in Occupied Europe: (1939–1945)*, Gent: Academia Press, 208.

6 Hionidou 2006: 130; much of my discussion in this section is based on Hionidou's study.

7 Eleanor Roosevelt Diary entry 10 June 1942. Franklin D. Roosevelt Presidential Library, on-line archive. http://fdrlibrary.tumblr.com/post/88760863723/day-23-visit-of-king-george-ii-of-greece-on.

8 Quoted in Eudes 1974: 6.

9 E. C. W. Myers (1985), *Greek Entanglement*, London: Alan Sutton, 280–1.

10 Skalidakis 2015: 166.

11 Quoted in Mazower 1992: 129–30.

12 Skalidakis 2015: 169.

13 C. M. Woodhouse (1948), *Apple of Discord: A Survey of Recent Greek Politics in the International Setting*, Reston: W. B. O'Neill, 47.

14 Quoted in Chiclet 1990: 209.

15 Quoted in Collard 1990: 236, 238.

Chapter 10

1 Wittner 1982: 137.

2 Quoted in Wittner 1982: 103.

3 B. Sweet-Escott (1954), *Greece: A Political and Economic Survey 1939–1953*, Oxford: Oxford University Press, 94, 98, 143.

4 W. H. McNeill (1978), *The Metamorphosis of Greece Since World War II*, Oxford: Basil Blackwell, 143–4.

5 E. Friedl (1962), *Vasilika: A Village in Modern Greece*, New York: Holt, Rinehart, Winston.

6 I. Sanders (1962), *Rainbow in the Rock. The People of Rural Greece*, Cambridge: Harvard University Press.

7 J. K. Campbell (1964), *Honour, Family and Patronage. A Study of Institutional and Moral Values in a Greek Mountain Community*, Oxford: Oxford University Press.

8 This news report by Nancy Crawshaw appeared in the *Manchester Guardian* in April 1953 and was reproduced in Sweet-Escott 1954: 132 (see note 3).

9 Sutton 1983: 243.

10 Sanders 1962: 296 (see note 6).

11 *The Times*, 2 June 1956, p. 1, col. 2.

12 Quoted in C. M. Woodhouse (1982), *Karamanlis: The Restorer of Greek Democracy*, Oxford: Clarendon Press, 45.

13 Quoted in Dreanos 2012: 119.

14 Dreanos 2012:153.

Chapter 11

1 P. Murtagh (1994), *The Rape of Greece: The King, the Colonels and the Resistance*, New York: Simon and Schuster, 118.

2 Veremis 1997: 153.

3 Interview published in the *New York Times*, 19 October 1983.

4 Lazaridis 1995: 114.

Chapter 12

1 Karakatsanis 2014: 197–204.

2 Economou et al. 2014: 8. The figures cited in this section all derive from this WHO report.

Glossary

Glossary words are shown in bold in the text.

AMAG The American Mission of Aid to Greece was established in 1947 to assist Greece in the civil war and to coordinate the country's post-war reconstruction.

Autochthonous Greek Refers to people who were born and resided in the territory that became the independent Kingdom of Greece.

Ayan Muslim notables who played critically important roles in local society as landowners and government officials during the period of Ottoman rule.

Balkan League An alliance between Greece, Bulgaria, Serbia and Montenegro that fought the Balkan Wars against the Ottoman Empire.

Bipolar World A term deployed during the Cold War (1945–89) that referred to the rough division of the world into two camps, the West and the Soviet Bloc.

Byzantine Empire The Eastern Roman Empire after the sixth century CE with its capital being Constantinople.

Concert of Europe The arrangement devised by Austrian Foreign Minister Klemens von Metternich after the fall of Napoleon to keep the peace in Europe. It entailed cooperation between Great Britain, France, Austria, Prussia and Russia.

Danubian Principalities The Ottoman provinces of Wallachia and Moldavia, strategically located along the borders with Austria, Hungary and Russia.

Dedilomeni The political principle that states that the party in Parliament that holds the majority of seats must be given the mandate to form a government.

Demarchy An administrative district in Greece that is a subdivision of an Eparchy; it most closely resembles a county.

Demotic Greek The vernacular version of Greek spoken by the common people (see Katharevousa).

Devş irme The child levy imposed on the Orthodox population of the Balkans by the Ottoman Empire from the fifteenth to the early eighteenth centuries.

Dhimmi Non-Muslims who practise one of the monotheistic faiths based upon the Old Testament.

Dowry The property that a woman brings into a marriage and that is provided to her by her family in lieu of an inheritance.

Ecumenical Patriarch The head of the Eastern Orthodox Church based in Constantinople.

Enlightenment A Western European intellectual movement of the eighteenth century.

Eparchy The primary administrative unit of Greece, equivalent to a province.

Exarchate The Bulgarian National Church established in 1870.

Eyalet The primary administrative unit of the Ottoman Empire, equivalent to a province.

Heterochtonous Greek Refers to people who were not born in the territory that became the independent Kingdom of Greece but who migrated there during or after the War of Independence.

Honour In Greek: *timi*. This was the central aspect of masculinity in traditional Greek society and it equated to a man's perceived reputation in his community.

Hospodar The governorship of one of the two **Danubian Principalities;** from the early eighteenth century onwards, the position was held by a **Phanariot Greek**.

Idionym (Law) A law passed in 1928 that made it illegal to agitate for the overthrow of the Greek state.

Irredentism An ideology that called for the expansion of a state territory to encompass the areas occupied by co-nationals.

Janissaries An elite corps of soldiers made up of men recruited through the **Devşirme.**

Junta A Spanish term that is used to refer to the Dictatorship of the Colonels (1967–74).

Katharevousa A new, 'purified' version of Greek that was intended to replace the vernacular spoken language as the official Greek language.

Kaza An administrative unit of the Ottoman Empire equivalent to a sub-county.

Kocabaşis Orthodox Christian notables who played critically important roles in local society as landowners and government officials during the period of Ottoman rule.

Megali Idea Greek irredentist ideology that stated that the boundaries of the country had to expand to encompass the territories occupied by the Greek nation in the Ottoman Empire.

Metapolitefsis The period of political restoration after the fall of the **Junta**.

Millet (Millet-i Rum) The term literally means nation, but it was used most frequently to denote one of the major denominational groups within the Ottoman Empire. The Orthodox religious community was referred to as the Millet-i Rum (the nation of the Romans).

National Schism The rift between Eleftherios Venizelos and King Konstantinos I over Greece's policy during the First World War.

Phanariot Greeks A group of wealthy and well-educated Greeks who occupied key positions in the Ottoman government; they took their name from the district in Istanbul where they lived. They monopolized the position of **Hospodar** of the **Danubian Principalities.**

Philhellene Someone who is a lover of all things Greek, usually relating to Ancient Greece. It was related to Romanticism.

Philiki Etaireia The 'Friendly Society'. It was the most important secret society in the years before the Greek War of Independence.

Regency When a sitting monarch has not yet reached the age of majority, a person or a Council called a regency rules in his or her place.

Romantic Nationalism A virulent form of nationalism that developed across Europe in the last quarter of the nineteenth century.

Sanjak An administrative unit of the Ottoman Empire equivalent to a county.

Sharecropping An agrarian system whereby a farming family works land owned by another and pays a portion of the agricultural produce as rent.

Sipahis A form of feudalism practised in the Ottoman Empire whereby cavalry warriors received grants of land in exchange for their military service.

Tanzimat The Ottoman reform programme during the nineteenth century that sought to modernize the Empire.

Theosebism A new, national religion proposed to replace Orthodoxy as the official faith of the new Greek state.

Suggestions for further reading

General reading

Calotychos, V. (2003), *Modern Greece: A Cultural Poetics*, London: Berg.
Clogg, R. (2013), *A Concise History of Greece*, 3rd ed., New York: Cambridge University Press.
Close, D. (2002), *Greece Since 1945: Politics, Economy, and Society*, New York: Longman.
Dertilis, G. (2009), *Ιστορία του Ελληνικού Κράτους, 1830-1920*, Athens: Estia.
Doumanis, N. (2009), *A History of Greece*, London: Palgrave Macmillan.
Featherstone, K. (ed.) (2014), *Europe in Modern Greek History*, London: Hurst and Company.
Fleming, K. E. (2008), *Greece – a Jewish History*, Princeton: Princeton University Press.
Gallant, T. W. (2001), *Modern Greece*, New York: Oxford University Press.
Gallant, T. W. (2015), *The Edinburgh History of the Greeks, 1768 to 1913: The Long Nineteenth Century*, Edinburgh: Edinburgh University Press.
Hatziiosif, C. (ed.) (2009), *Ιστορία της Ελλάδας του 20ού αιώνα. Όψεις πολιτικής και οικονομικής ιστορίας 1900-1940*, Athens: Bibliorama.
Kalyvas, S. (2014), *Modern Greece: What Everyone Needs to Know*, New York: Oxford University Press.
Koliopoulos, J. S. and T. Veremis (2002), *Greece: The Modern Sequel: from 1821 to the Present*, London: Hurst & Company.
Koliopoulos, J. S. and T. Veremis (2010), *Modern Greece: a History since 1821*, Malden, MA: Wiley-Blackwell.
Kostis, K. P. (2013), *'Τα κακομαθημένα παιδιά της ιστορίας'. Η διαμόρφωση του νεοελληνικού κράτους, 18ος-21ος αιώνας*, Athens: Polis.
Mazower, M. (2000), *The Balkans: A Short History*, New York: Modern Library.
Wagstaff, J. M. (ed.) (2002), *Greece, Ethnicity and Sovereignty, 1820-1994: Atlas and Documents*, Slough: Archive Editions.

Historiographical reviews

Lambropoulou, D., A. Liakos and Y. Yiannitsiotis (2006), *Work and Gender in Greek Historiography During the Last Three Decades*, Pisa: Edizioni Plus, Pisa University Press.

Liakos, A. (2004), 'Modern Greek Historiography (1974-2000). The Era of Tradition From Dictatorship to Democracy', in U. Brunbauer (ed.), *(Re)Writing History. Historiography in Southeast Europe After Socialism*, Munchen: Lang, 351–78.

Yannitsiotis, Y. (2007), 'Social History in Greece: New Perspectives', *East Central Europe*, 34, 1 (2), 101–30.

Chapter 1

Anastasopoulos, A. and E. Kolovos (eds) (2007), *Ottoman Rule and the Balkans, 1760-1850: Conflict, Transformation, Adaptation*, Rethymno: University of Crete: Department of History and Archaeology.

Anscombe, F. F. (ed.) (2006), *The Ottoman Balkans, 1750-1830*, Princeton: Markus Wiener Publishers.

Bintliff, J. (2012), *The Complete Archaeology of Greece: From Hunter-gatherers to the 20th Century AD*, Malden, MA: Wiley-Blackwell.

Davis, J. L. and S. Davies (eds) (2007), *Between Venice and Istanbul: Colonial Landscapes in Early Modern Greece*, Princeton: American School of Classical Studies at Athens.

Faroqhi, S. N. (ed.) (2006), *The Cambridge History of Turkey: Volume 3, The Later Ottoman Empire, 1603-1839*, New York: Cambridge University Press.

Faroqhi, S. N. and K. Fleet (eds) (2012), *The Cambridge History of Turkey: Volume 2, The Ottoman Empire as a World Power, 1453—1603*, New York: Cambridge University Press.

Finkel, C. (2005), *Osman's Dream: The History of the Ottoman Empire*, New York: Basic Books.

Greene, M. (2000), *A Shared World: Christians and Muslims in the Early Modern Mediterranean*, Princeton: Princeton University Press.

Greene, M. (2010), *Catholic Pirates and Greek Merchants: A Maritime History of the Mediterranean*, Princeton: Princeton University Press.

Greene, M. (2015), *The Edinburgh History of the Greeks, 1453 to 1774: The Ottoman Empire*, Edinburgh: Edinburgh University Press.

Hanioglu, M. (2008), *A Brief History of the Late Ottoman Empire*, Princeton: Princeton University Press.

Kardasis, V. A. (2001), *Diaspora Merchants in the Black Sea: The Greeks in Southern Russia, 1775-1861*, Lanham, MD: Lexington Books.

Karidis, D. N. (2014), *Athens from 1456 to 1920: The Town Under Ottoman Rule and the 19th-century Capital City*, Oxford: Archaeopress.

Kitromilides, P. M. (2013), *Enlightenment and Revolution: The Making of Modern Greece*, Cambridge, MA: Harvard University Press.

Kitromilides, P. M. and D. Arvanitakis (eds) (2008), *The Greek World under Ottoman and Western Domination: 15th–19th centuries*, New York, NY: Alexander S. Onassis Public Benefit Foundation (USA).

Kolovos, E. and P. H. Kotzageorgis (eds) (2010), *The Ottoman Empire, the Balkans, the Greek lands: Toward a Social and Economic History*, Istanbul: Isis Press.

Konortas, P. (1998), *Οθωμανικές θεωρήσεις για το Οικουμενικό Πατριαρχείο 17ος-αρχές 20ού αιώνα*, Athens: Alexandreia.

Kostantaras, D. J. (2006), *Infamy and Revolt: The Rise of the National Porblem in Early Modern Greek Thought*, New York: Columbia University Press.

Papademetriou, T. (2015), *Render unto the Sultan: Power, Authority, and the Greek Orthodox Church in the Early Ottoman Centuries*, New York: Oxford University Press.

Quataert, D. (2000), *The Ottoman Empire, 1700-1922*, New York: Cambridge University Press.

Vionis, A. K. (2013), *A Crusader, Ottoman, and Early Modern Aegean Archaeology: Built Environment and Domestic Material Culture in the Medieval and Post-medieval Cyclades, Greece (13th-20th Centuries AD)*, Leiden: Leiden University Press.

Vlami, D. (2015), *Trading with the Ottomans: The Levant Company in the Middle East*, London: I.B. Tauris.

White, S. (2011), *The Climate of Rebellion in the Early Modern Ottoman Empire*, New York: Cambridge University Press.

Zarinebaf, F., J. Bennet and J. L. Davis (eds) (2005), *A Historical and Economic Geography of Ottoman Greece: The Southwestern Morea in the 18th Century*, Princeton: American School of Classical Studies at Athens.

Primary sources

Murgescu, B. and H. Berktay (eds) (2009), *The Ottoman Empire. Workbook 1*, Thessaloniki: CDRSEE. Available at http://cdrsee.org/jhp/pdf/workbook1_eng_ed2.pdf

Chapter 2

Angelomatis-Tsougaraki, E. (2010), *1821. Η γέννηση ένος έθνους-κράτους. Α τόμος. Η προεπαναστατική Ελλάδα*, Athens: National Bank.

Anastasopoulos, A. and E. Kolovos (eds) (2007), *Ottoman Rule and the Balkans, 1760-1850: Conflict, Transformation, Adaptation*, Rethymno: University of Crete: Department of History and Archaeology.

Beaton, R. (2013), *Byron's War: Romantic Rebellion, Greek Revolution*, New York: Cambridge University Press.

Bitis, A. (2006), *Russia and the Eastern Question: Army, Government, and Society: 1815-1833*, New York: Oxford University Press.

Fleming, K. E. (1999), *The Muslim Bonaparte: Diplomacy and Orientalism in Ali Pasha's Greece*, Princeton: Princeton University Press.

Gourgouris, S. (1996), *Dream Nation: Enlightenment, Colonization, and the Institution of Modern Greece*, Stanford: Stanford University Press.

Güthenke, C. (2008), *Placing Modern Greece: The Dynamics of Romantic Hellenism, 1770-1840*, Oxford: Oxford University Press.

Kitromilides, P. and H. S. Ilicak (2010), *1821. Η γέννηση ένος έθνους-κράτους. Ε τόμος. Ιδεολογικά ρεύματα: Έλληνες-Οθωμάνοι. Α. Νεοελληνικός διαωτισμός. Β. Η αλλη όχθη*, Athens: National Bank of Greece.

Kostantaras, D. J. (2013), 'Christian Elites of the Peloponnese and the Ottoman State, 1715-1821', *European History Quarterly*, 43 (4), 628–56.

Michalidis, I. D. (2010), *1821. Η γέννηση ένος έθνους-κράτους. Γ τόμος. Ο αγώνας των Ελλήνων. Πολιτικές επιλογές και στρατιωτικές επεχειρήσεις 1821-1827*, Athens: National Bank of Greece.

Pizanias, P. (ed.) (2011), *The Greek Revolution of 1821: A European Event*, Istanbul: Isis Press.

Rizopoulos, C. A. and A. C. Rizopoulos (2008), *Φιλέλληνες και ελλήνες τεκτόνες Το 1821*, Athens: Tetraktys.

Rodriguez, M. E. (2009), *Under the Flags of Freedom: British Mercenaries in the War of the Two Brothers, the First Carlist War, and the Greek War of Independence (1821-1840)*, Lanham, MD: Hamilton Books.

Sakellariou, M. (2012), *Η απόβαση του Ιμπραήμ στην Πελοπόννησο*, Herakleion: University of Crete Press.

Stites, R. (2014), *The Four Horsemen: Riding to Liberty in Post-Napoleonic Europe*, New York: Oxford University Press.

Van Steen, G. (2010), *Liberating Hellenism from the Ottoman Empire: Comte De Marcellus and the Last of the Classics*, New York: Palgrave Macmillan.

Veremis, T. and Y. Koliopoulos (2010), *1821. Η γέννηση ενός έθνους-κράτους. Β τόμος. Η συγκρότηση εξουσίας στην επαναστατημένη Ελλάδα*, Athens: National Bank of Greece.

Yakovaki, N. (2014), 'The Philiki Etaireia Revisited: In Search of Contexts, National and International', *Historical Review/La Revue Historique*, 11, 171–87.

Primary sources

Hatzidimitriou, C. G. (ed.) (1999), *Founded on Freedom and Virtue: Documents Illustrating the Impact in the United States of the Greek War of Independence, 1821-1829*, New York: Aristide D. Caratzas Publishers.

Chapter 3

Aroni-Tsihli, K. (1989), *Αγροτικές εξεγέρσεις στην παλιά Ελλάδα, 1833-1881*, Athens: Papazisi.

Aroni-Tsihli, K. and L. Triha (eds) (2000), *Ο Χαριλάος Τρικούης και η εποχή του: Πολιτικές, επιδοχείς και κοινωινικές σύνθεκες*, Athens: Ekdoseis Papazese.

Carabott, P. (ed.) (1997), *Greek Society in the Making, 1863-1913: Realities, Symbols, and Visions*, Brookfield, VT: Variorum.

Diamandouros, N. P., T. Dragōna and C. Keyder (eds) (2010), *Spatial Conceptions of the Nation: Modernizing Geographies in Greece and Turkey*, London: I. B. Tauris.

Frangoudaki, A. and C. Keyder (2007), *Ways to Modernity in Greece and Turkey: Encounters with Europe, 1850-1950*, London: IB Tauris.

Gardkida, K., V. Kechriotis, C. Loukas, C. Lyrintzis and N. Marioniti (eds) (2008), *Η συγκρότηση του ελληνικού κράτους. Διεθνές πλαίσιο, εξουσία και πολιτική τον 19ο αιώνα*, Athens: Nefeli.

Gavrilis, G. (2008), *The Dynamics of Interstate Boundaries*, Cambridge; New York: Cambridge University Press.

Koliopoulos, J. S. (1987), *Brigands with a Cause: Brigandage and Irredentism in Modern Greece, 1821-1912*, Oxford: Clarendon.

McGrew, W. (1985), *Land and Revolution in Modern Greece, 1800-1881. The Transition in the Tenure and Exploitation of Land from Ottoman Rule to Independence*, Kent, OH: Kent State University Press.

Papageorgiou, S. P. (2005). *Άπο το γένος στο έθνος. Η θεμελίωση του ελληνικού κράτους, 1821-1862*, 2nd ed., Athens: Papasisi.

Petropoulos, J. A. (1968), *Politics and Statecraft in the Kingdom of Greece: 1833-1843*, Princeton: Princeton University Press.

Philliou, C. M. (2011), *Biography of an Empire: Governing Ottomans in an Age of Revolution*, Berkeley: University of California Press.

Triha, L. (2001), *Ο Χαρίλαος Τρικούπης και τα δημόσια έργα*, Athens: Kapon.

Triha, L. (2009), *Χαρίλαος Τρικούπης. Μία βιογραφική περιήγηση*, Athens: Kapon.

Chapter 4

Beaton, R. and D. Ricks (eds) (2009), *The Making of Modern Greece: Nationalism, Romanticism, & the Uses of the Past (1797-1896)*, Farnham, Surrey, UK: Ashgate.

Diamandouros, N. P., T. Dragōna and C. Keyder (eds) (2010), *Spatial Conceptions of the Nation: Modernizing Geographies in Greece and Turkey*, London: I. B. Tauris.

Fortna, B. C., S. Katsikas, P. Konortas and D. Kamouzis (eds) (2012), *State-nationalisms in the Ottoman Empire, Greece and Turkey: Orthodox and Muslims, 1830-1945*, New York: Routledge.

Gazi, E. (2000), *Scientific National History the Greek Case in Comparative Perspective (1850-1920)*, Frankfurt am Main: Peter Lang.

Just, R. (1989), 'The Triumph of the Ethnos', in J. Burke and S. Gauntlett (eds), *History and Ethnicity*, New York: Routledge, 71–88.

Kalliataki Merticopoulou, K. (1997), 'Literacy and Unredeemed Peasants: Late Nineteenth-century Rural Crete Faces Education', in P. Carabott (ed.), *Greek Society in the Making, 1863-1913: Realities, Symbols and Visions*, Brookfield, VT: Ashgate Publishing Company, 115–30.

Koliopoulos, J. S. (1987), *Brigands with a Cause: Brigandage and Irredentism in Modern Greece, 1821-1912*, Oxford: Clarendon.

Mackridge, P. (2009), *Language and National Identity in Greece, 1766-1976*, New York: Oxford University Press.

Papadakis, L. (2006), *Teaching of the Nation; Greek Nationalism and Education in Nineteenth Century Macedonia*, Thessaloniki: Institute for Balkan studies.

Tzanaki, D. (2009), *Women and Nationalism in the Making of Modern Greece: The Founding of the Kingdom to the Greco-Turkish War*, Basingstoke: Palgrave Macmillan.

Tzanelli, R. (2009), *The 'Greece' of Britain and the 'Britain' of Greece: Performance, Stereotypes, Expectations and Intermediaries in 'Neohellenic' and Victorian Narratives (1864-1881)*, Saarbrucken: VDM Verlag Dr. Müller.

Zervas, T. G. (2010), *Resurrecting the Past, Constructing the Future: A Historical Investigation on the Formation of a Greek National Identity in Schools, 1834-1913*, PhD Dissertation, Chicago: Loyola University.

Primary sources

Murgescu, M.-L. (ed.) (2009), *Nations and States in Southeast Europe*, Thessaloniki: CDRSEE. Available at http://cdrsee.org/jhp/pdf/workbook2_eng_ed2.pdf

Chapter 5

Brown, K. (2003), *The Past in Question: Modern Macedonia and the Uncertainties of Nation*, Princeton: Princeton University Press.

Doumanis, N. (2013), *Before the Nation: Muslim-Christian Coexistence and Its Destruction in Late Ottoman Anatolia*, Oxford: Oxford University Press.

Ekinci, M. U. (2009), *The Unwanted War: The Diplomatic Background of the Ottoman-Greek War of 1897*, Saarbrücken: VDM.

Exertzoglou, H. (2010), *Οι << χαμένες Πατρίδες>> Πέρα από τη νοσταλγία. Μια κοινωνική-πολιτισμική ιστορία των Ρωμίων της Οθωμανικής Αυτοκρατορίας (μέσα 19ου- αρχές 20ού αιώνα)*, Athens: Nefeli.

Fortna, B. C., S. Katsikas, P. Konortas and D. Kamouzis (eds) (2012), *State-nationalisms in the Ottoman Empire, Greece and Turkey: Orthodox and Muslims, 1830-1945*, New York: Routledge.

Frary, L. J. and M. Kozelsky (eds) (2014), *Russian-Ottoman Borderlands: The Eastern Question Reconsidered*, Madison, WI: University of Wisconsin Press.

Gallant, T. W. (2002), *Experiencing Dominion: Culture, Identity and Power in the British Mediterranean*, Notre Dame: University of Notre Dame Press.

Gavrilis, G. (2008), *The Dynamics of Interstate Boundaries*, New York: Cambridge University Press.

Gounaris, B. C. (2007), *Τα Βαλκάνια των Ελλήνων. Από το διαφωτισμό εως τον Α' παγκόσμιο πόλεμο*, Athens: Epikentro.

Gounaris, B. C., S. N. Kalyvas and I. D. Stefanidis (eds) (2010), *Ανορθόδοχοι Πόλεμοι. Μακεδονία, Εμφύλιος, Κύπρος*, Athens: Pataki.

Mazower, M. (2005), *Salonica, City of Ghosts: Christians, Muslims, and Jews, 1430-1950*, New York: Alfred A. Knopf.

Mylonas, H. (2012), *The Politics of Nation-building: Making Co-nationals, Refugees, and Minorities*, New York: Cambridge University Press.

Ozil, A. (2013), *Orthodox Christians in the Late Ottoman Empire: A Study of Communal Relations in Anatolia*, New York: Routledge.

Peckham, R. S. (2000), *National Histories, Natural States: Nationalism and the Politics of Place in Greece*, New York: I.B. Tauris.

Roudometof, V. (ed.) (2000), *The Macedonian Question*, New York: Columbia University Press, Eastern European Monographs.

Şenişik, P. (2011), *The Transformation of Ottoman Crete: Revolts, Politics and Identity in the Late Nineteenth Century*, London: I.B. Tauris.

Yosmaoğlu, I. (2014), *Blood Ties: Religion, Violence, and the Politics of Nationhood in Ottoman Macedonia, 1878-1908*, Ithaca, NY: Cornell University Press.

Chapter 6

Baruh, L. T. and V. Kechriotis (eds) (2010), *Economy and Society on Both Shores of the Aegean*, Athens: Alpha Bank.

Bintliff, J. L. and H. Stöger (eds) (2009), *Medieval and Post-Medieval Greece. The Corfu Papers*, Oxford: Archaeopress.

Doxiadis, E. (2012), *The Shackles of Modernity: Women, Property, and the Transition From the Ottoman Empire to the Greek State (1750-1850)*, Cambridge, MA: Harvard University Press.

Eldem, E. and S. Petmezas (eds) (2011), *The Economic Development of Southeastern Europe in the 19th Century*, Athens: Alpha Bank.

Forbes, H. (2007), *Meaning and Identity in a Greek Landscape: An Archaeological Ethnography*, New York: Cambridge University Press.

Gallant, T. W. (2002), *Experiencing Dominion: Culture, Identity and Power in the British Mediterranean*, Notre Dame: University of Notre Dame Press.

Gallant, T. W. (2008), '"When Men of Honor" Met "Men of Law": Violence, the Unwritten Law and Modern Justice', in S. d'Cruze, E. Avdela and J. Rowbotham (eds), *Crime, Violence and the Modern State, 1780-2000*, London: Edwin Mellen, 1–25.

Gallant, T. W. (2012), 'Women, Crime and the Courts on the Ionian Islands During the Nineteenth Century', *Historein*, 11, 137–56.

Gallant, T. W. (2014), *Βιώματα αποικικής κυριαρχίας. Πολιτισμός, ταυτότητα και εξουσία ετα Επτάνησα, 1817-1864*, Athens: Alexandreia Press.

Halstead, P. (2014), *Two Oxen Ahead: Pre-Mechanized Farming in the Mediterranean*, Malden, MA: Wiley Blackwell.

Harlaftis, G. (1996), *A History of Greek-owned Shipping: The Making of An International Tramp Fleet, 1830 to the Present Day*, New York: Routledge.

Kostis, K. and S. Petmezas (eds) (2006), *Η ανάπτυξη της ελληνικής οικονομίας κατά τον 19ου αιώνα (1830-1914)*, Athens: Alexandreia.

Kremmydas, V. (ed.) (2006), *Εισαγωγήστη νεοελληνική οικονομική ιστοριά (18ος-20ος Αιώνας)*, Athens: Typotheto.

Papataxiarchis, E. and S. D. Petmezas (1998), 'The Devolution of Property and Kinship Practices in Late- and Post-Ottoman Ethnic Greek Societies. Some Demo-economic Factors of 19th and 20th Century Transformations', *Mélaanges de l'Ecole française de Rome. Italie et Méditerranée*, 110 (1), 217–41.

Petmezas, S. (2003), *Η ελληνική αγροτική οικονομία κατά την 19ο αιώνα: Η περιφερειακή διάσταση*, Heraklio: University of Crete Press.

Sant Cassia, P. (2006), *The Making of the Modern Greek Family: Marriage and Exchange in Nineteenth-century Athens*, New York: Cambridge University Press.

Sigalos, E. (2004), *Housing in Medieval and Post-Medieval Greece*, Oxford: Archaeopress.

Vionis, A. K. (2013), *A Crusader, Ottoman, and Early Modern Aegean Archaeology: Built Environment and Domestic Material Culture in the Medieval and Post-medieval Cyclades, Greece (13th-20th Centuries AD)*, Leiden: Leiden University Press.

Chapter 7

Augustinos, G. (1977), *Consciousness and History: Nationalist Critics of Greek Society, 1897-1914*, New York: Columbia University Press, East European monographs.

Dakin, D. (1972), *The Unification of Greece, 1770-1923*, London: Ernest Benn Ltd.

Dalby, A. (2010), *Eleftherios Venizelos: Greece*, London: Haus Publishing.

Dragostinova, T. (2011), *Between Two Motherlands: Nationality and Emigration Among the Greeks of Bulgaria, 1900-1949*, Ithaca, NY: Cornell University Press.

Gallant, T. W., G. Treheles and M. Vitopoulos (2005), *The 1918 Anti-Greek Riot in Toronto*, Toronto: Dimitra and the Canadian Hellenic Historical Society.

Gingeras, R. (2009), *Sorrowful Shores: Violence, Ethnicity, and the End of the Ottoman Empire, 1912-1923*, New York: Oxford University Press.

Hall, R. C. (2000), *The Balkan Wars, 1912-1913: Prelude to the First World War*, New York: Routledge.

Hofmann, T., M. Bjørnlund and V. Meichanetsidis (eds) (2011), *The Genocide of the Ottoman Greeks: Studies on the State-sponsored Campaign of Extermination of the Christians of Asia Minor, 1912-1922 and Its Aftermath: History, Law, Memory*, New York: Aristide D. Caratzas.

Kitromilides, P. (ed.) (2006), *Eleftherios Venizelos: The Trials of Statesmanship*, Edinburgh: Edinburgh University Press.

Lyberatos, A. (ed.) (2013), *Social Transformation and Mass Mobilization in the Balkan and Eastern Mediterranean Cities, 1900–1923*, Herakleion: Crete University Press.

Macrakis, A. L. (1982), 'Eleftherios Venizelos in Crete, 1864-1910: The Main Problems', in N. Diamandouros and L. Macrakis (eds), *New Trends in Modern Greek Histiography*, New Haven: Modern Greek Studies Association, 85–104.

Macrakis, A. L. (2006), 'Venizelos' Early Life and Political Career in Crete, 1864-1910', in P. M. Kitromilides (ed.), *Eleftherios Venizelos: The Trials of Statesmanship*, Edinburgh: Edinburgh University Press, 37–86.

Maroniti, N. (2009), *Πολιτική εξουσία και 'εθνικό ζήτημα' στην Ελλάδα. 1880-1910*, Athens: Alexandreia.

Maroniti, N. (2010), *Το κίνημα στο Γουδί εκατό χρόνια μετά. Παραδοξές, ερωτήματα, νέες προοπτικές*, Athens: Alexandreia.

Papacosma, S. V. (1977), *The Military in Greek Politics: The 1909 Coup D'Etat*, Kent: Kent State University Press.

Yavuz, M. H. and I. Blumi (eds) (2013), *War and Nationalism: The Balkan Wars, 1912-1913, and Their Sociopolitical Implications*, Salt Lake City: The University of Utah Press.

Primary sources

Kolev, V. and C. Koulouri (eds) (2009), *The Balkan Wars. Workbook 3*, Thessaloniki: CDRSEE. Available at http://cdrsee.org/jhp/pdf/workbook3_eng_ed2.pdf

Chapter 8

Cliadakis, H. (2015), *Fascism in Greece: The Metaxas Dictatorship 1936-1941*, Wiesbaden: Otto Harrassowitz.

Clark, B. (2006), *Twice a Stranger: The Mass Expulsions That Forged Modern Greece and Turkey*, Cambridge, MA: Harvard University Press.

Doulis, T. (1977), *Disaster and Fiction: Modern Greek Fiction and the Impact of the Asia Minor Disaster of 1922*, Berkeley: University of California Press.

Higham, R. and T. Veremis (eds) (1993), *The Metaxas Dictatorship: Aspects of Greece 1936-1940*, Athens: The Hellenic Foundation for Defense and Foreign Policy.

Hirschon, R. (1998), *Heirs of the Catastrophe: The Social Life of Asia Minor Refugees in Piraeus*, New York: Berghan Books.

Hirschon, R. (ed.) (2003), *Crossing the Aegean: An Appraisal of the 1923 Compulsory Population Exchange Between Greece and Turkey*, New York: Berghan Books.

Kallis, A. (2010), 'Neither Fascist nor Authoritarian: The 4th of August Regime in Greece (1936-1941) and the Dynamics of Fascistisation in 1930s Europe', *East Central Europe*, 37, 2 (3), 303–30.

Kenna, M. E. (2001), *The Social Organisation of Exile: Greek Political Detainees in the 1930s*, Abingdon: Harwood Academic.

Kofas, J. V. (1983), *Authoritarianism in Greece: The Metaxas Regime*, New York: Columbia University Press, East European Monographs.

Koliopoulos, I. S. (1977), *Greece and the British Connection 1935-1941*, Oxford: Clarendon Press.

Koliopoulos, I. S. (2006), 'The Last Years, 1933-6', in P. M. Kitromilides (ed.), *Eleftherios Venizelos: The Trials of Statesmanship*, Edinburgh: Edinburgh University Press, 234–50.

Kontogiorgi, E. (2006), *Population Exchange in Greek Macedonia: The Rural Settlement of Refugees 1922-1930*, New York: Oxford University Press.

Liakos, A. (ed.) (2011), *Το 1922 και οι πρόσφυγες. Μια νέα ματιά*, Athens: Nefeli.

Llewellyn-Smith, M. (1998), *Ionian Vision: Greece in Asia Minor, 1919-1922*, Ann Arbor: University of Michigan Press.

Mackridge, P. A. and E. Yannakakis (eds) (1997), *Ourselves and Others: The Development of a Greek Macedonian Identity Since 1912*, Washington, DC: Berg.

Macmillan, M. O. (2002), *Paris 1919: Six Months That Changed the World*, New York: Random House.

Mavrogordatos, G. T. (1983), *Stillborn Rebublic: Social Coalitions and Party Strategies in Greece, 1922-1936*, Berkeley: University of California Press.

Pelt, M. (1998), *Tobacco, Arms and Politics: Greece and Germany From World Crisis to World War 1929-41*, Denmark: Museum Tusculanum Press.

Petrakis, M. (2011), *The Metaxas Myth: Dictatorship and Propaganda in Greece*, London: I. B. Tauris.

Vatikiotis, P. J. (1998), *Popular Autocracy in Greece, 1936-41: a Political Biography of General Ioannis Metaxas*, London, Portland, OR: Frank Cass.

Yildirim, O. (2006), *Diplomacy and Displacement: Reconsidering the Turco-Greek Exchange of Populations, 1922-1934*, New York: Routledge.

Chapter 9

Antoniou, G. and N. Marantzidis (2003), 'The Greek Civil War Historiography, 1945-2001: Toward a New Paradigm', *Columbia Journal of History*, (fall), 1–12. http://hdl.handle.net/1814/2176

Chiclet, C. (1990), 'The Greek Civil War 1946-1949', in M. Sarafis (ed.), *Background to Contemporary Greece*, New York: Barnes & Noble, 201–22.

Clogg, R. (ed.) (2008), *Bearing Gifts to Greeks: Humanitarian Aid to Greece in the 1940s*, New York: Palgrave Macmillan.

Close, D. H. (ed.) (1993), *The Greek Civil War, 1943-1950: Studies of Polarization*, New York: Routledge.

Close, D. (2015), *The Origins of the Greek Civil War*, New York: Routledge.

Collard, A. (1990), 'The Experience of Civil War in the Mountain Villages of Central Greece', in M. Sarafis (ed.), *Background to Contemporary Greece*, New York: Barnes & Noble, 223–54.

Eudes, D. (1975), *The Kapitanios: Partisans and Civil War in Greece 1943-1949*, London: New Left Books.

Featherstone, K., D. Papadimitriou, A. Mamrelis and G. Niarchos (2011), *The Last Ottomans: The Muslim Minority of Greece, 1940-1949*, New York: Palgrave Macmillan.

Hionidou, V. (2006), *Famine and Death in Occupied Greece, 1941-1944*, Cambridge: Cambridge University Press.

Iatrides, J. O. (2005), 'Revolution or Self-Defense? Communist Goals, Strategy, and Tactics in the Greek Civil War', *Journal of Cold War Studies*, 7 (3), 3–33.

Iatrides, J. O. and L. Wrigley (eds) (1995), *Greece at the Crossroads: The Civil War and Its Legacy*, University Park, PA: Pennsylvania State University Press.

Kalyvas, S. N. (2006), *The Logic of Violence in Civil War*, New York: Cambridge University Press.

Marantzidis, N. and G. Antoniou (2004), 'The Axis Occupation and Civil War: Changing Trends in Greek Historiography, 1941-2002', *Journal of Peace Research*, 41 (2), 223–32.

Mazower, M. (1993), *Inside Hitler's Greece: The Experience of Occupation, 1941-1944*, New Haven, CT: Yale University Press.

Sakkas, J. (2013), *Britain and the Greek Civil War, 1944-1949: British Imperialism, Public Opinion and the Coming of the Cold War*, Mainz: Franz Philipp Rutzen.

Skalidakis, Y. (2015), 'From Resistance to Counterstate: The Making of Revolutionary Power in the Liberated Zones of Occupied Greece, 1943–1944', *Journal of Modern Greek Studies*, 33 (1), 155–84.

Van Boeschoten, R. (1997), *Αναποδα χρόνια. Συλλογική μνήμη και ιστορία στο Ζιάκα Γρεβενών (1900-1950)*, Αθήνα: Πλεύρον.

Voglis, P. (2002), *Becoming a Subject: Political Prisoners in the Greek Civil War*, New York: Berghahn Books.

Voglis, P. (2014), *Η αδύνατη επανάσταση. Η κοινωνική δυναμική του εμφυλίου πολέμου*, Athens: Alexandreia.

Primary sources

Clogg, R. (ed.) (2002), *Greece 1940-1949. Occupation, Resistance, Civil War. A Documentary History,* New York: Palgrave Macmillan.
Erdelja, V. (ed.) (2009), *The Second World War. Workbook 4,* Thessaloniki: CDRSEE. Available at http://cdrsee.org/jhp/pdf/workbook4_eng_ed2.pdf

Chapter 10

Avdela, E. (2013), <<*Νέοι εν κινδύνων>>: Επιτήρηση, αναμόρφωση και δικαιοσύνη ανηλίκων μετά τον πόλεμο,* Athens: Polis.
Danforth, L. M. and R. V. Boeschoten (2012), *Children of the Greek Civil War: Refugees and the Politics of Memory,* Chicago: University of Chicago Press.
Draenos, S. (2012), *Andreas Papandreou: The Making of a Greek Democrat and Political Maverick,* New York: I.B. Tauris: Distributed in the United States and Canada exclusively by Palgrave Macmillan.
Hatzivassiliou, E. (2011), *Greece and the Cold War: Front-Line State, 1952-1967,* New York: Routledge.
Holland, R. F. (2012), *Blue-water Empire: The British in the Mediterranean Since 1800,* London: Allen Lane.
Holland, R. F. and D. W. Markides (2006), *The British and the Hellenes: Struggles for Mastery in the Eastern Mediterranean 1850-1960,* Oxford: Oxford University Press.
Mazower, M. (ed.) (2000), *After the War was Over: Reconstructing the Family, Nation and State on Greece, 1943-1960,* Princeton: Princeton University Press.
Papadakis, Y., N. Peristianis, G. Welz, N. Peristianis and G. Welz (2006), *Divided Cyprus: Modernity, History, and An Island in Conflict,* Bloomington: Indiana University Press.
Roubatis, Y. P. (1987), *Tangled Webs: The US in Greece 1947-1967,* New York: Pella.
Stefanidis, I. D. (1999), *Isle of Discord: Nationalism, Imperialism, and the Making of the Cyprus Problem,* New York: New York University Press.
Stefanidis, G. D. (2007), *Stirring the Greek Nation: Political Culture, Irredentism and Anti-Americanism in Post-War Greece, 1945-1967,* Burlington, VT: Ashgate.
Sutton, S. B. (1983), 'Rural-Urban Migration in Greece', in M. Kenny and D. I. Kertzer (eds), *Urban Life in Mediterranean Europe: Anthropological Perspectives,* Urbana: University of Illinois Press, 225–52.
Vryonis, S. (2005), *The Mechanism of Catastrophe: The Turkish Pogrom of September 6-7, 1955, and the Destruction of the Greek Community of Istanbul,* New York, NY: greekworks.com.
Wittner, L. S. (1982), *American Intervention in Greece 1943-1949,* New York: Columbia University Press.

Chapter 11

Clogg, R. (ed.) (1983), *Greece in the 1980's*, London: Macmillan.

Clogg, R. (1988), *Parties and Elections in Greece: The Search for Legitimacy*, London: C. Hurst and Co.

Clogg, R. (ed.) (1993), *Greece, 1981-89: The Populist Decade*, London: St. Martin's Press.

Constas, D. and T. G. Stavrou (eds) (1995), *Greece Prepares for the Twenty-first Century*, Baltimore: Johns Hopkins University Press.

Couloumbis, T. A. (2004), *The Greek Junta Phenomenon: A Professor's Notes*, New York: Pella Pub.

Doulis, T. (2011), *The Iron Storm: The Impact on Greek Culture of the Military Junta, 1967-1974*, Bloomington, IN: Xlibris Corp.

Featherstone, K. and D. K. Katsoudas (eds) (1987), *Poltical Change in Greece: Before and After the Colonels*, London: Croom Helm.

Karakatsanis, N. M. (2001), *The Politics of Elite Transformation: The Consolidation of Greek Democracy in Theoretical Perspective*, Westport, CT: Praeger.

Kariotis, T. C. (ed.) (1992), *The Greek Socialist Experiment: Papandreou's Greece, 1981-1989*, New York: Pella Publishing Company.

Kornetis, K. (2013), *Children of the Dictatorship: Student Resistance, Cultural Politics, and the 'Long 1960s' in Greece*, New York: Berghahn.

Lazaridis, G. (1995), 'Aspects of Greek and Cretan Rural Development: The Implications of the Implementation of the Common Agricultural Policy and of the Integrated Mediterranean Programmes for Agricultural Development', *Journal of Mediterranean Studies*, 5 (1), 108–28.

Nafpliotis, A. (2013), *Britain and the Greek Colonels: Accommodating the Junta in the Cold War*, New York: I.B. Tauris.

Sotiropoulos, D. A. (1996), *Populism and Bureaucracy: The Case of Greece Under PASOK, 1981-1989*, Notre Dame, IN: University of Notre Dame Press.

Spourdalakes, M. (1988), *The Rise of the Greek Socialist Party*, Boston: Routledge & Kegan Paul.

Veremis, T. (1997), *The Military in Greek Politics from Independence to Democracy*, New York: Black Rose Books.

Woodhouse, C. M. (1982a), *Karamanlis: The Restorer of Greek Democracy*, Oxford: Clarendon Press.

Woodhouse, C. M. (1982b), *The Rise and Fall of the Greek Colonels*, London: Granada.

Chapter 12

Cheliotis, L. K. and S. Xenakis (eds) (2011), *Crime and Punishment in Contemporary Greece: International Comparative Perspectives*, New York: Peter Lang.

Diamanti-Karanou, P. (2003), 'Migration of Ethnic Greeks from the Former Soviet Union to Greece, 1990-2000: Policy Decisions and Implications', *Southeast European and Black Sea Studies*, 3 (1), 25–45.

Economou, C., D. Kaitelidou, A. Kentikelenis, A. Sissouras and A. Maresso (2014), *The Impact of the Financial Crisis on the Health System and Health in Greece*, Copenhagen: European Observatory on Health Systems and Policies, the World Health Organization.

Ellinas, A. A. (2013), 'The Rise of Golden Dawn: The New Face of the Far Right in Greece', *South European Society and Politics,* 18 (4), 543–65.

Ellinas, A. A. (2014), 'Neo-Nazism in an Established Democracy: The Persistence of Golden Dawn in Greece', *South European Society and Politics,* 19 (3), 1–20.

Featherstone, K. and K. Ifantis (1996), *Greece in a Changing Europe: Between European Integration and Balkan Disintegration?* New York: St. Martin's.

Featherstone, K. (ed.) (2001), *Europeanization and the Southern Periphery,* Portland, OR: F. Cass.

Featherstone, K. (ed.) (2006), *Politics and Policy in Greece: The Challenge of Modernisation,* London: Routledge.

Kalyvas, S., G. Pagoulatos and H. Tsoukas (eds) (2012), *From Stagnation to Forced Adjustment: Reforms in Greece 1974-2010,* London: Hurst & Company.

Karyotis, G. and R. Gerodimos (eds) (2015), *The Politics of Extreme Austerity: Greece in the Eurozone Crisis,* New York: Palgrave Macmillan.

Karakatsanis, L. (2014), *Turkish-Greek Relations: Rapprochement, Civil Society and the Politics of Friendship,* London: Routledge.

Knight, D. (2015), *History, Time, and Economic Crisis in Central Greece,* New York: Palgrave Macmillan.

Lazaridis, G. (2009), *Women's Work and Lives in Rural Greece: Appearances and Realities,* Burlington, VT: Ashgate.

Lytra, V. (ed.) (2014), *When Greeks and Turks Meet: Interdisciplinary Perspectives on the Relationship Since 1923,* Burlington, VT: Ashgate Publishing Company.

Mavroudeas, S. (ed.) (2014), *Greek Capitalism in Crisis: Marxist Analyses,* New York: Routledge.

Pelagidis, T. and M. Mitsopoulos (2011), *Understanding the Crisis in Greece,* New York: Palgrave Macmillan.

Pettifer, J. (2012), *The Making of the Greek Crisis,* New York: Penguin.

Salapatas, D. (2014), *The Aegean Sea Dispute Between Greece and Turkey the Consequences for NATO and the EU,* London: AKAKIA Publications.

Simitis, K. A. (2012), *The European Debt Crisis: The Greek Case,* Manchester: Manchester University Press.

Triandafyllidou, A., R. Gropas and H. Kouki (eds) (2013), *The Greek Crisis and European Modernity,* New York: Palgrave Macmillan.

Index